The Great Recession

The Great Recession

Lessons for Central Bankers

edited by Jacob Braude, Zvi Eckstein, Stanley Fischer, and Karnit Flug

The MIT Press
Cambridge, Massachusetts
London, England

MIT Press books may be purchased at special quantity discounts for business or sales promotional use. For information, please email special_sales@mitpress.mit.edu or write to Special Sales Department, The MIT Press, 55 Hayward Street, Cambridge, MA 02142.

This book was set in Times Roman by Toppan Best-set Premedia Limited, Hong Kong. Printed and bound in the United States of America.

Library of Congress Cataloging-in-Publication Data

The great recession : lessons for central bankers / edited by Jacob Braude ... [et al.].
    p. cm.
Conference proceedings.
Includes bibliographical references and index.
ISBN 978-0-262-01834-0 (hardcover : alk. paper)
1. Global Financial Crisis, 2008–2009—Congresses. 2. Monetary policy—Congresses. 3. Banks and banking–Congresses. 4. International finance—Congresses. I. Braude, Jacob.
HB37172008-2009 .G73   2013
330.9'0511–dc23
2012015227

10   9   8   7   6   5   4   3   2   1

Contents

Preface

The recent global crisis was the worst since the Great Depression of the 1930s, and it was deep enough to shake not only the global economy and the financial systems of most major economies, but also conventional wisdom and accepted practices of economic policy-making, regulation of financial markets, and more. The recovery and return to normality is certainly long and painful in most developed countries. Further, as protests against the role of banks in the crisis and other aspects of the economic situation on its eve are still unfolding, we do not yet know what the final effects of the Great Recession on the political economy of the future will be.

In the beginning the crisis seemed manageable. It began in July 2007 as the subprime crisis, a problem in a relatively small segment of the US financial system. Subsequently it spread to other markets and countries. Yet for over a year the extent and nature of the crisis were not fully appreciated. In mid-2008 the partial recovery in share prices and additional positive indications from the financial markets led to a sense of relief that a global financial crisis had been averted.

The collapse of Lehman Brothers in mid-September 2008 marks the moment at which the crisis worsened decisively from a primarily US to a truly global event. Mid-September also marks the turning point of the policy response, a change most dramatically reflected in the massive rescue of AIG immediately after Lehman was allowed to collapse. Policy makers now realized the severity of the crisis and what might happen if they did not act immediately. Worldwide, governments and central banks acted on an unprecedented scale. The policy response was unique not only in its magnitude, but also in the type and variety of the measures undertaken. Policy makers considered and adopted measures that had so far been almost unthinkable. Much of this change in thinking and action took place in real time, amid high uncertainty and in a rapidly changing environment.

The extraordinary policy response was a success. It prevented the deterioration of the crisis into a complete meltdown of the financial system and a prolonged collapse of the global economy. Thus the fear of another Great Depression, which was palpable in late September through November 2008, did not materialize. The global situation stabilized by the second quarter of 2009, and later that year—earlier than had previously been expected—recovery, albeit slow and fragile, began in most countries. Nonetheless, uncertainty about the sustainability of the recovery remained high and many problems in the financial system have remained unresolved.

This success, resulting from the aggressive policy response, however, came at a cost: budget deficits and the government debt of many countries increased dramatically; the unbalanced global recovery resulted in large capital flows that exerted pressure on exchange rates and raised concerns about the possibility of currency wars; and recovery remained highly dependent on the continuation and feasibility of effective fiscal and monetary stimuli.

The crisis has led to a re-evaluation of preventive and remedial policies, and to the questioning of both the conventional wisdom and fundamental concepts that have long guided policy makers. This is evident in the reassessment of preventive policies for reducing the risk of a crisis, with greater emphasis on macroprudential policies—a concept that barely existed before the crisis, and stronger regulation and supervision of financial markets and institutions. Such rethinking is true also of remedial policies for dealing with a crisis once it occurs. Notable examples include a generally more favorable view of fiscal expansions and interventions in various financial markets, a renewed debate on capital controls and exchange rate intervention, and a new understanding of the role of quantitative easing in pursuing further monetary expansion as the nominal interest rate approaches the zero bound.

This volume brings together selected papers from an international conference on *Lessons from the World Financial Crisis* held by the Bank of Israel in Jerusalem on March 31 to April 1 2011. Its participants were members of central banks and important international institutions. The volume is highly policy oriented and presents the experience and perspective of a variety of countries—advanced economies as well as emerging ones, countries that were hard-hit by the crisis and countries that weathered it rather successfully. The focus—in terms of writers and content—on central banks reflects the prominent role they played in responding to the crisis, as well as the major role that they should play in preventing or preparing for future crises.

The papers in the volume cover primarily monetary policy, macro-prudential policy, and issues of exchange rates, capital flows, banking and financial markets as these relate to the crisis and its lessons. The choice of papers retains the focus on monetary and financial policies while providing a broad enough mix to highlight the interactions among these issues, such as the interaction between monetary and macropru-dential policies. The importance of such interactions and the need for integration among policy areas is surely one of the important lessons of the crisis.

The issues covered in the volume were highlighted during the crisis itself, and many of them are currently at the center of events, debate and policy-making as countries around the world experience an uneven recovery. These include not only factors leading to the crisis and events and policies during the crisis, but also lessons for macroprudential policy and changes in the regulation of financial markets that would reduce the risk of future crises.

The timing of this volume combines the benefit of the still-vivid expe-rience of policy makers who participated in making the key decisions, as well as some longer term perspectives on events and policy measures taken, including negative side effects of some of these measures. However, it is by no means too early, as certain lessons should be implemented immediately and may serve to prepare for another crisis which—it seems at the end of 2011 as this introduction is being written—may come sooner rather than later.

The ten lessons for central banks from the global crisis, which Fischer offers in the Introduction, provide an interesting framework for the volume. These lessons come to mind time and again as one reads through the papers on various policy aspects and the experience of different countries. Some of the lessons refer to policy during a crisis such as feasibility of monetary expansion even as the nominal interest rate approaches zero, the crucial role of the central bank as a lender of last resort and exchange rate policies in small open economies. Other lessons focus on policies to reduce the risk of a crisis and increase the economy's resilience should a crisis occur. These include the importance of macro-prudential supervision, sound macroeconomic policies in normal times, and the need to deal with bubbles in a timely manner. The tenth lesson is a general call for open-mindedness on part of policy makers—*Never say never*. It reflects more than any particular lesson the change that had occurred during the crisis in both the practice and concept of policy-making. Previously unthinkable policies were and are being considered and adapted, and conventional wisdoms are being questioned.

Monetary policy during the crisis was aggressive and exceptional. Part I discusses the effectiveness and exceptional dimensions of monetary policy. Pill and Smets review the interaction between two of the most outstanding features of monetary policy during the crisis—nonstandard measures (NSMs), and the lower bound on nominal interest rates. They also analyze the effectiveness of NSMs in supporting monetary policy transmission in the euro area. While Turkey did not reach the zero bound, it pursued an aggressive monetary expansion. Alp and Elekdağ examine how much deeper would the recession in Turkey have been absent the sharp cuts in its interest rate. Soto assesses the effectiveness of monetary and other policies in Chile's response to the crisis. He pays special attention to the zero bound.

While part I discusses policies for dealing with the crisis once it occurs, part II focuses on macroprudential and financial policies for reducing the risk of a crisis occurring and for increasing the resilience of the financial system. Alberola, Trucharte, and Vega assess Spain's system of dynamic loan loss provisioning and find that to a certain extent the system has proved useful in mitigating the buildup of risks and in strengthening the loss absorbency capacity of financial institutions. Schuberth's chapter highlights the broad scope of financial stability policy and its interaction with other areas of policy. She examines the role of tax policies in increasing vulnerabilities, such as by encouraging high leverage and risk-taking, and also discusses taxes that might internalize negative externalities of financial sector activities.

Capital flows and controls and exchange rate policies have been central to the debate and to actual policies in many countries during the crisis. The debate intensified as global recovery began, because the recovery was very unbalanced. Some countries, particularly emerging and several developed ones, recovered relatively rapidly, thereby attracting significant capital inflows. The corresponding pressures for the appreciation of their currencies raised concerns about potential currency wars.

Part III addresses these issues. Ostry reviews arguments about the management of capital inflow surges and focuses on the conditions under which capital controls may be justified. As he notes, the debate on this is hardly new but the recent crisis has revived it. He concludes that under certain conditions such controls are justified as part of the policy tool kit to manage the macroeconomic risks that inflow surges may bring. The next chapter provides a concrete example of dealing with capital flows. Chung and Kim describe the capital inflows into Korea during the 2000s and the policy responses to them. They then examine the effectiveness of Korea's foreign exchange policy, especially as related to capital outflow liberalization and foreign reserves accumulation, in terms of confronting the recent crisis. The challenge that sharp reversals in capital flows pose to emerging economies also motivates the third chapter in this section. Capistrán, Cuadra, and Ramos-Francia use a New Keynesian model to illustrate how credible monetary and fiscal policies increase policy makers' degrees of freedom to respond to adverse external shocks. This helps to explain why during the crisis, emerging economies, with better economic fundamentals, were able to implement countercyclical policies.

The last part of the book describes the experience and lessons of four countries. Three of them—Australia, Norway, and Israel—are developed economies that were affected rather mildly by the crisis. Their recessions were relatively moderate and short-lived; they did not suffer from failures of financial institutions, and their currencies appreciated during much of 2009. The lessons from the experience of such countries are no less instructive than those of the countries that were badly hurt. One may find certain similarities among these more successful countries, such as solid growth, fiscal discipline and conservative and tightly regulated financial systems in the years preceding the crisis. All of this underlines the importance of the initial conditions under which a country enters difficult times. All these countries also took timely and significant policy measures during the crisis. Yet conclusions based on such similarities should be drawn with caution, and these countries too need to learn and apply lessons from the crisis.

As Kearns points out, Australia and Canada are similar in many respects but fared quite differently through the crisis, largely due to luck—Canada's exports are oriented toward the United States, while Australia's toward East Asia. Berg and Eitrheim note that while the financial stability measures taken in Norway during the crisis sufficed this time, they would not have been adequate if Norwegian banks faced the same degree of distress that some banks in other countries had faced. Braude notes that Israel benefited from strong macroeconomic fundamentals and certain features of its financial system as well as from a fortunate timing of the shock following five years of rapid growth. However, the crisis also highlighted the vulnerabilities of its financial system, particularly in the nonbank credit market.

Ireland's case is different—it suffered a major financial crisis that later evolved into a public debt crisis. Browne and Kelly trace the origins of the crisis in Ireland (as well as in Spain, Greece, and Portugal) to the large differences between them and the core euro countries when they joined the eurozone. The ensuing convergence processes created distortions and dislocations that eventually brought them to a severe financial crisis or the brink of such a crisis.

At the time of writing this preface, there is considerable concern that we may be facing another round of the global crisis, this time triggered by the European debt crisis. This may make the volume particularly relevant and put to immediate test some of the lessons and insights offered here. It may render some of them obsolete or wrong. However, regardless of whether the immediate threats materialize, we believe that this volume should be of much interest to policy makers and to students of monetary and financial policies, as well as of crises more generally. We hope and believe that it should make a significant contribution to the lively debate on the lessons from the crisis and—most important—help in improving policy-making in relevant areas.

Introduction: Central Bank Lessons from the Global Crisis

Stanley Fischer

During and after the Great Depression many central bankers and economists concluded that monetary policy could not be used to stimulate economic activity in a situation in which the interest rate was essentially zero, as it was in the United States during the 1930s—a situation that later became known as the liquidity trap. In the United States it was also a situation where the financial system was grievously damaged. It was only in 1963, with the publication of Friedman and Schwartz's *Monetary History of the United States* that the profession as a whole[1] began to accept the contrary view, that "The contraction is in fact a testimonial to the importance of monetary forces" (Friedman and Schwartz 1963: 30).

Twenty years later, in 1983, Ben Bernanke presented the view that it was the breakdown of the credit system that was the critical feature of the Great Depression (Bernanke 1983: 257–76)—that it was the credit side of the banks' balance sheets, the failure or inability to make a sufficient volume of loans, rather than the behavior of the money supply per se, that was primarily responsible for the breakdown of the monetary transmission mechanism during the Great Depression. The Bernanke thesis gained adherents over the years, and must recently have gained many more as a result of the Great Recession.

In this introductory chapter, I present preliminary lessons—ten of them—for monetary and financial policy from the Great Recession. I do this with some trepidation, since it is possible that there will later be an eleventh lesson: that given that it took fifty years for the profession to develop its current understanding of the monetary policy transmission mechanism during the Great Depression, just two and a half years after the Lehmann Brothers bankruptcy is too early to be drawing even preliminary lessons from the Great Recession. But let me join the crowd and begin doing so.

Lesson 1: Reaching the zero interest lower bound is not the end of expansionary monetary policy.

Until the 2008 crisis the textbooks said that when the nominal interest rate reaches zero, monetary policy loses its effectiveness and only fiscal policy remains as an expansionary policy instrument—the pure Keynesian case. Now we know that there is a lot that the central bank can do to run an expansionary monetary policy even when it has cut the central bank interest rate essentially to zero—as did the Fed, the Bank of England, the Bank of Japan, and other central banks during this crisis.

In the first instance there is the policy of *quantitative easing*—the continuation of purchases of assets by the central bank even when the central bank interest rate is zero. Although these purchases do not reduce the short-term interest rate, they do increase liquidity. Further, by operating in longer term assets, as in QE2, the central bank can affect longer term interest rates, which may have an additional impact on the private sector's demand for longer term assets, including mortgages and corporate investment.

During the crisis several attempts were made to calculate how much quantitative easing was needed at a particular point in time. The calculation used a Taylor rule to calculate what the (negative) interest rate should have been in the given circumstances, combined that with an estimate of the increase in the money supply or central bank assets that would normally be needed to reduce the interest rate by one percentage point, and thereby calculated the needed increase in central bank assets. This is a logical approach, but we should note that it extrapolates economic behavior far beyond the range of the experience on which the estimated Taylor rule is based (Hatzius 2009).

Second, there is the approach that the Fed unsuccessfully tried to name "credit easing"—actions directed at reviving particular markets whose difficulties were creating serious problems in the financial system. For instance, when the commercial paper market in the United States was collapsing, the Fed entered on a major scale as a purchaser, and succeeded in reviving the market. Similarly it played a significant role in keeping the mortgage market alive. In this regard the Fed became the *market maker of last resort.*[2]

In a well-known article, James Tobin in 1963 asked in which assets the central bank should conduct open market operations. His answer was the market for capital—namely the stock market—since that way it could have the most direct effect on the cost of capital, later known as Tobin's q, which he saw as the main price through which the central bank could affect economic activity. Although central banks have occasionally operated in the stock market—notably the Hong Kong Monetary Authority in 1997—this has not yet become an accepted way of conducting monetary policy.[3]

Lesson 2: The critical importance of having a strong and robust financial system.

This is a lesson that we have all thought we understood for a long time—not least since the financial crises of the 1990s—but whose central importance has been reaffirmed by the recent global crisis.

This crisis has been *far* worse in many of the advanced countries—among them the United States, the United Kingdom, and some other European countries—than it has been in the leading emerging market countries. This was not the situation in the financial crises of the 1990s, and it is not a situation that I expected would ever occur.

The critical difference between countries that have suffered from exceptionally deep crises and those that had a more or less standard business cycle experience during this crisis traces to what happened in their financial sectors. Those countries that suffered financial sector crises had much deeper output crises.

In their important book, *This Time Is Different*, Carmen Reinhart and Kenneth Rogoff (Reinhart and Rogoff 2009) document the fact that over many centuries, downturns that also involved a financial crisis were more severe than those that did not. This is not coincidental, for the collapse of the financial system not only reduces the efficiency of financial intermediation but also has a critical effect on the monetary transmission mechanism and thus on the ability of the central bank to mitigate the real effects of the crisis.

If the financial system is intact, the standard anticyclical monetary policy response of cutting interest rates produces its response in the encouragement of purchases of durables, ranging from investment goods and housing to consumer durables. This happened during this crisis, in that many countries that did not suffer from a financial crisis but had cut interest rates sharply to deal with the negative effects of the global crisis returned to growth more rapidly than other countries, and soon found asset prices, particularly the price of housing, rising rapidly. Among these countries are Australia, Canada, China, Israel, Korea, Norway, and Singapore.

The main question is: What needs to be done to maintain a strong and robust financial system? Some of the answers to this question are to be found in the blizzard of recommendations for financial sector and regulatory reform coming out of the Basel Committee—now extended to include all the G-20 countries plus a few more—and the Financial Stability Board (the FSB).

In particular the recommendations relate to the capital requirements of the banks, which the Basel Committee and the FSB recommend raising sharply, including by toughening the requirements for assets to qualify as tier 1 and tier 2 capital. In addition there are recommendations on the structure of incentives, on corporate governance, on the advisability of countercyclical capital requirements, on risk management, on resolution mechanisms including eventually on how to resolve a SIFI (systemically important financial institution, typically a bank with major international operations) —and much more.[4] Further there has been a focus on systemic supervision and its organization, a topic to which I will return shortly.

These recommendations make sense, and the main question relating to them is whether and how they will be implemented, and whether political pressures will either prevent their implementation and/or lead to their gradual weakening. There is already cause for concern in that some of the recommendations are to be implemented only by 2019—a period sufficiently long for everyone to forget why such drastic changes are regarded as essential, and why they are indeed essential. One element of the conflicting pressures can be seen in the concern in many countries that the banks not tighten capital requirements too fast, since an expansion in credit is needed to fuel the recovery.

Lesson 3:   The need for macroprudential supervision.[5]

There is not yet an accepted definition of macroprudential policy or supervision, but the notion involves two elements: that the supervision relates to the entire financial system; and that it involves systemic interactions. Both elements were evident in the global financial crisis, with analyses of the crisis frequently emphasizing the role of the shadow banking system and of the global effects of the Lehman bankruptcy.

Thus, in discussing macroprudential supervision, we are talking about regulation of the financial system at a very broad level, going beyond the banking system. We are also going beyond bank supervision in considering macroprudential policy instruments—and we are therefore also discussing an issue that requires coordination among different regulators.

It is not clear whether the inclusion of a responsibility for (or contributing to) financial stability in modern central bank laws, such as those of the ECB, the Bank of England and many others, including the Bank of Israel, reflects the concerns that have led to the emphasis on macroprudential supervision, or rather primarily the traditional role of the central bank as lender of last resort. No one who has read Bagehot on panics can think that understanding of the potential for systemic crises is a new problem. However, its importance has been reinforced by the dynamics of the most recent crisis, in which a problem initially regarded as manageable—the subprime crisis—gradually developed into the worst financial crisis since the Great Depression, involving financial instruments built on mortgages, and after the Lehman bankruptcy which revealed interactions among financial institutions to be much stronger than policy makers must have thought at the time.

What macroprudential policy tools do central banks have? In the first place they have their analytic capacities and their capacity to raise policy makers' and the public's awareness of critical issues. These are reflected in the financial stability reports that some central banks have been producing for over a decade.

What about other macroprudential policy tools? Central banks have been engaged in a search for them since the financial crisis, but the search has not been especially fruitful. Some have defined countercyclical capital requirements[6] as a macroprudential policy tool, presumably because they reflect a macroeconomic assessment and because they apply to the entire banking system. Nonetheless, they are not particularly aimed at moderating systemic interactions, and thus it is not clear that they are the archetypal macroprudential policy tool.

More generally, it seems that there are few specifically macroprudential policy tools, and that the main tools that central banks and financial supervisors will be able to deploy to deal with systemic interactions will be their standard microprudential instruments or adaptations thereof.

Like other economies that did not suffer from a domestic financial crisis during the global crisis, Israel has had to deal with the threat of a housing price bubble in the wake of the global crisis. Housing prices, after falling gradually for over a decade, grew by around 40 percent in the last two years. The Bank's housing sector model suggests that while prices in the middle of 2010 were not far above their long-run equilibrium level, a continuation of their recent rapid rates of increase would definitely put them well above the equilibrium level. Further the atmosphere in the housing market was becoming increasingly bubble-like, with discussion of the need to buy before prices rose even further.

Because the exchange rate had been appreciating rapidly, the Bank preferred if possible not to raise the central bank interest rate too rapidly. Since bank supervision is located within the Bank of Israel, policy discussions in the Bank resulted in the supervisor undertaking measures that in effect increased mortgage interest rates, without affecting other interest rates. These, together with tax and other measures undertaken by the government, and with government measures to increase the supply of land for building, appear to have begun to dampen the rate of increase of housing prices—though it will take some time yet to know whether that has happened.

In announcing the new measures, the Bank of Israel emphasized that they were macroprudential, and that our aim was to ensure financial stability. In speeches we noted that our measures operated on the demand for housing, and that it would be preferable to undertake measures that would increase the supply—as some of the measures undertaken by the government soon afterwards were designed to do.

In this case the central bank was in the fortunate position of having at its disposal policy measures that enabled it to deal directly with the potential source of financial instability. Further the banks are the main source of housing finance, so the Bank of Israel's measures were unlikely to be circumvented by the responses of other institutions not supervised by the central bank. Even so, we in the Bank of Israel knew there were better ways of dealing with the price rises, and that it was necessary to cooperate with the government to that end.

Even within a central bank that is also the banking supervisor, questions arise about how best to coordinate macroprudential policy. In the case of the Bank of Israel, which still operates under the single decision maker model (but will shortly cease to do so as a new central bank law goes into effect), it was relatively easy to coordinate, since it was possible to include the bank supervisor in the nonstatutory internal monetary policy advisory committee, and to use the enlarged committee as the advisory body on macroprudential decisions.

More generally, macroprudential supervision could require actions by two or more supervisory agencies, and there then arises the issue of how best to coordinate their actions. A simple model that would appeal to those who have not worked in bureaucracies would be to require the supervisors to cooperate in developing a strategy to deal with whatever problems arise. However, cooperation between equals in such an environment is difficult, which is to say inefficient, all the more so in a crisis.

It is thus necessary to establish mechanisms to ensure that decisions on macroprudential policy are made sufficiently rapidly and in a way that takes systemic interactions into account. The issue of the optimal structure of supervision was discussed well before the recent crisis, with the FSA in the United Kingdom being seen as the prototype of a unitary regulator outside the central bank, the twin peaks Dutch model as another prototype, and various models of coordination and noncoordination among multiple regulators providing additional potential models.

The issue of the optimal structure of supervision came into much sharper focus in the wake of the financial crisis, with the failure of the FSA to prevent a financial crisis in the United Kingdom having a critical impact on the debate. Major reforms have now been legislated in the United States, Europe, and the United Kingdom. In the Dodd–Frank bill, the responsibility for coordination is placed in a committee of regulators chaired by the secretary of the treasury. In the United Kingdom, the responsibility for virtually all financial supervision is being transferred to the Bank of England, and the responsibility will be placed with a Financial Policy Committee, chaired by the Governor. The structure and operation of the new Committee will draw on the experience of the Monetary Policy Committee, but there are likely to be important differences between the ways in which the committees will work. In other countries, including France and Australia, the coordination of financial supervision is undertaken in a committee chaired by the Governor.

At this stage it is clear that there will be many different institutional structures for coordinating systemic supervision, and that we will have to learn from experience which arrangements work and which don't—and that the results will very likely be country dependent.

It is also very likely that the central bank will play a central role in financial sector supervision, particularly in its macroprudential aspects, and that there will be transfers of responsibility to the central bank in many countries.

Lesson 4: Dealing with bubbles.

One casualty of the crisis has been the Fed doctrine that the central bank should not react to asset prices and situations that it regards as bubbles until the bubble bursts. This is known as "the mopping up approach" —which is to say, to wait for the bubble to burst and then to mop up the mess that results.

The origin of this approach may lie in the expansion and stock market boom of the 1990s. As is well known, Chairman Alan Greenspan announced in a speech in 1996, at a point when the Dow Jones was about 6,400, that the stock markets were showing "irrational exuberance." Despite the Chairman's authority, the markets paused for only a few days before resuming their upward climb, eventually rising above 10,000.

The Fed was widely praised for allowing the boom to continue during that period, based on their conclusion that the rate of productivity growth had increased, and that the economy could grow faster than previously thought without generating inflation.

When the dot-com bubble burst in 2000, the mopping up approach appeared to have been successful. The Fed cut interest rates rapidly and the recession was relatively mild. The damage seemed to have been slight. There is, of course, much debate about whether in the wake of the recession the Fed kept the interest rate too low for too long, thus laying the groundwork for the next—and far more serious—crisis. But even those who argue that way do not suggest that the subsequent crisis was an inevitable result of the decision not to try to prick the bubble in the late 1990s.

I believe that the mopping up discussion was misleading. The issue was generally put as "should the central bank try to prick the bubble?" with the "no" side of the debate arguing that the interest rate would have had to be raised by so much to prick the bubble that doing so would have caused a serious recession. If the question had been "should the Fed react to asset prices in setting the interest rate?" the answer might well have been yes, though it would likely have been provided through the lens of the inflation targeting approach—that is to say, if excessively high asset prices were expected to influence future price or output levels, the central bank would be justified in taking them into account in its interest rate decision.

If the same question were asked today, it would likely be answered in terms of macroprudential supervision, and with reference to the possibility that regulatory measures might be employed to supplement the effects of the interest rate on asset prices.

It seems clear from the general acceptance of the need for macroprudential supervision that the mopping up doctrine is in retreat, though there could be circumstances—particularly a stock-market boom whose collapse would have no major implications for the rest of the financial system—in which the approach could be justified.[7]

Lesson 5: The lender of last resort, and too big to fail.

The view that the central bank should be the lender of last resort has a long and distinguished heritage, and central banks operated as lender of last resort in several countries in the recent crisis. The case for the central bank to be the lender of last resort is clear in the case of a liquidity crisis—one that arises from a temporary shortage of liquidity, typically in a financial panic—but less so in the case of solvency crises.

The key difference is that in the case of a liquidity crisis, decisive central bank action along the lines advocated by Bagehot can resolve the situation without a long-term financial cost to the public sector.[8] In the case where a financial institution is insolvent, intervention to restructure it may cause a long-term financial cost to the public sector—although in several crises in which the central bank and the government intervened massively to deal with a panic, the public sector ended up making a profit from the intervention.[9]

Given that the profits of the central bank are generally sooner or later transferred to the government, almost every financial action that the central bank takes has fiscal implications for the government. This is particularly so when the central bank is involved in actions to support financial stability, such as providing emergency liquidity to specific banks or to the financial system as a whole.

In principle, the distinction between liquidity and solvency problems should guide the actions of the central bank and the government in a crisis. For instance, in Israel, the law provides that the central bank can intervene on its own to deal with a liquidity problem but needs the authorization of the Treasury and the government to take over an insolvent financial institution. However, in practice, the distinction between a liquidity problem and a solvency problem is rarely clear-cut during a crisis, and what initially appears to be a liquidity crisis can very rapidly become an insolvency crisis. In short, judgment is needed at every stage of a financial crisis—as it is in central banking in general.

The too big to fail issue and the associated issue of moral hazard have been recurrent problems in dealing with financial crises. If a financial institution has what is purely a liquidity problem, then the central bank in its financial stability role should act as lender of last resort to that institution in case of need. Special difficulties arise when the institution is "too big" or "too interconnected" to fail. That is to say, causing it to fail will significantly worsen the financial crisis, for instance—to put the issue dramatically—by turning a recession into a depression.

Ideally the regulatory and legal systems should have developed a resolution mechanism whereby an institution judged to be insolvent can be allowed to fail and to be wound down in an orderly process. We have not yet seen such systems in operation for large financial institutions (SIFIs), though one of the key lessons drawn from the recent crisis has been the need to develop a framework of this type. The difficulties are manifold, especially for global banks, which operate in many jurisdictions and under different sets of laws and organizational frameworks (e.g., branches versus subsidiaries). The Basel Committee and the Financial Stability Board are working on this issue, and finding it to be among the thorniest with which they have to contend.

Moral hazard is usually present when governments intervene to help stabilize a financial system—or under any system of insurance. In the case of a lender of last resort, the valid concern is that the mere existence of such a lender encourages financial institutions to take more risks, since they know that in an emergency they will be bailed out; that is, they will be saved. The question here is: Who is "they"? It is generally accepted—and appropriately so—that equity holders should not be saved when a financial institution goes bankrupt.[10] Generally, it is assumed that to preserve the payments mechanism, deposit holders up to a certain size of deposits should be saved, perhaps up to deposit insurance limits—though frequently in financial crises governments extend deposit safety nets well beyond their normal limits.

The most difficult issue concerns bondholders. If a financial institution goes bankrupt, the bondholders will and should share in the losses. Nonetheless, governments sometimes extend guarantees to holders of nondeposit claims on banks, for instance, short-term paper. Why? The answer may that in a financial crisis, governments are willing to go a long way to prevent a cascade of bankruptcies, which is likely to develop if the bondholders have an incentive to run. Or, to put it more simply, it may be difficult to draw the line between deposit-like obligations of banks and equity-like claims. Further it may be argued that once the markets realize that bonds—particularly short-term paper—are likely to be written down in a crisis, the costs of bank financing in normal times are likely to rise.

A similar issue was discussed about a decade ago, when the IMF pursued the possibility of a sovereign debt-restructuring mechanism (SDRM). It was argued at the time that it should be easier to restructure sovereign bonds than it typically was in bonds issued in New York, which required unanimity among their holders to be restructured. Accordingly it was proposed that sovereign bonds should include CACs, collective action clauses, which would permit majority (or at least less than 100 percent) approval for restructuring. This issue was highly controversial, and potential borrowers objected that its inclusion would increase their financing costs. In the event it turned out that CACs already existed in some bonds issued in London (so-called British Trust Deed instruments) and that their effects on the cost of financing appeared to be small. Since then some sovereigns, including Mexico, have included CACs in their bonds, apparently without important effects on their cost of financing.

In the case of financial institutions, some banks have begun to issue *contingent capital*, bonds that automatically convert into equity when some objective criterion so signifies. In the last two years both Rabobank and Lloyd's have issues such bonds. Appealing as this approach may be, the systemic dynamics of the triggering of these bonds in a crisis remains to be tested in practice.

Nonetheless: while the use of contingent capital and other forms of financing that become more equity-like in a crisis—and more generally, the development of resolution mechanisms—will all help deal with moral hazard issues, the mere existence of a lender of last resort raises moral hazard issues. That is true. But there is nothing that says that the optimal reaction to moral hazard is to stop selling insurance. Rather, its existence is one factor to be taken into account in dealing with any situation where the state provides explicit or implicit forms of insurance—just as it has to be taken into account in private sector insurance contracts, for instance, the provision of fire insurance.

After having had to decide how to deal with moral hazard issues in a variety of financial crises, I have arrived at the following guide to conduct: *if you find yourself on the verge of imposing massive costs on an econ-omy—that is, on the people of a country or countries—by precipitating a crisis in order to prevent moral hazard, it is too late. You should not take the action that imposes those costs.* Rather, in thinking through how a system will operate in a crisis, you need to take into account the likeli-hood of facing such choices, and you need to do everything you can in designing the system to keep that likelihood very small.

Lesson 6:   The importance of the exchange rate for a small open economy.

The (real) exchange rate is one of the two most important macroeco-nomic variables in a small open economy, the (real) interest rate being the other. No central banker in such an economy can be indifferent to the level of the exchange rate. But there are no easy choices in exchange rate management.

There is first the choice of the exchange rate system, a choice that is tied up with the question of capital controls. If capital flows can be con-trolled, then there may be advantages for a country in trying to fix its nominal exchange rate. Nonetheless, and without entering the long-running debate over exchange rate systems, I believe that it is better to operate with a flexible exchange rate system and with a more open capital account.

"Flexible" does not mean that a country should not intervene in the foreign exchange market, or that the capital account should be completely open. Rather, it means that the country should not draw an exchange rate line in the sand and declare "thus far, and no further"; countries should not commit themselves to defending a particular exchange rate.

Market participants often say that the central bank cannot stand against market forces. However, we need to recognize the asymmetry between defending against pressures for depreciation and appreciation of the currency. In the case of pressures for depreciation, at the existing exchange rate the market wants more foreign exchange. The central bank has a limited supply of foreign exchange, and thus cannot stand against the pressure of the market for very long—though as the recent crisis has shown, large foreign exchange reserves can help the central bank deal with market pressures, for example, as in Brazil, Korea, and Russia during the Great Recession.

In the case of appreciation, at the existing exchange rate the markets want more domestic currency. The central bank can produce unlimited amounts of domestic currency—that is, it can intervene to buy the foreign exchange flowing into the country. Of course, to prevent inflation, it will have to sterilize the foreign exchange inflow. But that can be done, as the Bank of Israel and other central banks have shown over the last three years.

In the case of pressures for appreciation, the central bank has to balance the net costs of holding additional reserves against the benefits of preventing unwanted appreciation. This is a complicated calculus,[11] one that has led to the development of various rules for reserve holdings: when the current account was the dominant factor in the exchange market, the rule was specified in terms of holding reserves equal to the value of X months of imports; now that the capital account is at least as important, reserve-holding rules of thumb relate to capital flows, generally based on some form of the Greenspan–Guidotti rule that a country's reserves should at least cover the economy's short-term obligations falling due over the next year. The recent crisis has resulted in many countries deciding to hold more reserves than the previous conventions implied. In addition country-specific factors may be relevant; for instance, in the case of Israel the central bank has explicitly noted our geopolitical situation in discussing our reserve holdings.

Central bankers used to say that they have only one instrument — the interest rate — and thus can have only one target — the inflation rate. That view, which is based on the Tinbergen result that there should be as many instruments as there are goals of policy, is not generally correct (Fischer 2010b: 38–41). But in any case, I see the instrument of intervention in the foreign exchange market as in effect giving the central bank an extra instrument (or at least an extra half-instrument) of policy, which enables it not only to target inflation but also to have some influence on the behavior of the exchange rate.

As the pressures for appreciation increase, a country may want to limit further intervention, and is likely to turn to the use of capital inflow controls. Such controls are rarely elegant, are typically difficult to administer, and are continually being undermined by private sector attempts to circumvent them. Central banks prefer to do without them. But sometimes they are needed, as many countries faced with large short-term capital inflows — including Israel — have concluded in recent months.

Exchange rate management can be difficult in a growing small open economy with a strong financial system. Capital flows are likely to be very sensitive to interest rate differentials, which leads to the exchange rate bearing more of the burden of adjustment to inflation and aggregate demand than may be optimal from the viewpoint of policy makers. In such a case the country may be tempted to join a currency bloc.

Membership of a currency bloc demands disciplined management of the domestic economy — of fiscal policy, and of the financial system. The exchange rate cannot be changed without leaving the bloc, a step with unknown but certainly major, probably massive, consequences for the economy. At this time many expound on the constraints that membership of the euro area impose on countries that cannot devalue. These constraints clearly matter. But it is rarely noted that when countries did have the freedom to devalue, changes in exchange rates were frequently disruptive of trade with their neighbors — and further that some countries that did have that freedom mismanaged it, and paid a significant price in terms of economic performance. Or to put it differently, whatever type of exchange rate arrangement a country has, there will be times when it wished it had a different one.

I have emphasized the exchange rate problems likely to face small open economies, for that is the type of economy in which I operate. But the truth is that most of what I have said about exchange rate management in a small open economy is true of any open economy, large or small.

Lesson 7:   The eternal verities—Lessons from the IMF.

While I have emphasized lessons that we central bankers have learned from the crisis, many of them lessons that our predecessors knew long ago, the crisis has also reinforced lessons *we* learned long ago. In particular, this crisis has reinforced the obvious belief that a country that manages itself well in normal times is likely to be better equipped to deal with the consequences of a crisis, and likely to emerge from it at lower cost.

Indeed we should continue to believe in the good housekeeping rules that the IMF has tirelessly promoted. In normal times countries should maintain fiscal discipline and monetary and financial stability. At all times they should take into account the need to follow growth-promoting structural policies. And they need to have a decent regard for the welfare of all segments of society.

The list is easy to make. It is more difficult to fill in the details, to decide what policies to follow in practice. And it is very difficult to implement such measures, particularly when times are good and when populist pressures are likely to be strong. But a country that does not do so is likely to pay a very high price.

Lesson 8:   Target inflation, flexibly.

How to summarize all these conclusions? Simply: *flexible* inflation targeting is the best way of conducting monetary policy. The tripartite set of goals of monetary policy set out in modern central bank laws provide the best current understanding of what a central bank should try to achieve. Namely a central bank should aim:

• to maintain price stability;

• to support the other goals of economic policy, particularly growth and employment, so long as medium-term price stability—over the course of a year or two or even three—is preserved; and

• to support and promote the stability and efficiency of the financial system.

It is noteworthy that these goals of the central bank were defined well over a decade ago, that they were in place in the ECB, the Bank of England, and other central banks before the global crisis and during it, and that there is no reason to change them now, despite the lessons we have been discussing. Rather, we have learned better ways of trying to achieve those goals.

Lesson 9: In a crisis, you do not panic.

Consistent with the title of this lecture, all the lessons so far are reflections on the most recent crisis. Nonetheless, I would like to add a lesson I learned in an earlier crisis, the first financial crisis in whose management I was deeply involved, that of Mexico in 1994–95. At the end of January 1995, the IMF was asked late one night to come up at very short notice—about nine hours—with an extra twenty billion dollars of loans to Mexico. The senior management of the Fund met in Managing Director Michel Camdessus' office very early the next morning, to find a solution. The first words of the Managing Director at that meeting were: "Gentlemen: this is a crisis, and in a crisis, you do not panic."

This advice has stood the test of time and experience.

Lesson 10:   And the final lesson.

In a crisis, central bankers (and no doubt other policy makers) will often find themselves deciding to implement policy actions that they never thought they would have to undertake—and these are frequently policy actions that they would prefer not to have to undertake. Hence a few final words of advice for central bankers:
"Never say never."

Notes

This chapter formed the basis for a dinner lecture delivered at the Bank of Israel conference on Lessons of the Global Crisis, in Jerusalem, on March 31, 2011. It is slightly modified from a series of lectures given during the preceding months: the Brahmananda Lecture at the Reserve Bank of India in February 2011; a lecture at the CEPR/ESI conference in Izmir on October 28, 2010; and a lecture at the conference of the Cyprus Economic Society in October 2010. I am grateful to colleagues at the Bank of Israel with whom I have discussed and lived through the issues of monetary policy during the last five years, and to Joshua Schneck of the Bank of Israel for research assistance.

1. The qualification relates to the fact that some researchers, for example, Clark Warburton, had emphasized this view before the publication of Friedman and Schwartz's work (e.g., see the papers reprinted in Warburton 1963).

2. This term appears to have been introduced into the literature by Willem Buiter and Anne Siebert.

3. It is sometimes objected that such actions would require excessively detailed intervention by the central bank, since it would have to decide which companies' assets to buy. However, it could simply buy very broad stock indexes.

4. For example: Financial Services Authority (2009), Group of Thirty (2009), and HM Treasury (2010).

5. In this section I draw extensively on comments I made in a panel discussion at a Norges Bank symposium (Fischer 2010a).

6. Although these capital requirements vary procyclically, the intent is to be anticyclical in terms of their effects on the economy. Hence they are usually defined as countercyclical.

7. This circumstance is sometimes invoked to explain why the mopping up approach was successful in the recession of 2001–2002.

8. This leaves aside the moral hazard issue, which will be discussed shortly.

9. It is tempting to say that a liquidity crisis can be defined as one in which the public sector makes a profit from its intervention. However, the public sector's profit depends on how its interventions are priced and structured, so that the question is more complicated.

10. Presumably the same goes for nonfinancial institutions.

11. One complication in measuring the costs of holding reserves relates to the numéraire in which the reserves are valued. Typically and appropriately, the central bank presents its accounts in local currency terms. Any central bank that has intervened to moderate appreciation pressures is likely to show a capital loss in terms of the local currency value of the reserves. However, some of the reserves are held to enable the country to purchase foreign goods if the need arises, and in terms of the purpose for which the reserves are held, it is thus not clear that the numéraire should be the local as opposed to a foreign currency. Further, if capital flows reverse, the country may find itself intervening to prevent depreciation. One central bank colleague has remarked that his reserve holdings, at mark to market value, generally show a loss, but that whenever he has intervened in a crisis, he has made a profit.

References

Bernanke, Ben S. 1983. Non-monetary effects of the financial crisis in the propagation of the Great Depression. *American Economic Review* 73: 257–76.

Financial Services Authority. 2009. *The Turner Review: A Regulatory Response to the Global Banking Crisis* (March).

Fischer, Stanley. 2010a. Where do central banks go from here? In Sigbjørn Atle Berg, Øyvind Eitrheim, Jan F. Qvigstad, and Marius Ryel, eds., *What Is a Useful Central Bank?* Norges Bank occasional papers 42. Oslo: The Norges Bank, 179–87.

Fischer, Stanley. 2010b. Panel discussion. In Christopher Kent and Michael Robson, eds., *The Reserve Bank of Australia: Fiftieth Anniversary Symposium.* Sydney: Reserve Bank of Australia, 38–41.

Friedman, Milton, and Anna J. Schwartz. 1963. *A Monetary History of the United States, 1867–1960.* Princeton: Princeton University Press.

Group of Thirty. 2009. *Financial Reform—A Framework for Financial Stability.* Washington, DC.

Hatzius, Jan. 2009. The specter of deflation. *US Economics Analyst—Goldman Sachs Global ECS Research.* New York.

HM Treasury. 2010. *A New Approach to Financial Regulation*. London.

Reinhart, Carmen M., and Kenneth S. Rogoff. 2009. *This Time Is Different*. Princeton: Princeton University Press.

Tobin, James. 1971. An essay on the principles of debt management. In *Essays in Economics*. Vol. 1: *Macroeconomics*. Chicago: Markham.

Warburton, Clark. 1963. *Depression, Inflation, and Monetary Policy; Selected Papers, 1945–1953*. Baltimore: Johns Hopkins University Press.

I   MONETARY POLICY IN VIEW OF THE CRISIS

1 Monetary Policy Frameworks after the Great Financial Crisis

Huw Pill and Frank Smets

1.1 Introduction

The great financial crisis of the new millennium and its fallout on economic activity has, in the eyes of some observers, raised questions on the appropriateness of the price-stability oriented monetary policy frameworks that, until only a few years ago, were credited with supporting a long period of global nominal and real economic stability. For example, in view of the existence of a lower bound on policy-controlled nominal interest rates and the constraints this implies for active macrostabilization policies, the appropriateness of the pursuit of a small, but positive inflation objective around 2 percent has been challenged.[1] Moreover the neglect of explicit financial stability objectives in monetary policy frameworks and the mandates of central banks has been widely criticized on the ground that monetary policy can—and should—contribute to containing financial imbalances and instabilities.[2]

In this chapter we argue that the conduct of monetary policy should neither be changed fundamentally nor overburdened with additional objectives. Rather, it should remain focused on maintaining price stability over the medium term. Nonetheless, we recognize the need for some refinement of the existing policy framework in order to avoid and reduce the costs of large financial crises. In the interest of clarity, we flag three important elements of our argument from the outset.

First, the depth and persistence of the recent recession is related to the malfunctioning of financial markets throughout the crisis period: mortgage markets, markets for asset-backed securities (ABS), sovereign debt markets, and—perhaps most important (at least for the 2008 to 2010 period on which we focus)—interbank money markets have all seized up to a greater or lesser extent.[3] The presence of these financial market dysfunctionalities has impaired the conventional interest rate channel of monetary policy transmission and thus threatened the effectiveness of monetary policy. In the absence of other measures, large interest rate cuts would have been required to achieve macroeconomic stabilization and offset the contractionary effect of the rise in implicit or explicit market spreads. Large interest rate changes alone can induce instability and volatility. We argue, first, that nonstandard policy measures targeted at repairing malfunctioning markets are potentially more efficient instruments in stabilizing the economy. By re-establishing transmission, they complement and enhance the effectiveness of the standard interest rate policy instrument and thus serve to achieve macrostabilization without inducing greater interest rate volatility.

Second, we argue that the solid anchoring of inflation expectations that resulted from the establishment of credible price stability-oriented policy frameworks played a crucial role during the financial crisis, both as an automatic stabilizer and in preventing the emergence of a depression-like debt-deflation spiral. We suggest that this automatic-stabilizer role can be strengthened, notably by emphasizing the appropriate medium-term orientation of monetary policy in the pursuit of price stability. Indeed, going further, we could consider, for example, that paying greater attention to the price *level*—and not letting "bygones-be-bygones" by focusing solely on price *changes* (as reflected in inflation developments)—may yield substantial benefits.

Third, we argue that the source of the current crisis lies in the buildup of financial imbalances during the early part of the millennium. Newly established macroprudential policies are geared at preventing the buildup of excessive leverage and strengthening the resilience of the financial sector.[4] But, through the analysis of monetary and credit developments a stability-oriented monetary policy should avoid contributing to the buildup of financial imbalances and fragilities.

This chapter illustrates these points on the basis of the ECB experience during the 2008 financial crisis. We draw on a body of papers in which we have collaborated with a number of other colleagues.[5] Our empirical analysis focuses on the euro area during the period between the collapse of Lehman Brothers (in September 2008) and the onset of the European sovereign debt crisis (in May 2010). Such a focus is limiting as the ECB's experience inevitably reflects the specifics of the euro area: its financial structure, conjunctural perspective, and institutional setup. And many important monetary policy issues have arisen as government debt tensions subsequently intensified throughout Europe.[6] Yet maintaining a focus on the euro area during the immediate post-Lehman period also has a number of advantages for our purposes: available empirical analysis is more mature, and the euro area specificities create cross-sectional variation that allows lessons to be drawn by comparison with the experience of other countries.

After briefly recalling in section 1.2 some salient features of the recent financial crisis as they purport to the European experience, the remainder of the chapter is organized as follows. First, in order to shed light on the desirability of defining the central bank's objective in terms of a low rate of consumer price inflation and to motivate the subsequent analysis of NSMs, in section 1.3 we present some evidence on whether the lower bound on short-term nominal interest rates was binding in the euro area following Lehman's demise. We find this constraint to have been of lesser relevance than has typically been thought, and apparently of less relevance in the euro area than in the United States, United Kingdom, or Japan.

In section 1.4 we analyze the effectiveness of the ECB's nonstandard measures (NSMs) in supporting monetary policy transmission in the euro area so as to assess whether other policy actions can substitute for lowering short-term policy rates toward their lower bound in pursuit of macrostabilization. Although by nature exceptional and limited in extent and duration, we find that the ECB's NSMs were effective in addressing bank funding problems and ensuring a better transmission of policy rates.

In section 1.5 we complement our analysis of these operational and tactical issues with some strategic considerations surrounding the implementation and effectiveness of NSMs. We focus on two points: (1) we show how the stability of medium-term inflation expectations has helped stabilize the economy and reduce the likelihood of hitting the lower bound and discuss how the benefits of the stability-oriented approach could be further enhanced, for example by considering focusing on the price level (rather than the inflation rate) so as to induce an even more self-stabilizing mechanism in price and macroeconomic dynamics; (2) we emphasize that "prevention is better than cure." Information extracted from an enhanced analysis of monetary and credit developments can support a medium-term, stability-oriented strategy whereby monetary policy naturally "leans against" credit and liquidity booms, thereby helping to avoid the buildup of intrafinancial sector leverage and financial imbalances that can eventually destabilize the financial system and macroeconomy (including the price level). But such an approach is unlikely to be sufficient to prevent financial crises: embryonic macroprudential initiatives remain crucial.

Against this background, in section 1.6 we conclude with some final policy-oriented remarks pointing to the lessons that can be drawn by other central banks and policy makers from the ECB's experience.

1.2   Recalling the Facts: Features of the Financial Crisis in Europe

Financial turmoil first erupted in Europe with the emergence of money market tensions on August 9, 2007, following the announcement that a number of investment funds had to close as they could no longer value their portfolios owing to the illiquidity of asset-backed securities markets. These tensions escalated into a deep financial crisis after the collapse of Lehman Brothers on September 15, 2008, once it became clear that even prominent and systemically important institutions could fail. At that point financial markets froze, economic activity was disrupted, and the global economy appeared on the verge of collapse.

This threat gave rise to a significant and prompt policy response. Monetary authorities, governments, and supervisory authorities across the world acted decisively so as to avoid a recurrence of the collapse of the financial system, output, and prices seen during the Great Depression of the 1930s. Following the coordinated interest rate cut of October 8, 2008, the major central banks continued to ease monetary policy by substantially reducing policy-controlled short-term interest rates, in many cases close to their effective lower bound. At the same time a wide variety of unconventional or nonstandard monetary policy measures were introduced.[7]

As background, it is useful to divide the financial crisis and its aftermath into three periods. Figures 1.1 and 1.2, which show interbank money market spreads and government debt CDS spreads respectively, identify the following phases: (1) an initial period of turmoil after August 2007, during which tensions focused on ABS markets (in particular, those for subprime mortgages) and spilt over via the exacerbation of liquidity and credit risk into interbank money markets; (2) a period of intense global crisis following the failure of Lehman Brothers in September 2008, which led to the seizing up of money markets and significant disruptions in other market segments (including sovereign bonds); and (3) the emergence of a sovereign crisis specific to the euro area as from late April 2010, when the Greek situation deteriorated significantly.

During the first phase (August 2007 to September 2008), interbank money market spreads widened from a few basis points to between 50

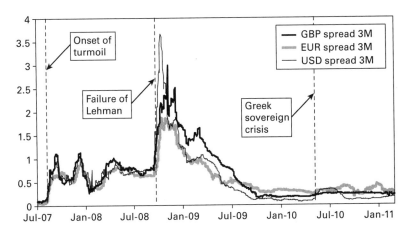

Figure 1.1
Money market spreads. Spread between EURIBOR/LIBOR and OIS rates, percentage points.
Sources: Bloomberg, ECB

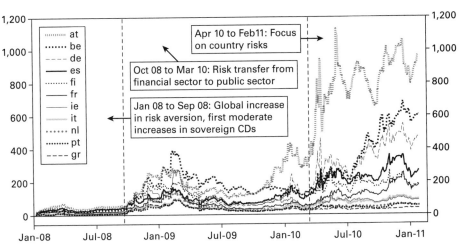

Figure 1.2
Government debt CDS spreads. Five-year CDS spreads, basis points.
Source: Datastream

and 100 basis points while sovereign CDS spreads, albeit increasing somewhat, remained contained.

Following the failure of Lehman, the spread between the three-month Euribor and the equivalent OIS rate—a common indicator of money market tension[8]—increased dramatically, more than doubling in the euro area. (The equivalent spread reached more than 350 basis points in the United States.) Owing to the comprehensive and substantial policy response, toward the end of 2009 this spread subsequently fell back. During this period government debt CDS spreads increased significantly in Europe, in particular in those countries where deficits rose substantially owing to the impact of automatic stabilizers in the face of a deep recession, discretionary expansionary fiscal policy, and interventions to shore up the banking sector. In short, at least to some extent risk was transferred from the financial sector onto public sector balance sheets, leading to a deterioration of the fiscal position.

Finally, in May 2010 the Greek sovereign debt market seized up following a large revision of the reported government deficit for 2009 and a loss of market confidence in the authorities' ability and willingness to address the large rise in Greek government debt. This shock soon spilt over into other "peripheral" countries (at that time, in particular, Ireland, Portugal, and Spain), as well as leading to an across-the-board rise in government debt CDS spreads as sovereign markets came under generalized pressure. At the time of writing (end of 2011), the sovereign debt crisis has turned into a twin sovereign debt and banking crisis as many banks are affected by considerable mark-to-market losses in their holdings of sovereign bonds.

As we noted above, in this chapter we focus on the middle period, between Lehman's demise and the onset of the European sovereign debt crisis. Even within this period it is useful to distinguish two phases. From September 2008 through the spring of 2009, monetary policy was mainly characterized by aggressive interest rate cutting by all the major central banks. Unconventional measures focused on supporting market functioning (even if their design varied across jurisdictions, according to the structure of the financial sector, the central bank's operational framework and the starting point from which such measures departed).[9] But as money market spreads came down from spring of 2009, policy-controlled interest rates remained much more stable. Nonstandard measures came to the forefront of the policy response, becoming more heterogeneous across countries as they did so. It is this heterogeneity that motivates the analysis in the next section.

1.3   Empirical Relevance of the Lower Bound on ECB Policy Rates during 2009

Broadly speaking, two motivations for the introduction of unconventional monetary policy measures have been offered by central banks: (1) that they represented the continuation of monetary policy easing "by other means," once the lower bound on short-term policy rates had been reached, and (2) that they supported the transmission of monetary policy in the face of financial market malfunctioning, so as to ensure that the selected policy stance (as reflected in the settings of policy rates) passed through to the real economy.[10]

From the spring of 2009 the policy discussion in the United States and the United Kingdom was motivated by the first consideration: how to stimulate the economy in an environment where a further easing of short-term nominal interest rates was constrained by the zero lower bound.[11] In this light the Federal Reserve's Large-Scale Asset Purchase (LSAP) program and the Bank of England's Quantitative Easing (QE) program were presented as ways to provide additional monetary easing once standard means were exhausted. By contrast, less emphasis was placed on such lower bound constraints in the euro area. For example, in his introductory statement to the regular monetary policy press conference in May 2009 then-ECB President J.-C. Trichet stated: "we did not decide today that the new level of our policy rates was the lowest level that can never be crossed, whatever future circumstances may be," suggesting—at least *prima facie*—that lower bound considerations were not yet binding. Rather, the ECB's nonstandard measures—labeled "enhanced credit support"—were motivated by the second consideration described above, and were thus aimed at maintaining monetary policy transmission in the face of financial market blockages and dislocations.[12]

One should not overstate this distinction: in general, all nonstandard measures aimed at avoiding the transformation of immediate and self-evident liquidity problems into deeper solvency problems (notably the bankruptcies, asset fire sales and collapse of financial markets that would have disrupted the flow of financing from private savers to private borrowers in a more lasting and fundamental way). But drawing such a distinction is useful in making an assessment of the measures, since one needs to establish an appropriate metric for their effectiveness. Moreover the distinction is relevant in drawing strategic conclusions from recent experience: for example, to assess whether an inflation target is "too low" given the potential incidence of the lower bound, one must take a view of whether such a constraint is inevitable in the face of a big adverse shock such as a financial crisis or whether it can be avoided by getting "more bang for your buck" through NSMs, directly aiming at addressing the financial market malfunctioning and thereby increasing the effectiveness of policy transmission at low rates when financial tensions are intense.

With these considerations in mind, in this section we analyze empirically the extent to which the ECB's policy-controlled short-term interest rates hit their effective lower bound in the euro area in the months following the collapse of Lehman Brothers. This is a necessary preliminary to understand the design of the ECB's nonstandard measures. We present three exercises that suggest that the lower bound on interest rates may have been less binding in the euro area than in the United States or the United Kingdom.

The first exercise is based on the work of Orphanides (2003, 2010). These papers demonstrate that a simple first-difference interest rate policy rule—where policy rates are determined by one-year-ahead forecasts of output growth and inflation taken from the ECB's survey of professional forecasters[13]—has accurately characterized the setting of the ECB's standard interest rate.[14] The simple policy rule is given by the following equation:

$$\Delta i_t = 0.5(E_t \pi_{t+1} - \overline{\pi}) + 0.5(E_t \Delta y_{t+1} - \Delta \overline{y}),$$

where Δi_t is the change in the main refinancing rate, $E_t \pi_{t+1} - \overline{\pi}$ is the deviation of the one-year-ahead inflation forecast from the inflation objective, and $\Delta y_{t+1} - \Delta \overline{y}$ is the deviation of the one-year-ahead forecast of real GDP growth from potential output growth.

Figure 1.3 (taken from Orphanides 2010) plots the ECB's main refinancing (MRO) rate[15] against the path for this rate prescribed by the simple real-time policy rule, which Orphanides (2003) found to also describe Fed behavior during the Volcker–Greenspan period very well. The shaded area reflects variants stemming from different assumptions for the inflation objective and the long-term potential growth rate.

Two conclusions are worth highlighting. First, this simple rule captures the developments of the ECB's main refinancing rate very well, as also noted by Smets (2010). This continues to be the case during the financial crisis. There are only two recent periods in which a deviation is apparent: (1) in the summer of 2008 the rule suggests a gradual easing of monetary policy, whereas the ECB increased its policy rate by 25 basis points—

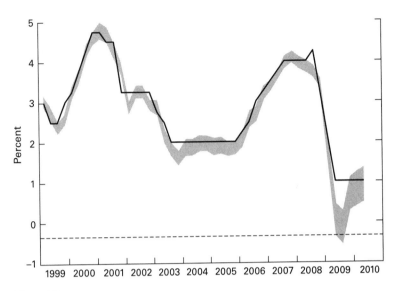

Figure 1.3
The Orphanides rule in the euro area
Source: Orphanides (2010)

this tightening was a preemptive move in the light of the high expected headline inflation due to a rise of oil and commodity prices and the risk of second-round effects in wages, and (2) the Orphanides rule points to a cut toward zero of the main refinancing rate in the summer of 2009, whereas the MRO rate was kept constant at 1 percent. However, this deviation is less obvious once one considers the EONIA rate as an alternative measure of the short-term interest rate. In normal times the MRO and EONIA rates are closely aligned. But, following the ECB's decision to fully satisfy the markets' demand for liquidity at the main refinancing rate via its fixed rate/full allotment (FRFA) tenders as part of its enhanced credit support, the EONIA rate dropped considerably below the MRO rate (owing to the generous liquidity conditions created by the switch in tender procedures) and traded close to the deposit rate which during this time stood at 25 basis points. Second, although there is a period in mid-2009 where some variants of the rule point to negative MRO rates, the Orphanides rule rate does not fall decisively or for a prolonged period below the zero lower bound through the financial crisis period. This contrasts with similar exercises conducted for the United States or United Kingdom.

The second exercise is summarized in figure 1.4, which plots the probability over the projection horizon of hitting the lower bound on nominal

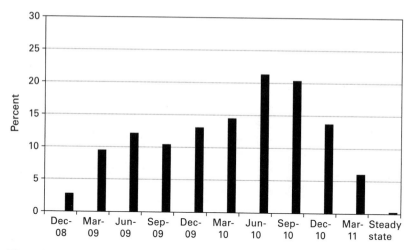

Figure 1.4
Incidence of lower bound based on stochastic simulations around projections. Probability over two-year forecast horizon.
Source: ECB calculations

interest rate in the ECB's published baseline macroeconomic projections derived using stochastic simulations of the ECB's new areawide model (NAWM) of the euro area.[16] The probability of hitting the lower bound rises significantly as the policy rate is reduced to 1 percent and attains a peak of slightly above 20 percent in June 2010. This is not a negligible figure. But the main point to take away is that the maximum probability remained relatively low throughout the episode and was only around 10 percent during the crucial period in the middle of 2009.

The third exercise employs the techniques developed in Giannone et al. (2011a). This paper presents an empirical model of the euro area economy, which—in addition to the normal set of macroeconomic variables—captures the joint cyclical behavior of a large number of monetary and credit aggregates, as well as interest rate spreads, yields and asset prices. More specifically, the paper constructs a very general multivariate linear model for thirty-nine euro area monthly time series, using a vector autoregressive (VAR) specification with 13 lags for the (log-)level of these variables. The so-called curse of dimensionality is addressed using Bayesian shrinkage methods, as suggested in De Mol et al. (2008) and Banbura et al. (2010). This model can be seen as a very flexible way of capturing the interactions between a large set of macroeconomic and financial variables in the euro area.

In order to assess the importance of the lower bound on nominal interest rates in the euro area, we conduct the following exercise. First, the model is estimated over the pre-crisis sample, from January 1991 to August 2007. This estimation should be understood as establishing the statistical regularities or "stylized facts" inherent in the "pre-crisis" euro area economy. In particular, implicit in the estimated dynamics of the model is a "policy rule" (more complex than that suggested by Orphanides above, but of the same character), which relates the short-term interest rate[17] to macroeconomic and financial variables. Second, using this model, we construct a conditional forecast of the short-term interest for the period from January 1999 through August 2010. This forecast is conditional on the actual path of the variables capturing economic activity in the model. We interpret this forecast as capturing what the historical pattern of policy-making would have implied for the level of short-term interest rates in the event of a recession like that seen in the aftermath of Lehman's failure.

The results of this exercise are shown in figure 1.5. Two messages are apparent. First, the actual path of short-term interest rates mimics quite closely that of the forecast. This suggests that the ECB has continued to set interest rates in line with historical regularities even in the face of the financial crisis. To the extent that discrepancies emerge, actual rates have tended to be lower than the implicit policy rule embodied in the

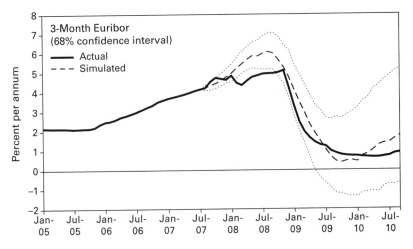

Figure 1.5
Evidence on lower bound. Actual and simulated three-month EURIBOR. Percent per annum; 68 percent confidence interval.
Sources: Bloomberg; simulations based on the Giannone et al. (2011b) model

conditional forecast would suggest. The only exception to this pattern occurs in the second half of 2009, where actual rates were modestly (less than 50 bp) above the rule/forecast-consistent level. Second, the confidence intervals surrounding the forecast give some impression of the extent that a lower bound may have constrained the evolution of short-term rates. The median conditional forecast (shown by the dashed line in figure 1.5) remains above the literal lower bound of zero throughout the forecast horizon through August 2010. That said, a significant portion of the probability distribution (around 25 percent) does lie below zero in the second half of 2009, an estimate comparable to that derived from the simulations of the ECB's NAWM discussed above.

Summing up the conclusions we draw from these exercises, we find that empirical evidence developed using three very different techniques points to little immediate impact of a lower bound constraint on nominal interest rates on the ECB's standard monetary policy decisions. Our analysis suggests that, on the basis of various characterizations of the ECB's normal pre-crisis policy making behavior, the probability of hitting the lower bound rose to a *maximum* of 20 to 25 percent during 2009, with the *modal* prescribed rate remaining above zero.

While such results do not rule out that concerns about encountering the lower bound in the future did enter current policy decisions, they do suggest that throughout the crucial post-Lehman period the ECB's policy rule did not dictate negative rates and therefore a need to pursue monetary policy easing via nonstandard means as a substitute for lower interest rates. Rather, these results are consistent with the view that the ECB set interest rates in line with its normal practice and pursued non-standard measures in order to ensure that the stance of monetary policy established in this way was effectively transmitted to the real economy. This conclusion motivates the analysis in the next section.

1.4   Effectiveness of NSMs in Supporting Monetary Policy Transmission in the Euro Area

Since (on the basis of the preceding section) we view the lower bound on nominal short-term interest rates as having been a secondary concern for monetary policy makers in the euro area throughout the post-Lehman crisis period, the ECB's NSMs can be characterized as a mechanism to *complement* standard interest rate decisions, rather than substitute for them. In line with its historical practice, the ECB decided on an interest rate level appropriate to fulfill its price stability mandate prior to the crisis and then implemented its NSMs to ensure that this policy stance was effectively transmitted to the economy as a whole. Against this background, evaluation of the effectiveness of the ECB's NSMs should focus on whether, in the face of the financial crisis, monetary policy transmission has been maintained. The technical challenges faced in making such an assessment are formidable. For example, we face the usual policy identification problem: since the ECB acted promptly to the onset of crisis, distinguishing the macroeconomic impact of the policy response from the underlying shock that triggered that response is inherently very difficult.

Rather than address these challenges head on, here we again present empirical exercises conducted using the Giannone et al. (2011a) machinery discussed above. These exercises are in the same spirit as the interest rate policy rule analysis: they do not attempt to identify policy shocks, but rather make a reduced-form assessment of whether key macro and financial variables behaved aberrantly during the crisis period. To conduct this analysis, we estimate a very rich model of macroeconomic and financial dynamics in the pre-crisis data, so as to establish a characterization of what constitutes "normal" behavior of the euro area economy and financial system. We then use this model to produce forecasts of macro variables central to monetary policy transmission and compare these with the observed behavior of these variables. Importantly, the forecasts we produce are conditional on the actual behavior of those variables capturing the business cycle.

Our interpretation of this exercise is as follows. The conditional forecast (labeled "simulated" in figures 1.6, 1.7, and 1.8) reflects the anticipated evolution of key monetary and financial variables given the observed path of economic activity during the financial crisis, assuming that the historical pre-crisis regularities in the euro area data are maintained. This represents the benchmark behavior of the monetary and credit sector in the face of a marked fall in economic activity against which we can compare observed outcomes. By their nature, the observed paths of monetary and credit variables (labeled "actual" in figures 1.6 through 1.8) are also conditional on the observed path of economic activity. But they are also conditional on two other factors: (1) the actual behavior of the monetary and financial sector over this period and (2) the impact of the nonstandard monetary policy measures by the euro system. The former is not (necessarily) "normal"—indeed, in a context of financial crisis, one would anticipate that financial institutions and markets behave abnormally: it is precisely such behavior that

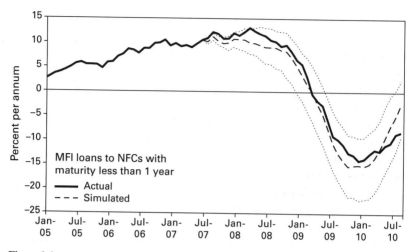

Figure 1.6
Transmission via short-term corporate loans. Actual (solid line) and simulated (dashed line) MFI loans to NFCs with maturity less than 1 year. Percent per annum; 68 percent confidence interval.
Sources: Bloomberg; simulations based on the Giannone et al. (2011b) model

characterizes the crisis. The latter—again, by their nature—are not part of "normal" pre-crisis behavior captured by the model.

Comparing the actual path with the simulated path offers an insight into monetary policy transmission. Divergence between the actual and simulated paths can be interpreted as a measure of the extent to which the introduction of nonstandard measures failed to offset the impact of the financial crisis on the banking sector, resulting in an overall ("reduced form") impact on money and credit growth and their relationship with other macroeconomic variables. By the same token, convergence between actual and simulated paths can be seen as evidence of the success of the nonstandard measures in insulating macroeconomic monetary and credit dynamics from the immediate impact of the financial crisis on financial institutions and markets.

Here we focus on three key macrofinancial variables: short-term loans to nonfinancial corporations (NFCs) (figure 1.6), narrow money (M1) (figure 1.7), and the interest rate on bank loans to small and medium-sized enterprises (figure 1.8).

Short-term loans to NFCs are typically seen as crucial at times of economic distress, since they play an important buffering role in corporate cash flows. Such loans are typically used to finance working capital and the forced accumulation of inventory as the business cycle turns down. Concerns about the impact of a "credit crunch" on economic activity are often associated with the potential drying up of the flow of such loans and its significant adverse consequences for economic activity and employment. Figure 1.6 suggests that the behavior of short-term corporate loans during the crisis closely mimics that which would have been anticipated by the model in the event of a sharp fall in economic activity. This result supports the view that the euro system's nonstandard monetary policy measures were effective in supporting financial intermediation, preventing the forced liquidation of such loans as bank funding conditions and the interbank money market seized up, and thus they maintained monetary policy transmission in the face of market dislocations. Long-term loans to firms (not shown here, but see Giannone et al. 2011a for details) appear more significantly affected by the financial crisis (in both economic and statistical senses), especially from the middle of 2009. While prima facie this raises some doubts about the effectiveness of the nonstandard measures, one possible explanation is a shift out of longer term bank borrowing to the issuance of debt securities by large euro area companies. And such loans are less central to the immediate transmission of monetary policy.

Turning to figure 1.7 and the behavior of M1, the evolution of narrow money after the collapse of Lehman Brothers is statistically

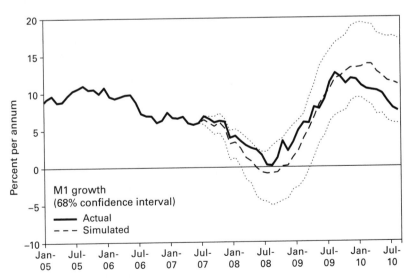

Figure 1.7
Transmission via narrow money. Actual (solid line) and simulated (dashed line) M1 growth. Percent per annum; 68 percent confidence interval.
Sources: Bloomberg; simulations based on the Giannone et al. (2011b) model

indistinguishable from the model's conditional forecast. This reflects the strong liquidity effect driving the behavior of M1 — the sharp fall in short-term interest rates both observed in the data and predicted by the model (given the contraction of real activity) gives rise to stronger demand for the overnight deposits and currency comprising M1.[18] The availability of short-term monetary liquidity to the nonfinancial sector was therefore not impaired by the crisis itself, again suggesting that monetary policy transmission was maintained. By contrast, M3 growth (again, not shown, but see Giannone et al. 2011b) behaves quite differently during the financial crisis than would have been anticipated on the basis of pre-crisis regularities. More generally, in seeking behavior that differs from pre-crisis historical regularities, our analysis focuses attention on the liability side of bank balance sheets, rather than the asset side. In consequence one might ask — in contrast with much of the existing literature — whether the propagation of the 2007 to 2010 financial crisis should be seen as via a "bank funding crunch," rather than as a "bank credit crunch." As with short-term corporate loans, the evidence suggests that the immediate impact of the financial crisis on economic activity was contained by the ECB's NSMs but that the underlying behavior of the wider financial sector — as reflected in balance sheet structure — was more significantly affected, with (as yet, at end of 2011) unknown results.

Figure 1.8 shows the results for the interest rate on bank short-term loans to NFCs. It can be read in conjunction with figure 1.6: it has been argued that widening interest rate spreads on bank borrowing are a more important channel for propagating a credit crunch than the flow of loans itself.[19] Remarkably, the figure suggests that observed bank lending rates were *below* what would have been anticipated conditional on pre-crisis regularities. Since the behavior of the benchmark money market rate has broadly followed the path anticipated by the conditional forecast (as shown in figure 1.5), we can conclude that the spread of bank loan rates over money market rates has followed historical regularities in the face of the financial crisis. Again, this suggests that the ECB's NSMs were effective in insulating the corporate sector from the impact of the crisis on the banking and financial system, at least in the immediate aftermath of Lehman's failure.

Of course, these reduced-form exercises do not shed light on the channels through which the ECB's NSMs have served to maintain crucial financial flows to the real economy through the financial crisis. We understand their main effect to have been through the expansion of central bank intermediation, which substituted for financial transactions that

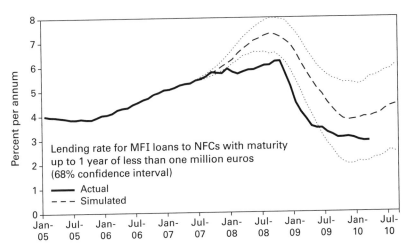

Figure 1.8
Transmission via bank interest rates on loans to NFCs. Actual (solid line) and simulated (dashed line) lending rate for MFI loans to NFCs for maturity up to 1 year of less than EUR 1 million. Percent per annum; 68 percent confidence interval.
Sources: Bloomberg; simulations based on the Giannone et al. (2011b) model

could no longer take place in malfunctioning private markets. In particular, the ECB expanded its role in (1) *maturity transformation* by increasing the average maturity of its repo operations, (2) *liquidity transformation* by accepting as collateral assets that had become illiquid in private markets and thereby offering cash against them, and (3) the provision of *transactions services* via its interaction with a very large number of counterparties, which allowed the ECB to act as a central counterparty for bank transactions. Taken together, these measures allowed much greater intermediation across the ECB balance sheet (which expanded significantly as a result) and in turn prevented a collapse of the financial sector and mitigated the impact of the financial crisis and market turmoil on the real economy.

1.5   Some Strategic Considerations

1.5.1   Defining Monetary Policy Objectives

The effectiveness of the NSMs in mitigating the impact of the financial crisis on the real economy, and implied reduction of the likelihood of hitting the lower bound on short-term interest rates, suggests that calls for reviewing the optimality of central banks pursuing a small positive inflation objective may be overstated. In this section we argue, on the contrary, that the stability of inflation expectations which resulted from the credibility of central banks' stability-oriented pre-crisis approach was an important asset for the effectiveness of the standard monetary policy response. Overburdening monetary policy with other objectives may endanger this credibility.

From the beginning of EMU, the ECB has defined price stability as annual HICP inflation below 2 percent, to be maintained over the medium term. In 2003 it was clarified that the ECB's Governing Council aimed at keeping inflation below, but *close to,* 2 percent. At the time the establishment of a small inflation buffer was partly justified on the argument that it would reduce the likelihood of hitting the lower bound and thereby lead to greater macroeconomic and price stability.[20] The ECB has achieved its objective remarkably well: from the establishment of EMU in 1999 till the end of 2010, the average HICP inflation rate has been 2 percent. Figure 1.9 shows that annual headline inflation has fluctu-

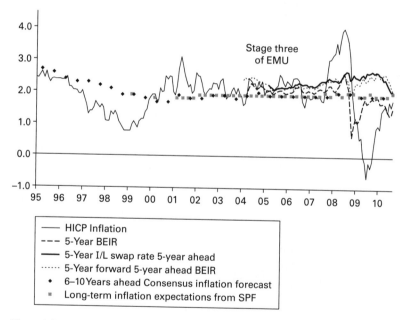

Figure 1.9
Inflation and inflation expectations. BEIR is breakeven inflation rate from comparison of inflation indexed to conventional sovereign bonds; last observation: September 2010.
Sources: Consensus; ECB Survey of Professional Forecasters; Eurostat; Reuters; ECB calculations

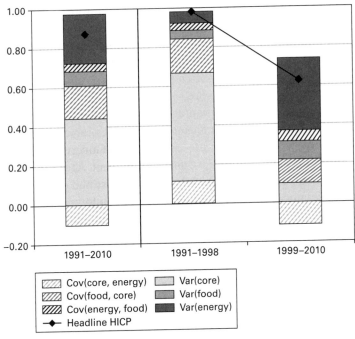

Figure 1.10
Inflation volatility and its components. Core refers to headline inflation excluding food and energy. Var is variance, Cov is twice the covariance between the respective measures in order to sum up to overall variance of the headline measure. See Fahr et al. (2011). Sources: ECB; Eurostat

ated around the 2 percent level, in some cases reaching almost 4 percent such as in 2008 and in other cases temporarily falling to 0 percent such as in 2009. Overall, the volatility of HICP inflation has fallen from 1 percent in the decade before EMU to less than 0.8 percent in the EMU period. Figure 1.10 taken from Fahr et al. (2011) shows that the volatility of core inflation (HICP inflation excluding volatile food and energy prices) has dropped even more dramatically from more than 0.5 to 0.1 percent, while the volatility of energy prices has increased quite substantially. Compared to the pre-EMU period, the correlation between energy prices and core inflation has turned negative, also contributing positively to the fall in overall volatility of HICP inflation.

The combination of the ECB's stability-oriented institutional framework based on central bank independence and a clear price stability mandate and its impeccable track record has led to a strong anchoring of inflation expectations. Figure 1.9 shows that long-term inflation expectations as measured from surveys of professional forecasters have been stable around 2 percent since the start of EMU and remained so despite large fluctuations in both headline and short-term forecasts of inflation in the most recent period. Inflation expectations, as measured by breakeven inflation rates or inflation swaps, show more volatility but have also remained close to 2 percent.

The stability of medium-term inflation expectations has been a strong stabilizing factor in the recent financial crisis and the great recession that followed. It increased the effectiveness of standard monetary policy by ensuring that the easing of nominal interest rates following the failure of Lehman Brothers translated into a fall of the real interest rate, which ultimately determines the real cost of capital and spending and investment decisions. The stability of inflation expectations also avoided the risk of a debt deflation spiral, whereby falling prices increase the real debt burden of households and firms, leading them to deleverage and postpone spending decisions. In turn this would reduce aggregate demand, put further downward pressure on prices, and increase the debt burden. By increasing the effectiveness of the standard monetary policy response and reducing the risk of a debt deflation spiral, the anchoring of inflation expectations lowered the risk of a binding lower bound on nominal short-term interest rates.

Figure 1.11 illustrates the quantitative importance of the stability of long-term inflation expectations for macroeconomic stability. It shows the actual behavior of consumer price inflation, real GDP growth and the short-term nominal interest rate (Euribor rate) from the first quarter of 2008 till the first quarter of 2010 under the assumption that the long-term inflation anchor is fixed at 1.9 percent, as well as two counterfactual simulations based on the ECB's NAWM.[21]

The baseline shows how following the onset of the great recession in the last quarter of 2008 inflation dropped from more than 3 percent to almost minus 1 percent in a year's time, while annual GDP growth dropped to almost minus five percent. In response, the short-term nominal interest rate was eased to close to the effective lower bound, which is assumed to be somewhat above zero reflecting the risk premium embedded in the three-month Euribor interest rate.

In the two alternative scenarios, the economy is simulated under the assumption that the long-term inflation anchor shifts downward in response to the fall in headline inflation, as shown in the lower right panel of figure 1.11. In this counterfactual simulation two scenarios are entertained: in the first one, it is assumed that the lower bound on inter-

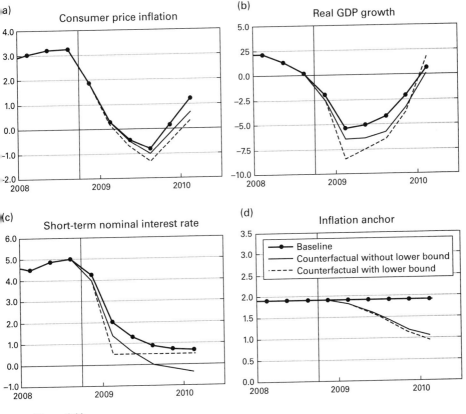

Figure 1.11
Impact of a downward shift in the inflation anchor. Simulations with new areawide model (NAWM). In the baseline the NAWM is used to replicate the actual euro area developments in HICP inflation, real GDP growth, and the short-term euribor rate under the assumption of a constant inflation anchor. The counterfactuals assume that the inflation anchor responds to past inflation with and without a lower bound on the short-term interest rate. See Christoffel, Coenen, and Warne (2008).

est rates is not binding; in the second, it is assumed to bind. From these scenarios, two conclusions are worth mentioning. First, under the estimated policy reaction function in the NAWM a quite modest downward shift in medium-term inflation expectations would have led to the short-term nominal interest rate hitting its effective lower bound already in the first quarter of 2009, as shown by the dashed line in the lower left panel of figure 1.11. Second, the downward shift in the long-term inflation anchor would have deepened the fall in inflation and particularly in real GDP growth, ceteris paribus, as it pushes up the long-term real interest rate putting further downward pressure on spending. This effect is particularly powerful if the lower bound on nominal short-term interest rates is binding. In this case the maximal impact of the recession on GDP growth would have been 3 percentage points larger. These counterfactual simulations are likely to be a lower bound of the impact of a downward shift in long-term inflation expectations because the NAWM does not explicitly incorporate a debt deflation spiral as discussed above.

Overall, we conclude that the ECB's primary focus on maintaining price stability over the medium-term contributed to the solid anchoring of inflation expectations, which in turn allowed for a prompt and effective monetary policy response to the financial crisis and alleviated the incidence of hitting the lower bound on nominal interest rates. In light of this finding, one should be very cautious in overburdening monetary policy with other objectives or with changing the inflation objective, letting it endanger the stability of inflation expectations. In contrast, it may be worthwhile to consider enhancing the stabilizing role of inflation expectations by moving toward a greater focus on the price level (rather than the inflation rate) and not letting bygones be bygones. As extensively discussed in Gaspar et al. (2010), in such a credible policy regime, agents would automatically expect a return of the price level to its predetermined path following an initial disinflationary shock. This would in turn stabilize the economy and prices by reducing the real interest rate and correcting the initial rise in the real debt burden.

1.5.2   The Role of Monetary Analysis

A distinguishing feature of the ECB's monetary policy strategy has been its emphasis on monetary analysis.[22] How does the financial crisis affect the role of monetary analysis in a stability-oriented monetary policy? The source of the current crisis lies in the buildup of financial imbalances during the early part of the millennium. In this section we argue that the analysis of monetary developments can help identify the excessive credit expansion underlying the creation of financial imbalances and fragilities, as well as recognize the potential contribution of excessively loose monetary policy stance to these developments. If anything, the experience of the financial crisis has therefore strengthened the role of monetary analysis, although its scope needs to be broadened beyond the quantity-theory-based long-term relationship between money growth and inflation.[23] Under the motto that "prevention is better than cure," the analysis of monetary and credit developments provides an appropriate framework for a stability-oriented monetary policy to lean against the buildup of financial imbalances.

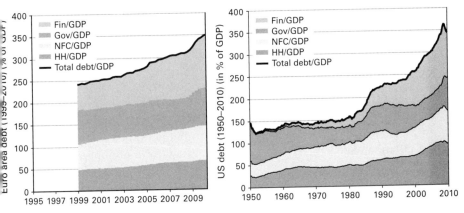

Figure 1.12
Debt in the euro area and the United States. Debt is defined as loans for euro area households (credit market instruments in the United States); for NFCs and financial corporations debt is credit, securities excluding equity, and pension liabilities, net of intercompany loans (credit market instruments in the United States). Debt by governments are loans and securities.
Sources: Fahr et al. (2011); Quarterly Euro Area Accounts Eurostat; Flow of Funds Federal Reserve; BEA

In what follows we review some evidence of the usefulness of money and credit indicators as early warning signals and of the role of monetary policy as a source of excessive credit developments. Figure 1.12 shows the large buildup of debt in the euro area and the United States since the beginning of the new millennium. While the data from the financial accounts may not be directly comparable across both areas, it is clear that in both economies overall debt rose in the order of more than 100 percent of GDP. This accumulation of debt is particularly striking in the financial sector: intrafinancial sector leverage provided the fuel for the credit boom. The longer time series for the United States also illustrates that a similar sized deepening of the financial system took place in the 1980s following the deregulation of the financial sector and culminating in the savings and loans crisis of the late 1980s.

The role of money creation in fueling the credit boom in the euro area is also illustrated in figure 1.13. It shows the negative association between the increasing annual growth rate of M3 corrected for portfolio shifts and the fall in a measure of the external finance premium in the run-up to the financial crisis.

This suggestive evidence is confirmed by increasing formal empirical evidence that money and credit developments are good early-warning indicators for financial crises and provide robust signals for unsustainable

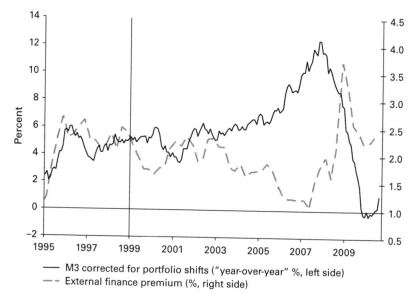

Figure 1.13
M3 growth and external finance premium. M3 is corrected for portfolio shifts. The external finance premium is measured as an average of spreads between lending rates, including corporate bond yields, and measures of risk-free rates of corresponding maturities, in percentage points.
Sources: Fahr et al. (2011); BIS; ECB; Dow Jones; ECB calculations

asset price developments and growing financial imbalances.[24] One example is the study by Alessi and Detken (2011), which shows that a real-time global credit-to-GDP gap is the single best indicator for asset price bubbles that are followed by costly busts. Other ECB studies that provide additional evidence are summarized in Detken et al. (2010).

To what extent can excessive credit creation be related to the monetary policy stance? Also here there is increasing theoretical and empirical evidence that keeping policy rates low for too long may have contributed to excessive credit creation and risk taking. The growing theoretical literature includes model-based analysis as in Adrian and Shin (2010), Dell'Ariccia et al. (2010), De Nicolo et al. (2010), and Boissay (2010), as well as the more general conceptual discussion in Rajan (2005) and Borio and Zhu (2008). For example, Boissay (2010) shows how low interest rates may worsen the adverse selection problem in credit markets by encouraging less productive investors to enter the market. This may ultimately lead to a financial crisis as the deteriorating quality of the investor pool leads to a breakdown of the credit market. Similarly there is increasing empirical evidence from a wide variety of financial markets and country experiences that keeping interest rates too low for too long encourages risk-taking. Examples are the studies by Altunbas et al. (2010), Gambacorta and Marques-Ibanez (2011), Maddaloni and Peydro (2010), Ciccarelli et al. (2011), Jimenez et al. (2011a, b), Ioannidou et al. (2009), and Bekaert et al. (2010). For example, Maddaloni and Peydro (2010) use the ECB's Bank Lending Survey to show that an easing of monetary policy leads to an easing of lending standards by banks not only because of the improved financial situation of borrowers but also via a so-called bank lending channel, namely the improved liquidity of the banks themselves.

In the light of this evidence, it is natural that an enhanced analysis of liquidity developments is part of the central bank's tool kit in order to avoid that the monetary policy stance become a source of growing financial imbalances. At the same time it is unlikely that monetary policy alone can prevent a buildup of such imbalances. It is therefore important to further develop the macroprudential policy framework geared at containing systemic risk.[25]

1.6   Concluding Remarks

The great financial crisis and its large costs in terms of reduced economic activity, high unemployment and increased government debt has led some observers to question the appropriateness of the price-stability oriented monetary policy frameworks which until recently were often credited with the long period of low inflation and stable growth before the crisis. In this chapter we argued that, if anything, the focus on maintaining price stability over the medium term should be strengthened. This is based on three arguments.

First, the stability of inflation expectations built up over the past decades has been instrumental in making the standard monetary policy response more effective by avoiding a deflationary spiral and allowing the central bank to embark on nonstandard policy measures without igniting inflationary fears. As we discussed above, the role of inflation expectations as automatic stabilizers could be further enhanced by a greater focus on the price level rather than the inflation rate.

Second, the use of NSMs targeted at addressing malfunctioning financial markets has been effective in reducing the impact of the financial crisis on the real economy and ensuring the transmission of standard monetary policy. In this way NSMs have alleviated the potential constraint imposed by the zero lower bound on nominal interest rates and reduced the need for a higher average inflation objective. However, because NSMs typically involve increased central bank intermediation in private markets, they also imply taking more risk on the central bank's balance sheet. In order to avoid that those intermediation activities and their overlap with fiscal policy risk endangering the price stability objective, it is important that (1) they are carried out fully in line with the price stability objective and (2) they are temporary and limited in nature, in line with temporary nature of the financial market malfunctioning.

Third, under the motto that prevention is better than the cure, and in line with their medium-term orientation, central banks are advised to actively use monetary analysis to avoid making the monetary policy stance a source of growing financial imbalances.

This way a stability-oriented monetary policy framework will act in a symmetric way by not only providing the necessary tools to respond to a financial crisis but also by reducing the probability of such a crisis occurring. However, monetary policy does not act in a vacuum. In order for it to be successful, it is important that other policy domains also play their roles. In particular, fiscal policy needs to be guided by an analogous stability-oriented approach as illustrated by the complications caused by the sovereign debt crisis. Moreover one of the lessons from the great financial crisis is the need for a new macroprudential policy framework geared at avoiding systemic risk. The development of a new, effective macroprudential tool set will also contribute to a successful price-stability-oriented monetary policy framework.

Notes

European Central Bank, Kaiserstrasse 29, D-60311 Frankfurt, Germany. This chapter was prepared for the Bank of Israel conference "Lessons from the World Financial Crisis" held in Jerusalem on March 31 to April 1, 2011. Thanks are due to conference participants, to many colleagues at the ECB, to participants in the ECB central bank workshop "Macroeconomic Impact of Nonstandard Monetary Policy Measures" held in Frankfurt on March 23 to 24, 2011, and to the BGIE seminar at Harvard for helpful comments. The views expressed are our own and should not be attributed to the European Central Bank.

1. See, for example, Blanchard, Dell'Ariccia, and Mauro (2010).

2. See the discussion in Ingves (2011).

3. See, for example, Bank of England (2009) and Galati and Moessner (2011).

4. See, for example, Gorton and Metrick (2012) and Brunnermeier (2009).

5. Particular thanks are due to our co-authors in the following papers: Lenza et al. (2010), Giannone et al. (2011a), and Fahr et al. (2011). We are also grateful to Günter Coenen and his colleagues for use of the simulations of the ECB's new area wide model.

6. See, for example, Durre and Pill (2010).

7. See, for example, Aït-Sahalia et al. (2012) for an overview of the market response to policy initiatives during the global financial crisis, and Borio and Disyatat (2009) for a classification of unconventional policies.

8. The Euribor rate is an unsecured interbank rate, whereas the OIS rate is a cash-settled derivative (where no principal is exchanged). The spread between these rates therefore offers a measure of market participant's perceived counterparty credit risk, the most important driver of money market tensions in this period (see Heider et al. 2009).

9. See Lenza et al. (2010).

10. See Pill (2010).

11. See, for example, Bernanke (2010): "Notwithstanding the fact that the policy rate is near its zero lower bound, the Federal Reserve retains a number of tools and strategies for providing additional stimulus."

12. Trichet (2009).

13. More specifically, Orphanides (2010) uses the one-year-ahead forecasts of HICP inflation and real GDP growth from the ECB's Survey of Professional Forecasters.

14. See also Smets (2010).

15. The rate at the ECB's main refinancing operation (the weekly repo) is labeled the MRO rate and is usually seen as the key policy rate signaling the ECB's monetary policy stance.

16. See Christoffel et al. (2008).

17. In this exercise, the three-month EURIBOR rate is the modeled short-term interest rate. While this is not a policy instrument, nonetheless it can be seen as indicative of what historical behavior would imply about the appropriate policy setting.

18. The analysis presented in Giannone et al. (2010) shows that the effect of a monetary policy shock on euro area M1 is large and persistent in normal ("pre-crisis") times; that is, there is a strong liquidity effect. In the exercise presented in figure 1.7, the underlying structural shock is not identified. Nonetheless, we find that M1 behaves during the crisis period as expected by the model conditionally on the cycle. This suggests that there was no change in the liquidity effect, a conclusion supported by the analysis of Lenza et al. (2010).

19. See, for example, Bernanke and Blinder (1988).

20. See, for example, Coenen (2003).

21. See Christoffel et al. (2008) for a description of the NAWM.

22. See, Fischer et al. (2007).

23. See Papademos and Stark (2010).

24. See, for example, Borio and Lowe (2002).

25. In the European Union this role is taken up by the European Systemic Risk Board which started its operations in January 2011.

References

Adrian, Tobias, and Hyun S. Shin. 2010. Financial intermediaries and monetary economics. In Benjamin M. Friedman and Michael Woodford, eds., *Handbook of Monetary Economics* 3 (12): 601–50.

Aït-Sahalia, Yacine, Jochen Andritzky, Andreas Jobst, Sylwia Nowak, and Natalia Tamirisa. 2012. How to stop a herd of running bears? Market response to policy initiatives during the global financial crisis. *Journal of International Economics,* 87(1): 162–77.

Alessi, Lucia, and Carsten Detken. 2011. Quasi real time early warning indicators for costly asset price boom/bust cycles: a role for global liquidity. *European Journal of Political Economy,* 27(3): 520–33.

Altunbas, Yunus, Leonardo Gambacorta, and David Marques-Ibanez. 2010. Does monetary policy affect bank risk-taking? Working paper 1166. ECB, Frankfurt.

Banbura, Marta, Domenico Giannone, and Lucrezia Reichlin. 2010. Large Bayesian VARs. *Journal of Applied Econometrics* 25 (1): 71–92.

Bank of England. 2009. *The Role of Macroprudential Policy.* London: Bank of England.

Bekaert, Geert, Marie Hoerova, and Marco Lo Duca. 2010. Risk, uncertainty and monetary policy. Working paper 16397. NBER, Cambridge, MA.

Bernanke, Ben S., and Alan S. Blinder. 1988. Credit, money and aggregate demand. *American Economic Review* 78 (2): 435–39.

Bernanke, Ben S. 2010. The economic outlook and monetary policy. Speech at the FRB Kansas City Jackson Hole Symposium. http://www.federalreserve.gov/newsevents/speech/bernanke20100827a.htm.

Blanchard, Olivier, Giovanni Dell'Ariccia, and Paulo Mauro. 2010. Rethinking macroeconomic policy. Staff position note 10/03. IMF, Washington, DC.

Borio, Claudio, and Piti Disyatat. 2009. Unconventional monetary polices: An appraisal. Working paper 292. BIS, Basel.

Borio, Claudio, and Philip Lowe. 2002. Asset prices, financial and monetary stability: Exploring the nexus. Working paper 114. BIS, Basel.

Borio, Claudio, and Haibin Zhu. 2008. Capital regulation, risk-taking and monetary policy: A missing link in the transmission mechanism? Working paper 268. BIS, Basel.

Boissay, Frederique. 2010. Financial imbalances and financial fragility. Mimeo. ECB, Frankfurt.

Brunnermeier, Markus K. 2009. Deciphering the liquidity and credit crunch 2007–08. *Journal of Economic Perspectives* 23 (1): 77–100.

Christoffel, Kai, Günter Coenen, and Anders Warne. 2008. The new area-wide model of the euro area: A micro-founded open-economy model for forecasting and policy analysis. Working paper 944. ECB, Frankfurt.

Ciccarelli, Matteo, Angela Maddaloni, and Jose Luis Peydro. 2011. Trusting the bankers: A new look at the credit channel of monetary policy. Working paper 1228. ECB, Frankfurt.

Coenen, Günter. 2003. Zero lower bound: Is it a problem in the euro area? In Otmar Issing, ed., *Background Studies for the ECB's Evaluation of Its Monetary Policy Strategy.* Frankfurt: ECB, 139–56.

Dell'Ariccia, Giovanni, Luc Laeven, and Roberto Marquez. 2010. Monetary policy, leverage, and bank risk-taking. Working paper 10/276. IMF, Washington, DC.

De Mol, Christine, Domenico Giannone, and Lucrezia Reichlin. 2008. Forecasting using a large number of predictors: Is Bayesian regression a valid alternative to principal components? *Journal of Econometrics* 146 (2): 318–28.

De Nicolo, Gianni, Giovanni Dell'Ariccia, Luc Laeven, and Fabian Valencia. 2010. "Monetary policy and bank risk taking. Staff policy note 10/09. IMF, Washington, DC.

Detken, Carsten, Dieter Gerdesmeier, and Barbara Roffia. 2010. Interlinkages between money, credit and asset prices and their implications for consumer price inflation: Recent empirical work. In Otmar Issing, ed., *Enhancing Monetary Analysis*. Frankfurt: ECB, 307–54.

Durre, Alain, and Huw Pill. 2010. Non-standard monetary policy measures, monetary financing and the price level. www.ecb.de/events/pdf/conferences/ecb_mopo_fipo/Pill.pdf?5a906b97f488ab51fe98d5d47eb201c5.

European Central Bank. 2003. The ECB's monetary policy strategy. Press release May 8. ECB, Frankfurt.

Fahr, Stephan, Roberto Motto, Massimo Rostagno, Frank Smets, and Oreste Tristani. 2011. Lessons for monetary policy strategies from the recent past. In Marek Jarociński, Frank Smets, and Christian Thimann, eds., *Approaches to Monetary Policy Revisited: Lessons from the Crisis*. Frankfurt: ECB, 26–66.

Fischer, Bjorn, Michele Lenza, Huw Pill, and Lucrezia Reichlin. 2007. Money and monetary policy: The ECB experience 1999-2006. In Andreas Beyer and Lucrezia Reichlin, eds., *The Role of Money: Money and Monetary Policy in the 21st Century*. Frankfurt: ECB, 102–75.

Galati, Gabriele and Richild Moessner. 2011. Macroprudential policy—A literature review. Working paper 337. BIS, Basel.

Gambacorta, Leonardo, and David Marques-Ibanez. 2011. The bank lending channel: Lessons from the crisis. Working paper 1334. ECB, Frankfurt.

Gaspar, Vitor, Frank Smets, and David Vestin. 2010. Is the time ripe for price-level path stability? In Pierre Siklos, Martin Bohl, and Mark Wohar, eds., *Challenges in Central Banking*. Cambridge, UK: Cambridge University Press, 21–51.

Giannone, Domenico, Michele Lenza, and Lurcrezia Reichlin. 2010. Money, credit, monetary policy and the business cycle in the euro area. ECB. http://www.ecb.int/events/conferences/html/moneymechanism.en.html.

Giannone, Domenico, Michele Lenza, Huw Pill, and Lucrezia Reichlin. 2011a. Non-standard monetary policy measures and monetary developments. In Jagjit Chadha and Sean Holly, eds., *Interest Rates, Prices and Liquidity*. Cambridge, UK: Cambridge University Press, 195–221.

Giannone, Domenico, Michele Lenza, Huw Pill, and Lucrezia Reichlin. 2011b. Monetary policy and financial stability. In S. Claessens, D. D. Evanoff, G. G. Kaufman, and L. E. Kodres, eds., *Macroprudential Regulatory Policies: The New Road to Financial Stability*? Singapore: World Scientific, 103–20.

Gorton, Gary B., and Andrew Metrick. 2012. Securitized banking and the run on repo. *Journal of Financial Economics*, 104 (3): 425–51.

Heider, Florian, Marie Hoerova, and Cornelia Holthausen. 2009. Liquidity hoarding and interbank market spreads: The role of counterparty risk. Working paper 1126. ECB, Frankfurt.

Ingves, Stefan. 2011. Central bank governance and financial stability. BIS study group report for the Central Bank governance group, http://www.bis.org/publ/othp14.pdf.

Ioannidou, D., Steven Ongena, and Jose-Luis Peydro. 2009. Monetary policy, risk-taking, and pricing: Evidence from a quasi-natural experiment. Discussion paper 2009–31S. Tilburg University, The Netherlands.

Jimenez, Gabriel, Steven Ongena, Jose-Luis Peydro and Jaime Saurina. 2011a. Credit supply and monetary policy: Identifying the bank balance sheet channel with loan applications. *American Economic Review,* forthcoming.

Jimenez, Gabriel, Steven Ongena, Jose-Luis Peydro, and Jaime Saurina. 2011b. Hazardous times for monetary policy: What do twenty-three million bank loans say about the effects of monetary policy on credit risk? Discussion paper 6514. CEPR, London.

Lenza, Michele, Huw Pill, and Lucrezia Reichlin. 2010. Monetary policy in exceptional times. *Economic Policy* 62: 295–339.

Maddaloni, Angela, and Jose-Luis Peydro. 2010. Bank risk-taking, securitization, supervision and low interest rates: Evidence from the euro area and the U.S. lending standards. *Review of Financial Studies,* forthcoming.

Orphanides, Athanasios. 2003. Historical monetary policy analysis and the Taylor rule. *Journal of Monetary Economics* 50 (5): 983–1022.

Orphanides, Athanasios. 2010. Monetary policy lessons from the crisis. Presented at the ECB conference "The Great Financial Crisis: Lessons for Financial Stability and Monetary Policy: A Colloquium in Honour of Lucas Papademos."

Papademos, Lucas, and Jürgen Stark. 2010. *Enhancing Monetary Analysis.* Frankfurt: ECB.

Pill, Huw. 2010. Monetary policy in a low interest rate environment: A checklist. *International Seminar on Macroeconomics* 6: 335–45.

Rajan, Raghu. 2005. Has financial development made the world riskier? Presented at the FRB Kansas City Jackson Hole symposium.

Smets, Frank. 2010. Comment on chapters 6 and 7. In Marco Buti, Servaas Deroose, Vitor Gaspar, and J. Nogueira Martins, eds., *The Euro: The First Decade.* Brussels: European Commission, 259–79.

Trichet, Jean-Claude. 2009. The ECB's enhanced credit support. Address at the University of Munich annual symposium. http://www.ecb.europa.eu/press/key/date/2009/html/sp090713.en.html.

2 The Role of Monetary Policy in Turkey during the Global Financial Crisis

Harun Alp and Selim Elekdağ

2.1 Introduction

Distinct features of the global financial crisis that intensified during September 2008 include a sharp slowdown in global economy activity — including severe recessions across many countries — along with an episode of acute financial distress across international capital markets. Another departure from past global downturns was the coordination of unprecedented countercyclical policy responses to the crisis, which seems to have supported the rebound in economic activity.

Turkey was one of the hardest hit countries by the crisis. Real GDP contracted sharply for four quarters, reaching a year-over-year contraction of 14.7 percent during the first quarter of 2009, resulting in a –4.8 percent annual growth rate for that year. At the same time, anticipating the fallout from the crisis, the Central Bank of the Republic of Turkey (CBRT) decreased policy rates by an astounding 1,025 basis points over the November 2008 to November 2009 period.

The recent Turkish experience differs from the past in several dimensions. As discussed in section 2.2, Turkey suffered from an intense financial crisis in 2001. While the 2001 crisis was certainly harsh, it was followed by at least two important reforms. First, the pegs and heavily managed exchange rate regimes of the past were replaced by a flexible exchange rate regime. Second, and relatedly, the policy framework of the CBRT gradually transitioned into a full-fledged inflation targeting regime.

Against this backdrop, this chapter focuses on the macroeconomic implications of these two monetary policy reforms, particularly during the recent global financial crisis. Our principle objective is to explore how these changes to the monetary policy framework mitigated the severity of the recent recession. More specifically, we seek to address the following set of questions: (1) In contrast to the fixed exchange rate regimes of the past, what was the role of exchange rate flexibility in helping insulate the economy from the crisis? (2) Relatedly, consistent with the attainment of the inflation targets, what was the role of the CBRT's countercyclical interest rate cuts in softening the impact of the crisis?

To this end we develop and estimate a small open economy dynamic stochastic general equilibrium (DSGE) model designed to capture salient features of the Turkish economy. The model contains a number of nominal and real frictions such as sticky prices, sticky wages, variable capital utilization, investment adjustment costs, habit persistence, and incorporates a financial accelerator mechanism à la Bernanke and others (1999) in an open economy setup to better fit the data. Details regarding the setup of the model, the estimation procedure, its robustness, and its dynamics are briefly covered in sections 2.3 through 2.5.[1]

By means of this estimated structural model, we find that if an inflation targeting framework underpinned by a flexible exchange rate regime was not adopted, the recent recession would have been much deeper and thus substantially more severe.

Our model-based counterfactual simulations represent the basis for our main policy implications and are discussed in detail in sections 2.6 and 2.7. We contrast the actual real GDP (the baseline scenario) with other counterfactual scenarios that, for example, consider the how the economy would have responded if the CBRT had not implemented any discretionary monetary policy loosening.

To more intuitively convey our quantitative results, we consider the growth rate during the most intense year of the global financial crisis, namely 2009, as our baseline. In this regard our counterfactual simulations indicate that without the discretionary interest rate cuts (expansionary monetary policy shocks) possible under the inflation targeting regime, growth in 2009 would have decreased from the actual realization of −4.8 to −5.9 percent, a difference of 1.1 percentage point. This lies within the range found by Christiano and others (2008), who find growth contributions of monetary policy of 0.75 and 1.27 percent for the United States and the euro area, respectively.

Other insightful counterfactual experiments are possible. For example, if there was absolutely no countercyclical responses to the crisis—in other words, the CBRT did not take the output gap into account and at the same time did not implement any discretionary policy loosening (no expansionary monetary policy shocks) — then the 2009 growth outcome would have been –6.2 percent. Moreover, if a fixed exchange rate regime would have been in place instead of the current inflation targeting regime, which operates with a flexible exchange rate, the results indicate that growth in 2009 would have been –8.0 percent, a difference from the actual outcome of 3.2 percentage points.

In sum, without the adoption of the flexible exchange rate regime, and active countercyclical monetary policy guided by an inflation targeting framework, the impact of the recent global financial crisis would have been substantially more severe. As emphasized in the final section of the chapter, the inflation-targeting framework underpinned by a flexible exchange rate seems to have increased the resilience of the Turkish economy to shocks. The inflation-targeting framework allowed the CBRT to implement countercyclical and discretionary interest rate cuts, while exchange rate flexibility acted as a shock absorber, both of which increased the resiliency of the economy. The latter result echoes the favorable output stabilization properties of exchange rate flexibility that can be traced back to at least to the seminal contributions of Mundell and Fleming.

Our chapter builds on a tradition of small open economy DSGE models popularized by Mendoza (1991). Over time these real models were augmented with nominal rigidities to motivate and then explore the implications of monetary policy (e.g., Gali and Monacelli 2005). To capture financial frictions more appropriately, building on Bernanke and others (1999) and others, a financial accelerator mechanism was added to these models (e.g., see Cespedes et al. 2004; Gertler et al. 2007; Elekdağ and Tchakarov 2007).

Subsequently, with the growing feasibility and popularity of Bayesian method, building on the closed economy studies of Smets and Wouters (2003, 2007), small open economy models were estimated (Lubik and Schorfheide 2007; Teo 2009; Christensen and Dib 2008). Then Elekdağ, Justiniano, and Tchakarov (2006) estimated a small open economy model with a financial accelerator for an emerging market, which motivated others do follow suit using richer modeling structures (e.g., see Garcia-Cicco 2010). Against this backdrop, this chapter takes Elekdağ, Justiniano, and Tchakarov (2006) as a starting point, and augments their model with some of the features in Gertler et al. (2007) and Smets and Wouters (2007) to improve the model fit and to facilitate the counterfactual simulations discussed below.

2.2 Economic Developments in Turkey: The Role of Macroeconomic Reforms

In this section we discuss some key developments regarding the Turkish economy over the last decade. In particular, we focus on a few key macroeconomic policy reforms that we argue helped soften the impact of the global financial crisis that intensified after the Lehman Brothers bankruptcy.

To highlight how the recent Turkish experience differs from the past, we take the intense financial crisis of 2001 as our point of departure, which was associated with fragilities in the banking system and a speculative attack on the fixed exchange rate regime in place at the time. A severe recession ensued.

After the 2001 crisis Turkey embarked on a new IMF-supported arrangement. For the purpose of our simulations the two major reforms implemented in the aftermath of the crisis that we consider are, first, the floating exchange rates that replaced the heavily managed and fixed exchange rates regimes of the past and second, the officially implemented full-fledged inflation targeting regime that the CBRT started in 2006 and that would serve as the economy's nominal anchor.

Over the next 26 quarters, from the first quarter of 2002 to mid-2008, the Turkish economy grew by over 5 percent (year-over-year), and inflation declined markedly.[2] While global economic and financial conditions were favorable, it is hard to argue that the reforms mentioned above did not contribute positively toward achieving these growth rates.[3]

With the intensification of the global financial crisis during the fall of 2008, synchronized downturns coupled with financial stress affected international capital markets and economies across the world. As expected, the Turkish economy was severely affected by this abrupt collapse of the global economy. The contraction in world demand in fact hit Turkish exports severely with dire implications for the rest of the economy. The shock to global financial markets had resulted in a collapse of asset prices (including the currency), an increase in spreads, and sizable capital outflows. The heightened uncertainty associated with the unprecedented nature of this global financial crisis had reinforced foreign demand and financial shocks, additionally suppressing consumption, investment, and credit extension. The collapse in foreign demand, the distress across international capital markets, and the heightened uncertainty hit Turkey hardest among the countries unfavorably affected by the crisis.

In Turkey real GDP contracted sharply for four quarters, and reached a year-to-year contraction of 14.7 percent during the first quarter of 2009, which amounted to a –4.8 percent annual contraction. The CBRT grasped the urgency of this situation relatively early on. Anticipating substantially reduced levels of resource utilization, and in an attempt to mitigate the impact of the crisis on the economy, the CBRT cut interest rates by an astounding 1,025 basis points over the November 2008 to November 2009 period. But to what end? We attempt to address this question below.

2.3 The Model

This section presents an overview of the structural model underpinning our quantitative results. Readers primarily interested in the main policy implications of the chapter could directly proceed to sections 2.7 and 2.8. The goal here is to present the general intuition of the model; the details are relegated to the working paper version of this study (Alp and Elekdağ 2011). The structural framework builds upon a core (New) Keynesian model. The model used is an open economy variant of what the literature refers to as a New Keynesian dynamic stochastic general equilibrium (DSGE) model. However, to better fit the data, the model is augmented with a number of features including real and nominal rigidities (e.g., investment adjustment costs and sticky wages), as well as a financial accelerator mechanism (to capture financial market imperfections).[4]

The model consists of several agents: households, producers, and the government. There are three types of producers: entrepreneurs, capital producers, and retailers. The government is responsible for implement monetary and fiscal policy. Rather than elaborate on all aspects of the model, in this section we focus on the transmission of certain shocks and the role of monetary (and exchange rate) policy.

2.3.1 The Transmission of Shocks

By our argument above, during the global financial crisis, the Turkish economy was unfavorably affected by a collapse in foreign demand, distress across international capital markets, and heightened uncertainty. To assess this impact on the Turkish economy, we capture these disturbances in our model by an export demand shock, a sudden stop shock, and a (financial) uncertainty shock. We first review each of these and then provide quantitative evidence that appraises the relative growth contribution of these three shocks (as well as the other structural shocks) during the recession which intensified in the first quarter of 2009.

2.3.2 The Export Demand Shock

The export demand shock, or perhaps equivalently, the foreign demand shocks propagates through the model via the market-clearing condition

$$Y_t^H = C_t^H + C_t^{eH} + I_t^H + C_t^{H*} + G_t.$$

Leaving aside differences in notation, this is basically the standard aggregate demand identity for home (domestically produced) goods, which posits that domestic output is equal to the sum of consumption of domestically produced goods (which is the sum of both household and entrepreneurial consumption, $C_t^H + C_t^{eH}$), domestic investment goods, I_t^H, government expenditures, G_t, and exports, C_t^{H*}. Therefore, leaving the other details to the complete model description in Alp and Elekdağ (2011), a collapse in export (foreign) demand is simply represented by a decline in C_t^{H*}.

2.3.3 The Sudden Stop Shock

Turkey's experience during the global financial crisis was also associated with a reversal of capital inflows (a sudden stop in the parlance of Calvo et al. 2004), as well as a sharp depreciation of the exchange rate. To capture these interrelated disruptions, we augment the uncovered interest parity (UIP) condition with a shock as

$$i_t = i_t^* E_t \left[\frac{S_{t+1}}{S_t} \right] \Phi_t,$$

where i_t and i_t^*, represent the domestic and international (gross) interest rates, respectively, S_t denotes the nominal exchange rate (Turkish lira per US dollar—an increase represents a depreciation), E_t is the expectations operator (conditional on information up to time t), and Φ_t is the sudden stop shock (also referred to as an exchange rate shock or UIP shock). Therefore, as in Gertler et al. (2007), a shock that triggers large capital outflows is captured by this exogenous term and appended to an otherwise standard UIP condition. This sudden stop shock would serves to capture an important dimension of the financial aspect of the recent crisis: the (financial) uncertainty shock.

2.3.4   The (Financial) Uncertainty Shock

The description of this shock warrants some background. In our model the real cost of capital departs from the standard representation in other studies because of the existence of an external finance premium. Consider the equation

$$E_t \left[R_{t+1}^k \right] = \chi_t (\cdot) E_t \left[R_{t+1} \right],$$

where we have that the real cost of capital, R_t^k, is equal to the real interest rate, R_t, augmented by the external finance premium represented by the term $\chi_t(\cdot)$. In turn the external finance premium depends on the leverage ratio (assets scaled by net worth) of the entrepreneurs:

$$\chi_t = \chi_t \left(\frac{Q_t K_{t+1}}{N_{t+1}} \right).$$

Note that total assets, $Q_t K_{t+1}$, depends on the price of equity, Q_t, which is not sticky (by contrast to goods prices or wages). This implies that the leverage ratio is quite sensitive to asset price fluctuations.

The precise specification of the evolution of net worth, N_{t+1}, is complex (and shown in the working paper version of this study), so here we use an abridged version:

$$N_{t+1} = Q_t V_t + W_t^e,$$

where W_t^e and V_t denote the entrepreneurial wage bill and the value of the firm, respectively. The (financial) uncertainty shock is an exogenous process, represented by the term, Q_t, which by construction has direct impact on the level of aggregate net worth and therefore the external financial premium. Put differently, the net worth shock could be interpreted as a shock to the rate of destruction of entrepreneurial financial wealth (in line with several other studies). This shock directly affects entrepreneurial net worth and has been used in various forms by Elekdağ et al. (2006), Curdia (2007), and Christiano et al. (2010). Another way to think about this shock is that it could capture counterparty risk—owing part to Knightian uncertainty—a key consideration during the global financial crisis. Such heightened uncertainty regarding cash flows, for example, would impair assets and thus disrupt the financial system.

2.3.5   What Role for Monetary Policy?

In our model the central bank alters interest rates in an attempt to achieve certain policy objectives. Before proceeding to the details, note that the policy rule to be described below implies that the monetary authority sets the nominal interest rate, with regard to the inflation rate deviation from the time-varying inflation target, the output gap, the rate of exchange rate depreciation, and the previous period's interest rate (policy smoothing).

A simplified version of the interest rate rule takes the following (log-linear) form (see the working paper version for further details):

$$\hat{i}_t = \rho_i \hat{i}_{t-1} + \tau_\pi \left(E_t \hat{\pi}_{t+1} - \rho_{\bar{\pi}} \hat{\pi}_t^T \right) + \tau_y \hat{y}_t + \tau_s \Delta \hat{S}_t + \epsilon_t^i,$$

where, in this flexible specification, $\hat{i}_t$, $\hat{\pi}_{t+1}$, $\hat{y}_t$, and $\hat{S}_t$ denote the (short-term policy) interest rate, the (core CPI) inflation rate, the output gap, and the nominal exchange rate, respectively. Note that ϵ_t^i denotes the monetary policy shock—interest rate changes that deviate from the (empirical) interest rate rule would be captured by this disturbances and could be considered discretionary monetary policy. The time-varying inflation target, $\hat{\pi}_t^T$, is assumed to evolve according to the following stochastic process:

$$\hat{\pi}_t^T = \rho_{\bar{\pi}} \hat{\pi}_{t-1}^T + \epsilon_t^\pi.$$

The time-varying inflation target captures the reality that the inflation target in Turkey was changed over time. However, it has also been used in the literature to capture structural changes in the conduct of monetary policy that are not captured otherwise (see Adolfson et al. 2007 for more details).

Anticipating the results to follow, notice that when the output gap is negative—that is, output is below potential—strict adherence to the rule above would imply that the interest rate decreases by an amount dictated by the coefficient τ_y. However, the monetary authority might decrease interest rates by more than what the systematic component of the rule would imply. Recall that this deviation from the rule is capture by the error term, ϵ_t^i, which is the monetary policy shock—thereby capturing discretionary monetary loosening. As will be discussed below, during the most intense episode of the global financial crisis, interest rates decreased by more than the amount the empirical counterpart of the rule would have implied, which helped softening some of the global financial crisis.

2.4   Estimation

This section gives an overview of model estimation. It briefly reviews issues pertaining to data, parameter calibration, the choice of prior distributions, the resulting posterior distributions, model fit, and sensitivity analysis. An extensive discussion of these issues is provided in Alp and Elekdağ (2011).

2.4.1 Data

Our log-linearized model is estimated using Bayesian methods primarily developed by Schorfheide (2000), and later popularized by Smets and Wouters (2003, 2007). For our estimates we use quarterly data from the first quarter of 2002 to the second quarter of 2010 in the series shown in figure 2.1. In line with many other studies, we match the following set of twelve variables: the levels of the domestic policy and foreign interest rates, the inflation rates of domestic GDP deflator and core consumer price and foreign consumer price indexes, as well as the growth rates of GDP, consumption, investment, exports, imports, foreign GDP, and the real exchange rate. We use the sample period for our estimations, 2002 to 2010, which is the period when the CBRT was transitioned to an inflation targeting regime (initially implicitly, and the explicitly starting in 2006).

2.4.2 Model Parameters

We followed the literature and calibrate certain parameters (e.g., see Christiano et al. 2010), threating them as infinitely strict priors. Most of the parameters we chose were to pin down key steady state ratios; the remaining parameters are taken from the literature as summarized in table 2.1.

The parameters, shown in table 2.2, determine the degree of the real and nominal rigidities, the monetary policy stance, as well as the persistence and volatility of the exogenous shocks. The table shows the assumptions pertaining to the choice of distribution, the means, standard deviations, or degrees of freedom. The choice of priors is in line with the literature.

The posterior estimates of these variables are also shown in table 2.2. The table reports the means along with the 5th and 95th percentiles of the posterior distribution of the estimated parameters obtained through the Metropolis–Hastings sampling algorithm. In general, the parameter estimates are in line with those found in other studies.

2.4.3 An Initial Assessment of Model Fit and Sensitivity Analysis

In assessing the fit of the model, we start by comparing the data with the baseline model's one-sided Kalman filter estimates of the observed

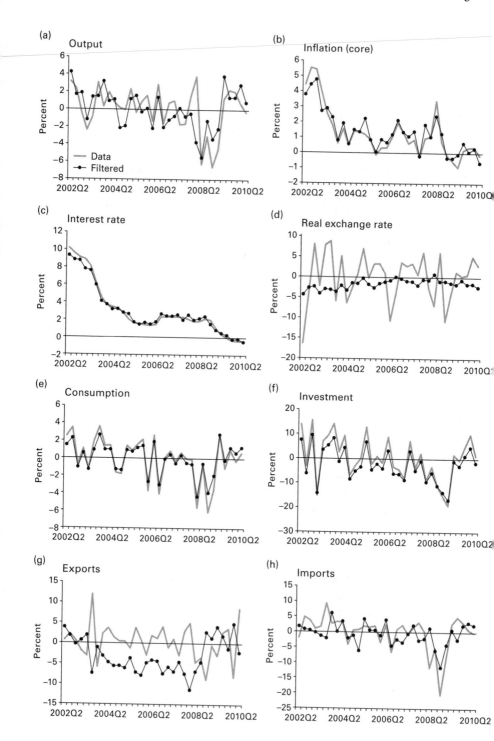

Table 2.1
Calibrated parameters

Parameter	Symbol	Value
Discount factor	β	0.9928
Consumption intra-temporal elasticity of substitution	ρ	1
Share of domestic goods in consumption	γ	0.75
Investment intra-temporal elasticity of substitution	ρ_i	0.25
Share of domestic goods in investment	γ_i	0.77
Inverse of the elasticity of work effort with respect to the real wage	σ_l	1
Share of capital in production function	α	0.4
Elasticity of marginal depreciation with respect to utilization rate	ϵ	1
Steady state markup rate for domestically produced goods	μ^H	1.15
Steady state markup rate for imported goods	μ^F	1.15
Steady state markup rate for wages	μ^W	1.15
Share of entrepreneurial labor	$1-\Omega$	0.01
Steady state external finance premium	χ	1.03
Number of entrepreneurs who survive each period (at steady state)	Q	0.9728
Variance of idiosyncratic shock to entrepreneur production	σ_ω	0.4
Fraction of monitoring cost	μ_ω	0.15
Depreciation rate (at steady state)	δ	0.035
Elasticity of country risk premium with respect to net foreign debt	Φ	0.01

variables; we consider the model's robustness in the following section. The data and the filtered variables are shown in figure 2.1, and indicate that the sample fit is quite satisfactory overall.

To assess the robustness of the estimated model, we consider a battery of alternative specifications which include different monetary policy rules and alternative structural features. The results are summarized in table 2.3, which depicts the log data density of the various models, and the posterior odd ratio contrasting the baseline and the alternative model specifications. While the details are discussed extensively in the appendix at the end of this chapter, the main takeaway is that we consider 18 alternative specifications, and the results are very strongly, if not decisively, in favor of the baseline.

Figure 2.1
Model predictions (thin lines with circles) versus actual data (thick gray lines)

Table 2.2
Estimated parameters

Parameter description	Symbol	Prior distribution			Posterior distribution		
		Type	Mean	Standard deviation	Mean	Confidence interval	
						5%	95%
Calvo parameter							
Domestic prices	θ_H	Beta	0.50	0.10	0.306	0.177	0.435
Import prices	θ_F	Beta	0.50	0.10	0.554	0.434	0.679
Wages	θ_W	Beta	0.50	0.10	0.558	0.387	0.739
Indexation							
Domestic prices	γ_H	Beta	0.50	0.10	0.460	0.296	0.623
Import prices	γ_F	Beta	0.50	0.10	0.475	0.313	0.641
Wages	γ_W	Beta	0.50	0.10	0.562	0.400	0.731
Others							
Export demand elasticity	χ	Normal	1.00	0.20	0.182	0.090	0.271
Export demand inertia	ϖ	Beta	0.50	0.20	0.883	0.794	0.979
Habit formation	b	Beta	0.70	0.20	0.904	0.850	0.958
Investment adjustment cost	ψ	Normal	4.00	0.50	3.625	2.769	4.511
Monetary policy							
Interest rate smoothing	ρ_i	Beta	0.70	0.20	0.724	0.639	0.808
Inflation response	τ_π	Normal	1.40	0.10	1.537	1.383	1.685
Output gap response	τ_y	Normal	0.25	0.10	0.021	-0.022	0.064
Nominal exchange rate response	τ_s	Normal	0.10	0.05	0.173	0.101	0.242
Shock persistence							
Stationary technology	ρ_a	Beta	0.80	0.10	0.767	0.593	0.939
Unit-root technology	ρ_ς	Beta	0.80	0.10	0.497	0.386	0.604
Investment specific technology	ρ_{inv}	Beta	0.80	0.10	0.916	0.893	0.940
Domestic markup	ρ_μ^h	Beta	0.80	0.10	0.774	0.609	0.945
Import markup	ρ_μ^f	Beta	0.80	0.10	0.713	0.545	0.881
Foreign inflation	ρ_{π^*}	Beta	0.80	0.10	0.623	0.459	0.792
Foreign interest rate	ρ_{i^*}	Beta	0.80	0.10	0.847	0.751	0.948
Country risk premium	ρ_ϕ	Beta	0.80	0.10	0.895	0.836	0.956
Foreign demand	ρ_{y^*}	Beta	0.80	0.10	0.928	0.892	0.962
Preference	ρ_c	Beta	0.80	0.10	0.721	0.556	0.888

Table 2.2
(continued)

Parameter description	Symbol	Prior distribution			Posterior distribution		
		Type	Mean	Standard deviation	Mean	Confidence interval	
						5%	95%
Labor supply	ρ_l	Beta	0.80	0.10	0.762	0.605	0.931
Exogenous spending	ρ_g	Beta	0.80	0.10	0.868	0.791	0.944
Net worth	ρ_N	Beta	0.80	0.10	0.715	0.574	0.856
Inflation target	ρ_π	Beta	0.80	0.10	0.769	0.620	0.931
Shock volatility							
Stationary technology	σ_a	Inverse gamma	0.03	1.00	0.015	0.009	0.022
Unit-root technology	σ_ξ	Inverse gamma	0.03	1.00	0.047	0.036	0.057
Investment specific technology	σ_{inv}	Inverse gamma	0.03	1.00	0.421	0.334	0.504
Domestic markup	σ_μ^h	Inverse gamma	0.03	1.00	0.020	0.009	0.030
Import markup	σ_μ^f	Inverse gamma	0.03	1.00	0.052	0.032	0.072
Foreign inflation	σ_{π^*}	Inverse gamma	0.03	1.00	0.008	0.007	0.010
Foreign interest rate	σ_{i^*}	Inverse gamma	0.03	1.00	0.005	0.004	0.005
Country risk premium	σ_ϕ	Inverse gamma	0.03	1.00	0.011	0.007	0.015
Foreign demand	σ_{y^*}	Inverse gamma	0.03	1.00	0.063	0.048	0.077
Preference	σ_c	Inverse gamma	0.30	1.00	0.429	0.218	0.642
Labor supply	σ_l	Inverse gamma	0.03	1.00	0.016	0.007	0.024
Exogenous spending	σ_g	Inverse gamma	0.03	1.00	0.046	0.036	0.055
Net worth	σ_N	Inverse gamma	0.05	1.00	0.061	0.035	0.086
Inflation target	σ_π	Inverse gamma	0.02	1.00	0.012	0.005	0.020
Monetary policy	σ_i	Inverse gamma	0.03	1.00	0.007	0.005	0.008

* For the inverse gamma distribution, the mean and the degrees of freedom are reported in the table.

Table 2.3
Sensitivity analysis

		Log data density	Log data density	Log data density
	Baseline	802.482		
	Sensitivity to frictions			
1	Financial accelerator	779.963	6.025E+09	No
2	Low price stickiness	787.606	2.888E+06	No
3	Low stickiness including wages	726.449	1.049E+33	No
4	Low habit persistence	719.789	8.193E+35	No
5	Low investment costs	753.752	1.456E+21	No
	Sensitivity to shocks			
6	Technology (all)	619.305	3.573E+79	No
7	Labor supply	706.645	4.185E+41	No
8	Investment-specific technology	664.178	1.161E+60	No
9	Preference	664.068	1.296E+60	No
10	Government	699.794	3.951E+44	No
11	Financial (uncertainty and UIP)	796.283	4.924E+02	No
12	Unit-root inflation target	794.754	2.272E+03	No
	Sensitivity to policy rules			
13	Add change in output and inflation	798.223	7.073E+01	No
14	Baseline rule, but without ΔS rule	796.913	2.622E+02	No
15	Same as (13), but without ΔS	792.821	1.570E+04	No
16	No interest rate smoothing	779.072	1.469E+10	No
17	Strict inflation targeting	776.368	2.193E+11	No
18	Fixed exchange rate regime	752.835	3.644E+21	No

2.5 Model Dynamics

This section aims to explore the dynamics of the estimated model. It starts off by exploring the implications of a monetary policy shock, and then provides an overview of the dynamics associated with the other shocks relegating the details to the working paper version of this study.

2.5.1 The Monetary Transmission Mechanism

Monetary tightening is effected via three main channels:

• The first channel operates as interest rates affect domestic demand, which primarily comprises of consumption and investment. Working through the Euler equation, higher real interest rates foster an increase in saving as consumption is postponed to later periods. At the same time higher real interest rates increase the opportunity cost of investment, decreasing the rate of capital accumulation (a channel that is operational in models with capital). As a result domestic demand and output decreases, putting downward pressure on inflation.

• The second channel brings out the open economy features of the model as it works via the exchange rate. Because of the nominal rigidities, the increase in the nominal interest rate translates into higher real interest rates and is associated with an increase in the real exchange rate. In turn this appreciation of the real exchange rate suppresses net exports (the expenditure switching effect), further decreasing aggregate demand.

• The third channel is characterized by the financial accelerator mechanism. Higher interest rates depress asset prices (the real price of capital) bringing about a deterioration in net worth. Weaker balance sheet fundamentals cause an increase in the external finance premium thereby raising the opportunity cost of investment above and beyond the initial effect generated by the monetary tightening. In turn, this brings about an even sharper contraction in investment, which is the primary determinant of the deeper contraction. As discussed in Bernanke, Gertler, and Gilchrist (1999), the financial accelerator mechanism can amplify the effects of certain shocks.

To more openly communicate the degree of uncertainty regarding the monetary transmission mechanism in Turkey during a sample period that encompasses the global financial crisis, we present in figure 2.2 the Bayesian impulses response functions for a selected set of variables along with their 90 percent bands, which take into consideration parameter uncertainty. As shown in the table 2.2, a one standard deviation contractionary monetary policy shock corresponds to a 70 basis point (quarterly) increase in the nominal interest rate—in other words, an annual increase in the policy rate of about 3 percent. The impulse response functions indicate that the output gaps dips below the steady state by 70 basis points, whereas the year-over-year inflation rate reaches a trough of about 140 basis points below steady state after four periods.

2.6 Historical Decompositions

To better illustrate the contributions of the structural shocks to output growth, the key structural shock we focus on is the monetary policy shock. In this section we quantify the role of monetary policy shocks

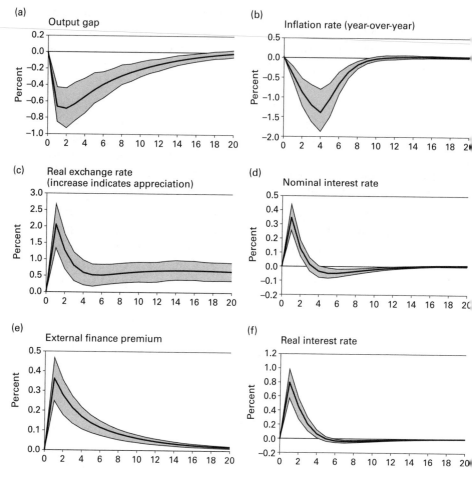

Figure 2.2
Turkey's monetary transmission mechanism. Shown are interest rates, inflation rates, and the external finance premium as absolute deviations from their steady states; other variables are percentage deviations from their steady states.

on output growth, and therefore provide one of our main policy implications.

We categorize the fifteen structural shocks in the model into three groups to reinforce intuition. The first group consists of the monetary policy shocks. The second group comprises the crisis shocks, namely shocks to foreign demand, financial uncertainty, and the uncovered interest rate parity (the sudden stop shock), and the final group contains the remaining supply and demand shocks. Our interest isto assess the role of these groups of shocks on (yearly) output growth over the 2005 to 2010 period, which includes the run-up and the most intense episode of the global financial crisis.

2.6.1   What Was the Growth Contribution of the Monetary Policy Shocks?

The main takeaway of this section is shown in figure 2.3. The figure plots real (year-over-year, demeaned) GDP growth, as well as the growth contributions of the three groups of shocks described above. The figure shows the growth contribution of the monetary policy shocks. The monetary policy shocks are in black, and as is clear, they positively contributed to output growth during the crisis episode.

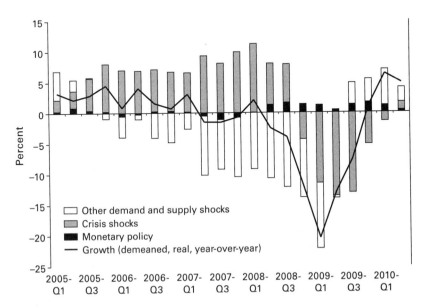

Figure 2.3
Historical decomposition of the role of money policy (demeaned yearly real GDP growth and shock contributions)

Note that the average growth contribution of the monetary policy shocks during the crisis episode is about 1.1 percent. To put this number in perspective, recall that the yearly real GDP contraction in Turkey in 2009 was –4.8 percent. Our model indicates that without these monetary policy shocks—that is, discretionary departures from the estimated interest rate rule—the growth rate for this year would have been –5.9 percent instead. In other words, monetary policy seems to have markedly contributed the softening the impact of the global financial crisis. We contrast this growth contribution of 1.1 percent to those in the literature in the section below.

2.6.2   What Was the Role of the Other Structural Shocks?

Consider first the role of the crisis shocks. To better understand the effects of the second group of shocks (foreign demand, risk premium, and financial uncertainty), each of these shocks is shown separately along with real (demeaned, year-over-year) GDP growth in figure 2.4. Note that the sudden stop (UIP or risk premium) shock does not seem to have an important effect on growth during the crisis. A key reason could be that in contrast to Cespedes, Chang, and Velasco (2004) as well as Elekdağ

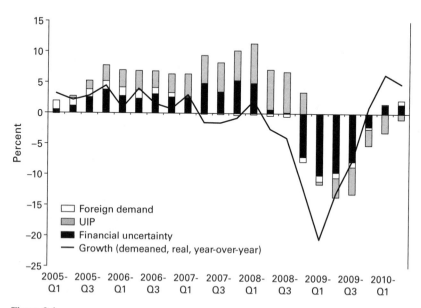

Figure 2.4
Historical decomposition of crisis shocks (demeaned yearly real GDP growth and shock contributions)

and Tchakarov (2007), we follow the initial specification of Gertler et al. (2007) and posit that entrepreneurs borrow in domestic- rather the foreign-currency-denominated debt. This arguably could reduce the role of risk premium (UIP) shocks, an important determinant of exchange rate dynamics. However, because foreign currency exposure in Turkey had generally decreased markedly after 2002, and because it was never as serious an issue as in some Latin American countries, for example, we do not pursue this (straightforward) extension in our simulation.

We analyzed the role of the crisis shocks depicted in figure 2.4 in three phases. First there was the run-up to the global financial crisis. During the period starting around 2005, the positive contribution of the foreign demand shocks to growth starts gaining momentum. The healthy growth rate of the global economy that solidified in 2005 certainly is one reason why foreign demand seems to have supported Turkish growth during this period. Then, during the last quarter of 2008, emerging markets started feeling the brunt of the global crisis. As the figure shows, it was initially the financial uncertainty shock that negatively impacted Turkish growth, followed by the foreign demand shock. The last phase corresponds to the onset of the recovery lead by a decrease in the financial uncertainty shocks. We find that the financial uncertainty shock explains a large fraction of the downturn among the three crisis shocks. It is also interesting to see the lingering effects of the foreign demand shock. The depressed growth trajectory in Turkey's main trading partner—the euro area— surely contributed to these dynamics.

The growth contributions of the remaining supply and demand shocks are shown in figure 2.5. The two prominent supply shocks are the unit-root and investment-specific technology shocks. In contrast to some other studies, there seems to be a limited role for the cost push (markup) and stationary technology shocks. By contrast, the unit-root technology shock seems to be the most important of the supply shocks, as in the result of Aguilar and Gopinath (2007) who argue that these types of trend shocks are important determinants of business cycle fluctuations across emerging markets. There also seems to be an important contribution by the investment-specific technology shocks, a point made by Justiniano et al. (2010). The demand shocks consist of the government spending, preference, and time-varying inflation target shock. The latter has a negligible role, and the remaining two demand shocks usually tend to offset each other to varying degrees over time. Overall, we see that the net effect of these shocks acted as a drag on growth, particularly in the early phase of the global financial crisis.

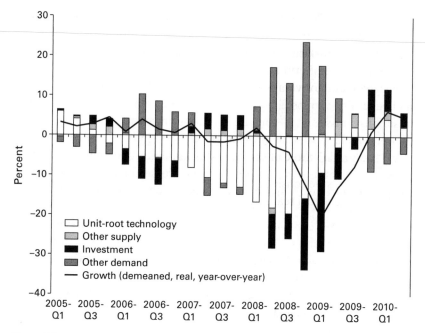

Figure 2.5
Historical decomposition of other supply and demand shocks (demeaned yearly real GDP growth and shock contributions)

2.7 The Role of Monetary Policy during the Crisis

We conducted some counterfactual experiments to see if the adoption of the flexible exchange rate regime and the implementation of active countercyclical monetary policy within an inflation targeting framework were not carried out, how much deeper would the recent recession been.

It turned out that the recession would indeed have been significantly more severe. The counterfactual experiments we discuss below indicate that the countercyclical and discretionary interest rate cuts implemented by the CBRT within an inflation-targeting regime underpinned by a flexible exchange rate added at least 3.2 percentage points to the 2009 real GDP growth.

Before proceeding, it may be useful to recall that after the 2001 financial crisis, two monetary policy reforms were carried out: (1) the fixed and heavily managed exchange rate regimes of the past were abandoned in favor of a flexible exchange rate and (2) the CBRT started implementing an inflation targeting regime—implicit initially, then officially as of 2006. Against this backdrop, as a by-product of our modeling setup, we can also take a first pass at assessing the possible role of the post-2001 financial reforms. As we saw in section 2.2, with these reforms, the risk profile of the Turkish economy—led by the banking sector—decreased markedly in the aftermath of the 2001 crisis. Based on a cross section of firms, the average leverage ratio decreased to a value of two in 2007 from a value of three in 2000. To illustrate, we will quantify below the impacts of these reforms by altering the steady state leverage ratio.

2.7.1   Setting up the Counterfactual Simulations

In what follows we consider four counterfactual simulations and compare them with the actual realization which is our baseline. The baseline monetary policy framework operates under a flexible exchange rate regime, follows the estimated baseline interest rate rule as it reacts to the output gap, and allows for deviations from the rule (in the form of the monetary policy shocks discussed above). Therefore the four counterfactual experiments are as follows:

• *No monetary policy shocks.*   This scenario posits strict adherence to the baseline empirical interest rate rule. It is a simulation that excludes the monetary policy shocks, that is, the monetary policy shocks, ϵ_t^i, are all set to zero in this simulation. It serves to address the following question: What would the dynamics of output growth have been if the CBRT did not implement any discretionary policy (deviations from the interest rate rule) during the crisis? While the previous section answered this question, here we seek to underscore this result and provide further context.

• *No response to the output gap.*   In this scenario the output gap coefficient in the empirical interest rate rule is set to zero ($\tau_y = 0$). Furthermore, as these counterfactuals are "cumulative," this scenario also sets the monetary policy shocks to zero. It serves to address the following question: What would the dynamic of output growth have been if the CBRT did not implement any discretionary policy and did not take into consideration the state of the output gap when formulating its policy decisions during the crisis?

• *Peg.*   In this scenario the CBRT is assumed to implement a strict fixed exchange rate regime.[5] Intuitively, monetary policy does not react to the output gap, and there are no discretionary deviations from the rule (which solely focuses on stabilizing the nominal exchange rate). Here we seek to address the following question: What would the dynamic of output growth have been if the CBRT was implementing a fixed exchange rate regime?

• *Peg with heightened financial vulnerability.*   In this last scenario the CBRT is presumed to operate under a fixed exchange rate regime as above, but the leverage ratio is calibrated to correspond to the case where it equals three in line with the situation during 2000. While not the main focus of the chapter, out modeling framework allows us to construct such an illustrative counterfactual serving to address the following question: What would the dynamic of output growth have been if the CBRT was implementing a fixed exchange rate regime *and* the economy was financially more vulnerable?

2.7.2   Results Based on the Counterfactual Simulations

Figure 2.6 depicts the level of real GDP with the first quarter of 2008 (the pre-crisis peak) normalized to 100 to allow the reader to better distinguish the (cumulative) effects of each counterfactual. The figure depicts (1) the actual realization of real GDP (the baseline scenario), (2) the counterfactual scenario without the monetary policy shocks, (3) the counterfactual scenario without the monetary policy shocks and with

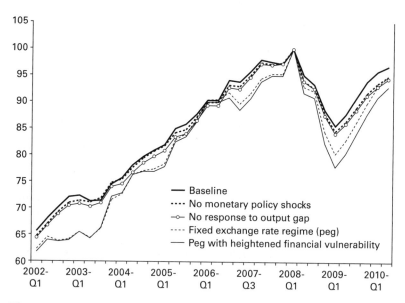

Figure 2.6
Counterfactual scenarios of the role of monetary policy and real GDP (levels), 2008Q1 = 100

the output gap coefficient in the empirical interest rate rule is set to zero, (4) the counterfactual scenario with the fixed exchange rate regime (peg), and (5) an illustrative counterfactual scenario with the peg under heightened financial vulnerabilities.

As clearly seen from figure 2.6, the inflation-targeting framework underpinned by a flexible exchange rate regime softened the impact of the global financial crisis. More specifically, there are three main results:

• First, as expected, output growth declines the most under the fixed exchange rate regime. The lack of the exchange rate to serve as a shock absorber decreases the resiliency of the economy to the shocks that ensued during the global crisis. Intuitively, the illustrative counterfactual experiment with heightened financial vulnerabilities, and thereby a more pronounced balance sheets channel, leads to an even sharper decline in output. These counterfactual experiments highlight the role of the exchange rate flexibility as well as financial reforms that promote the soundness of the financial system.

• Second, giving weight to the output gap seems to have a more limited role, but that is to be expected as the estimated coefficient (of 0.02) is quite low. In other words, the interest rate rule coefficient implies a small systematic response of policy rate to output gap, and a large discretionary (nonsystematic) response as summarized by the expansionary monetary policy shocks which we discuss next.

• Third, as discussed in the previous section, there is an important role for the discretionary departure from the interest rate rule, which helped soften the impact of the crisis. At first glance, while they may seem small, the role of these discretionary departures from the interest rate rule (the monetary policy shocks) is very much in line with the literature.

While our results suggest that the inflation targeting framework underpinned by a flexible exchange rate supported growth during the global financial crisis, clearly other policies also played a role. For example, it should be noted that we do not capture the direct effects of the liquidity measures enacted by the CBRT starting in the fourth quarter of 2008. Some of these policies include extending the terms of repurchase (repo) transactions, restarting foreign exchange auctions, and reducing reserve requirements on foreign exchange deposits. Moreover fiscal policy is modeled along the lines of many other studies in this strand of the literature, and is admittedly cursory. Therefore it is important to recognize that it might be possible that some of the contributions of expansionary fiscal policy and some of the liquidity measures implemented during the crisis (and not directly captured by our model) could have been attributed to the monetary policy shocks.

2.7.3 How Do Our Results Compare with Those in the Literature?

The precise contributions to growth under the various counterfactuals are shown in table 2.4. Our intention is for the table to focus on the most intense period of the crisis, but this could be open to interpretation. Therefore, in the context of the Turkish economy, we consider two alternative crisis episodes: 2008Q4 to 2009Q4 or 2009Q1 to 2009Q4.

Before investigating the details, it would be useful to clarify the information contained in table 2.4. The values under columns show either the average or cumulative contributions to growth during these two episodes. The table presents our results as well as the results of Christiano et al. (2007), the most closely related study to our in terms of conducting counterfactual experiments. The number of quarters in each episode and the quarterly cut in interest rates is also presented. Columns 1 through 5 indicate the incremental contribution to growth owing to the consecutive implementation of each policy. For example, consider the 2009:Q1 to 2009:Q4 episode. As column 4 indicates, reducing financial vulnerabilities added, on average, 1.45 percentage points to growth. In addition to this effect, the incremental growth contribution of adopting a flexible exchange rate regime, denoted under column 3, is 1.86 percentage points.

It would be useful to first compare the results in table 2.4 with the literature. In column 1 we see that the average contribution of the monetary shocks (discretionary deviations from the empirical interest rate rule) to output growth of around 1 percent (1.14 or 1.18 percent depending on the episode chosen) lies in between the values found by Chrisitiano et al. (2007) for the United States (0.75 percent) and the euro area (1.27 percent). The cumulative growth contributions also seem reasonable, and give some context as to the role of monetary policy in softening the impact of the crisis.

2.7.4 Summary of Main Results

To more intuitively summarize the findings in the counterfactuals above, we focus on the most intense year of the crisis, namely 2009. As shown in table 2.5, the actual growth rate for 2009 was –4.8 percent. Our model-based simulations suggest that if the CBRT had not departed from the empirical interest rate rule, growth would have instead been –5.9 percent,

Table 2.4
Role of monetary policy and financial reforms (in percent)

| | Quarters | Cut in policy rate | Growth contributions of monetary policy owing to: | | | | |
			(1) Monetary policy shocks	(2) Responsiveness to the output gap	(3) Flexible exchange rate regime	(4) Reduced financial vulnerability	(5) All factors, (1)–(4)
Average							
2008Q4–2009Q4	5	1.98	**1.18**	0.32	2.22	1.69	5.42
2009Q1–2009Q4	4	2.40	**1.14**	0.35	1.86	1.45	4.81
Christiano et al. (2008)							
United States (2001Q2–2002Q2)	4		0.75				
Euro area (2001Q4–2004Q4)	13		1.27				
Cumulative							
2008Q4–2009Q4	5	9.90	5.92	1.60	11.11	8.44	27.08
2009Q1–2009Q4	4	9.59	4.56	1.42	7.45	5.81	19.23
Christiano et al. (2008)							
United States (2001Q2–2002Q2)	4		3.00				
Euro area (2001Q4–2004Q4)	13		17.00				

Table 2.5
Measuring the severity of economic contractions (in percent; calculations relative to actual 2009 annual real GDP growth)

	Growth	Growth difference	Growth cumulative difference
Baseline (actual)	–4.8		
No monetary policy shocks	–5.9	–1.1	–1.1
No response to output gap	–6.2	–0.3	–1.4
Fixed exchange rate regime (peg)	–8.0	–1.8	–3.2
Peg with heightened financial vulnerability	–9.3	–1.3	–4.5

a difference of 1.1 percentage points. Furthermore, if instead of the inflation-targeting regime, a peg was in place, the results imply a growth rate of –8.0 percent, a difference from the actual of 3.2 percentage points. In sum, without the adoption of the flexible exchange rate regime, and active countercyclical monetary policy guided by an inflation targeting framework, the impact of the recent global financial crisis would have been substantially more severe.

2.8   Conclusion

In this chapter we developed and estimated a structural model using Turkish time series over the 2002 to 2010 period corresponding to the Central Bank of the Republic of Turkey (CBRT)'s gradual transition to full-fledged inflation targeting. Turkey is an interesting emerging economy case study because it was one of the hardest hit countries by the crisis, with a year-over-year contraction of 14.7 percent during the first quarter of 2009. At the same time, anticipating the fallout from the crisis, the CBRT decreased policy rates by an astounding 1025 basis points over the November 2008 to November 2009 period.

To this end, we addressed the question whether the recent recession would have been much deeper if an inflation-targeting framework under-pinned by a flexible exchange rate regime was not adopted. The main result is that the recession would have been substantially more severe.

This finding is based on counterfactual simulations derived from an estimated dynamic stochastic general equilibrium (DSGE) model that includes a financial accelerator mechanism in an open economy frame-work. These counterfactual situations allow us to quantify the differences in terms of growth between outcomes, for example, where the CBRT did not implement any countercyclical and discretionary interest rate cuts.

The most intuitive way to communicate our quantitative results is by taking the growth rate during the most intense year of the global financial crisis, namely 2009, as our baseline. In this context, our counterfactual simulations indicate that without the countercyclical interest rates cuts implemented by the CBRT, growth in 2009 would have decreased from the actual realization of –4.8 percent to –6.2 percent. Moreover, if a fixed exchange rate regime would have been in place instead of the current inflation targeting regime (which is underpinned by a flexible exchange rate), the results show that growth in 2009 would have been –8.0 percent, a difference from the actual outcome of 3.2 percentage points. In other words, these simulations underscore the favorable output stabilization properties owing to the combination of countercyclical interest rate cuts (consistent with the inflation target) and exchange rate flexibility.

In sum, without the adoption of an inflation-targeting framework underpinned by a flexible exchange rate regime, the impact of the recent global financial crisis would have been substantially more severe.

Notes

The views expressed in this chapter do not represent the views of the International Monetary Fund (IMF) or the Central Bank of the Republic of Turkey (CBRT). We thank Anella Munro, Zahid Samancıoğlu, Ümit Özlale, Fatih Özatay, Hakan Kara, Özer Karagedikli, Güneş Kamber, Cecilia Lon, and Refet Gürkaynak, as well as conference participants at the Bank of Israel, CBRT, Koç University, Reserve Bank of New Zealand, TOBB University of Economics and Technology, and the Turkish Economic Association for their insightful comments.

1. Alp and Elekdağ (2011).

2. The Turkish banking system was nearly completely overhauled after the 2001 crisis. Excessive leverage, maturity, and currency mismatches that intensified the severity of the 2001 crisis declined markedly (see Alp and Elekdağ 2011 for further details).

3. The economy proved resilient after successfully coping with the crisis in mid-summer 2006 brought on by a sell-off of assets in many emerging economies.

4. Theoretically our model brings together elements from Adolfson et al. (2007), Bernanke et al. (1999), Elekdağ and Tchakarov (2007), and Gertler et al. (2007) and, quantitatively we build on the work of Smets and Wouters (2003, 2007) and Elekdağ et al. (2006).

5. Just as the model-based framework assumes that the inflation targeting regimes are fully credible, it also assumes that the exchange rate regimes are fully credible. While the latter assumption is harder to justify, the credibility of both regimes is needed for comparability. For a lack of a better term, credibility was used, but perhaps sustainability is a more related or even more appropriate characterization.

References

Adolfson, Malin, Stefan Laseen, Jesper Linde, and Mattias Villani. 2007. Bayesian estimation of an open economy DSGE model with incomplete pass-through. *Journal of International Economics* 72: 481–511.

Aguilar, Mark, and Gita Gopinath. 2007. Emerging market business cycles: The cycle is the trend. *Journal of Political Economy* 115 (1): 69–102.

Alp, Harun, and Selim Elekdağ. 2011. The role of monetary policy in Turkey during the global financial crisis. Working paper 11/150. IMF, Washington, DC.

Bernanke, Ben, and Mark Gertler, and Simon Gilchrist. 1999. The financial accelerator in a quantitative business cycle framework. *Handbook of Macroeconomics,* vol. 1C. Amsterdam: Elsevier, 1341–93.

Calvo, Guillermo, and Alejandro Izquierdo. and Luis. F. Mejia. 2004. On the empirics of sudden stops: The relevance of balance-sheet effects. Working paper 10520. NBER, Cambridge, MA.

Cespedes, Luis F., Roberto Chang, and Andres Velasco. 2004. Balance sheets and exchange rate policy. *American Economic Review* 94: 1183–93.

Christiano, Lawrence J., Roberto Motto, and Massimo Rostagno. 2008. Shocks, structures, or monetary policies? The euro area and U.S. after 2001. *Journal of Economic Dynamics and Control* 32: 2476–2506.

Christiano, Lawrence J., Roberto Motto, and Massimo Rostagno. 2010. Financial factors in economic fluctuations. Working paper 1192. EBC, Frankfurt.

Curdia, Vasco. 2007. Monetary policy under sudden stops. Staff report 278. Federal Reserve Bank of New York.

Dib, Ali, and Ian Christensen. 2008. The financial accelerator in an estimated New Keynesian model. *Review of Economic Dynamics* 11: 155–78.

Elekdağ, Selim, Alejandro Justiniano, and Ivan Tchakarov. 2006. An estimated small open economy model of the financial accelerator. *IMF Staff Papers* 53: 219–41.

Elekdağ, Selim, and Ivan Tchakarov. 2007. Balance sheets, exchange rate policy, and welfare. *Journal of Economic Dynamics and Control* 31: 3986–4015.

Gali, Jordi, and Tommaso Monacelli. 2005. Monetary policy and exchange rate volatility in a small open economy. *Review of Economic Studies* 72 (3):707–34.

Garcia-Cicco, Javier. 2010. Estimating models for monetary policy analysis in emerging countries. Working paper 561. Central Bank of Chile, Santiago.

Gertler, Mark, Simon Gilchrist, and Fabio Natalucci. 2007. External constraints on monetary policy and the financial accelerator. *Journal of Money, Credit and Banking* 39 (2/3): 295–330.

Justiniano, Alejandro, Giorgio E. Primiceri, and Andrea Tambalotti. 2010. Investment shocks and business cycles. *Journal of Monetary Economics* 57 (2): 132–45.

Lubik, Thomas A., and Frank Schorfheide. 2007. Do central banks respond to exchange rate movements? A structural investigation. *Journal of Monetary Economics* 54: 1069–87.

Mendoza, Enrique. 1991. Real business cycles in a small open economy. *American Economic Review* 81: 797–818.

Schorfheide, Frank. 2000. Loss function-bases evaluation of DSGE models. *Journal of Applied Econometrics* 15: 1–48.

Smets, Frank, and Rafael Wouters. 2003. An estimated stochastic general equilibrium model of the euro area. *Journal of the European Economic Association* 1: 1123–75.

Smets, Frank, and Rafael Wouters. 2007. Shocks and frictions in US business cycles: A Bayesian DSGE approach. *American Economic Review* 97 (3): 586–605.

Teo, Wing. 2009. Estimated dynamic stochastic general equilibrium model of the Taiwanese economy. *Pacific Economic Review* 14 (2): 194–231.

3 An Assessment of Chile's Monetary and Fiscal Policy Responses to the Global Crisis

Claudio Soto

3.1 Introduction

During 2008 to 2009 we witnessed a period of unprecedented financial turmoil that led to a major financial crisis and a global recession. In response, many governments around the world implemented a wide set of countercyclical policies using conventional and nonconventional policy instruments. In this chapter I describe and analyze the fiscal and monetary policies taken by the Chilean authorities to deal with the crisis and the global recession.[1]

The most immediate measures taken by the Central Bank of Chile shortly after the Lehman collapse were intended to provide and ensure liquidity to the banking system. After some weeks of turmoil, with clear sign of liquidity contraction, different liquidity spreads returned back to their pre-shock level. However, credit risk remained considerably above its historical level. Then a second line of action by the monetary authority consisted in aggressively adjusting its main policy instrument, the overnight lending rate, in order to produce a clearly expansionary monetary stance. The reduction in the policy rate proceeded at a much faster speed than it would have been under the historical behavior of the Central Bank. Simultaneously the government announced a stimulus package of about 2.5 percent of GDP, which combined direct government spending, tax cuts, and transfers to the private sector. Finally, in mid-2009 the Central Bank implemented a nonconventional policy by extending its lending facility up to six months at the given policy rate. This measure was taken so as to increase the monetary policy impulse at a moment where the monetary policy rate had reached its technical zero lower bound.

Despite these policy measures, GDP fell about 1.5 percent during 2009 and aggregate demand contracted by 6 percent. However, the rebound was relatively fast and strong. Already by the last quarter of 2009 the economy was growing again, and during 2010 it grew by more than 5 percent despite a severe earthquake that hit the country at the beginning of the year.

There are several questions regarding the consequences of the policy actions implemented by the Chilean authorities in this crisis. For example, was the liquidity provision by the Central Bank successful? Did the nonconventional monetary policy measure have an impact on the monetary stimulus? How would the economy have responded had these policy measures not been implemented?

In the chapter I attempt to answer some of these questions. In particular, I show that the liquidity measures taken right after the Lehman collapse in October 2008—which clearly had an impact on the Chilean market—allowed the money market to work relatively smoothly after a couple of weeks. Then the aggressive reduction in the monetary policy rate starting in January 2009 led to a substantial reduction in market lending rates, which avoided a sharp contraction in credit and allowed domestic demand to recover relatively fast. The nonconventional policy did reduce long-term market rates, producing an extra monetary stimulus. According to the counterfactual scenario constructed with a DSGE model, the fact that the policy rate was reduced at a much faster speed than under the historical behavior of the Central Bank avoided a drop of about 2 percent in GDP. In turn the substantial fiscal stimulus package launched at the beginning of 2009 contributed to prevent a further drop in output of about the same magnitude.

The rest of the chapter is organized as follows. Section 3.2 discusses the impact of the global shock on domestic liquidity and the actions implemented by the Central Bank. Section 3.3 analyzes the monetary policy response to the contraction in demand and inflation, triggered by the surge in risk perception and the abrupt downward adjustment in expectations. Section 3.4 describes and analyzes the effect of the fiscal stimulus package, and section 3.5 concludes.

3.2 Liquidity Shock and Immediate Policy Actions

As in most economies, financial tensions in Chile were severe after the collapse of Lehman Brothers in September 2008. From mid-September to mid-October different measures of liquidity reflected the fears of financial market participants and their desire to hold liquidity. The prime-swap spread, for example, went up from around 50 basis points at the end of September to more than 300 basis points at the beginning

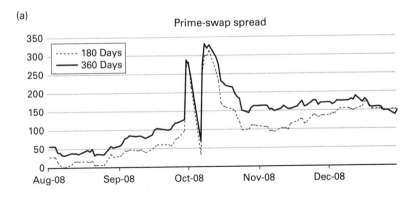

(a)

Prime-swap spread

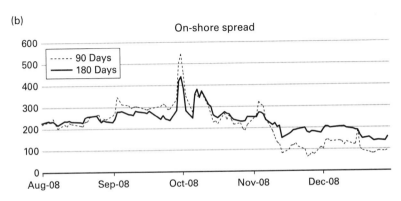

(b)

On-shore spread

Figure 3.1
Liquidity shock
Source: Central Bank of Chile

of October. Also foreign-currency shortages were reflected in on-shore spreads, which spiked during the first week of October (figure 3.1).

Together with the appetite for liquidity, there was a sharp increase in the price of risk and in the external perception of the country's risk. The EMBI went up from less than 200 basis points at the end of August to almost 400 basis points in October. In turn external borrowing condition for local banks became tighter. The spread at which domestic banks could borrow from abroad increased more than 100 basis points (figure 3.2). The shortage of foreign currency liquidity and the increased risk perception of the country led to a large depreciation of the currency of about 30 percent during a couple of weeks (figure 3.3).

The first line of action taken by the Central Bank was to ensure the provision of liquidity both in domestic and foreign currency. On September 29, the Central Bank announced the ending of the international

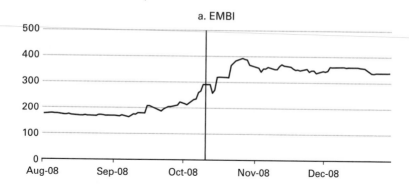

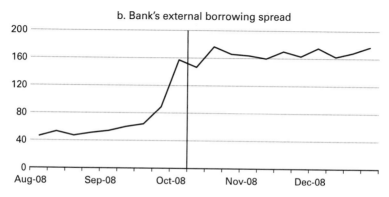

Figure 3.2
Chile's external premium
Sources: Bloomberg; Superintendency of Banks and Financial Institutions

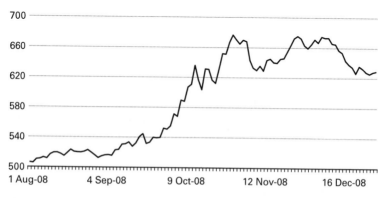

Figure 3.3
Nominal exchange rate
Source: Central Bank of Chile

reserves accumulation program launched in April 2008. Also repo and swap operations were implemented to boost domestic and foreign currency liquidity. On October 10, the set of eligible collaterals for the repo operations was expanded, and the foreign currency swap program was extended from one to six months. These policy actions were intended not only to mitigate liquidity tensions, but also to ensure foreign currency financing, should foreign loans become scarce (De Gregorio 2011). The fiscal authority complemented these measures by allocating its excess liquidity in deposits with local banks.

On December 3, the Central Bank extended its auctions of foreign currency swaps from 60 and 90 days up to 180 days, and on December 10, the liquidity provision program through repos and swaps was extended until the end of 2009. Simultaneously a new liquidity provision mechanism was introduced by allocating credit against collaterals that included public bonds and bank deposits.

Local money market conditions normalized rapidly over a period of weeks as is reflected in different spread measures (see figure 3.1). The additional liquidity facilities put in place were not used extensively by financial institutions, reflecting their sustained access to external markets. For example, not all the foreign currency liquidity offered though the swap operations was demanded by market participants, suggesting that quantitative restrictions were not biding at that moment. What the liquidity provision achieved was the reduction of uncertainty. By doing that, the on-shore spread fell substantially to levels even lower than those at the beginning of September, and the same occurred to the prime-swap spreads. In other words, the Central Bank allowed the money market to keep on working with fewer tensions.

3.3   Monetary Policy Response to the Crisis

Beyond the stressful episode in local money markets, the confidence crisis that swept around the world had an important impact in Chile. The events in developed financial markets prompted a deep and widespread revision of investment and spending plans of businesses and households, bringing expenditure to a halt (De Gregorio 2011). Domestic demand and economic activity dropped significantly as lending standards tightened. The increase in financial spreads amplified the effects of the initial shock on demand and activity (García and Medina 2009).

In this context the inflation outlook changed radically. Initially, the dramatic fall in the international oil price was quickly passed through to

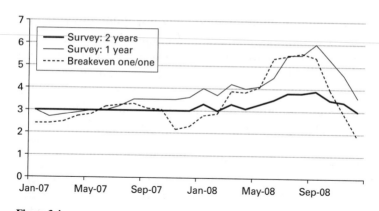

Figure 3.4
Inflation expectations
Source: Author's calculation based on Central Bank of Chile data

the domestic price of gasoline. Inflation expectations declined abruptly by the end of 2008 (figure 3.4). Subsequently the contraction in aggregate demand led to a widening in the output gap that, combined with the fall in the price of oil and the reduction in inflation expectations, pushed prices down. This was the case even despite the nominal depreciation of the currency depicted in figure 3.3.

Monetary policy reacted forcefully. Initially the Central Bank stopped its process of monetary tightening. In fact in the baseline case discussed in the Inflation Report of September 2008, before the Lehman collapse and when inflation was approaching a double-digit figure, further monetary policy rate hikes were required in order to bring inflation under control (figure 3.5, bold line). Then, in an update of the Inflation Report published in November 2008, a change in outlook and the bias for monetary policy was communicated, inducing an important decline in market rates at all horizons (figure 3.5, dashed line).

In January 2009, with a clearer assessment of the reduced inflationary pressures, the Central Bank started a process of monetary policy loosening by lowering the monetary policy rate by 100 basis points. Later, with the evidence of alleviated inflationary pressures and a sharp contraction in demand, the Central Bank decided to cut the monetary policy rate by 250 basis points at both its meetings of February and March.

The monetary easing process continued and completed 775 basis points in seven monthly meetings, bringing the monetary policy rate to 0.5 percent in July 2009, the minimum level deemed adequate for a normal functioning of money markets (De Gregorio 2011). Each of the rate cuts

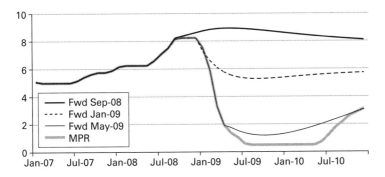

Figure 3.5
Monetary policy rate and forward curve
Source: Author's calculation based on Central Bank of Chile data

from January onward was larger than what the market was expecting as can be seen in the different forward curves during this period (figure 3.5).

The last policy rate cut was in July 2009. The monetary policy rate reached 0.5 percent, which was considered the minimum value it could attain without causing problems in the financial system (Central Bank of Chile 2009). At that moment, however, the forward curve became steeper. There was clearly a bias regarding the direction of the next policy move, and there was uncertainty regarding the precise moment at which such a move could occur. Both elements introduced premiums, which implied that medium- to long-term market rates had started to increase.

In response, and given the evaluation that a substantial monetary impulse was still required in order to ensure the economic recovery, the monetary authority decided to use an unconventional monetary policy. Basically the Central Bank announced that the monetary policy rate would be held constant at the minimum level for a prolonged period of time, and in order to strengthen its commitment to this announcement, it extended the overnight liquidity facility for banks at the monetary policy rate to a 180-days' term through a term liquidity facility (*Facilidad de Liquidez a Plazo*, FLAP). As a result of the implementation of the FLAP program, the forward curve shifted down by 100 basis points approximately, thus providing an extra monetary impulse to the economy (figure 3.6). This extraordinary liquidity measure was phased out during mid-2010.

As mentioned, the global financial crisis not only generated a short-term liquidity squeeze that was alleviated with extraordinary liquidity measures by the Central Bank. The increase in uncertainty and risk

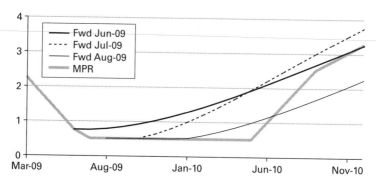

Figure 3.6
Monetary policy rate and forward: Pre- and post-FLAP
Source: Author's calculation based on Central Bank of Chile data

perception also triggered a credit crunch, which was reflected in sharp increases in credit spreads. In this context, what monetary authority did by aggressively lowering its policy rate was to—partially—offset the contraction in credit. The lowering of the policy rate was in fact quickly transmitted into the economy by a reduction in commercial lending rates. These rates had increased in response to the previous tightening cycle of monetary policy, but also in response to an increased risk perception in the domestic financial market.

Figure 3.7 depicts the evolution of two of the most representative lending rates together with the fitted value of a model for these rates that incorporates the monetary policy rate as an explanatory variable (see Becerra et al. 2010). In the case of the commercial short-term lending rate, it is clear that the sharp fall at the beginning of 2009 was in large part due to the aggressive monetary policy response to the financial shock. If the monetary policy rate had remained at its December 2008 level, the commercial lending rate would have fallen only marginally (dashed line in figure 3.7). In the case of the consumer lending rate, a large fraction of its increase at the beginning of the crisis is associated with a transitory increase in risk perception on concerns about household default probabilities. If the monetary policy rate had remained high, this lending rate would have still fallen significantly since risk perception was quickly reduced (probably as a result of the monetary policy response and additionally the fiscal policy discussed below).

The speed at which the monetary authority proceeded during the crisis was faster than what a policy rule estimated using historical data would predict (Calani et al. 2011; García 2010). This deviation from the histori-

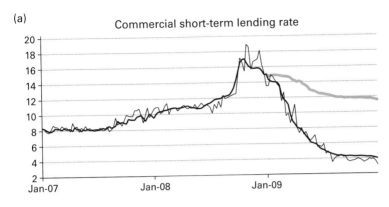

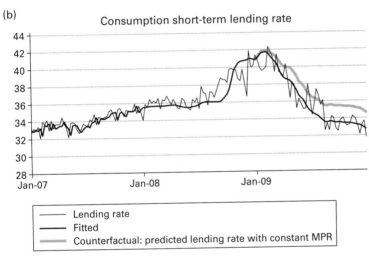

Figure 3.7
Lending rates
Source: Becerra et al. (2010)

cal behavior of the monetary authority was fully consistent with the inflation-targeting regime and under full confidence that the exchange rate posed no threat. The quick and strong reaction of monetary policy led to a much more muted contraction in inflation and activity than would have been the case if conservative measures were effected.

To quantify the contribution of this deviation from historical behavior in the monetary policy conduction, I use a structural DSGE model tailored to the Chilean economy to evaluate what would have happened with the main macro variables of the economy if the Central Bank had followed its historical policy rule.[2] The results are depicted in figure 3.8.

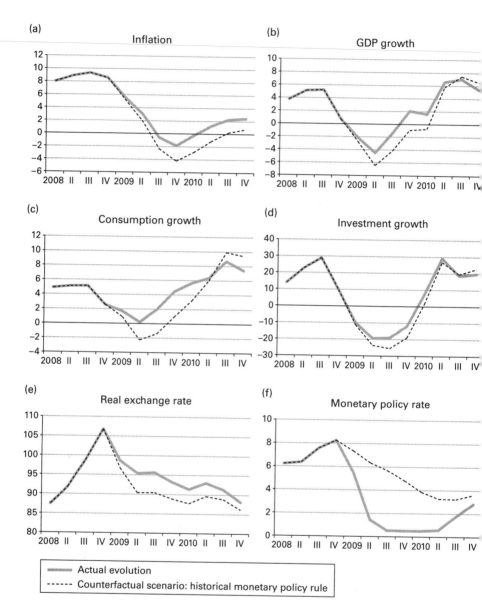

Figure 3.8
Counterfactual scenario: more aggressive monetary policy
Source: Author's simulations using the MAS model of the Central Bank of Chile

The bold line in the figure corresponds to the actual evolution of each variable. The dashed line depicts the counterfactual scenario of what would have happened if the Central Bank had reduced its policy rate in a smooth fashion, as it would have based on its historical behavior. As can be seen from the figure, in this case inflation would have fallen by 200 basis points more than it actually did, the real exchange rate would have appreciated 5 percent more, and GDP would have contracted by almost 2 percent more. Also, by being more aggressive at lowering the policy rate, the Central Bank avoided negative growth in consumption and an even stronger contraction in investment.

3.4 Fiscal Stimulus Response

The shift to a countercyclical policy stance was also taken forcefully by the fiscal authority. In January 2009 the government announced a sizable fiscal stimulus package, amounting to US$4 billion for that year, equivalent to 2.5 percent of GDP. The fiscal package consisted of three broad measures. The first was a transitory expansion in government expenditure consistent with a temporary reduction in the target for the structural public balance of 0.5 percent of GDP (the target was reduced from 0.5 to 0 percent of GDP), coupled with a permanent increase in public expenditures of another 0.5 percent of GDP. The latter was justified on the grounds that structural public revenue at the end of 2008 was larger than previously estimated, providing room for a fiscal expansion consistent with the guidelines of the structural rule.[3]

The second measure was a transitory reduction in the stamp tax on financial transactions. The tax rate was reduced from 1.2 percent to 0 percent in January 2009 and then partially increased back to 0.6 percent in January 2010. The tax rate was originally scheduled to be back to its original level in June 2010. However, the government passed a law to keep the rate at 0.6 percent permanently. The impact of this measure on fiscal revenues was not considered in the accounting of the structural balance since it was an ex ante transitory measure. The third measure consisted of a tax credit for small and medium-size firms, intended to enhance their liquidity.

Evaluating the incidence of the expansion of public spending on activity depends on the assessment of the size of the standard multiplier of fiscal expenditure. However, evaluating the effect of the transitory elimination of the stamp tax on financial transactions and the tax credit to small- and medium-sized firms is less obvious. In principle, the stamp-tax reduction would temporarily lower the financial cost of credit to both firms and households. Depending on the inter-temporal elasticity of substitution, this will boost consumption and investment. However, since the stamp-tax affects credits at different horizons to a different degree (it is a tax that affects the total amount of credit), it affects different types of agents differently depending on their borrowing horizons. Finally, the degree of pass-through of the lower tax rate to the marginal financing cost of final borrowers was not obvious. It was possible for the credit institution to partially offset the reduction in the tax rate by increasing the lending rate where the supply of credit was somehow elastic. For the same reason the impact of the tax credit was not obvious enough to evaluate.

As in the case of monetary policy, I make use of the DSGE model to construct a counterfactual scenario to answer the question: What would have happened if the government had not implemented the stimulus package? Key to the results discussed below are values of some of the parameters of the model. For example, the model assumes that a share of households is non-Ricardian. This share is calibrated so as to obtain a fiscal multiplier of about 1.3, which is consistent with VAR evidence for Chile (Restrepo and Rincón 2006). The whole set of parameters of the model is described in Medina and Soto (2007a).

Figure 3.9 presents the actual evolution of the data and the counterfactual scenario that would be obtained without the stimulus package. In this analysis the combined effects of all the fiscal measures are taken into account. Accordingly, the fiscal stimulus avoided a drop in output of about 2 percent. It also prevented inflation from falling further than it did. Without the stimulus package, the real exchange rate would have remained a bit more depreciated throughout the last two years.

The smaller contraction in GDP is basically explained by the fact that the fiscal measures allowed consumers to sustain a higher level of consumption during the recession. The stimulus package had in fact a much smaller impact on investment. Notice that under the counterfactual scenario, monetary policy would have been slightly more expansionary than it actually was. Indeed, if the stimulus package had not have been in place, the monetary policy would have reached its zero lower bound for the interest rate one quarter before (assuming that the same departure from the historical behavior of the Central Bank would have occurred without the fiscal stimulus package).

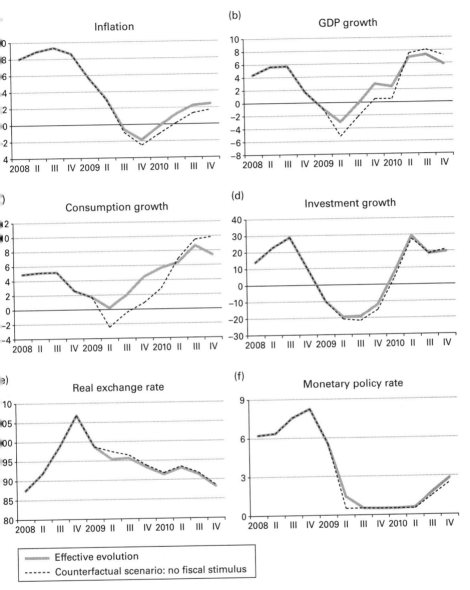

Figure 3.9
Actual and counterfactual scenario without fiscal stimulus
Source: Author's simulations using the MAS model of the Central Bank of Chile

3.5   Conclusions

In this chapter I described and evaluated the policy measures implemented by the Chilean authorities in response to the global financial crisis of 2008. The Central Bank of Chile adopted a series of liquidity measures and conducted a very aggressive monetary policy, which was complemented with the use of unconventional measures. The government in turn introduced a stimulus package of about 3 percent of GDP.

I showed that the liquidity measures taken following the Lehman collapse in October 2008 allowed the money market to work relatively smoothly after a couple of weeks. Then the aggressive reduction in the monetary policy rate, starting in January 2009, led to a substantial reduction in market lending rates, which avoided a sharp contraction in credit and allowed domestic demand to recover relatively fast. According to the counterfactual scenario constructed with the DSGE model, the fact that the policy rate was reduced at a much faster speed than it would have been under the historical behavior of the Central Bank, avoided a drop of about 2 percent in GDP. In turn the substantial fiscal stimulus package launched at the beginning of 2009 also contributed to prevent a further drop in output of about the same magnitude.

Notes

The opinions expressed in this chapter do not necessarily represent those of the Central Bank of Chile. I thank José De Gregorio and Luis Ceballos for valuable discussions, Roque Montero and Sebastián Becerra for their technical assistance, and Yan Carrière-Swallow for editorial assistance. All remaining errors are mine.

1. Another detailed account of the policies adopted in response to the crisis and their impact can be found in De Gregorio (2011).

2. The model is a small open economy model in the spirit of Christiano, Eichenbaum, and Evans (2005). The economy includes two types of households: Ricardian households that make choices about consumption and borrowing, and set wages; and non-Ricardian households that consume all their labor income and neither save nor borrow. Production technology uses labor, capital, and oil. Both prices and wages are sticky (subject to nominal rigidities à la Calvo), with partial indexation to past inflation. There are adjustment costs to investment, and the pass-through from the exchange rate to the domestic price of imports is imperfect in the short run. The model also includes a commodity sector whose production—based on natural resources—is completely exported. This sector is meant to characterize the copper sector in the Chilean economy. Monetary policy is conducted through a policy rule for the interest rate, while fiscal policy is conducted through a structural balance rule. For specific details of the model, see Medina and Soto (2007a).

3. For a discussion on the structural fiscal rule, see Marcel et al. (2001) and Medina and Soto (2007b).

References

Becerra, Sebastián, Luis Ceballos, Felipe Córdova, and Michael Pedersen. 2010. Market interest rate dynamics in times of financial turmoil. *Economía Chilena* 13 (1): 5–21.

Calani, Mauricio, Kevin Cowan, and Pablo Garcia. 2011. Inflation targeting in financially stable economies: Has been flexible enough? In Luis F. Céspedes, Roberto Chang, and Diego Saravia, eds., *Monetary Policy under Financial Turbulence*. Santiago: Central Bank of Chile, 283–368.

Central Bank of Chile. 2009. Política monetaria no convencional. *Inflation Report* (December): 11–12.

Christiano, Lawrence, Martin Eichenbaum, and Charles Evans. 2005. Nominal rigidities and the dynamic effects of a shock to monetary policy. *Journal of Political Economy* 113 (1): 1–45.

De Gregorio, José. 2011. Chile: Policy response to the global crisis. Presentation delivered at the Conference Monetary Policy and Central Banking in the Post Crisis Environment, Central Bank of Chile and Global Interdependence Center, January 17, Santiago, Chile. http://www.bcentral.cl/politicas/presentaciones/consejeros/pdf/2011/jdg17012011.pdf.

García, Benjamin, and Juan P. Medina. 2009. Efecto de las primas financieras en la actividad agregada. *Economía Chilena* 12 (3): 89–101.

García, Benjamín. 2010. Empirical evidence on the variability of the degree of persistence of the policy rule in inflation targeting countries. Working paper 592. Central Bank of Chile, Santiago.

Marcel, Mario, Marcelo Tokman, Rodrigo Valdés, and Paula Benavides. 2001. Balance estructural: La base de la nueva regla de política fiscal chilena. *Economía Chilena* 4 (3): 5–27.

Medina, Juan P., and Claudio Soto. 2007a. The Chilean business cycle through the lens of a general equilibrium model. Working paper 457. Central Bank of Chile, Santiago.

Medina, Juan P., and Claudio Soto. 2007b. Copper price, fiscal policy and business cycle in Chile. Central Bank of Chile Working paper 458. Central Bank of Chile, Santiago.

Restrepo, Jorge, and Hernán Rincón. 2006. Identifying fiscal policy shocks in Chile and Colombia. Working paper 370. Central Bank of Chile, Santiago.

II MACROPRUDENTIAL AND FINANCIAL POLICIES

4 Central Banks, Macroprudential Policy, and the Spanish Experience

Enrique Alberola, Carlos Trucharte, and Juan Luís Vega

4.1 Introduction

The global financial crisis erupted in a context of financial excesses and an underlying financial fragility fostered by loose economic and financial conditions, low inflation, high-risk appetite, lack of due diligence by some investors, and inadequate regulation and supervision. The magnitude of the damage forced central banks, financial authorities, and many other policy institutions throughout the world to react swiftly in order to mitigate its fallout, a process in which advanced economies, in particular, are still engaged. Moreover the financial origin of the crisis strengthened the commitment of central banks to improve their surveillance and reinforcement of financial stability, a process still underway.

Central banks had traditionally maintained a clear division of tasks: financial stability was mostly achieved through financial supervision and regulation — microprudential policy — while price stability was the role of monetary policy. Central bank monetary policy therefore contributed to financial stability in a setting that had attained macroeconomic stability. In the aftermath of the 2008 crisis, this proved not enough, and spawned a growing consensus that monetary policy and financial stability should be more integrated within the general policy framework of central banks. However, this move is being plagued by a complexity that could interfere with the paramount monetary policy objective of achieving price stability.

Given this situation, a key building block in the new policy environment would appear to be a macroprudential policy — that is, the set of instruments to prevent the buildup of financial imbalances that could lead to a crisis and/or mitigate its impact. An adequate macroprudential policy design would address financial stability objectives, and through interactions with central bank monetary policy and the microprudential policies, it could adjust the goals and improve the instruments in the central bank policy framework.

The integration of a macroprudential framework in the policy toolbox of central banks would consist of surveillance as well as tools. In the area of surveillance there have been remarkable advances in the last two years both at the global level—for example, the Financial Stability Board (FSB) and the Basel Committee—and at the national or regional levels, with the establishment of the European Systemic Risk Board (ESRB) in the European Union. In the implementation of instruments, there has been some lag, due in part to the assessments that these institutions are making of the macroprudential instruments and their practical applications.

Spain is among those countries where macroprudential instruments have already been applied for over a decade. Thus the Spanish experience with the dynamic provisions is being treated in international economic discussions as a reference example. However, as this "domestic" tool is to be implemented within the euro area, the monetary policy would be set at the supranational level. This is a feature that is worth examining.

In this chapter we describe and assess the Spanish dynamic provision. We frame it in the context of the current role of central banks in promoting financial stability, in general, and in the euro area, in particular.

4.2   Central Banks, Monetary Policy, and Financial Stability

Maintaining price stability over the medium term in the euro area is the primary objective of the monetary policy strategy of the Eurosystem. That notwithstanding, as an important financial authority, the Eurosystem devotes substantial effort to promoting European financial integration and financial stability. Indeed the European Central Bank´s Statute states that, without prejudice to the primary objective of price stability, the Bank will contribute to financial stability. This institutional framework was not to be affected by the creation of the European Financial Stability Board, in which officers of both the ECB and the central banks of the ESCB participate.

4.2.1   The Interaction between Monetary and Financial Stability: The Conventional Pre-crisis View

When thinking about the relationship between monetary policy and financial stability it is useful to distinguish between two time horizons:

the short and the long term. In the long term, as economic theory makes clear, there can be no trade-off between monetary stability and financial stability because the two concepts are mutually reinforcing: low and stable inflation and a monetary policy strategy dedicated to this goal tend to promote financial stability.[1] Empirical evidence also supports this view, since historically monetary instability is one of the main factors causing episodes of financial instability.[2]

This complementarity over the long term suggests that the monetary policy stance that is considered appropriate for the maintenance of price stability need not be in contradiction with financial stability requirements. However, history and recent experience show that financial imbalances can develop in an environment of stable prices. Price stability should therefore be seen as a necessary but not a sufficient condition for financial stability and the short-term relation between the two objectives is more complex than suggested by the long-term link between them. As argued by Issing (2003), "there may be situations where it is optimal to deviate from the desired rate of inflation in the short-run in order to best maintain price stability over the medium run." Hence, how should monetary policy deal with potential conflicts that might arise at shorter horizons?

The so-called Tinbergen principle advocates that only one policy instrument be assigned to each objective supporting the idea that monetary policy should remain firmly anchored in the objective of price stability. Policy instruments other than interest rate, including regulatory and supervisory tools but also the provision of liquidity by the central bank, would, in principle, be better suited for coping with problems of financial stability.

However, it should be noted that monetary policy has a legitimate interest in the financial stability objective, as this is a necessary condition for the proper functioning of the transmission mechanism. Moreover a second principle of monetary policy is that excessive emphasis on short-term inflation targeting is not optimal and entails risks. Indeed, by deviating from short-term inflation targeting, the monetary policy strategy of the ECB does accommodate financial stability considerations. In particular, the ECB's monetary analysis is concerned about, among other things, the evolution of monetary and credit indicators, which are potentially useful indicators to assess risks to financial stability. But above all, it is the medium-term orientation (and the abstention from specifying a fixed-term horizon for policy) that permits sufficient weight to be assigned to medium- to long-term risks and thus for possible conflicts that may arise between these two objectives to be accounted for in the short term. Nonetheless, when navigating these conflicts, the central bank must attend to its primary price stability objective, as loss of credibility on this front can have serious consequences.

4.2.2   The Case of Asset Prices

The evolving view about the role of monetary policy in counterbalancing the excessive growth of asset prices provides a good example of the conventional position of central bankers in the years before the crisis and how that position has changed in the aftermath of the crisis.

Asset prices constitute, together with agents' balance sheets, an important channel in the transmission mechanism of monetary policy. If, for example, stock or housing prices increase, a central bank that is targeting, say, a weighted average of inflation and the output gap would raise interest rates. The rationale for that rather uncontroversial policy action is that, ceteris paribus, wealth effects would make aggregate demand increase too fast and would cause an intensification of inflationary pressures.

There is also a relative consensus as to whether monetary policy should react to movements in asset prices beyond their indirect effects on price stability when asset prices reflect current and expected value of fundamentals. In those cases economic theory suggests that given their character of endogenous variables, monetary policy should not react to their evolution as such but to the underlying, not directly observable shocks.[3]

By contrast, however, the views of economists have diverged, sometimes dramatically, when misalignments occur, namely when asset prices detach from fundamentals. While some in the profession have long promoted a more active role of monetary policy in that context,[4] the majority of academics and policy makers have until recently favored a more hands-off approach.[5] This latter group had tended to emphasize that monetary policy should not be overburdened with objectives that may prove to be overambitious and for which it does not have the appropriate instruments either. Adjusting monetary policy to prick a financial bubble on the basis of financial stability considerations would require an increase in interest rates that would possibly be incompatible with macroeconomic stability, in particular as bubbles can only be identified relatively late. Moreover this group of economists had claimed that attempts to identify misalignments early enough are hopeless, giving rise to numerous false positives. As Blinder has put it, the central bank ". . . may see bubbles where there are none, or fail to recognize them until it's too late—or probably both."[6] This line of reasoning has led to the conclusion that central banks should remain focused on its primary objective of preserving price stability and act only ex post, as aggressively as necessary, to counter the fallout of the bubble burst, limiting collateral damage and ensuring financial stability.[7]

The response of the Federal Reserve following the burst of the tech bubble in 2000 followed that script and was successful: the financial damage was limited without prejudice to price stability and the country confronted only a very mild recession. The then majority view had been vindicated and the debate vanished in the years prior to the crisis. However, the burst of the subprime bubble in August 2007 has given rise to a protracted period of severe financial instability and the largest global recession since World War II. Not only the strategy to let financial bubbles deflate according to their own dynamics and restrict the action of monetary policy to damage control has not worked this time, but the aggressive monetary response to mitigate the impact of the dotcom bubble led to a period of loose global financing conditions, which has is now seen by some as a contributor of the financial excesses behind the current crisis.

This recent experience is leading to a profound reassessment of the prior consensus, which goes beyond the asset price management to encompass whole area of financial stability. As a consequence the view that central banks should be assigned a stronger role in preserving financial stability is gaining considerable ground.

4.2.3   The Reassessment of the Role of Central Banks in Providing Financial Stability after the Crisis

From today´s perspective it is clear that the long period of stable, non-inflationary growth experienced by the global economy during the so-called Great Moderation made us forget that the vulnerabilities that lead to macroeconomic instability are conceived precisely in good times, characterized by excessive optimism. The so-called Great Recession, from which the advanced economies are recovering, has been a powerful reminder of the enormous welfare costs that financial instability inflicts on societies and illustrates the difficulties of monetary policy to counter episodes of severe financial turmoil. With the benefit of hindsight, we can conclude that these elements at the root of the previous consensus were not well calibrated. The rethinking of monetary policy is spreading to other dimensions as well and will impact the evolving position of central banks.

First, the events since August 2007 show that the structural changes through which the financial system has gone in recent decades bring new challenges for economic policies. Those changes underline the importance of proper regulation and supervision as the first and main lines of defense against financial instability. But they also highlight the strengthened link between financial stability and macroeconomic policies, bringing back to the fore the potential role of monetary policy to counteract financial excesses and safeguard financial stability.[8] Regarding bubbles, recent empirical analysis suggests that we can be now confident that at least those asset price misalignments for which consequences would be the most severe can be detected sufficiently early to allow preemptive action.[9] Furthermore research is continuing on the effects that loose financing conditions could have on risk-taking and financial stability.[10]

Finally, comparisons of the recent crisis with past crises have shown that not all bubbles are alike. In the case of the dot-com bubble in the late nineties, and other past bubbles which affected areas in which central banks did not have a particular expertise , it is doubtful that monetary policy would have been the appropriate means to counter the excesses in the valuation of technology companies or, more generally, stock prices. By contrast, in the case of the bubbles that originated in the banking system, central banks are well positioned to observe and understand banking practices. Therefore, one could argue that their perspective to identify speculative excesses fueled by inadequate bank behaviour is better than any other institution´s, in particular when the central bank is also the supervisory authority.

Against this evolving backdrop, central banks have become increasingly convinced of the need for them to take a more a pro-active stance in the area of financial stability beyond their traditional roles as regulators or supervisors. However, issues are not settled at the operational level yet, as regards in particular the relative role to be played by monetary policy tools vis-à-vis macroprudential tools. As regards the former, there is growing support for preemptive adjustments in official interest rates when circumstances so warrant, to counter medium- and long-term risks arising from macrofinancial imbalances. Already, as we mentioned earlier, its monetary policy strategy gives the ECB enough flexibility to *lean against the wind* of the financial cycle in exceptional circumstances.[11] That flexibility is not unconstrained, however, since the objective of price stability remains paramount. Moreover the ECB is well aware of the communication challenges and risks of confusion that may arise in the event of conflicting objectives. Also interest rates may eventually prove to be too blunt an instrument to deal with specific risks to financial stability. In those cases monetary policy tools will, with all likelihood, need to be complemented by microprudential and macroprudential tools.

4.3 The Role of Macroprudential Policy and the Spanish Experience

4.3.1 Concept and Goals of Macroprudential Policy

The intention behind a macroprudential policy is to combat the fallacy that if each individual bank is sound, the whole banking system must be sound. The current financial crisis has shown that correlations across assets and banks' balance sheets can sharply increase and pose systemic risk. Therefore the microprudential approach to supervision needs to be complemented with a macroprudential approach.

So far no formal definition of macroprudential policy exists. However, most approaches to prudential concepts concentrate on the following basic features. A macroprudential policy should be preventive in orientation and should provide the economy with specific instruments that can be implemented in times of crisis to minimize its impact on the financial and real sector. The macroprudential policy should,in effect, help the financial system withstand shocks and continue functioning in a stable way without depending on an emergency form of public aid.

Conceptually, there are two main objectives to be considered: on the one hand, effort should be made to reinforce the resilience of the financial system and, on the other, means should be established for moderating the financial cycle, commonly referred to as an objective intended to lean against the financial cycle.

By the first objective, the financial system's resilience would be strengthened by endowing it with adequate levels of loss absorbency capacity rather than handling the buildup of risks. By the second objective, attempts would focus on reducing the probability of a crisis occurrence. As these objectives are not exclusive, the question is how extensive an application would be appropriate for each.

The implementation of the macroprudential policy to achieve both objectives depends on a systemwide adaptation of microprudential instruments, and this requires adequate assessment at the systemic level. Building resilience into individual financial systems would extend the microprudential function to the entire financial system and strengthen each individual institution's loss absorbency capacity. At the whole system level correlations of shocks and risk factors would then be made from individual institutions to the total system. Moderating the financial cycle involves the application of dynamic elements in response to the creation of vulnerabilities as they are building up with the final purpose of using the loss absorbency buffers created during the upswing as the risk of contraction starts to materialize.

Countercyclical elements such as dynamic provisions are the type of tools more orientated toward this macroprudential objective.[12] Dynamic provisions reinforce the resilience of banks and help limit the buildup of risks. They help mitigate part of the pro-cyclicality of the banking system supporting the aim of moderating the credit cycle. They enable earlier detection and coverage of potential credit losses in banks' loan portfolios building up a buffer in lending booms to be used during recessions.

4.3.2   The Spanish Dynamic Provision: Motivation and Functioning

Worldwide, the experience of bank supervisors reveals that bank lending mistakes are more prevalent during upturns. Borrowers and lenders become overconfident about investment projects, and overoptimistic banks lower their lending standards. During recessions banks suddenly turn very conservative and tighten their lending standards, prompting credit crunches.

Financial markets have their own imperfections, as the current financial crisis has reminded us.[13] From time to time, significant mispricing of risk (i.e., credit risk or liquidity risk) may occur and not be quickly arbitraged away. The main theoretical arguments used to rationalize fluctuations in credit policies are based on information imperfections (disaster myopia, herd behavior, agency problems).[14] The value of collateral, which tends to be pro-cyclical, also has a role in credit cycles. For certain types of loans and borrowers, it may happen that in boom periods collateral requirements are relaxed while the opposite takes place during recessions. Furthermore too much competition among financial intermediaries can worsen financial stability.[15] There is robust empirical evidence of looser credit standards during expansions. For instance, Jiménez and Saurina (2006) show that there is a direct, although lagged, relationship between credit growth and credit risk, so that a rapid increase in loan portfolios is positively associated with an increase in nonperforming loan ratios later on. Moreover loans granted during boom periods have a higher default rate than those granted during periods of moderate credit growth. Finally, a sustained period of low interest rates and volatility—such as the one previous to the 2008 crisis—in a context of low inflation pressures tends to stimulate risk-taking by banks (looking for yield).[16]

Overall, the risk in bank portfolios builds up during the expansion periods. In recessions, the ex ante credit risk increase materializes in ex post credit losses, so that banking supervisors' concerns are well rooted on theoretical, empirical, and prudential grounds. For prudential reasons it is important that banks recognize the increase in credit risk/credit losses in their loan portfolios as the risk builds. In doing so, bank managers and shareholders will be kept apprised of the financial state of the bank and have more incentive to control the risks. Loan loss provisions, an accounting item to cover credit losses, is the natural tool to be used in this case. A proper recognition of credit risk and credit losses along the lending cycle will enhance the soundness of each bank as well as that of the banking system as a whole, thus help curb pro-cyclicality in lending. There is nothing more pro-cyclical than an improperly managed bank (Caruana 2005). Therefore loan loss provisions that account for the increase in credit risk in the upturn can help, by increasing the resilience of banks, cope with the damage that lending cycles can potentially inflict on the real economy, its growth potential, and the level of employment and welfare of any society.

Spain has had such a system of loan loss provisions for over a decade, referred to as a "general provision" (provisión genérica)—although it is sometimes considered to be dynamic, statistical, or countercyclical[17]—and it has drawn global attention from regulators and supervisors as an exemplary macroprudential tool to advance financial stability.

The current provisioning framework in Spain is based on the concept of collective assessment for impairment. This concept refers to losses that are incurred in credit portfolios, but have not yet been identified in specific loans but where statistical experience shows that a certain proportion will materialize in the future. In other words, the provisioning framework recognizes that credit risk may be incurred during expansions when loan portfolios are mainly being built, and that the loan losses may be already lurking on the balance sheets of banks, although they have not yet been identified in a specific loan.

Moreover regulation requires institutions to develop internal methodologies to estimate impairments in the loan portfolio (whether specific transactions or collective assessment). For banks which do not have their own model, the Banco de España provides a model based on loss data information for homogenous groups of loans, so that it can be used for collective assessment. This historical credit loss information is obtained from its Credit Register (CIR), a comprehensive database that covers information on any loan granted in Spain by any bank operating in Spain above 6,000 euros.[18] The Banco de España model applies to cover incurred losses only for credit activity in Spain.

Dynamic provisions were introduced in Spain in 2000. In 2005 to comply with IFRS, the provisioning system was slightly changed with respect to the original one.

The basic formula describing how the flow of general provision is currently computed is as follows:

$$\text{General provision} = \alpha \Delta C_t + (\beta C_t - \text{Specific provision}_t),$$

where C_t is the stock of loans at the end of period t and $\emptyset C_t$ its variation from end of period $t - 1$ to the end of period t (positive in a lending expansion, negative in a credit crunch). α and β are previously defined parameters set by the Banco de España. This is a simplification of the full formula—described in the box on the next page—that discriminates among six credit risk groups, each with different parameters.[19]

The formula is based on four components. The first is called component alpha, and it is obtained as the product of a certain parameter times the change in the amount of the loans granted: $\alpha \emptyset C$. This component alpha reflects the inherent losses of the transactions granted in the period. The parameter α is the average estimate of the credit loss in a period (the collective assessment for the impairment in a year that is neutral from the cyclical perspective).

However, as incurred losses not yet identified materialize at a different rate, depending on the business cycle, α has to be supplemented by another parameter, β, giving rise to the second component of the provision. This second component, beta, is the product of the parameter β, times the total amount of outstanding loans in the period, C. β reflects the average specific provision[20] over a business cycle, so that its comparison with the current specific provision is indicative of the economy's current position in the economic cycle.

The third component consists of the combination of the specific net provisions made in the period, that is, the provisions that account for actual detected impairments of assets in order to correct their value in a certain period. The interconnection of this and beta components allows to take into account the effect of the business cycle on inherent losses,

Computing the Dynamic Provision

The formula above is a simplification. Banco de España, based on historical information of credit losses, identifies six risk buckets, or homogeneous groups of risk, to take into account the nature and risk of different types of credit products (distinct segments of types of loans), each of them with a different α and β parameter. The groups (in ascending order of risk) are as follows:

1. Negligible risk: includes cash and public-sector exposures (both loans and securities) as well as interbank exposures.
2. Low risk: made up of mortgages with a loan-to-value (LTV) ratio below 80 percent and exposures to corporations with an A or higher rating.
3. Medium-low risk: composed of mortgages with an LTV ratio above 80 percent and other collateralized loans not previously mentioned.
4. Medium risk: made up of other loans, including unrated or below-A rated.

The values for α are (moving from lower to higher risk levels) 0, 0.6, 1.5, 1.8, 2, and 2.5 percent, and those for β are 0, 0.11, 0.44, 0.65, 1.1, and 1.64 percent. The final formula to be applied by each bank is therefore

$$dot.gen_t = \sum_{i=1}^{6} \alpha_i \Delta C_{it} + \sum_{i=1}^{6} \left(\beta_i - \frac{dot.espe_{it}}{C_{it}} \right) C_{it}$$

$$= \sum_{i=1}^{6} \alpha_i \Delta C_{it} + \left(\sum_{i=1}^{6} \beta_i C_{it} - dot.espe_t \right),$$

where *dot.gen* is the general provision and *dot.espe* is the specific provision.

The parameters above imply, for instance, that for a traditional mortgage with LTV above 80 percent a bank has to set aside 0.71 percent (0.6 percent alpha plus 0.11 percent beta) of its amount as a general provision. Assuming a 15 percent of loss, given default, the commented amount would be sufficient to cover for a nonperforming loan ratio of close to 4.75 percent, which is comparable to the 3.85 percent ratio for mortgages at the peak of the last recession in 1993.

and therefore these last two components form the basis of the macro-prudential dimension of the provision.

To obtain an idea of how the provisioning system works, note that during expansion periods, nonperforming loans and specific provisions are very low; thus the difference between the beta and the third component, the term in brackets in the expression above, is positive. That amount is charged against the profit and loss account, increasing the general loan loss provision fund and therefore accumulating provisions. During recession, nonperforming loans surge and so do specific provisions; in this case the difference between the second and third components becomes negative. Additionally, if credit declines, the first component, alpha, becomes negative. The overall negative amount is drawn down from the general fund, provided that the fund has a positive balance, and credited in the profit and loss account (i.e., a reversal of impairment or back to the P&L).

The three components cited above are used to calculate the theoretical general provision. The resulting number is not necessarily the final provision to be made, since there is a limit to the general provision (the fourth component of the provisioning system), fixed at 125 percent of the product of parameter α and the total volume of credit exposures. The objective of this cap is to avoid excess provisioning.[21]

It is worth noting that the rules-based system of loan loss provisions presently in place enhances transparency and comparability across banks. Loan loss provisions are fully transparent. Banks must publish the amount of their general provisions so that investors and analysts can isolate the impact of dynamic provisions. Banks are required to disclose the amount of the dynamic provision, apart from the specific provision. Thus users of accounting statements can "undo" its impact on the P&L statement. The ultimate aim, from an accounting point of view, is that financial statements properly inform users about the true financial situation of the bank, namely that they recognize the credit risk/losses when they appear, in order to avoid biases in profits, dividends, and bonuses as well as to deliver the proper incentives to bank managers and investors.

Finally, regarding the tax treatment, general provisions are tax-deductible expenses up to 1 percent of the increase in gross loans, as long as they are not mortgages. Nondeductible amounts (i.e., those above that threshold) are accounted for as deferred tax assets because they will become specific provisions in the future, and therefore deductible, when the impairment is assigned to an individual loan. Tax deductibility made dynamic provisions more popular among banks. Nevertheless, the Spanish experience shows that they can still be implemented even if they are not fully tax deductible.

4.3.3 Facts and Results

Using data from July 2000 to December 2010, we show the mechanism and functioning of dynamic provisions, in particular the buildup of the countercyclical provision and its use in the downturn. It is important to clarify that the data and figures provided are based on individual bank data, as opposed to consolidated figures. It should also be noted that in principle, dynamic provisions mostly apply to domestic exposures. Furthermore, when referring to provisions as such, we mean the flow of provisions, otherwise mention will be made of the consideration of provision funds (the stock of provisions). Finally, the data scope refers to the group of Spanish deposit institutions (commercial banks, savings banks and credit cooperatives).

Figure 4.1 shows the economic expansion and the high credit growth rates—over 25 percent year-over-year rates at some point—that took place in the early years of this century and that allowed banks to have low levels of nonperforming loans and, at the same time, to experience a declining path in the level of the ratio of specific loan loss provisions to total loans. However, by the second half of 2007, economic growth and lending started a significant slowdown, with a sharp rise in the nonperforming loan (NPL) ratio since 2008, as the Spanish economy headed for

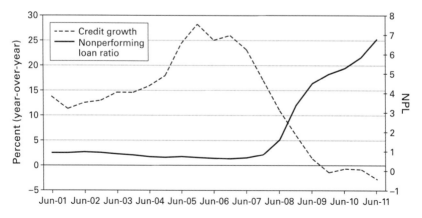

Figure 4.1
Credit growth and nonperforming loan ratio
Source: Banco de España

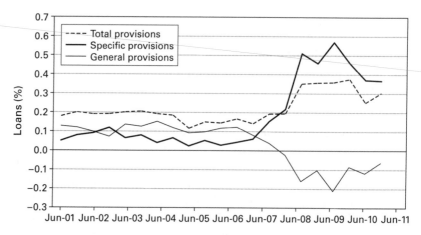

Figure 4.2
Loan loss provisions (flow) as a percentage of total loans
Source: Banco de España

its deepest recession in more than 60 years. By mid-2011 credit growth had become negative and the NPLs ratio was above 7 percent.

Figure 4.2 presents provisions in relative terms (i.e., as the percentage of total credit to the private sector). Specific provisions (over total loans granted) represented a very small share of credit exposures (around 0.05 percent) during the expansion years, while the dynamic or general provisions were more than twice that figure during the same period. However, in 2008, due to the change in general economic conditions, a deep and rather sharp change took place in the lending cycle and specific provisions increased very rapidly while statistical provisions moved into negative territory, with the final result of a much less pronounced increase in total provisions.

More precisely figure 4.2 illustrates the countercyclical nature of dynamic provisions. If Spain had had only specific provisions, in around two years these would have jumped from around 0.05 percent of total credit to more than 0.5 percent (a tenfold increase). However, total provisions have evolved from a minimum of around 0.15 percent of total loans to up to 0.4 percent. Loan loss provisions therefore have an impact on the profit and loss account of banks, but a much smaller one thanks to the countercyclical mechanism which contributes to the resilience of the whole banking sector. This corresponds to the graphical description of how the macroprudential dimension of dynamic provisions operates.

The loan loss provision fund (stock) has evolved accordingly (figure 4.3). The countercyclical nature of dynamic provisions can also be seen

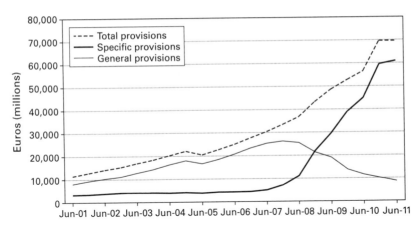

Figure 4.3
Breakdown of provision funds (stock) into specific and general
Source: Banco de España

in the changes in the stock of the general fund, which starts to be depleted as the effects of the crisis gained momentum. The buffer of provisions accumulated in the expansion phase was used in the downturn; therefore it starts to be depleted since 2008. It was not the idea of the regulator to build up a permanent buffer of provisions. Subsequently the general fund built up in the upturn can be depleted as specific provisions keep growing as a result of the increase in nonperforming loans.

It is also interesting to analyze the stock of provisions in relative terms. The specific provision fund relative to the overall amount of nonperforming loans is around 50 percent for almost the whole period under study, while the most relevant changes are for the general fund, as expected. During the upturn, the coverage of doubtful loans with general loan loss provisions reached a maximum of around 250 percent, which reflects the very low level of problematic loans in good times as well as the fact that the latent credit risk in banks' balance sheets had not yet materialized in individual loans. As those losses materialized, the coverage of the general provision fund relative to nonperforming loans started, as expected, to decline sharply because the former increased significantly forcing the latter to start to be depleted. Following the same path, the stock of total provisions has also declined. Although much smaller than in previous years, the total provision fund currently offers an acceptable level of coverage taking into account the average loss given default expected for the aggregated Spanish bank portfolios.

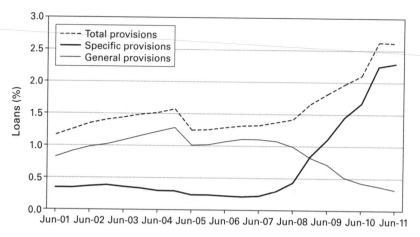

Figure 4.4
Provision funds (stock) over total loans
Source: Banco de España

In terms of total loans, figure 4.4 shows that a countercyclical loan loss provisioning system smoothes the total loan loss provision coverage. As it can be seen, the specific provision fund relative to total loans has increased more than sixfold over the last three years whereas the total loan loss provision fund in relation to total loans has only increased by 50 percent as a result of the application of the general provisions set up for this purpose. Again, this shows the macroprudential aspect of dynamic provisions.

If we focus on those exposures subject to positive general or dynamic provisioning requirements (i.e., excluding exposures to the public sector as well as interbank exposures) the ratio of general provisions to total loans was 1.1 percent and relative to credit subject to positive dynamic provisioning requirements was 1.44 percent at the end of 2007 at a consolidated level.[22]

At the end of 2007, before dynamic provisions started to being depleted, the stock of total loan provisions was 1.33 percent of total consolidated assets (excluding branches from EU countries, not subject to dynamic provisions). This number compares with a ratio of 5.78 percent between bank capital and those total assets. Therefore the total loan loss provision buffer meant an additional 27.1 percent of core capital or 26.6 percent addition to the tier 1 figure. It should be taken into account that Spanish banks did not have conduits or SIVs; thus the amount of off-balance sheet assets was much more limited than in other banking systems,

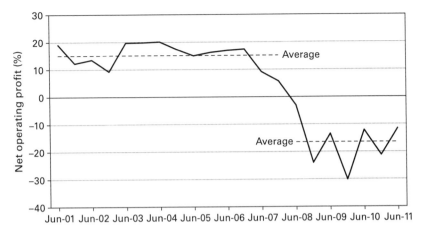

Figure 4.5
General loan loss provisions (flow) over net operating income
Source: Banco de España

which reinforces the importance of the buffer coming from loan loss provisions.

Arguably, the relevant benchmark to assess the impact of Spanish dynamic provisions is not consolidated data but rather individual data centered on the Spanish lending market. The ratio of general provisions to total credit subject to the general provision at the end of 2007 for individual balance sheets was 1.22 percent. If we exclude those exposures with a 0 percent weighting, the coverage ratio climbs to 1.59 percent. For nonconsolidated data in Spain, the general provisions were 78.9 percent of total provisions at the end of 2007.

Another interesting issue about dynamic provisions is their impact on the profit and loss account. Figure 4.5 shows that the impact of the flow of general provisions on net operating income is material, accounting in average terms for around 15 percent of it during the period before the general provision fund started to be used. This explains why banks are usually not much in favor of them in an expansionary phase. It can also be seen that when dynamic provisions are used (i.e., when the general fund is being drawn down), the impact on net operating income is also very significant, helping banks to protect their capital during recessions.

4.3.4 Assessment

The analysis of dynamic provisions in Spain has shown that they can help to deal with part of the pro-cyclicality inherent in the banking system.

By allowing earlier detection and coverage of credit losses in loan port-folios, they enable banks to build up a buffer in good times that can be used in bad times. Loan loss provisions, in particular those that are made earlier in the cycle increasing the resilience of each individual bank and that of the whole system. Thus, based on the experience gained, a coun-tercyclical loan loss provision should be part of the tool kit for macro-prudential oriented supervision.

However, countercyclical loan loss provisions are not the perfect silver bullet for dealing with a classical lending cycle. Counterfactuals are not possible in economics, thus we do not know what credit growth in Spain would have been without the dynamic provisions. It is clear from figure 4.1 that credit growth was strong in Spain during the period when dynamic provisions were being built up by banks. It could be argued that the parameters of the Spanish system were too low, but considering coverage ratios, the fact that they were calibrated using data from the early 1990s recession, and given the impact of general provisions on net operating income (around 15 percent), it is difficult, even ex post, to argue for requiring more stringent parameters.

Moreover, while for the Spanish financial institutions there is no doubt that the provisioning buffer has helped them withstand the shock and deal with the crisis from a much better starting point, there is no guar-antee that, on their own, they will suffice to cope with all the credit losses of the downturn. Clearly, for some institutions the answer is no, and they will need to make additional provisions further impacting their profit and loss accounts or, at an extreme, denting their capital buffers.

4.4   Conclusions: The Spanish Experience in the New European and International Context

The case for macroprudential policies—institutions, surveillance, and tools—is well established in the aftermath of the financial crisis. The policy frame and tool kit of macroprudential policy is not completely settled yet, and how it interacts with other policies, in particular mone-tary policy, is not neatly established either. Central banks are key players in this process, given their privileged position in the surveillance of the banking and financial system and as the monetary policy makers.

In this chapter we have reviewed the Spanish dynamic provision expe-rience, in order to contribute to the debate in two different spheres: its value as an instrument in the macroprudential policy tool kit and its interaction of this type of tool with the overall economic policy framework. This interaction is determined in the euro area context by the supranational nature of the monetary policy and the macroprudential institutional framework.

As a macroprudential tool, dynamic provisions have proved useful in Spain during the current financial crisis in the two dimensions that have been identified for macroprudential tools: mitigating the buildup of risks—albeit to a limited extent—and, above all, providing substantial loss absorbency capacity to the institutions of the system. In this regard they could be an important prudential tool for other banking systems.

But dynamic provisioning is not the macroprudential panacea, since the lending cycle is too complicated to be dealt with using only loan loss provision policies. Indeed the Spanish experience shows that even well targeted and calibrated instruments cannot cope perfectly with the narrow objective for which they are designed, among other things because the required size to fully achieve its goals would have inhibited and distorted financial and banking activity. Thus the management of the lending cycle, and more in general the reinforcement of financial stability, should be consistently complemented with other instruments, either within the macroprudential sphere—tighter control over lending standards and concentration of risks, countercyclical capital buffers or provisions, for instance, with microprudential policies and in the broader context of macroeconomic management, including monetary policies.

Regarding the general framework of macroprudential policies, it follows that a thorough assessment of the design, intensity, scope, and use of the macroprudential tools and their compounded impact is required. In this sense, the settlement of new macroprudential institutions to assess macrofinancial vulnerabilities should also devote efforts to assess these issues.

In addition in the European Union, and in particular in the euro area, there is a clear differentiation between assessment and implementation. The European Systemic Risk Board (ESRB), the new institution to assess systemic and macroprudential risks is supranational. The ESRB—whose secretariat is located within the ECB and is chaired by the ECB president—has just started to function, and it will issue warnings and recommendations. National authorities will remain in charge of macroprudential policies,[23] even when they heed the recommendations of the ESRB, which is consistent with their regulatory and supervisory expertise in their domestic markets.

Regarding the link of macroprudential tools with other economic policies, a first guideline is that they should be consistent. In particular, the role of monetary policy to support financial stability, complementing macro- and microprudential policies, has been strengthened after the crisis, as discussed above. However, it faces limits, not only due to the paramount objective of achieving price stability but also to the potency of the available instruments (interest rates) to deal with specific financial stability imbalances—be it credit booms or price assets.

Moreover, in the context of EMU, the use of monetary policy instruments to deal with financial stability issues would meet with additional difficulties, since interest rates are set on the basis of regional considerations while experience shows that credit and asset price developments in member countries can differ considerably.

The setting of monetary policy at the euro area level and macroprudencial policy at the domestic level suggests that countries can adapt their macroprudential regulations to their specific circumstances. Indeed dynamic provisions were introduced in Spain in 2000, just after the Single Monetary Policy started to operate, although other considerations related to the domestic banking sector were at play in their inception. It could hence be argued that macroprudential instruments can be used to modulate the effects that the one-size-fits-all monetary policy has on domestic credit and asset prices developments.

While recognizing that macroprudential tools can adapt common financial conditions to domestic situations, some challenges arise, so a thorough assessment of the risks and externalities of macroprudential policies should be made. First, there is a risk of overburdening macroprudential policy with additional goals that might displace their central role. Second, it is important that the expected extension and higher intensity of their use does not translate into barriers to financial integration in Europe. Risks to financial integration arise because domestic-oriented macroprudential policies are likely to be more effective in sectors where financial integration is not complete (e.g., banking). It is hence important to ensure that attempts to maximize the effectiveness of domestic policies are without prejudice to European financial integration.

All in all, the proved usefulness of Spanish provisions and the acknowledgment of their limitations is a key consideration for macroprudential policy in the euro area and also at the global level in this new phase of financial regulation where macroprudential tools may be quintessential to improve the resilience of the financial system.

Notes

The views expressed in this chapter are those of the authors and not necessarily those of the Banco de España. This chapter was prepared for the Conference "Lessons from the World Financial Crisis" at the Central Bank of Israel, March 31 to April 1, 2011. The assistance of Silvia Gutiérrez and comments at the conference, the internal seminar at Banco de España, and the SEACEN-CEMLA seminar in Kuala Lumpur are gratefully acknowledged. A previous version of this chapter appeared in the Banco de España Occasional Papers series (Documentos Ocasionales 1102).

1. See, for instance, Schwartz (1988).

2. See, for instance, Bordo et al. (2000) or the experience of the previous decades in Latin America. There are several channels by which this can occur. First, high and volatile inflation conceals expected returns, contributing to the information asymmetry between lenders and borrowers. Second, cyclical expansions that are accompanied by high inflation are often the breeding ground of overinvestment and asset prices bubbles. And third, excess credit and excess liquidity are frequently at the very core of financial instability.

3. Rising asset prices do not always point to inflationary pressures. There are a number of disturbances such as productivity shocks and certain structural reforms that may increase asset prices while reducing, in parallel, inflationary pressures, at least at short- to medium-term horizons.

4. See Borio and Lowe (2002), Cechetti et al. (2000), or Walsh (2010).

5. See, for instance, Bernanke and Gertler (1999).

6. *New York Times*, June 15, 2008 Economic View: "Two bubbles, two paths."

7. See Blinder and Reis (2005).

8. See, for instance, Blanchard et al. (2010).

9. See, for instance, Borio and Drehmann (2009) or Alessi and Detken (2009).

10. For instance, recent research shows that not only the current level of interest rates explains loan defaults but also the (low) level of interest rates when the loan was granted is also important (Jiménez et al. 2008).

11. Such possibility was clearly admitted well before the crisis erupted; see, for instance, Trichet (2005).

12. Additional examples of countercyclical elements can be found in Repullo et al. (2010).

13. See the Turner Review (FSA 2009) for a detailed catalog of recent imperfections.

14. Jiménez and Saurina (2006) contains a more detailed discussion of the literature. Rajan (1994) analyses the impact of market imperfections on the fluctuations of the lending cycle.

15. An erosion of the franchise value of the bank, as a result of more competition, may motivate the bank to increase risk-taking and also leverage (Keeley 1990; Salas and Saurina 2003).

16. See BIS (2009) for a more extended discussion and Jiménez et al. (2008) for empirical evidence in Spain.

17. In Spain this provision was known as a "statistical provision" when it was introduced in 2000. After a 2005 revision in order to comply with the IFRS, it changed to "general provision."

18. This means that virtually any loan granted to any firm as well as any mortgage is in the CIR. For consumer loans the coverage is not full, but a significant amount of those loans should be reported. The CIR contains information, among other items, on whether or not the loan is in default and how long its status has been such.

19. More details and further explanation about Spanish dynamic provisions can be found in Saurina (2009 a, b).

20. Specific provisions are those provisions set aside in a certain period that account for actual detected impairments of assets in order to correct their value.

21. Excessive provisioning might occur in a long expansionary phase as the term in brackets in the formula would remain positive, and the alpha component positively would contribute further to the accumulation of provisions in the fund. The cap is intended to avoid a fund that keeps growing indefinitely producing unnecessarily high coverage ratios of nonperforming loans through provisions.

22. Not all consolidated assets are subject to credit risk and, therefore, do not require a loan loss provision If we focus on the assets which require general loan loss provisions, at the end of 2007 Spanish banks at a consolidated level had 1.20 percent of general provisions for total credit granted. General provisions were 73.2 percent of total loan loss provisions at that time.

23. The ESRB functions will be complemented, at the supervisory level, by the three new European supervisory authorities, which complete the new financial oversight framework at the EU level. The new ESAs will be the European Banking Authority, the European Insurance and Occupational Pensions Authority, and the European Securities and Markets Authority.

References

Alessi, Lucía, and Carsten Detken. 2009. Real-time early warning indicators for costly asset price boom/bust cycles: A role for global liquidity. Working paper 1039. EBC, Frankfurt.

Bank for International Settlements. 2009. *79th Annual Report.* Basel: BIS.

Bernanke, Ben, and Mark Gertler. 1999. Monetary policy and asset price volatility. In *New Challenges for Monetary Policy.* Federal Reserve of Kansas City.

Blanchard, Olivier, Giovanni dell'Ariccia, and Paolo Mauro. 2010. Rethinking macroeconomic policy. Staff position note 10/03. IMF, Washington, DC.

Blinder, Alan, and Ricardo Reis. 2005. Understanding the Greenspan standard. In *The Greenspan Era: Lessons for the Future.* Federal Reserve of Kansas City, 11–96.

Bordo, Michael D., Michael J. Dueker, and David C. Wheelock. 2000. Aggregate price shocks and financial instability: A historical analysis. Working paper 7652. NBER, Cambridge, MA.

Borio, Claudio, and Mathias Drehmann. 2009. Assessing the risk of banking crises—Revisited. *BIS Quarterly Review* (March): 29–46.

Borio, Claudio, and Philip Lowe. 2002. Assessing the risk of banking crises. BIS Quarterly Review (December): 43-54

Caruana, Jaime. 2005. Monetary policy, financial stability and asset prices. Occasional paper 0507. Banco de España, Madrid.

Cechetti, Stephen G., Hans Genberg, John Lipsky, and Sushil Wadhwani. 2000. Asset prices and central bank policy. In *Geneva Report on the World Economy*, vol. 2. London: Centre for Economic Policy Research (CEPR).

Financial Services Authority. 2009. The Turner Review: A regulatory response to the global banking crisis." London.

Issing, Otmar. 2003. Monetary and financial stability: Is there a trade-off? In *Monetary Stability, Financial Stability and the Business Cycle*. Basel: Bank for International Settlements, 28–29.

Jiménez, Gabriel, and Jesús Saurina. 2006. Credit cycles, credit risk, and prudential regulation. *International Journal of Central Banking* 2 (2): 65–98.

Jiménez, Gabriel, Steven Peydró Ongena, José Luis, and Jesús Saurina. 2008. Hazardous times for monetary policy: What do twenty-three million bank loans say about the effects of monetary policy on credit risk? Working paper 0833. Banco de España, Madrid.

Keeley, Michael C. 1990. Deposit insurance, risk and market power in banking. *American Economic Review* (80): 1183–1200.

Rajan, Raghuram. 1994. Why bank credit policies fluctuate: A theory and some evidence. *Quarterly Journal of Economics* 109 (2): 399–441.

Repullo, Rafael, Jesús Saurina, and Carlos Trucharte. 2010. Mitigating the pro-cyclicality of Basel II. *Economic Policy* 25 (64): 659–702.

Saurina, Jesús. 2009a. Dynamic provisioning: The experience of Spain. Crisis response, note 7. World Bank, Washington, DC.

Saurina, Jesús. 2009b. Loan loss provisions in Spain: A working macro-prudential tool. *Bank of Spain, Revista de Estabilidad Financiera* (17): 11–26.

Schwartz, Anna J. 1988. Financial stability and the federal safety net. In William S. Haraf and Rose Marie Kushneider, eds., *Restructuring Banking and Financial Services in America*. Washington, DC: American Enterprise Institute, 34–62.

Salas, Vicente, and Jesús Saurina. 2003. Deregulation, market power and risk behavior in Spanish banks. *European Economic Review* 47: 1061–75.

Trichet, Jean-Claude. 2005. Asset price bubbles and monetary policy. Speech at the *Fifth MAS Lecture*, Singapore.

Walsh, Carl E. 2010. Using monetary policy to stabilize economic activity. In *Financial Stability and Macroeconomic Policy*. Federal Reserve Bank of Kansas City, Jackson Hole 2009 Symposium, 245–96.

5 Tax Policies and Financial Stability: Lessons from the Crisis

Helene Schuberth

5.1 Introduction

In rejecting the recurring perception that "this time is different," Reinhart and Rogoff (2009) show that in a historical perspective, financial crises exhibit remarkable parallels in areas such as leverage, the development of assets, and in particular housing prices, growth patterns, and current account deficits. The majority of historical crises were preceded by financial liberalization and deregulation (Kaminsky and Reinhart 1999). And the current financial crisis is again a "no lessons learned" event, given the numerous examples of regulatory forbearance foremost vis-à-vis the growing shadow banking system with its complex securitization-based lending processes and further relaxations of regulatory standards in the period following the crises that swept through emerging markets in the late 1990s.

But each crisis is exceptional as well, with unpredictable triggering events, and each crisis evolves from quite different financial market microstructures and market interaction with other parts of the domestic and global macroeconomy. Given the exceptional characteristic of each financial crisis, it is not advisable to solely base reform on past experience, for example, by adjusting regulation in areas that had played a role as explanatory factors; in fact it is harmful. The current reform initiatives are a case in point: they address issues that have played a certain role in the current crisis—such as lack of transparency, undercapitalization of financial institutions, securitization, the role of rating agencies, a lack of coordination among regulatory authorities, and to some extent, procyclicality—but they bear the huge risk of missing explanatory factors of future crises.

A related argument for a comprehensive approach can be derived from the application of Heisenberg's uncertainty principle to the subject of regulation. This quantum physics principle states that uncertainty is a fundamental and unavoidable property in physical systems that are generally stationary and invariant because the process of measuring or observing a particular phenomenon in nature changes the trajectory of the object observed. In highly dynamic financial markets this effect seems to be even more relevant. Focusing attention on particular factors that explain the recent crisis might shift risks to other areas beyond the recognition of economists and regulators alike.

Furthermore an all-encompassing approach is substantiated by the systemic nature of the crisis, which stands in stark contrast to debates immediately after the outbreak of the financial turmoil in 2007 when the crisis was perceived as a minor accident caused by easy monetary policies and the moral indiscretions of bank managers. The concept of stability being destabilizing by itself, of financial instability being an inherent systemic feature of our economies that cannot be legislated away by adjusting some of the regulatory screws, features prominently in the work of Hyman Minsky (1975, 1982, 1992), who was probably the most astute observer of the financial system of the past century. The more recent economic research on the causes of the financial crisis increasingly acknowledges that we have to combine a variety of direct and indirect explanatory factors to form a mosaic that gives a complete picture, where the pieces constituting the mosaic are drawn from a wide range of areas, such as regulatory issues, the international macroeconomy, monetary policy, the tax system as well as issues of distribution, financial governance, and finally political economy considerations. Much controversy arises when determining the relative importance of those factors: some economists consider tax policies, for instance, to be unimportant or negligible, a view that the present chapter intends to challenge.

Reform is required not only for financial stability reasons. Benjamin Friedman (2009) reminded us that we are in dire need of a real discussion of what function our financial system is supposed to perform and how well it is doing that job. On that note, all regulatory reform should be built on a normative view of which financial system serves society best in terms of growth, efficiency, and equity.

Overall, it follows that preventing financial crises in the future requires addressing the pieces of the mosaic: first, the systemic and structural roots of crises, such as deficiencies in the regulatory framework (only one cause, albeit a predominant one), and second, several phenomena that might have reinforced some of these causal factors. One such root cause is the distortive and incoherent design of our tax systems. While taxes were not the major proximate cause of the recent financial crisis, the biases embedded in the current tax systems might have exacerbated the crisis and might have a greater impact in future crises unless tax systems are thoroughly reformed.

The chapter is structured into two parts. The first surveys the literature on incoherence and distortions of the tax codes that may serve as an independent source of excessive leverage, risk-taking, and financial instability. Those mechanisms work even in the absence of irrational exuberance or traditional leverage cycles and work under the general assumption of the efficient market hypothesis. The second part starts from the premise of systemic instability inherent in finance and discusses whether regulation should be complemented with taxes internalizing negative externalities.

First, I discuss the causes of the crisis in 2007 and the role of the tax system (section 5.2). In section 5.3, I examine the key channels through which tax policies have contributed to vulnerabilities of the financial and nonfinancial sectors, in particular to high leverage and high risk-taking. The best-known example is the favorable tax treatment of owner-occupied housing together with mortgage interest relief, factors that created a tax bias toward housing and that in some cases contributed to a rise in housing prices. However, housing bubbles were not limited to countries with large tax preferences for home ownership. Another channel through which tax distortions impact financial stability is the preferential treatment of debt over equity. Tax systems that typically favor corporate debt finance over equity finance encourage excessive leverage by corporates and financial institutions. Furthermore the different treatment of interest, dividends, and capital gains affects firms' financing choices. A well-known case in point is the incentive that international tax arbitrage opportunities provide to increase leverage and to take on more risky investment. Finally, I evaluate proposals to reduce tax distortions and inconsistencies.

In section 5.4, I discuss the rationale of various taxes that are supposed to internalize negative externalities stemming from financial sector activities to align private incentives with the social cost of activities. The corrective taxes under consideration include a systemic risk levy on large and complex financial institutions, a financial activities tax, and financial transaction taxes. Each of these taxes is meant to target quite distinct externalities. I critically evaluate the corrective potential of those taxes and discuss the relative merits of, and complementarities between, taxation and regulation. In general, if taxes are properly designed, there is a strong case for using them as a macroprudential instrument. Section 5.5 concludes.

5.2 On the Causes of the Recent Financial Crisis and the Role of the Tax System

The economic literature has identified various roots of the crisis that can be classified under one of three interconnected domains: macroeconomic aspects (Borio and White 2004; Borio and Zhu 2008; Adrian and Shin 2008, 2009, 2010), political economy considerations (Mooslechner et al. 2006, Levine 2010, Rajan 2010, Warwick Commission 2009), and regulation. Most of the research on the financial turmoil has analyzed the transformation of the world financial system in the years preceding the crisis, such as the advance of arcane financial innovations (Stein 2010), the increasing complexity of financial networks exacerbating the financial system's fragile characteristics and amplifying uncertainty (Haldane 2010), and the emergence of a shadow banking system that fueled credit extended to households and nonfinancial business sectors (Pozsar et al. 2010). The Great Moderation was accompanied by the Great Leverage (Clarida 2010).

However, the factors mentioned above were symptoms rather than causes. Being a causal factor requires independent behavioral changes — but we have few indications of this. Much rather, behavioral changes were an endogenous response to policy changes, to a large degree in the field of regulation but also in taxation. The interaction of new capital adequacy rules and tax wedges set up arbitrage opportunities for financial institutions and contributed to the rise in financial innovation and leverage (Blundell-Wignall and Atkinson 2009). The regulatory system with an exclusive focus on the traditional banking system, in particular the procyclical effect of risk-calibrated bank capital requirement rules, has not only failed to mitigate but might have been a factor in fueling the recent cycle in leverage, credit expansion and housing prices (Hellwig 2010). Furthermore the possibility of using credit default swaps (CDS), which were introduced in 1996, to reduce risk weights of bonds lowered capital requirements and increased leverage (Levine 2010). The inherent procyclicality of the capital requirement rules in place was further exacerbated by fair value accounting, the accounting principle set up by the International Accounting Standards Board (Plantin et al. 2008). The unprecedented high degree of global interconnectedness and vulnerability was, above all, furthered by the "originate and distribute" strategy that was achieved through a new wave of securitization and resecuriti-zation (Stein 2010).[1]

What has been less recognized in research[2] is that these regulatory changes interacted with tax arbitrage opportunities that reinforced each other with respect to the surge in securitization and the strong growth of CDS contracts. In particular, low-tax jurisdictions were used for special purpose vehicles (SPVs) and collateralized debt obligations (CDOs) to obtain tax benefits. The rapid growth of debt, above all mortgage debt, was further reinforced by fiscal measures to increase the affordability of home ownership, such as preferential tax treatment of housing, thereby creating increased demand despite rising housing prices.

5.3 Key Channels of Tax Policies to Leverage and Risk Taking

5.3.1 Tax-Induced Bias in Home Ownership

The Character of Tax Incoherence in Housing

Tax policies interact with the dynamics of housing finance markets in a number of ways. Deregulation and product innovations in mortgage markets that expanded borrowing opportunities and lowered borrowing costs for housing resulted in a substantial increase in the supply of mortgage loans in many countries. This phenomenon was reinforced by various features of the prevailing tax regimes that contributed to the favorable tax treatment of housing in an effort to stimulate home owner-ship (IMF 2009; Lloyd 2010; Hemmelgarn and Nicodéme 2010).

Tax preferences for homeownership are often justified on the ground that it has positive externalities, namely encouraging investment in neighborhoods. But negative externalities are not only strong with re-spect to the overall financial and macroeconomic stability consequences of rising household mortgage debts. Among the other negative externali-ties are the need to compensate the shortfall in tax revenue with other (distortionary) taxes, crowding out of more productive investments than housing, limited mobility, and unfavorable distributional consequences when fiscal subsidization is mainly reflected in higher house prices gen-erating potential capital gains for homeowners at the expense of new-comers on the market thereby preventing some financially constrained and poor households from owning homes.

Tax-preferential treatment of housing tends to increase house prices, households' leverage, as well as the share of housing in the aggregate capital stock (IMF 2009). As assets are shifted to tax-favored uses, these features can contribute to an overinvestment in real estate, thus lead to less diversification of households' investments and excessive leverage by homeowners. Another consequence of the tax-preferential treatment of housing is that the steady-state level of house prices rises compared to a situation with tax neutrality where the choice between renting and buying a domicile is not affected by tax considerations. The expectation of house prices increasing further raises the anticipated return on borrowing to acquire housing. Yet another consequence is that the high volatility of house prices can amplify shocks to the supply and demand of housing. The theoretical rationale is provided by Poterba (1991). In his model, house prices are, above all, influenced by a combination of the (short-term) price-inelastic supply of newly built houses and the preferential tax treatment of housing, where the latter—together with lower interest rates and expectations of further housing price inflation (or capital gain)—contributes to a lower price elasticity of housing demand, because the impact of price increases on demand will be (partly) offset by the tax break.

It is important to recognize that tax incentives alone are not the root of volatility in house prices, except in the event of a change in the tax regime where prices adjust to their new equilibrium. But tax incentives interact with and magnify the shocks that impinge on house prices, such as demographic change, bottlenecks in urban planning, and variations in real disposable incomes. Van den Noord (2005) tested the hypothesis of higher housing price volatility due to preferential tax treatment for eight European countries for the time span between 1970 and 2001. He finds evidence of higher housing price volatility in countries with lower housing taxes, taking into account information on tax interest deductibility, tax credits, and imputed income from housing. But it has to be noted that prior to the crisis, household debt and house prices rose in many countries, notwithstanding variations in tax incentives (Lloyd 2010). House prices were also rising in countries with tax regimes with relatively high housing taxes.

Tax deductibility for interest on mortgage loans is evident in many OECD countries and involves quite remarkable gaps between the market rate and the after-tax debt-financing cost (highest in the Netherlands, lowest in Italy).

There seems to be a positive relation between the tax wedge, measured as the gap between the market interest rate and the after-tax financing cost, with the growth in real house prices, while there is no correlation between the tax wedge and residential mortgage indebtedness.

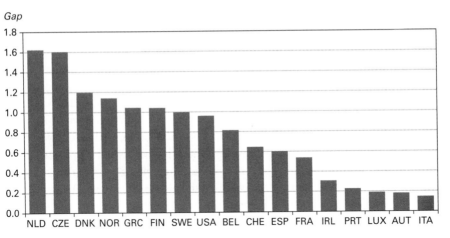

Figure 5.1
Tax relief on debt financing cost of homeownership, 2009. Note: This indicator takes into account if interest payments on mortgage debt are deductible from taxable income and if there are any limits on the allowed period of deduction or the deductible amount, and if tax credits for loans are available.
Source: OECD (2011).

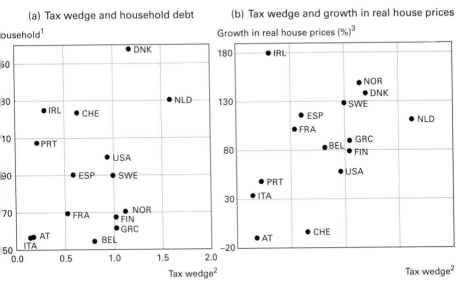

Figure 5.2
(a) Tax wedge and household debt; (b) tax wedge and growth in real house prices: (1) In percentage of GDP for 2009; (2) gap between market interest rate and after tax financing cost (the larger the gap, the greater the tax relief), (3) change in real house prices, 1995Q1 to 2007Q4
Sources: OeNB; ECB; OECD

In some countries, interest deductibility is targeted to specific house-holds, while in other countries, all households are eligible. Tax deduct-ibility tends to favor the better-off, since in most of the countries, tax relief is a tax deduction against earned income and not a tax credit. Tax deductibility seems to subsidize house purchases by higher income households, since such households take the mortgage interest deduction at a higher marginal rate; moreover they are more likely to own a prop-erty without this subsidy. Only a few countries have tax credits for owner-occupancy. The experience of the United Kingdom, which experienced a housing price bubble despite the phaseout of mortgage interest relief in 2001, suggests that other factors might also have an effect, such as regulatory limits of loan-to-value ratios (IMF 2009).

Equal treatment with other investment categories would require the imposition of a *tax on imputed rental income*. Only a few countries, such as Belgium, the Netherlands, Italy, and Luxemburg, levy taxes on imputed rents (Wolswijk 2010), but these countries often underestimate rental values (Lloyd 2010). The taxes currently levied on immovable property are not perfect substitutes for taxes on imputed rents because in most of the countries, the ratio of taxes on real estate to overall tax revenues appears to be small, barring the United Kingdom, United States, and Japan.

The bias toward housing created by tax deductibility is reinforced by the preferential treatment of *capital gains*, where the gains are often entirely or partly exempted from taxation or assessed at a lower tax rate. Owners of primary residences are often exempted, in particular if they have occupied a property for a number of years before selling it or if capital gains are only taxed beyond a high threshold. This favors owner-occupation over renting.

Policy Perspective

The current tax preference for housing embedded in most OECD coun-tries has contributed also to the buildup of financial imbalances—an unintended consequence.[4] Mitigating tax distortion may help avoid mac-roeconomic imbalances, but the timing and size of the measures are crucial to avoid disruptions in the housing markets. The social objectives behind the tax incoherencies could possibly be achieved through better-targeted policies, namely public housing or allowances for rental accom-modations. Many countries are experienced in providing public housing to enhance housing opportunities for low-income households. This may also serve the function of a shock absorber helping to contain housing

Table 5.1
Recurrent taxes on immovable property (2009)

	Percent of GDP	Percent change 1995 to 2009	Percent of total tax revenue
United Kingdom	3.6	0.6	10.3
Canada	3.1	−0.1	9.8
United States	3.1	0.2	12.7
Israel	2.4	0.1	7.7
France	2.4	0.5	5.7
Japan	2.1	0.1	13.6
New Zealand	2.0	0.3	6.4
Iceland	1.8	0.5	5.3
Ireland	1.6	0.8	5.7
Denmark	1.4	0.3	2.8
Korea	0.8	0.2	3.3
Sweden	0.8	0.0	1.7
Spain	0.8	0.1	2.5
Italy	0.6	−0.1	1.5
Chile	0.6	0.0	3.2
Finland	0.6	0.1	1.3
Slovenia	0.5	0.1	1.3
Germany	0.5	0.1	1.2
Slovak Republic	0.4	—	1.4
Belgium	0.4	0.0	0.9
Hungary	0.3	0.2	0.9
Norway	0.3	0.0	0.8
Austria	0.2	0.0	0.6
Turkey	0.2	0.2	0.8
Switzerland	0.2	0.0	0.6
Czech Republic	0.2	−0.1	0.5
Luxembourg	0.1	0.0	0.2

Source: OECD Tax Statistics.
Note: Recurrent taxes on immovable property: Cover taxes levied regularly in respect of the use or ownership of immovable property. These taxes are levied on land and building, in the form of a percentage of an assessed property value based on a national rental income, sales price, or capitalized yield; or in terms of other characteristics of real property, such as size and location, from which are derived a presumed rent or capital value. Such taxes are included whether they are levied on proprietors, tenants, or both. Unlike taxes on net wealth, debts are not taken into account in their assessment.

market shocks if rents do not instantaneously react to house price rises (Wolswijk 2010). Denmark, the Netherlands, and Austria stand out with shares of public housing amounting to more than 20 percent of the total dwelling stock (OECD 2011a).

Recommendations to correct for tax incoherencies in housing have a long tradition in public finance economics. One such recommendation is to tax imputed rents. An alternative may be to raise taxes on immovable property. If property taxes (and taxes on imputed rents) are designed such that the tax base is derived from some proxy of the market value of dwellings that are regularly adjusted to market developments, this might also serve as an automatic stabilizer. During a housing boom, tax revenues and housing prices would increase and at the same time lower demand. To prevent low-income households from being affected by housing price shocks, a progressive design of this tax is recommended (Wolswijk 2010). The reduction or phasing out of mortgage interest relief may lower the price elasticity of housing demand and reduce house price volatility.

The recommendations to correct for tax incoherencies aim at reducing housing market volatility on a structural basis. This is different from fine-tuning. The recent financial crisis has stimulated a new and controversial debate on the use of tax policies as a *macroprudential instrument,* where taxes are discretionarily varied in an anticyclical manner, in particular to correct housing market imbalances. Proponents of this approach point to advantages of taxation compared to prudential regulatory in-struments (i.e., Ahearne et al. 2008). Primarily there is the possibility of targeting specific assets, as well as the high degree of heterogeneity of housing market structures and developments across as well as within countries; this makes tax policy—together with structural policies—a reasonable instrument. Tax policy can be implemented at the national level, taking account of the respective cyclical and imbalance positions, whereas banking or financial market regulation are, in general, intended to be uniform across countries to avoid regulatory arbitrage.[5]

Loan-to-value ratios (LTVs) imposed by regulators, for example, are an important macroprudential tool because they have a direct influence on the sensitivity of the supply of credit to the assets used as collateral (Borio 2009). Lowering LTVs would reduce procyclicality but will prob-ably not be fully effective given borrowing abroad. To target a regional housing boom, tax instruments could complement regulatory devices such as LTVs. During the housing boom, a few countries used tax mea-sures to taming the boom. Korea introduced a national property tax in

2005 with progressive rates on housing and land whose values exceeded a certain threshold and then, in 2007, raised the gains tax rate applicable to owners of two houses and to owners of land held for nonbusiness use. Similarly Ireland introduced a tax of 2 percent for the market value of homes other than primary residences (IMF 2009).

Tax measures, however, have often been procyclical—take, for example, several incentives for homeowners to take out mortgages in the United States.[6] The discretionary use of taxes to smooth the housing cycle has been criticized because of the difficulty of predicting the precise impact of tax changes on housing market developments, timing issues, and unintended consequences (IMF 2009). Furthermore fine-tuning measures might be anticipated and then become a source of volatility.

5.3.2   Biases in Income Taxation

Debt Financing versus Equity Financing

Tax considerations have a decisive impact on corporate financial policies. Tax legislation classifies the broad range of financial instruments with varying features into two categories: debt and equity. Interest on debt repayments is deductible for tax purposes against corporate profits, while returns to equity finance are nondeductible. This implies that profits may be taxed both at the corporate and at the personal level when they are distributed as dividends. Debt-financed corporate earnings are generally taxed only once, and at the debtholder's rather than the corporate issuer's marginal rate. The different taxation of debt and equity generates a systemic income tax bias in favor of corporate debt financing over equity financing. The tax preference for corporate debt financing may to some extent be offset by preferential individual tax treatment of the returns to equity through reduced taxation of dividends and capital gains on shares (Lloyd 2010).

A tax preference for debt over equity yields a departure from the Modigliani–Miller irrelevance theorem, which states that investors are indifferent to the capital structure. Tax allowances for debt repayments lower the cost of debt for the firm at each level of leverage and have various implications. The level of leverage is higher than that achieved with tax neutrality, increasing the volatility of profits (interest payments have to be paid regardless of profits), the vulnerability to economic shocks, and in the end also the risk of bankruptcy as well as higher undertakings of risk (as marginally unviable projects become viable due to the ability to finance them more cheaply by exploiting the tax benefit).

Especially for financial institutions, negative externalities arise from the fact that they should take account of their own bankruptcy risk in their financing decisions (leaving aside the too-big-to-fail issue), but that they fail to take account of the macroeconomic consequences of contagion effects. Implicit government guarantees provided for large financial institutions are the source of an additional externality. If debt has a tax advantage over equity, increasing equity requirements is equivalent to a loss in tax subsidies through a reduction in leverage. Hence requiring banks to use less debt financing can raise banks' cost of capital—provided that dividends or capital gains on shares are not taxed at a lower rate than interest income at the level of personal income taxation (Admati et al. 2010).

Hybrid Financial Instruments

The debt bias has contributed to constructing hybrid instruments such as convertible bonds or preferred securities, which have become very important in corporate financing. Hybrid instruments are treated like debt obligations for tax purposes: interest payments are deductible but are treated as capital under bank regulations. In the financial sector, the debt bias jeopardizes the effectiveness of regulatory objectives, such as the resilience of financial institutions through adequate capital requirement rules. The issuance of hybrid instruments not only reduces corporate income tax revenues; it increases complexity and opacity and blurs the distinction between debt and equity (IMF 2009). Moreover hybrid instruments have encouraged less secure forms of capital.

Tax Preference for Capital Gains

In addition to the different tax treatment of debt and equity financing, the preferential treatment of capital gains creates a further bias—in this case, a bias in favor of more risky investment. One consideration is that exempting capital gains from taxation or levying a lower tax rate than on alternative sources of income, such as interest income, may distort portfolio investment decisions of households in favor of assets generating tax-exempt capital gains. This may imply a tax distortion, encouraging risk-taking above levels consistent with tax neutrality (OECD 2006).

Many tax systems favor assets that are expected to appreciate. The whole return is classified as capital gains for tax purposes. In general, capital gains of individuals are subject to lower tax rates than other forms of capital income, such as dividends or interest rates.[7] Several countries exempt capital gains from taxation or have special provisions that tax-exempt returns from home sales, pension savings, life insurance, or municipal bonds. If such returns are not exempt, they are taxed upon realization rather than accrual, which defers tax liability.[8] The realization-based capital gains tax system creates a "lock-in" effect for investors in postponing the sale of assets with appreciation as well as a "lock-out" effect in selling assets with losses. A further characteristic of capital gains taxation is that capital losses are usually only written off against other capital gains or, alternatively, against other income on a limited basis. With a full loss offset (when losses are deductible at the same effective rate applied to tax gains), governments share not only the income earned by the investor but effectively fully share the losses. Loss deductions are thus equivalent to a deduction for the cost of risk from returns (Mintz 2003).

Capital taxation that provides a symmetric tax treatment of capital gains and losses may encourage excessive risk-taking, with the government providing a risk subsidy. A full loss offset together with a preferential tax rate for capital gains may be a policy intended to encourage risk-taking in investment in certain asset classes, compared to more risk-averse types of savings (OECD 2006). With a full loss offset against capital gains, the incentive to invest in risky assets is particularly high. A full loss offset is often limited, which should somehow reduce the incentive to invest in risky assets, since it introduces a form of progressivity in taxing capital gains. However, this would only apply if investors consider possibilities of price declines (Slemrod 2009). But during episodes of a long-lasting boom, the expectation of appreciation seems to prevail.

With regard to financial institutions, capital gains and income are often treated as ordinary trading income; losses are fully deductible in this case (Mintz 2003).

Under the realization-based system a high degree of symmetry in the treatment of capital gains and losses provides tax-planning and tax-minimizing opportunities (OECD 2006). Taxpayers have considerable opportunity to defer capital gains taxes, while obtaining up-front relief for realized capital losses. Taxes may be minimized, for instance, by selling assets with appreciation gains just sufficient to fully absorb deductions taken on capital losses incurred through the sale of loss-producing assets. Furthermore, if capital losses can be offset against a wide range of income types, this may give investors an incentive to characterize certain consumption activities as business activities so that certain expenses may translate into capital losses that can in turn be deducted from income taxes or capital gains taxes.

The tax preference for capital gains affects not only the relative attractiveness of assets, resulting in an inefficient allocation of resources and tax arbitrage opportunities, but also favors the activities of private equity and hedge funds whose managers' or partners' compensation is taxed as a return on investment ("carried interest") and not as income subject to marginal income tax rates. Also hedge fund managers usually benefit from similar tax-privileged "carried interest" treatment.

Derivatives and Securitization

Tax incoherencies give rise to use of derivatives to minimize tax liabilities (Shaviro 2009). One incoherency arises from asymmetries in the treatment of counterparties, as investor types are subject to different tax rates and rules, depending on the status and the nature of their investment. A traditional nonfinancial (buy-and-hold) investor is likely to be taxed at income tax rates on interest income, while gains and losses of the principal invested are taxed at preferential capital gains rates. A financial sector investor is likely to be taxed at income tax rates without a distinction between interest and principal, and a tax-exempt investor will not be taxed. This generates opportunities for tax arbitrage, as the same risk pattern of returns is treated differently by the tax code depending on how it is packaged and structured. The differential treatment of capital gains and interest, for instance, may create an incentive to use derivatives to reduce taxes. Instead of a security that pays interest, the investor may choose to purchase a zero coupon bond and an option. If the interest is fully taxable and the options are treated as capital gains or losses taxed at preferential rates, the investor may exploit these differences to reduce income recognition.

A further incoherence lies in the inconsistent treatment of the fundamental position of a taxpayer depending on how this position is structured and which instruments are used. A taxpayer will be able to minimize tax payments by using some derivatives. Finally, an imbalance lies in the realization-based taxation of capital gains and losses, where losses can be readily realized (typically deducted against ordinary income or capital gains) while gains can, in principle, be deferred indefinitely.

Derivatives may exacerbate the consequences of incoherencies in capital income taxation (Slemrod 2009). As a response to tax distortions, any portfolio can be replicated in such a way as to tailor the nature of returns to the tax preferences of the investor, for instance by transforming interest into lightly taxed principal. However, whether the incoherencies embedded in the tax code have played a prominent role in encouraging the growth of derivatives markets is controversial.[9]

According to the tax arbitrage feedback theory (TAFT) formulated by Eddins (2009), tax incoherencies were a crucial factor in structuring the credit securitization process. Banks' traditional "originate and hold" model could not compete with the "originate and distribute" model because the latter has improved the tax efficiency of investments in securitized products. Tax arbitrage opportunities are created through the application of different tax rules (capital gains vs. ordinary income) to different types of investors (traditional buy-and-hold investors versus financial investors) on the identical loss of a credit default. Since this arbitrage is tax based rather than price based, it cannot be eliminated. While the theoretical arguments of the TAFT are appealing, the empirics remain speculative. The future challenge is to empirically test this theory.

International Tax Arbitrage and Low-Tax Jurisdictions

The exploitation of differences between national tax systems to structure a transaction, entity or arrangement in a manner that reduces tax liabilities has played a growing role in tax planning (Ring 2002; Mintz 2003). International tax arbitrage opportunities provide incentives for increased leverage and excessive risk-taking. Tax deductibility of interest on debt creates incentives for multinational corporate groups to use debt to shift net taxable income from high-tax to low-tax jurisdictions. Lending from an affiliate in a low-tax jurisdiction allows a corporate in the high-tax country to deduct interest at a high rate and pay tax at a low rate. One widely studied example that adds to the debt bias is the use of hybrid entity structures to exploit "double-deduction" (double-dip) schemes. The latter refers to arrangements that allow a taxpayer to obtain tax relief in more than one jurisdiction mostly due to different entity or income qualifications. Often hybrid entities or hybrid financial instruments are used to perform a double dip: a hybrid entity is taxable as a corporation in its country of incorporation, and chooses to be treated as a branch or partnership (rather than a subsidiary) in another country.

While one motivation for setting up complex corporate structures across the globe might be tax avoidance, these structures were also used to bypass domestic financial regulation.[10] Low-tax jurisdictions facilitate regulatory and tax arbitrage-driven complexity and opaqueness

of financial arrangements, making ultimate risk exposures less comprehensive to regulators. Low-tax jurisdictions have probably played some
role in inflating the bubble and in transmitting the financial crisis shock,
as they were hosting parts of the parallel banking system, such as conduits, structural investment vehicles, hedge funds, and other nonbank
financial institutions. The significant degree of financial interconnections
with advanced economies, in particular large financial centers, is a
concern for financial stability, as a nontrivial fraction of global capital
flows pass through entities resident in these countries en route to ultimate investment destinations (Lane and Milesi-Ferretti 2010).

Policy Perspective

The significant negative macroeconomic externalities of excessive leverage have strengthened the criticism against the preferential tax treatment
of debt. Debt neutrality with respect to the debt–equity choice is one of
the most frequent demands in discussions about corporate tax reforms.
Given the particular negative externalities associated with high leverage
of financial institutions, tax policies should be designed to make banks
internalize the social costs imposed by high leverage.

Alleviating the tax bias can be achieved either by limiting the extent
of interest deductibility or by keeping deductibility but allowing for a
deduction for a notional cost of equity finance (ACE).[11] When applied
to banks, accumulating capital would no longer be tax penalized. One of
the downsides of the ACE approach is the likely shortfall in corporate
income tax that cannot be easily compensated by an increase in the tax
rate.[12] Removing the debt bias by adjusting corporate income taxation
by means of limiting interest deductibility or, alternatively, by allowing
corporates to deduct a notional return to shareholders' equity would still
leave elements of distortions in financial investment decisions, as long
as tax neutrality does not apply to alternative forms of return on financial
investment, such as interest and dividend income.

Unless all forms of capital income are taxed at a single marginal rate,
domestically as well as internationally, there will be tax arbitrage opportunities. In this respect the preferential tax treatment of capital gains
deserves particular attention. Lower tax rates than those applicable to
other forms of capital income as well as the favorable tax treatment
stemming from the realization-based principle of taxation at the personal
level are the focal points of reform proposals. Introducing an accrual-
based taxation on capital gains, however, incurs problems of valuation,
for instance, of infrequently traded assets, as well as possible hardship

for taxpayers who do not have the means to pay for the lax liabilities unless they sell their assets (Mintz 2003).

The only tax-related subject matter the G20 addressed in its effort to overhaul the regulatory framework was the role of low-tax jurisdictions in the run-up to the crisis.[13] However, the measures taken focused on tax information exchange on request and transparency in order to avoid tax evasion and recover tax revenue lost from the nondeclaration of proceeds (OECD 2011b). The measures are not meant to have a direct impact on the existing tax arbitrage-induced incentives to leverage, where the latter are also contingent on practices in high-tax countries (Lloyd 2010).

5.4   Use of Corrective Taxes as a Tool of Financial Sector Prudential Policy

The tax incoherencies described above are a source of financial instability through tax-induced incentives for excessive leverage and risk-taking that unfold these effects even if financial markets work efficiently and the financial system properly performs its main functions—efficient intermediation, shock absorption, as well as transformation and diversification of risk—cross-sectional and across time (Allen and Gale 2000)—to name the most important. Financial sector activities generate various forms of financial system externalities that are amplified by the prevailing tax codes. Negative externalities can be internalized through regulatory measures or through taxation. Traditionally statutory regulation and financial sector supervision have been the regulatory control at the microprudential level. In the wake of the financial crisis, it was suggested to not only conceptualize the systemic outcome of financial system instabilities and inefficiencies in terms of negative externalities but also to apply the concept of a Pigouvian tax to financial sector externalities (Slemrod et al. 2010; Jeanne and Korinek 2010; Weder di Mauro 2010). The notion of financial sector externality was, in particular, analyzed with respect to internalizing externalities arising from systemic risk associated with excessive risk-taking of systemically important financial institutions. In the following, I use a broader notion of externalities and discuss financial system characteristics that give rise to externalities in three broad areas: endogenous shock propagation within the financial system, the failure of the financial sector to fulfill an efficient intermediation function, and finally, the increased tendency of the financial system to transfer risk across sectors, markets, and regions to those who are not always capable to absorb it.

5.4.1   Financial System Externalities

Shock Absorption versus Shock Propagation

Rather than absorbing shocks from outside the financial system the financial crisis has lead bear the mechanisms that make the financial system a location of a source of shocks. The view of the financial system being a source of fundamental instability leading to leverage cycles where the boom sows the seeds for the bust with severe real economic disruptions features prominently in the work of Hyman Minsky (1959, 1975, 1982, 1992), written at a time when finance was not important in macroeconomic research.[14] In contemporaneous research following the recent financial crisis, the *credit or leverage cycle* is studied as an important source of endogenous risk (Adrian and Shin 2009) taking into account rather recent institutional changes of the financial system. The leverage cycle then acts as a financial accelerator for business cycles. Endogenous risk refers to risk from shocks that are generated and amplified within the system rather than originating from outside the system (Danielsson and Shin 2003). The credit cycle is amplified by risk management and regulatory techniques, insofar as these techniques rely on market price valuation (e.g., mark-to-market valuation of assets and market-based measures of risk in internal risk models or external credit ratings that form the basis for the calculation of capital requirements; see Hellwig 2010). These valuation practices appear to have contributed to an increase in the procyclicality of leverage in the financial system.

Further the prevalence of collateralized borrowing and the resulting interaction between debt accumulation and asset prices contribute to magnifying the boom and bust cycle, since increases in borrowing and in collateral prices feed each other during booms and when the crisis hit asset prices plummet and the feedback loop works in the opposite direction (Geanakoplos 2009). Financial innovations and, in particular, securitized and re-securitized assets were a source of previously nonavailable collateral and contributed to further leveraging up the financial system. Also CDSs provided an opportunity to leverage (Geanakoplos 2009; Baily et al. 2008). Boom and bust cycles have been further reinforced by the combination of a high degree of aggregate maturity transformation[15] and traded securitized credit (Turner 2010).

Built-in procyclical mechanisms encourage excessive risk-taking in the expansionary phase of the cycle, by making it a rational response in a competitive environment. These mechanisms were particularly disruptive during periods of market strain that were exacerbated by the extensive use of fair value accounting. Mark-to-market losses eroded banks' core capital, causing balance sheet leverage to rise. Banks sold assets in an attempt to offset the rise in balance sheet leverage, but such sales only pushed credit spreads wider, causing more mark-to-market losses.

It follows that lending decisions of (rationally behaving) individual banks are collectively suboptimal. Banks fail to internalize the externalities their lending actions impose on others. Internalizing the spillovers that arise across banks over the credit cycle is an important task of macroprudential policies and lies at the heart of the reform proposal in banking regulation, including countercyclical capital buffers, restrictions on leverage, liquidity requirements, and remuneration packages that align managers' compensation to long-term performance.

In the current academic discourse models of a credit or leverage cycle that have attracted a lot of attention and have made their way into regulatory reform initiatives have overshadowed externalities arising from pure *irrational exuberance bubbles.* Mishkin (2011) distinguishes the irrational exuberance bubble from the credit boom bubble described above, where the major difference is that the former does not involve the cycle of leveraging against higher asset values, and would consequently involve less severe bank balance sheet and macroeconomic disruptions if the bubble bursts. As an example of an irrational exuberance bubble Mishkin mentions the bubble in the technology stocks in the late 1990s. The large upward swing in commodities prices in the first half of 2008 as well as their sharp rise since autumn 2010 would also match Mishkin's typology. While it is questionable whether boom–bust episodes can be attributed exactly to one of these cycle categories,[16] a conceptual distinction between the irrational exuberance and the credit boom bubble is useful because it relates asset price swings to factors other than leveraging up against collateral (this has featured prominently in the research on the credit crisis), such as exuberant expectations about economic prospects, herding behavior, fads, and in particular, myopia (Akerlof and Shiller 2009). These are psychological factors that have been identified by behavioral economists and that may also be prevalent in amplifying credit boom cycles (Shefrin 2009).

It is the influence of myopia that had led Keynes (1936) in the *General Theory* to compare the stock market to a casino. There is reason to believe that certain structural features of financial markets further encourage short-termism. Algorithmic trading (black-box trading), and in particular high-frequency trading methods that have evolved out of electronic trading systems, have markedly increased productivity and have become common in major financial markets (Dodd 2010; Cardella et al. 2010).[17] For the United States it is estimated that in the last quarter of 2010, about half of the daily equity share trading volume was related to high-speed, high frequency trading as compared to 15 percent in 2006 (Easthope 2009).[18] The focus of regulators is on avoiding price manipulation or errors in the construction of algorithms. But from the perspective of fundamental valuation efficiency (Tobin 1984), a critical evaluation of those techniques is warranted, in particular with respect to the implication of such techniques for the efficiency of the price discovery process and for the short-term volatility as well as long-term swings in asset prices. The extremely rapid pace of this trading probably may result in larger and more sudden changes in market prices in response to significant events and news (short-term volatility). Whether this may feed into long-term swings of asset prices is open to debate and cannot be excluded axiomatically. The wide use of trend-following technical analysis[19] rather than fundamental analysis may lead to over- and undershooting of equilibrium price levels because the more highly correlated behavior of the models may reinforce each other to the extreme and herewith lengthen price trends (AFM 2010). The sequence of short-term price trends may accumulate to long-term trends if a bullish or bearish sentiment prevails in the market (Schulmeister 2010).

The dominant wisdom claims that forms of high-speed trading are beneficial because they add liquidity, which is especially useful in times of financial stress.[20] However, high-frequency trade participants assume the role of "quasi-" market makers with no official liquidity-providing function; they can always decide to stop making quotes (AFM 2010). Further, as emphasized by Turner (2010), the view of liquidity always being beneficial in every market is interpreted in an axiomatic way. In general, the debate about high-frequency trading illustrates the divide between the proponents of the view of financial markets being informationally efficient or efficient in a strong sense and those who reject the validity of the efficient market hypothesis even in the weak and semi-strong form.[21] As John Maynard Keynes famously put it: "Of the maxims of orthodox finance none, surely, is more anti-social than the fetish of liquidity and the doctrine that it is a positive value on the part of institutional investors to concentrate their resources on the holding of 'liquid' securities'" (Keynes 1936: 155). Liquidity might be beneficial up to a specific optimal point, which is difficult to determine (Haberer 2004). But adding extra liquidity might be associated with decreasing marginal utility. At a specific point it may be socially harmful since abundant liquidity may reinforce the boom and bust pattern of asset price dynamics (Turner 2010). Further it may be a source of moral hazard because it generates a deceptive sense of self-confidence leading to mispricing of risk: ". . the illusion of permanent market liquidity is probably the most insidious threat to liquidity itself" (BIS 2000: 45).

Efficient Intermediation versus Waste, Opaqueness, and Interconnectedness

The financial system has performed rather *poorly in fulfilling its intermediation function*, the transfer of financial resources to the most productive investments. In the developed countries prior to the crisis, the strong credit expansion relative to GDP growth has mainly reflected residential mortgages, and it has supported leveraged purchases of already existing assets. In parallel, the rapid rise of credit was largely refinanced by short-term funding, creating refinancing risk as well as the risk of liquidity runs. Further it seems that the financial system has created its own circular flows and has extracted rents from the real sector. In a remarkable speech held about a quarter of a century ago, James Tobin (1984) warned that developed economies were "throwing more and more human and financial resource, . . . , into financial activities remote from the production of goods and services, into activities that generate high private rewards disproportionate to their social productivity" (Tobin 1984: 14). Tobin's concerns about what he has framed "functional" efficiency are much more valid today. At the peak of the boom in 2007, 40 percent of all corporate profits in the United States were accruing to the financial sector, which accounted for 7 percent of overall GDP.

When Tobin wrote about the efficiency of the financial markets and argued that the financial sector was virtually milking the productive sector, the US financial sector had a 7 percent share in overall domestic profits and accounted for 4 percent of overall GDP (Philippon 2009). High rents in the financial sector that can be the result of lower refinancing costs due to too-big-to-fail or of informational advantages when conducting opaque and complex operations, can indicate excessive risk-taking. The latter may be a consequence of limited liability, of enjoying the upside risks while shifting the downside risk onto society as a whole. A related concern was expressed by Stiglitz (1989) and reformulated by Subrahmanyam (1998) who argued that excessive rent-seeking occurs in financial markets. Scarce skilled resources are diverted to acquiring information hours or seconds before other agents, which as such represents a deadweight loss to society. In general, the growth of the financial sector has been strongly biased toward highly skilled individuals. The flow of highly skilled employees into the financial sector may be undesirable because social returns may be higher in other occupations (Philippon 2007). Concerning renumeration, there is evidence that wages are higher in the financial sector than in other sectors. Philippon and Reshef (2009) found for the United States that rents account for 30 to 50 percent of the wage differentials observed since the late 1990s.

Financial conglomerates have emerged that generate conditions for systemic importance and bailout prerogatives creating moral hazard and incentives for excessive risk-taking ("too big to fail"; Thomson 2009).

Risk Transformation versus Inefficient Redistribution of Risk

Financial intermediaries are supposed to transform risk by having a large number of borrowers, which allows them to absorb default losses because they earn interest on other loans. Further, the pooling of risks and their allocation to those most able and willing to bear them is an important aspect of functional efficiency of the financial system (Tobin 1984). Financial intermediaries have increasingly developed instruments that allow them to transfer and redistribute risk. Risk transfer across sectors and regions was highly welcomed because it was thought to spread risk away from the center of the financial system—in line with the prerogatives of functional efficiency. Securitization was viewed as a means to enhance the financial system's resilience to defaults by borrowers, but in fact it did the opposite. It enhanced systemic risk. Particularly harmful were the recent innovations in securitization (Baily et al. 2008). Financial stability was furthermore impeded by the way in which the securitization process enabled excessive intermediation through higher leverage of the financial system as a whole. Securitization was aided by CDS that grew exponentially in the years prior to the crisis.

5.4.2   Corrective Taxes

Systemic Risk Levy (SRL)

Financial institutions generate systemic risks like counterparty risk, fire sales, increases in the cost of liquidity transfers in interbank markets, or risk refinancing through wholesale funding that may lead to disruptive liquidity runs (Acharya et al. 2010). The extent of systemically relevant excessive risk-taking is exacerbated by the bailout prerogative of systemically important financial institutions (SIFIs). Since the latter enjoy the benefits of a free-of-charge implicit state guarantee—lower refinancing costs and a higher probability of being bailed out—financial institutions have an incentive to become large, interconnected, and opaque and to take on correlated risk (Thomson 2009). A bank tax levied on certain balance sheet positions (including off balance sheet positions) is meant to internalize negative externalities, to correct for the distortions stemming from the implicit state guarantee, and to help contribute to more equal burden sharing between the private and the public sector (Weder di Mauro 2010). Further the tax rate may be varied over the cycle, thus making financial institutions' activities less procyclical. A bank tax may also be implemented with the aim of improving financial intermediation through steering effects, for instance, if the tax treats macroeconomically desirable financial instruments preferentially such as by differentiating commercial real estate lending from other corporate lending.

Preferably, the size of the tax should reflect the contribution of the individual financial institution to systemic risk. Several proposals on how to proxy the respective systemic risk contribution have been made; they depend on how sources of systemic risk are identified. Perotti and Suarez (2009) suggest measuring the individual risk contribution using financial institutions' exposure to wholesale funding, in particular short-term funding, but also foreign exchange funding. A Pigouvian tax on short-term refinancing, which grew significantly in the years prior to the crisis, may be levied to internalize an externality that arises because individual financial institutions' funding decisions may well account for the banks' own refinancing risk but fail to consider systemic implications. The "liquidity charge" suggested increases in the maturity mismatch between assets and liabilities. Charge revenues are collected by an Emergency Liquidity Insurance Fund that provides emergency liquidity support, guarantees, or capital injections during a systemic crisis.

One influential strand of literature that is to some extent congruent with the liquidity charge proposal of Perotti and Suarez (2009) takes a comprehensive approach and suggests considering a broad range of criteria for systemic risk externalities. In 2009 the German Council of Economic Experts (GCEE 2009) recommended imposing a tax on SIFIs that increases with their systemic relevance. Further it was suggested that part of the proceeds from the tax would accrue to a systemic risk fund that is endowed with control rights for early intervention and resolution of SIFIs. This proposal was further refined in Weder di Mauro (2010), Doluca et al. (2010), and the IMF (2010b). If the tax base comprises all liabilities excluding deposits, which are already insured by deposit insurance funds, and capital, the tax may, in principle, unfold effects similar to those of the liquidity charge because it penalizes unsecured short-term refinancing sources. To avoid shifting risk to other types of financial institutions, the tax should apply to all SIFIs, including insurance companies and parts of the parallel banking system. Determining the size of the tax rate that increases with the size of the externality requires, first, determining the systemic relevance of a financial institution. Because of the sizable discrepancy between the theoretical concepts of systemic relevance of financial institutions and the empirical tools available to measure relevance,[22] risk score methods have been proposed that combine relevant quantitative indicators such as size, interconnectedness and complexity with qualitative assessments, namely by using a scoring system based on supervisory information to derive an overall risk score for a financial institution. Second, a range of average tax rates is set that reflect the too-big-to fail subsidy to capture the externality. Several ways of approximating corrective taxes come up with a reference value in the range of 10 to 50 basis points.

At present, ten EU countries are levying a tax on certain balance sheet items of financial institutions.[23] The approximated range of optimal tax rates of 10 to 50 basis points is significantly higher than the levies on financial institutions that are currently charged in some European Union countries; almost all of the levies charged are within a one-digit range. While to some minor extent, systemic risk considerations might have played a role, the main motivation behind the imposition of the tax was to partly recoup the direct fiscal costs of the crisis. The levy applies also to other financial institutions, such as insurance companies, in only a few countries. It follows that at present, a systemic risk levy as envisaged by its architects is not broadly used as a macroprudential instrument.

Financial Transactions Tax (FTT)

Several countries, including some major financial centers, are levying a tax on selected financial transactions, with tax revenues on average being low—with the exception of the United Kingdom and Hong Kong (IMF 2010b). Tax rates, tax bases, and tax eligibility exhibit significant differences across respective countries. The most common form of FTT is a securities tax on secondary trading in equity shares; a few countries also tax derivatives.[24] Proposals for a common design of this tax have been made, including a harmonized definition of the taxable transactions, of the taxable event and a range of tax rates, and of the geographical scope of imposition, both for a currency transaction tax (CTT) as well as for a general FTT.[25] Some of the proposals could generate quite a substantial amount of tax revenues.

While the idea of throwing some sand in the wheels of speculation originally envisaged in Keynes (1936) and in Tobin (1978) has recently attracted renewed academic support,[26] it is not overly accepted as an instrument capable of correcting negative externalities. On the contrary, an FTT is supposed to exert negative externalities on the real economy. An increase in the cost of capital, a reduction in the trading volume and a corresponding increase in volatility as well as unfavorable incidence effects are the main arguments put forward against an FTT (e.g., IMF 2010a; EC 2010). Since a credit-driven boom was at the heart of the recent crisis, an argument claims that higher transaction costs would not have significantly mitigated the boom but would rather have exacerbated the liquidity squeeze when the bubble burst. Proponents view a transaction tax, either in the form of a CTT or an FTT, as an instrument to raise the "fundamental valuation" as well as the "functional" efficiency of financial markets by crowding out market participants that behave irrationally, increase volatility, and waste social resources in a speculative zero-sum game in terms of its payoffs.[27] However, in providing deterrents to short-term holdings of financial instruments and larger rewards for fundamental long-term investors, technical or trading efficiency may decline—which is the main argument against the use of taxes that increase transaction costs. It follows that the corrective potential of an FTT fundamentally depends on the impact of higher transaction costs on short-term volatility, and even more important, on long-term swings of asset prices.

The literature on the relationship between an FTT and volatility almost exclusively examines short-term volatility. Theoretical considerations view the impact of an FTT on short-term volatility as ambiguous. An FTT will reduce trading volume depending on the size of the tax rate, the definition of the tax base and the geographical scope of the tax implementation. The size of the elasticities of trading volume with respect to the FTT rises with opportunities of migration. Migration to nontaxed financial instruments may be avoided if the tax base comprises traditional spot as well as derivative transactions, if transactions are carried out on organized exchanges, and if OTC transactions are included in the tax base. A multilateral imposition that also covers the major financial centers and low-tax jurisdictions would reduce opportunities for avoidance.

Whether the reduction in trading volume and liquidity in the markets increases volatility and herewith reduces technical efficiency (Tobin 1984), that is, the possibility to buy or sell large quantities at very low transaction costs without a significant impact on the market price, depends on the efficiency of the respective market's microstructure. If the market exhibits excess liquidity, for instance, because fundamentalists are outweighed by noise traders (Shleifer and Summers 1990) who exacerbate market price swings on account of bandwagon effects that push prices away from equilibrium, increasing transaction costs through an FTT would dampen short-term volatility and increase fundamental valuation efficiency. Subrahmanyam (1998) provides a model of price formation with asymmetrically informed traders that shows that transaction taxes can reduce short-termism in information acquisition and increase traders' incentives to acquire fundamental information, thereby enhancing long-term price discovery. When traders are allowed to have different investment horizons within agent-based financial market models Demary (2010) shows that they abstain from short-term trading in favor of longer investment horizons. This leads to less excess volatility provided the tax rate is small. With a tax rate exceeding a certain threshold value excess volatility will increase. However, in a technically inefficient market, liquidity provision might be crucial to stabilize prices and to achieve efficiency.[28] The empirical literature is equally inconclusive: most studies show either no significant effect or a positive effect of an increase in transaction costs on short-term volatility;[29] a negative impact has been found in a recent study by Liu and Zhu (2009). Some studies show that trading activities generate short-term volatility.[30]

But these studies consider only short-term volatility. Long-term swings in asset prices may generate large negative externalities in the form of severe real economic disruptions, whereas the short-term volatility more generally increases uncertainty and may reduce the level of investment and consumption (Romer 1988). However, short-term deviations of asset prices from their intrinsic value may well translate into the longer term if irrational exuberance prevails,[31] or if technical trading strategies are highly correlated, exacerbating price trends. The use of electronic trading platforms, financial innovation, and deregulation has dramatically decreased transactions costs. In parallel, financial transactions have risen sharply relative to real activity. Proponents of an FTT argue that the tax might partly offset the sharp decline in transaction costs and herewith limit implicit (excessive) leverage in derivatives markets.

Short-termism in trading activities is often blamed for wasting resources that could otherwise be invested more effectively. Subrahmanyam (1998) examines the impact of an FTT on rent-seeking behavior when traders try to obtain private information earlier than others. He finds that an FTT lowers the advantage of receiving information early, thereby freeing society's resources for probably more productive uses. But others claim that it is difficult to distinguish between desirable and undesirable short-term trading (IMF 2010a).

Financial Activities Tax (FAT)

There is some evidence of undertaxation of the financial sector, which may contribute to misallocation of funds to financial sector activities, excessive rents and risk-taking (IMF 2010b; EC 2010). While the financial sector contributed to a substantial share of all corporate income tax revenue,[32] it is common practice to exempt financial services from VAT. While the financial sector in many countries does not charge VAT on most of its services to the purchaser, it cannot deduct the VAT charged on its inputs; hence financial services are "input-taxed."[33] Sector-specific taxes such as financial transaction taxes only generate rather small amounts of revenues. To offset the usually favorable treatment of financial institutions under VAT and to correct for systemic risk stemming from excessive rents and a financial sector that has become too large, the IMF (2010a, b) proposes a financial activities tax whose tax base is profits plus compensation. In varying the tax base, quite different externalities may be addressed. If the tax base is defined as wages plus profits in cash-flow terms—that is, deducting investment while not deducting financing costs—the FAT1 (value-added FAT) resembles a VAT, being a tax on sales of goods and services less purchases of labor input (addition method for calculating VAT liability).[34] An FAT1 may offset undertaxation implied by VAT exemption and may help downsize the financial sector by making financial services more expensive.

If the economic purpose is to scale back rents accruing to owners and shareholders, the tax base of FAT2 (rent-taxing FAT) should include profits as defined above plus surplus wages, while the later are defined pragmatically as earnings exceeding those paid in the rest of the economy for similar jobs. A third option would be to tax surplus earnings as well as excess profits that are defined as excess net income in the financial sector above a benchmark return on average equity. The thresholds for defining surplus profits and wages are innately arbitrary. FAT3 (risk-taking FAT) is meant to target negative externalities stemming from excessive risk-taking.

In all three options an FAT, in effect, taxes financial institutions' net transactions (whereas an FTT taxes gross transactions). An FAT does not directly affect the market structure, nor does it discriminate between different products, though it has the potential to internalize negative externalities and generate a nonnegligible amount of tax revenue.[35] This is the main reason why the IMF favors an FAT over an FTT.

5.4.3   Complementarities or Conflicts between Regulation and Taxation?

Where might an SRL, an FTT, or an FAT have a corrective impact on the above-mentioned sources of financial sector externalities? Can these tax instruments be considered as indispensable complements to regulatory reform initiatives, such as the Basel framework, or are they substitutes that require a concise analysis of the relative merits of price and quantitative macroprudential tools? In principle, private and social costs can be aligned either through Pigouvian taxes or through controls on quantities. They are equivalent under conditions of perfect information and lack of uncertainty (IMF 2010b). Major differences arise if these preconditions are relaxed.

Following the regulatory reform initiatives, *endogenous shock propagation* within the financial system, which has been analyzed as the major source of financial system externalities, is addressed mainly through macroprudential tools applied to banks to prevent financial system cyclicality, in particular a credit boom cycle. These tools include countercyclical capital buffers, countercyclical or dynamic provisioning, and leverage ratios. Other tools that are broadly discussed in the literature are, for example, loan-to-value ratios, limits to credit growth, and loan-to-deposit ratios. These tools are meant to restrain excessive procyclical credit growth.

Three limitations regarding the scope and reach of these instruments have to be mentioned. The first limitation is that the irrational exuberance bubble is not directly addressed as one important source of externalities. An FTT might be a reasonable instrument to restrain such bubbles, provided that the remaining open research issues, in particular the implications of an FTT on technical efficiency, are resolved. The second limitation is that the inherent leverage of derivatives trade is only affected in as far as it is covered by capital requirement regulations. If leverage regulation is limited to banks, leveraged asset purchases may well migrate, which suggests that leverage limits at the security level are warranted. Leveraged trades could be discouraged either by imposing an FTT on derivatives, or, alternatively, through increased margins or through collateral requirements (Geanakoplos 2009). The third limitation is closely related to the second limitation, namely that countercyclical macroprudential instruments applied to banks may, in general, induce migration to other parts of the financial system. An SRL, for example, if varied in a countercyclical matter across the whole financial sector, would avoid migration and establish a level playing field among financial institutions covering the broad range of the financial sector.

Among the financial system externalities that are associated with *waste, opaqueness, and interconnectedness,* the regulatory reform initiatives so far have mainly addressed the externality that arises from financial institutions becoming too large, too interconnected, and too complex. One important reform proposal to internalize the related externality aimed at correcting perverse incentives is to impose capital surcharges on capital requirements for systemically important banks. Other instruments discussed are, for example, contingent capital,[36] limits on maturity mismatches,[37] or above all, splitting narrow banking (deposit taking and lending to nonfinancial corporations and households) from other banking activities, though this interferes directly with the market structure. As price-based corrective tool, an SRL can yield similar internalizing effects as the capital surcharge; however, an SRL differs from the latter in mainly three respects (Doluca et al. 2010; IMF 2010b). First, an SRL is levied on systemically relevant financial institutions of the whole financial sector, whereas capital surcharges are imposed on systemically important banks, allowing parts of the parallel financial sector to reap an implicit public subsidy. Thus the capital surcharge may induce migration of risks to less regulated parts of the financial sector. Second, the SRL imposes on the banks continuous costs whereas costs of raising additional capital to fulfill the capital surcharge requirement depend on the prevailing market conditions. Third, the capital surcharge creates an internal buffer and remains on the balance sheet of banks and somehow under the control of management and shareholders. Yet the proceeds of an SRL could partly back a systemic risk fund, while the other tranche might be transferred to the general budget. In general, forgoing the revenues of Pigouvian taxes, revenues that would then have to be raised through other taxes that cause undesirable distortions, must be weighed against any alternative.

With respect to limiting waste of resources as well as excessive rent-seeking the regulatory response so far has been soft, exceptions being restrictions on executive compensation or the proposal to limit dividend distributions as the banks' capital levels approach a minimum require-ment. Hence taxes are discussed as appropriate instruments that are complementary to quantitative control. Depending on the tax design, an FAT may correct for excessive rent-seeking and excessive risk-taking and it may result in a downsizing of the financial sector. Proponents argue that an FAT will be efficient in internalizing these kinds of externalities without interfering with the market structure, whereas it is claimed that an FTT may have similar effects but would distort the functioning of financial markets (IMF 2010b).

Macroprudential instruments to alleviate the phenomenon of *inefficient redistribution of risk* range from setting up financial market infra-structure to improving market transparency and supporting clearing and settlement arrangements for OTC derivatives and reducing counter-party and settlement risk, to ban or at least to restrict particular financial instruments, for example, to require that at least one of the parties involved in a derivatives transaction has an insurable interest. But the view prevails that as long as markets exist for particular instruments, they are considered to be welfare enhancing, provided that disclosure and transparency are sufficiently and that they are traded on organized exchanges. Distinguishing the hedging from the speculative interest is difficult in each instance. Increasing costs of transactions either through higher collateral or margin requirements or through taxes should reduce transaction volume without significantly burdening an investor with a hedging interest provided that technical or trading efficiency is not impaired.

5.5   Conclusion

While the more recent economic research on the causes of the financial crisis increasingly acknowledges that we have to combine a variety of explanatory factors drawn from a wide range of areas, taxes are still considered to be unimportant or negligible. But the tax system interacts with the financial system in important ways, directly and indirectly: together with regulatory changes, it has contributed to the buildup of financial institutions' and nonbanks' leverage, leading to a surge in finan-cial imbalances and excessive risk-taking. A more neutral tax system should contribute to financial stability.

The recent financial crisis has stimulated a debate about the use of tax tools as a macroprudential instrument, namely Pigouvian taxes, which have so far mostly been applied to environmental externalities. Negative externalities can, in principle, be internalized through regulatory measures or through taxation. But rather than being substitutes, tax instruments may complement regulation in various ways. While the most important macroprudential tools are envisaged to be applied to banks within the Basel III framework, taxes can be imposed on the whole financial sector, thereby avoiding migration of systemic risk to the less regulated parts of the financial system. In addition, from a broad and comprehensive perspective on financial system externalities, one may conclude that regulatory reform initiatives are ambitious but presumably partial, just to mention the rather soft regulatory response to externalities arising from irrational exuberance bubbles, excessive rents, or from inefficient redistribution of risk. Tax instruments may be implemented to target some of these externalities.

Notes

The views expressed are those of the author ad do not necessarily correspond with those of the Oesterreichische Nationalbank.

1. Resecuritization means that the collateral is not a pool of loans but rather a collection of tranches created out of earlier rounds of securitizations of loans.

2. Exceptions are reports issued by the IMF (2009a) and the OECD (Lloyd 2010) on how tax policies and secrecy jurisdictions boosted leverage and contributed to the buildup of complexity in the financial system. The two influential reports on the financial crisis, the Turner Review (FSA 2009) and the De Larosiere Report (De Larosiere 2009), do not mention the incoherence of the tax system as one of the causal factors for the crisis, an exemption being the role of low tax jurisdictions.

4. One of the recurrent patterns of the 18 financial crises since 1945 analyzed by Reinhart and Rogoff (2009) is the run-up of housing prices prior to the financial turmoil.

5. Exceptions are capital add ons that can be implemented as a microprudential instrument. Further, some macroprudential instruments within the Basel III framework may be varied at the national level.

6. The 1997 Taxpayer Reflief Act in the United States quadrupled the tax exemption for capital gains, giving further incentives to purchase houses—and the 2002 Single-Family Affordable Housing Tax Credit Act as well as the 2004 American Dream Downpayment Act provided further fiscal measures in favor of home ownership (Hemmelgarn and Nicodème 2010).

7. Lower tax rates for capital gains are sometimes justified on the ground that part of the appreciation gain of an asset held for a long time reflects inflation. Furthermore, because of a limited loss offset, capital gains taxes can result in higher effective tax rates, since the gains are fully taxed but the losses are only partly deductible. Thus a lower tax rate on

capital gains is meant to compensate for risk costs that would otherwise be fully shared through full loss write-offs (Mintz 2003).

8. The rationale for a realization-based capital gains tax is twofold: first, it is intended to avoid hardship for taxpayers (for those who would have to sell assets in order to pay the tax liability), and second, it avoids valuation problems in the case of infrequently traded assets (Mintz 2003).

9. Shaviro (2009), for instance, argues that at least for the United States, the incoherencies mentioned above might be less important because US tax law requires dealers in securities to use mark-to-market accounting and to treat all gains and losses as ordinary. With mark-to-market accounting by both sides, asymmetries, inconsistencies, and imbalances might become irrelevant.

10. Lane and Milesi-Ferretti (2010) point to the round-tripping phenomenon prevalent among the advanced economies, where financially sophisticated entities seek to maximize the gains from regulatory arbitrage.

11. Allowance for corporate equity.

12. For a discussion on the impact of an ACE approach on tax revenues, see Keen et al. (2010).

13. At their London summit, the G20 leaders agreed "to take action against non-cooperative jurisdictions, including tax havens. We stand ready to deploy sanctions to protect our public finances and financial systems. The era of banking secrecy is over." (G20 2009: 4).

14. While the contemporaneous economic research echoes much of Minsky's writings the major difference is the premise of fundamental instability and (Knightian) uncertainty in Minsky's cycle theory. By contrast, with the exception of behavioral finance, much of research on financial crises phenomena explains the root of financial market instabilities and externalities in terms of lack of transparency or of distorted incentives that rationally behaving financial institutions and individuals are faced with, such as adverse selection, moral hazard, asymmetric information, limited liability, implicit or explicit government guarantees, or strategic behavior such as predatory trading.

15. In particular, structured investment vehicles and conduits have funded contractually long-term securities with short-term commercial paper.

16. For example the surge in stock market prices prior to the bust in 1987 can to some extent be explained by leverage buy-out lending (Brady Commission 1988).

17. For an analysis of the impact of trading practices on asset prices, see Schulmeister (2010). The recent Triennial Central Bank Survey of Foreign Exchange and Derivatives Market Activity conducted in 2010 shows a 20 percent increase in global foreign exchange market activity over the past three years (King and Rime 2010). Eighty-five percent of the higher turnover is contributed to "other financial institutions," which include high-frequency traders, banks trading as clients of the biggest dealers, and online trading by retail investors. King and Rime mention market estimates suggesting that high-frequency trading accounts for around 25 percent of spot foreign exchange activity.

18. Regarding the scope of the market share of high-frequency trading in the European markets, there seems to be a cautious consensus for a percentage between 30 and 40 percent (AFM 2010).

19. For example, technical analysis is the most widely used trading technique in the foreign exchange market (Menkhoff and Taylor 2006).

20. A similar argument is made for derivatives trading in general. Even if we contend that a large part of derivatives trading is not based on a legitimate hedging interest but on a pure speculative motive, in this line of reasoning, derivatives trading is beneficial and delivers value added because it completes the market and allows particular contracts not previously available.

21. There are three major versions of the efficient market hypothesis (EMH): weak, semi-strong, and strong. Weak EMH claims that asset prices reflect all past publicly available information. Semi-strong EMH claims that prices reflect all publicly available information and that they immediately change to reflect new information. Strong EMH additionally alleges that prices instantly reflect the rational expectations of the future payments to which the asset gives title.

22. As noted by Weder di Mauro (2010) and Doluca et al. (2010), sophisticated new statistical methods of measuring systemic relevance (e.g., CoVAR models) as well as network models are not yet suited to incorporating all the propagation channels. Concerning the latter, the incomplete availability of data in particular on global interinstitutional exposure severely limits the use of these models to accurately determine the size of externalities. One major drawback of the statistical methods is that they rest on extensive use of market price data (i.e., CDS) that may be severely distorted and mispriced and that are hence unreliable indicators for measuring the systemic relevance of financial institutions.

23. The tax design varies with respect to the tax base, the tax rate as well as the perimeter. With a few exemptions, the tax base is defined as liabilities minus insured deposits and capital. Austria and Germany impose a reduced rate on the notional value of off balance sheet derivatives. Among the countries with a tax base as described above (liabilities minus insured deposits and capital), the tax rates range from 0.01 to 0.05 percent in Portugal, and from 0.055 to 0.085 percent in Austria. In Austria, Portugal, Hungary, and Germany, the rate varies with the size of the tax base. In the United Kingdom, the tax rate of 0.07 percent is reduced for longer maturity wholesale funding (Council of the European Union 2010).

24. Transactions in corporate and noncorporate shares are taxed, for example, in China, India, Indonesia, Italy, South Africa, South Korea, Hong Kong, Switzerland, Singapore, Taiwan, and the United Kingdom. A few countries also levy a tax on equity derivatives: Equity futures and options (tax base: premiums and strike prices) as well as the underlying shares are taxed in India. In the United Kingdom, a stamp duty is also levied on the strike price of equity options but not on premiums; it also applies to the delivery price of UK equities purchased via futures contracts. In the United States, the Securities and Exchange Commission (SEC) charges a small tax on stock market transactions. For further details, see IMF (2010b).

25. Among the more recent tax design proposals are Schulmeister et al. (2008) and the Leading Group on Innovative Financing for Development (2010). The latter examines a global CTT that would apply to traditional foreign exchange transactions—spot transactions, outright forward and foreign exchange swaps—on all major currency markets at point of global settlement. The annual tax revenue estimates range from USD 25 billion to USD 33.5 billion. Schulmeister et al. (2008) present a few scenarios on the revenue potential of an FTT. For example, with a tax rate of 1 basis point raised from trading in global spot and derivative transactions, the annual tax revenue will amount to about USD 200 billion, when exchange as well as OTC transactions are taxed. The FTT revenue estimates are based on the assumption of a decline in trading volume of spot transactions of exchange-traded stocks (5 percent) and bonds (3 percent); exchange traded derivatives are supposed to decline by between 30 and 40 percent (measured by the notional value), while the transactions traded over the counter are expected to decline by 40 percent. In September 2011

the European Commission proposed a harmonized FTT at European Union level (EC 2011).

26. Among the proponents are Paul Krugman (2009) and Joseph Stiglitz (Conway 2009).

27. Among the major contributions proposing a securities transaction tax are Stiglitz (1989) and Summers and Summers (1989). Eichengreen et al. (1995), for instance, discuss the merits of a uniform and universal CTT.

28. For a rationalization of both views within a general equilibrium framework with noise trading, see Song and Zhang (2005).

29. Only a few studies examine the effects of a change in transaction taxes; some study the impact of changes in transaction *costs*. For example, Aliber et al. (2003) show that volatility has declined with a decline in transaction costs. Endogeneity problems emerge, as noted by Werner (2003), because it is equally plausible to assume lower trading costs being the result of higher liquidity and reductions in uncertainty. However, the results of the studies examining historical episodes of changes in transaction taxes, such as the widely studied securities transaction tax in Sweden in the 1980s, cannot easily be applied when studying the effects of a multilateral, all-encompassing FTT that minimizes migration, both geographically and with respect to avoidance by substituting taxed financial instruments by nontaxed ones.

30. For an overview of the literature on transactions costs and volatility, see, for example, Schulmeister et al. (2008) and Matheson (2010).

31. In Froot et al. (1992), investors with short horizon choose to ignore some information about fundamentals but herd because they trade based on uninformative signals.

32. In the years between 2006 and 2008, the share of the financial sector in total corporate tax collection was around 18 percent in the United States, 23.5 percent in Canada, 20.9 percent in the United Kingdom, and 26.3 percent in Italy (IMF 2010b). The respective share of the financial sector in total value added was 8 percent (United States), 7.8 percent (Canada), 8.5 percent (United Kingdom), and 4.7 percent (Italy). The comparably high share in corporate income taxation is, however, not evidence of overtaxation, since it may well reflect overly high profitability (and/or rents).

33. Exemption means that final customers tend to be undertaxed while business users are overtaxed (IMF 2010b).

34. As mentioned by the IMF (2010b), several countries (Israel, Denmark, France, and Italy) have implemented some form of addition-based tax in the financial sector to offset the undertaxation implied by exemption.

35. Tax revenues differ across countries, depending on country size, profitability and wage structures. An FAT1 rate of 5 percent, for instance, is estimated to raise about 0.3 percent of GDP in the United Kingdom (IMF 2010b). The estimates of the tax revenues for FAT2 indicate a substantial reduction of the tax base. The estimates are based on the assumption that 12 percent of wage costs are excessive (this is 40 percent of the UK wage differential between the top 25 percent of employees in the financial sector and the top 25 percent in the rest of the economy). The calculations of FAT3 revenues are based on the assumption that excess profits are net income above a benchmark return on average equity of 15 percent.

36. Contingent capital is a form of hybrid capital that is, in the case of a particular stress event, turned into high-quality capital. It aims at increasing the solvency of the banking

system in periods of stress, reducing moral hazard, and it should make recapitalization of banks by taxpayers redundant.

37. A cap set on maturity mismatch aims at limiting the amount of long-term assets being funded with short-term refinancing instruments.

References

Acharya, Viral V., Lasse H. Pedersen, Thomas Philippon, and Matthew P. Richardson. 2010. Measuring systemic risk. Working paper 10-02. Federal Reserve Bank of Cleveland.

Admati, Anat R., Peter M. DeMarzo, Martin F. Hellwig, and Paul C. Pfleiderer. 2010. Fallacies 2020. Irrelevant facts, and myths in the discussion of capital regulation: Why bank equity is not expensive. Working paper 86. Rock Center for Corporate Governance at Stanford University.

Adrian, Tobias, and Hyun S. Shin. 2008. Financial intermediaries, financial stability, and monetary policy. Staff report 346. Federal Reserve Bank of New York.

Adrian, Tobias, and Hyun S. Shin. 2009. Liquidity and leverage. Staff report 328. Federal Reserve Bank of New York.

Adrian, Tobias, and Hyun S. Shin. 2010. The changing nature of financial intermediation and the financial crisis of 2007–2009. *Annual Review of Economics* 2: 603–18.

AFM (Netherlands Authority for the Financial Markets). 2010. *High Frequency Trading: The Application of Advanced Trading Technology in the European Marketplace.* Amsterdam: AFM.

Ahearne, Alan, Juan Delgado, and Jakob von Weizsäcker. 2008. A tale of two countries. Bruegel policy brief 11. Brussels.

Akerlof, George A., and Robert Shiller. 2009. *Animal Spirits, How Human Psychological Drives the Economy and Why It Matters for Global Capitalism.* Princeton: Princeton University Press.

Aliber, Robert Z., Baghwan Chowdhury, and Shu Yan. 2003. Some evidence that a Tobin tax on foreign exchange transactions may increase volatility. *European Finance Review* 7: 481–510.

Allen, Franklin, and Douglas Gale. 2000. *Comparing Financial Systems.* Cambridge: MIT Press.

Baily, Martin, Robert Litan, and Matthew Johnson. 2008. The origins of the financial crisis. Fixing finance series 3, Initiative on business and public policy at Brookings. Washington, DC.

BIS (Bank for International Settlement). 2000. Special feature: Market liquidity and stress. Selected issues and policy implications. *BIS Quarterly Review* November 2000: 38–52.

Blundell-Wignall, Adrian, and Paul Atkinson. 2009. Origins of the financial crisis and requirements for reform. *Journal of Asian Economics.* doi:10.1016/j.asieco.2009.07.009.

Borio, Claudio. 2009. Implementing the macroprudential approach to financial regulation and supervision. Financial stability review 9-09. Bank of France, Paris.

Borio, Claudio, and William White. 2004. Whither monetary policy and financial stability? The implications of evolving policy regimes. Working paper 147. BIS, Basel.

Borio, Claudio, and Haibin Zhu. 2008. Capital regulation, risk-taking and monetary policy: A missing link in the transmission mechanism. Working paper 268. BIS, Basel.

Brady Commission. 1988. Report of the Presidential Task Force on Market Mechanisms: Submitted to the President of the United States, the Secretary of the Treasury, and the Chairman of the Federal Reserve Board. US Department of the Treasury. Washington, DC.

Cardella, Laura, Jia Hao, and Ivalina Kalcheva. 2010. The floor trader vs. automation: A survey of theory and empirical evidence. Mimeo. University of Arizona.

Clarida, Richard. 2010. What has—and has not—been learned about monetary policy in a low inflation environment? A Review of the 2000s. Speech, Boston Federal Reserve Bank Conference, October 15.

Conway, E. 2009. Joseph Stiglitz calls for a Tobin tax on all financial trading transactions. *The Telegraph,* October 5. Available at: http://www.telegraph.co.uk/finance/financialcrisis/6262242/Joseph-Stiglitz-calls-for-Tobin-tax-on-all-financial-trading-transactions.html.

Council of the European Union. 2010. Report on financial levies. Brussels, June 17. Available at: http://register.consilium.europa.eu/pdf/en/11/st09/st09918.en11.pdf.

Danielsson, Jon, and Hyun S. Shin. 2003. *Endogenous Risk in Modern Risk Management: A History*. London: Risk Books.

De Larosiere, Jacques. 2009. Report of the High Level Group of Supervision in the EU. Brussels, February 25. Available at: http://ec.europa.eu/internal_market/finances/docs/de_larosiere_report_en.pdf.

Demary, Markus. 2010. Transaction taxes and traders with heterogeneous investment horizons in an agent-based financial market model. *Economics—The Open-Access, Open-Assessment e-Journal*. Kiel Institute for the World Economy 4(8): 1–44.

Dodd, Randall. 2010. Opaque trades. *Finance and Development* 47 (1): 26–28.

Doluca, Hasan, Ulrich Klueh, Marco Wagner, and Beatrice Weder di Mauro. 2010. Reducing systemic relevance: A proposal. Discussion paper 4-10. GCEE, Berlin.

Easthope, David. 2009. Demystifying and evaluating high frequency equities trading: fast forward or pause? *Celent Research Reports,* December 18. London. Available at: http://www.celent.com/reports/demystifying-and-evaluating-high-frequency-equities-trading-fast-forward-or-pause.

Eddins, Sam T. 2009. Tax arbitrage feedback theory. Available at: http://papers.ssrn.com/sol3/papers.cfm?abstract_id=1356159.

Eichengreen, Barry, James Tobin, and Charles Wyplosz. 1995. Two cases for sand in the wheels of international finance. *Economic Journal* 105: 162–72.

EC (European Commission). 2010. Innovative financing at a global level. Commission Staff Working Document SEC (2010) 409 final. Brussels.

EC (European Commission). 2011. Proposal for a Council Directive on a common system of financial transaction tax amending Directive 2008/7/EC. Brussels, 28.9.2011, COM(2011) 594 final.

Friedman, Benjamin. 2009. Overmighty finance levies a tithe on growth. *Financial Times,* August 26. Available at: http://www.ft.com/intl/cms/s/0/2de2b29a-9271-11de-b63b-00144feabdc0.html#axzz1u72igfgL.

Froot, Kenneth, David S. Scharfstein, and Jeremy S. Stein. 1992. Herd on the street: Informational inefficiencies in a market with short-term speculation. *Journal of Finance* 74 (4): 1461–84.

FSA (Financial Services Authority). 2009. The Turner Review: A regulatory response to the global banking crisis. FSA, London.

G20. 2009. Global plan for recovery and reform: The Communiqué from the London Summit. London, April 2. Available at: http://ukinsingapore.fco.gov.uk/en/news/?view=News&id=16082013.

GCEE (German Council of Economic Experts). 2009. Financial system on the drip: Challenging detoxification ahead. Jahresgutachten 2009/10. GCEE, Berlin.

Geanakoplos, John. 2009. The leverage cycle. *NBER Macroeconomics Annual* 24:1–65.

Haberer, Markus. 2004. Might a securities transactions tax mitigate excess volatility? Some evidence from the literature. Discussion paper 4–06. University of Konstanz, Baden-Württemberg.

Haldane, Andrew G. 2009. Rethinking the financial network. Speech, Financial Student Association, April 28.

Hellwig, Martin. 2010. Capital regulation after the crisis: Business as usual? Preprint 31-10. Max Planck Institute for Research on Collective Goods, Bonn.

Hemmelgarn, Thomas, and Gaetan Nicodème. 2010. The 2008 financial crisis and taxation policy. Taxation paper 20. European Commission, Brussels.

IMF (International Monetary Fund). 2009. Debt bias and other distortions: Crisis-related issues in tax policy. June 12. Memo. Fiscal Affairs Department, IMF, Washington, DC.

IMF (International Monetary Fund). 2010a. A fair and substantial contribution by the financial sector. Report to the G20. June. IMF, Washington, DC.

IMF (International Monetary Fund). 2010b. Financial sector taxation. The IMF's report to the G-20 and background material. September. IMF, Washington, DC.

Jeanne, Olivier, and Anton Korinek. 2010. Managing credit booms and busts: A Pigouvian taxation perspective. Discussion paper 8015. CEPR, Washington, DC.

Kaminsky, Graciela L., and Carmen M. Reinhart. 1999. The twin crises: The causes of banking and balance of payments problems. *American Economic Review* 89: 473–500.

Keen, Michael, Alexander Klemm, and Victoria Perry. 2010. Tax and the crisis. *Fiscal Studies* 31: 43–79.

Keynes, John M. 1936. *The General Theory of Employment, Interest, and Money*. London: Macmillan.

King, Michael R., and Dagfinn Rime. 2010. The $4 trillion question: What explains FX growth since the 2007 survey? *BIS Quarterly Review* (December): 27–42

Krugman, Paul. 2009. Taxing the speculators. *New York Times,* November 26: 39.

Lane, Philip. R., and Gian M. Milesi-Ferretti. 2010. Cross-border investment in small international financial centers. Working paper 38-10. IMF, Washington, DC.

Leading Group on Innovative Financing for Development. 2010. Globalizing solidarity: The case for financial levies. Report of the Committee of Experts to the Taskforce on International Financial Transactions and Development. Paris. Available at: http://www.leadinggroup.org/IMG/pdf_Financement_innovants_web_def.pdf.

Levine, Ross. 2010. The governance of financial regulation: Reform lessons from the recent crisis. Working paper 329. BIS, Basel.

Liu, Shinhua, and Zhen Zhu. 2009. Transaction costs and price volatility: New evidence from the Tokyo Stock Exchange. *Journal of Financial Services Research* 36 (1): 65–83.

Lloyd, Goeff. 2010. Moving beyond the crisis—Strengthening understanding of how tax policies affect the soundness of financial markets. Mimeo. Centre for Tax Policy and Administration, OECD, Paris.

Matheson, Thornton. 2010. Taxing financial transactions: Issues and evidence. Working paper 54-11. IMF, Washington, DC.

Menkhoff, Lukas, and Mark P. Taylor. 2006. The obstinate passion of foreign exchange professionals: Technical analysis. Discussion paper 352. Wirtschaftswissenschaftlichen Fakultät der Universität Hannover.

Minsky, Hyman. 1959. Monetary systems and accelerator models. *American Economic Review* 47: 859–83.

Minsky, Hyman. 1975. *John Maynard Keynes*. Columbia University Press.

Minsky, Hyman. 1982. *Can "It" Happen Again? Essays on Instability and Finance*. Armonk, NY: M.E. Sharpe.

Minsky, Hyman. 1992. The financial instability hypothesis. Working paper 74. Jerome Levy Economics Institute of Bard College, Annandale-on-Hudson, NY.

Mintz, Jack M. 2003. Taxing financial activity. International Tax Program paper 5-03. Institute for International Business, Joseph L. Rotman School of Management, University of Toronto.

Mishkin, Frederic. 2011. Monetary policy strategy: Lessons from the crisis. Working paper 16755. NBER, Cambridge, MA.

Mooslechner, Peter, Helene Schuberth, and Beat Weber. 2006. *The Political Economy of Financial Market Regulation: The Dynamics of Inclusion and Exclusion*. Cheltenham, UK: Edgar Elgar 2006.

OECD (Organisation for Economic Cooperation and Development). 2006. Taxation of capital gains of individuals: Policy considerations and approaches. Tax policy study 14. OECD, Paris.

OECD (Organisation for Economic Cooperation and Development). 2011a. Housing and the economy: Policies for renovation. Economic policy reforms 2011: Going for growth, January. OECD, Paris.

OECD (Organisation for Economic Cooperation and Development). 2011b. The global forum on transparency and exchange of information for tax purposes. Information brief, February 11. OECD, Paris.

Perotti, Enrico, and Javier Suarez. 2009. Liquidity insurance for systemic crises. Policy insight 31. CEPR, Washington, DC.

Philippon, Thomas. 2007. Financiers vs. engineers: Should the financial sector be taxed or subsidized? Working paper 13560. NBER, Cambridge, MA.

Philippon, Thomas. 2009. The evolution of the US financial industry from 1860 to 2007: Theory and evidence. Working paper. New York University.

Philippon, Thomas, and Ariell Reshef. 2009. Wages and human capital in the U.S. financial industry: 1909–2006. Working paper 14644. NBER, Cambridge, MA.

Plantin, Guillaume, Haresh Sapra, and Hyun S. Shin. 2008. Fair value accounting and financial stability. Research paper 15-08. Chicago Graduate School of Business.

Poterba, James N. 1991. House price dynamics: The role of tax policy and democracy. *Brookings Papers on Economic Activity* 2: 143–203.

Rajan, Raghuram G. 2010. *Fault Lines: How Hidden Fractures Still Threaten the World Economy*. Princeton: Princeton University Press.

Reinhart, Carmen, and Kenneth Rogoff. 2009. *This Time Is Different: Eight Centuries of Financial Folly*. Princeton: Princeton University Press.

Romer, Christina D. 1988. The Great Crash and the onset of the Great Depression. Working paper 2639. NBER, Cambridge, MA.

Ring, Diane M. 2002. One Nation Among Many: Policy Implications of Cross-Border Tax Arbitrage. *Boston College Law Review Rev* 44:79.

Schulmeister, Stephan. 2010. Boom–bust cycles and trading practices in asset markets, the real economy and the effects of a financial transactions tax. Working paper 364. WIFO, Vienna.

Schulmeister, Stephan, Margit Schratzenstaller, and Oliver Picek. 2008. A general financial transaction tax: Motives, revenues, feasibility and effects. Monograph 3-08. WIFO, Vienna.

Shaviro, Daniel. 2009. The 2008–09 financial crisis: Implications for Income Tax Reform. Law and Economics research paper 35-09. New York University.

Shefrin, Hersh M. 2009. How psychological pitfalls generated the global financial crisis. Research paper 10-04. Santa Clara University Leavey School of Business.

Shleifer, Andrei, and Lawrence H. Summers. 1990. The noise trader approach to finance. *Journal of Economic Perspectives* 4: 19–33.

Slemrod, Joel, Daniel Shaviro, and Douglas Shackelford. 2010. Taxation and the financial sector. *National Tax Journal* 63: 781–806.

Slemrod, Joel. 2009. Lessons for tax policy in the Great Recession. *National Tax Journal* 62 (3): 387–97.

Song, Frank M., and Junxi Zhang. 2005. Securities transaction tax and market volatility. *Economic Journal* 115: 1103–20.

Stein, Jeremy. 2010. Securitization, shadow banking, and financial fragility. *Daedalus* 139: 41–51.

Stiglitz, Joseph E. 1989. Using tax policy to curb speculative short-term trading. *Journal of Financial Services Research* 3: 101–15.

Subrahmanyam, Avanidhar. 1998. Transaction taxes and financial market equilibrium. *Journal of Business* 71: 81–118.

Summers, Lawrence H., and V. P. Summers. 1989. When financial markets work too well: A cautious case for a securities transactions tax. *Journal of Financial Services Research* 3: 261–86.

Thomson, James B. 2009. On systemically important financial institutions and progressive systemic mitigation. Policy discussion paper 7. Federal Reserve Bank of Cleveland.

Tobin, James. 1984. On the efficiency of the financial system. *Lloyd's Bank Review* 153: 1–15.

Tobin, James. 1978. A proposal for international monetary reform. Cowles Foundation discussion paper 506. Yale University.

Turner, Adair. 2010. What do banks do? What should they do? Why do credit booms and busts occur and what can public policy do about it? In Adair Turner, Andrew Haldane, Paul Woolley, Sushil Wadhwani, Charles Goodhart, Andrew Smithers, Andrew Large, John Kay, Martin Wolf, Peter Boone, Simon Johnson, and Richard Layard, eds., *The Future of Finance: The LSE Report*. London: London School of Economics and Political Science, 5–86.

Van den Noord, Paul. 2005. Tax incentives and house prices in the euro area: Theory and evidence. *Economie Internationale* 101: 29–45.

Warwick Commission. 2009. The Warwick Commission on International Financial Reform. In *Praise of Unlevel Playing Fields*. Coventry, UK: University of Warwick.

Weder di Mauro, Beatrice. 2010. Taxing systemic risk: Proposal for a systemic risk charge and a systemic risk fund. Mimeo. University of Mainz.

Werner, Ingrid M. 2003. Comment on "Some evidence that a Tobin tax on foreign exchange transactions may increase volatility." *European Finance Review* 7: 511–14.

Wolswijk, Guido. 2010. Fiscal aspects of housing in Europe. In Philip Arestis, Peter Moo-slechner, and Karin Wagner, eds., *Housing Market Challenges in Europe and the United States*. Basingstoke, UK: Palgrave Macmillan: 158–77.

III CAPITAL FLOWS, CAPITAL CONTROLS, AND EXCHANGE RATE POLICIES

6 Managing Capital Inflows: Old and New Debates

Jonathan D. Ostry

6.1 Introduction

The recent (sometimes acrimonious) debates over how to manage capital inflows to emerging market countries are hardly "new," but rather only the latest installment in what remains a highly unsettled issue among both professional economists and policy makers. Think back to the 1930s and 1940s when the two founding fathers of the International Monetary Fund, Lord Keynes and Harry Dexter White, were discussing these issues in crafting their vision for the IMF (and in a little known fact, White even took them up much earlier in his dissertation submitted to Harvard in 1930). And, skipping a few decades, think of the arguments in the 1960s and early 1970s over how to manage the international consequences of US monetary policy—with various capital control measures being adopted in a number of advanced economies, not unlike what we are seeing in the emerging market countries today.

One view of the historical debate in the 1940s is that Keynes was in favor of capital controls, White was against them, and the Fund's Articles of Agreement were an uneasy compromise between these two great minds. But this interpretation turns out to be incorrect. In fact both Keynes and White recognized that capital flows can bring tremendous benefits to countries (for investment and growth), but that large and sudden surges of inflows can create difficulties for recipient countries. This is why both men accepted the need for what White called "some measure of the intelligent control of the volume and direction of foreign investments."

Today's discussions need to be viewed in this context. At the IMF, following the sudden stop of late-2008, researchers began thinking anew about these issues, and in particular about what would constitute an "intelligent" use of controls, alongside other components of the policy tool kit—macro policies and macroprudential instruments. The framework that was developed should be viewed as preliminary, and very much open to debate among policy makers and the interested community more broadly. While the issues remain fraught with ideological overtones, there are also profoundly technical questions—and no one has yet worked out all the answers.

This chapter reviews some arguments on the appropriate management of inflow surges and examines, in particular, the conditions under which capital controls may be justified. A key conclusion is that if the economy is operating near potential, if the level of reserves is adequate, and if the exchange rate is not undervalued, then use of capital controls—in addition to both prudential and macroeconomic policy—is justified as part of the policy tool kit to manage the macroeconomic risks that inflow surges may bring.[1] Such controls can moreover retain potency even if investors devise strategies to bypass them, provided such strategies are more costly than the expected return from the transaction: the cost of circumvention acts as "sand in the wheels."

A key issue is, of course, whether capital controls have worked in practice.

The empirical evidence is mixed at best. Controls seem to be quite effective in countries that maintain extensive systems of restrictions on most categories of flows, but the present context relates mainly to the re-imposition of controls by countries that already have largely open capital accounts. The evidence appears to be stronger for capital controls to have an effect on the composition of inflows than on the aggregate volume (though empirical models linking aggregate inflows to controls are frequently subject to a host of objections, notably simultaneity bias).

For the current crisis, the results presented below suggest that controls aimed at achieving a less risky external liability structure paid dividends as far as reducing financial fragility. An interesting twist is that some foreign direct investment (FDI) flows may be less safe than usually thought. In particular, some items recorded as financial sector FDI may be disguising a buildup in intragroup debt in the financial sector and will thus be more akin to debt in terms of riskiness. This point resonates well with the experience of emerging Europe during the recent crisis.[2]

A significant caveat, however, to the use of capital controls by individual countries relates to the potential for adverse multilateral consequences. In the present circumstances global recovery is dependent on macroeconomic policy adjustments that could be undercut by capital controls. Widespread adoption of controls could exacerbate global imbalances and slow other needed reforms—a critical concern at present, as sustained recovery hinges on a rebalancing of global demand and the sources of growth in individual countries. In addition controls imposed by some countries may lead other countries to adopt them also: widespread adoption of controls could have a chilling impact on financial integration and globalization, with significant output and welfare losses. Multilateral dimensions clearly need to be taken into account in assessing the merits of controls at the country level.

6.2   Responding to Capital Inflows

Although capital flows to developing and emerging market countries are generally welcome—providing lower cost financing and indicating market confidence in the fundamentals of the economy—sudden surges can complicate macroeconomic management and create financial risks. On the macroeconomic front the concern is that the surge will lead to an appreciation of the exchange rate and undermine competitiveness of the tradable sector—possibly causing lasting damage even as inflows abate or reverse. The main worry from the financial fragility perspective is that large capital inflows may lead to excessive foreign borrowing and foreign currency exposure and fuel domestic credit booms (especially foreign-exchange-denominated lending) and asset bubbles (with significant adverse effects in the case of a sudden reversal). Can such concerns justify the imposition of controls on capital inflows—not only from the individual country's perspective but also taking account of multilateral considerations? The answer is yes—under certain circumstances. Although in practice, macroeconomic and financial fragility considerations are both relevant to a decision on whether to impose capital controls, it is analytically useful to think of each in turn (figure 6.1).

6.2.1   Macroeconomic Implications

How should a country respond to an inflow surge? The appropriate policy response is likely to be multifaceted, according to the circumstances facing the country.

Exchange Rate Appreciation

The first question is whether the exchange rate should be allowed to appreciate. Although countries are frequently concerned that an appreciation will damage competitiveness of the tradable sector, the

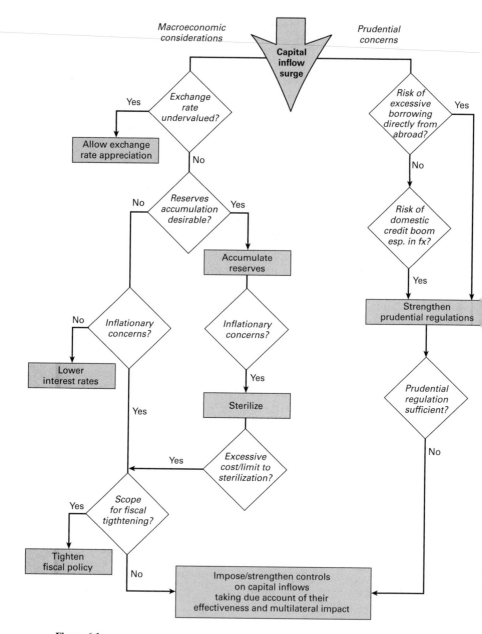

Figure 6.1
Coping with surges to capital inflows. Macroeconomic and prudential considerations from the perspective of an individual country, without taking account of multilateral considerations.

multilateral context is paramount here: if the exchange rate is undervalued from a multilateral perspective, the appropriate response would be
to allow the nominal exchange rate to appreciate passively in response
to the capital inflows. But when the exchange rate is already overvalued
(or roughly in equilibrium), and there are concerns about the impact of
an appreciation on competitiveness, a more proactive policy response is
required.

Reserve Accumulation . . .

The next question is whether the country has a relatively low level of
foreign exchange reserves (e.g., from a precautionary perspective) and
whether some further reserve accumulation would be desirable. If so, the
capital inflows may present a useful opportunity to augment the central
bank's reserve holdings.

. . . and Sterilization

If there are inflation concerns, the resulting increase in the money supply
can be sterilized through open market operations or, more generally, a
corresponding decrease in domestic credit. There are, however, limits to
sterilization.[3] Domestic financial markets may not be sufficiently deep
to absorb a significant increase in sterilization bonds, and there is a fiscal
cost associated with the differential between interest paid on domestic
bonds and interest earned on reserves (particularly in the current low-
yield environment). Moreover sterilization means that domestic interest
rates continue to be relatively high, perpetuating inflows (especially if
markets believe that because of fiscal costs, or otherwise, the policy of
reserve accumulation will eventually be abandoned and the exchange
rate will be allowed to appreciate).

   If the central bank has exhausted the sterilization possibilities and
risks losing monetary control, or if it does not want to accumulate further
reserves (and assuming that further exchange rate appreciation would
not be appropriate), it must try to reduce inflows through macroeconomic policies or more direct methods.

Monetary and Fiscal Policies

The policy response would be to lower interest rates, thus reducing incentives for inflows, and to tighten fiscal policy—particularly when capital
inflows are driven by fiscal expansion—thus reducing currency appreciation pressures.[4] However, if the economy is at risk of overheating and
there are inflation pressures, reducing interest rates is not an attractive

policy option, and both political considerations and implementation lags may limit the scope for fiscal consolidation.

Controls on Capital Inflows

In the face of substantial inflows, a purely macroeconomic policy response may not suffice in some country circumstances (as described above), and controls on capital inflows may form a useful part of the policy tool kit.[5] This is particularly true of transitory surges because the currency appreciation is likely to be temporary, whereas damage to the tradable sector (through hysteresis effects) may be more permanent. If the increase in flows is expected to be more persistent, by contrast, the economy should adjust to the (permanently) higher real exchange rate, particularly as controls lose their effectiveness over time and thus need to be continually strengthened, leading to increasing distortions.

6.2.2 Financial Fragility

Beyond their macroeconomic effects, capital inflows—especially certain types of liabilities—can make the country more vulnerable to financial crisis. An obvious example is debt versus equity flows, where the latter allows for greater risk sharing between creditor and borrower. Capital inflows might also fuel domestic lending booms, including foreign exchange denominated credit, which is especially dangerous if extended to borrowers lacking a natural hedge (e.g., households rather than exporters). More generally, it is not implausible that herd behavior and excessive optimism on the part of foreign lenders, coupled with myopic borrowers who underestimate foreign exchange and liquidity risks, can lead to foreign borrowing that is suboptimal from a financial fragility perspective. Based on these considerations, the theoretical literature yields a pecking order of capital inflows, in decreasing order of riskiness, with short-term instruments more risky than long-term ones within each category:

- foreign currency debt,
- consumer price indexed local currency debt,
- local currency debt,
- portfolio equity investment, and
- foreign direct investment.

During "normal" times prudential regulation of the domestic banking system—such as (possibly cyclical) capital requirements and limits on foreign exchange lending to unhedged borrowers—may suffice. But again, in the face of large capital inflows that may fuel credit booms, controls on inflows can buttress prudential regulations, particularly if it is possible to target the flows that lead to the greatest vulnerabilities.[6] For example, unremunerated reserve requirements on foreign exchange debt can be used to reduce external foreign exchange borrowing, and even if this encourages substitution into other forms of external debt, the risks are reduced.[7] Inflow taxes on short-term debt reduce the price differential between short- and long-term debt and induce longer maturities. The optimal size of the tax depends on the risk of liquidity panics, the size and social cost of the associated fiscal adjustment, and the elasticity of substitution between debt of different maturities. Financial transaction taxes are relatively more costly for short-term carry trades and may deter such flows. Minimum-stay requirements are a direct method of lengthening the maturity of liabilities.

6.2.3 Other Considerations

Even if an analysis along the lines sketched above points to the adoption of capital controls, several other factors need to be considered.

Effectiveness

The first and most obvious issue concerns the effectiveness of controls. This depends on whether the country has some existing controls and therefore the administrative apparatus is already in place. For countries that have a substantially closed capital account, strengthening controls will be easier (but there may be less need for such countries to further impede capital inflows). More relevant for present purposes is the case of countries with substantially open capital accounts. These countries will need to design and implement new controls and likely strengthen them over time in the face of circumvention, without creating excessive distortions. The importance of this factor is often underestimated.

Controls on Outflows

Second, though the discussion here is confined to controls on inflows, relaxing controls on outflows could also have an impact on aggregate net inflows, and hence on the exchange rate and other macroeconomic variables. But the direction of that impact is unclear. On the one hand, liberalizing capital outflows can reduce net inflows as some of the inflows are offset by outflows. On the other hand, greater assurance that capital can be repatriated may make the country an even more attractive destination for foreign investors.

Multilateral Considerations

As emphasized above, any decision to impose capital controls needs to take account of their multilateral repercussions.[8] At a most basic level the greatest concern is that widespread use of capital controls by EMEs could have deleterious effects on the efficient allocation of investment across countries, reducing gains from intertemporal (asset) trade much as tariffs limit the gains from goods (within-period) trade.

Widespread use of controls, especially by systemically important countries, could also impede necessary steps to address global imbalances. It might allow countries to avoid appreciation where currencies are undervalued and where appreciation is needed to support global demand rebalancing. Clearly, to the degree that currencies in some countries are undervalued relative to some notion of medium-term equilibrium (Lee et al. 2008), the first-best policy would be to allow currencies to strengthen in response to inflows; this would also have the welcome effect from a multilateral perspective of increasing current account deficits (reducing surpluses) in a manner consistent with reducing the extent of global current account imbalances. By contrast, adoption of controls by countries with undervalued currencies would be likely to redirect flows to countries less able to absorb them, thus adding to systemic pressures and running the clear risk of a bandwagon response in the form of generalized financial protectionism.

In addition the adoption of controls by some countries might lead others to follow suit: controls may thus be contagious. To the degree that capital controls complicate the management of inflows for other countries, which will likely see even more capital flowing in their direction, they can be considered a beggar-thy-neighbor policy. Finally, while these considerations generally caution against the imposition of controls, it bears emphasizing that multilateral considerations do not militate unambiguously against the imposition of controls. For instance, inasmuch as controls curtail especially risky forms of capital inflows, they may also reduce countries' precautionary demand for reserves, thus serving to reduce global imbalances and contributing to systemic stability.[9]

To summarize, there are two main reasons why governments might want to impose capital controls—to limit the appreciation of the exchange rate and to limit crisis vulnerability due to excessive or risky forms of foreign borrowing. While other tools—macroeconomic policies and prudential regulations—should always be deployed, logic suggests that appropriately designed controls on capital inflows could usefully complement them in certain circumstances, especially in the face of temporary inflow surges. Controls would normally be temporary, as a means to counter surges.[10] Long-term increases in inflows tend to stem from more fundamental factors and will require more fundamental economic adjustment—though, of course, it is not always easy to tell whether a surge is temporary or portends a persistent trend.[11]

6.3   Inflows, Fragilities, and Controls—Some Stylized facts

The discussion above suggests certain circumstances under which capital controls might be useful for macroeconomic management or prudential purposes. But are they effective in practice? This section takes a look at the stylized facts, surveying existing studies and exploiting the "natural experiment" of the global financial crisis to see whether capital controls had any bearing on how individual EMEs fared in the current crisis.

6.3.1   Existing Empirical Evidence

The effectiveness of capital controls needs to be judged against the objectives in imposing them, which may include reducing the volume of inflows and limiting the appreciation of the exchange rate, altering the maturity composition of inflows to reduce financial fragility, and providing additional monetary policy independence.

Although individual country studies often find little or no impact of capital controls on the aggregate volume of inflows (table 6.1), some cross-country analyses suggest that at least among countries that faced some surge in inflows, those with controls experienced smaller surges.[12] Obviously, all other things being equal, a country with a closed capital account will experience smaller inflows than a country with a largely open capital account. The effectiveness of controls in regulating inflows thus depends on how extensive they are, whether the country maintains the necessary administrative and institutional infrastructure to enforce the controls, and the incentives investors have to try to circumvent them. The lack of convincing evidence on the effectiveness of controls in reducing the total volume of inflows therefore likely reflects: (1) the relatively marginal control measures adopted by EMEs in recent years; (2) the fact that capital controls are often imposed or strengthened as part of an overall package of policy responses, making it difficult to isolate their effect; (3) difficulty in measuring the intensity of capital controls; and (4) econometric identification problems—for instance, if countries that are facing large inflows are the ones that impose controls, it is not surprising that econometric studies find no, or even a positive, relationship between controls and the magnitude of capital inflows. Further the recent wave of capital controls has also included restrictions on derivative positions (e.g., in Colombia), which highlights the deepening and sophistication of financial markets in EMEs and the potential complexity in assessing the effects of controls. Since most studies do not find much impact of controls on aggregate volumes of inflows, they usually do not find much effect on exchange rate appreciation either.[13]

6.3.2 Evidence from the Current Global Financial Crisis

Empirical studies are typically more successful at finding some impact of capital controls on monetary policy autonomy[14] and on the composition of inflows—particularly, lengthening their maturity (box 6.1, figure 6.1).[15] This raises the question of whether limiting (certain types) of capital inflows is useful for reducing financial fragility. The recent global financial crisis provides a natural experiment in this regard, with differences in how EMEs have fared possibly shedding light on whether certain types of capital inflows pose greater risk of financial fragility, and whether controls on inflows have indeed been associated with reduced vulnerabilities. A first look at the foreign liability structure of the EMEs and their resilience in the current crisis suggests that larger stocks of *debt liabilities* and of FDI in the financial sector (*financial FDI*) are associated with worse growth slowdowns. More formal regression analysis supports this finding: countries with larger stocks of debt liabilities or financial FDI fared worse in the current crisis, whereas those with larger stocks of nonfinancial FDI fared better. The findings in regard to debt and nonfinancial FDI conform to conventional wisdom: debt represents fixed obligations for the borrower, with limited risk sharing with the creditor, whereas FDI—especially greenfield FDI—is not only less likely to flee in a crisis, it may also be a source of fresh financing. More surprising is the greater vulnerability associated with financial FDI. Although financial FDI can be useful (many studies—e.g., Kose et al. 2006—find benefits of foreign bank ownership), the results indicate that some components of financial FDI bring added risks—for example, financial FDI may reflect lending from a parent bank to a branch or local affiliate, which may be more in the nature of debt flows than greenfield FDI.[16]

Why are debt and some components of financial FDI more risky? Both are strongly associated with credit booms and foreign exchange denominated lending by the domestic banking system, which in turn is associated with greater vulnerability. This is likely to be a key channel through which such flows make the country more susceptible to crisis. Interestingly, however, the greater crisis vulnerability associated with debt liabilities holds, even when controlling for credit booms and foreign-exchange-denominated lending—perhaps because households and firms may borrow directly from abroad (or flows are intermediated through nonbank financial institutions). Accordingly controls that limit debt inflows (and debt flows recorded as financial FDI) might usefully supplement prudential regulations aimed at curtailing domestic credit booms and unhedged foreign exchange denominated lending.

Empirically there does appear to be a negative association between capital controls that were in place prior to the global financial crisis and the output declines suffered during the crisis. Although causation is far from established, the empirical evidence suggests that the use of capital controls was associated with avoiding some of the worst growth outcomes associated with financial fragility.[17] Moreover, consistent with the discussion above, it is controls on debt flows that are significantly associated with avoiding crises. Although further study is needed, these controls are not associated with lower average growth in the pre-crisis period as well.

6.4 Conclusions

There is no surefire one-size-fits-all way to deal with the impact of potentially destabilizing short-term capital inflows. From an individual-country point of view, the usual elements of the tool kit to manage inflows include currency appreciation, reserves accumulation, adjustments in fiscal and monetary policy, and strengthening the prudential framework. In some circumstances, however, the usual macro policy remedies will not be appropriate (e.g., because inflation is a concern, so lowering domestic policy rates will be ill advised, the currency is already too strong, or reserves are more than adequate). In others, it may not be possible to quickly address financial fragility concerns through the domestic prudential framework alone. For both macroeconomic and prudential reasons, there may therefore be circumstances in which capital controls are a legitimate component of the policy response to surges in capital inflows.

Table 6.1
Selected cases of control measures on capital inflows

Country	Year	Controls	Study	Did controls on inflows:		
				Reduce the volume of net flows	Alter the composition	Reduce real exchange rate pressures
Brazil	1993–97	Explicit tax on capital flows on stock market investments, foreign loans, and certain foreign exchange transactions	Cardoso and Goldfajn (1998)	Yes (ST)	Yes (ST)	No
			Reinhart and Smith (1998)	Yes (ST)	Yes (ST)	No
			Ariyoshi et al. (2000)	No	No	
		Administrative controls (outright prohibitions against, or minimum maturity requirements for, certain types of inflows)	Edison and Reinhart (2001)	Yes (ST)		
			Carvalho and Garcia (2008)			
Chile	1991–98	Introduced URR on foreign borrowing, later extended to cover nondebt flows, American Depository Receipts, and potentially speculative FDI	Valdes-Prieto and Soto (1998)	No	Yes	No
			Le Fort and Budnevich (1997)	No	Yes	Yes
			Larran, Laban, and Chumacero (1997)	No	Yes	No
			Cardoso and Laurens (1998)	Yes (ST)	Yes (ST)	No
			Reinhart and Smith (1998)	Yes (ST)	Yes (ST)	No
			Edwards (1999)	No	Yes (ST)	No
		Raised the discount rate	Gallego, Hernández, and Schmidt-Hebbel (1999)	Yes (ST)	No	Yes (ST)
			Ariyoshi et al. (2000)	No	Yes	Yes
			De Gregorio, Edwards, and Valdes (2000)	No		
			Edwards and Rigobon (2009)			
Colombia	1993–98	Introduced URR on external borrowing (limited to loans with maturities up to 18 months) and later extended to cover certain trade credits	Le Fort and Budnevich (1997)	Yes (ST)	Yes	Yes
			Cárdenas (1997)	No	Yes	No
			Reinhart and Smith (1998)	No	No	
			Ariyoshi et al. (2000)	No	No	

Table 6.1
(continued)

Country	Year	Controls	Study	Did controls on inflows:		
				Reduce the volume of net flows	Alter the composition	Reduce real exchange rate pressures
	2007–08	Introduced URR of 40 percent on foreign borrowing and portfolio inflows	Concha and Galindo (2008)	No	Yes	No
			Crdenas et al. (2007)	No	Yes (ST)	
		Imposed limits on the currency derivative positions of banks (500 percent of capital)	Clements and Kamil (2009)	No	Yes	
Croatia	2004–08	Introduced prudential marginal reserve requirements on bank foreign financing	Jankov (2009)		Yes	
Malaysia	1994	Prohibition against sale of short-term debt securities and money market instruments to nonresidents, and against commercial banks' engagement in non-trade-related swaps or forward transactions with nonresidents. - Ceilings on banks' net liability position. - Non-interest-bearing deposit requirement for commercial banks against ringgit funds of foreign banks	Ariyoshi et al. (2000) Tamirisa (2004)	Yes	Yes	Yes (ST) No

Table 6.1
(continued)

Country	Year	Controls	Study	Did controls on inflows:		
				Reduce the volume of net flows	Alter the composition	Reduce real exchange rate pressures
Thailand	1995–96	URR imposed on banks' nonresident baht accounts. - Introduced asymmetric open-position limits to discourage foreign borrowing. - Imposed reporting requirements for banks on risk-control measures in foreign exchange and derivatives trading.	Ariyoshi et al. (2000)	Yes	Yes	Yes
	2006–08	URR of 30 percent imposed on foreign currencies sold or exchanged against baht with authorized financial institutions (except for FDI and amounts not exceeding US$20,000) Equity investments in companies listed on the stock exchange were made exempt from the URR				
Cross-country evidence			Reinhart and Smith (1998)	Yes (ST)		
			Montiel and Reinhart (1999)	No	Yes (ST)	
			Edison and Reinhart (2001)	No	Yes (ST)	
			Binici, Hutchison, and Schindler (2009)		No	No

Box 6.1
Country experiences with controls on short-term capital inflows

Recourse to capital controls to counter surges in capital inflows has been pervasive in emerging markets. Controls are often imposed to maintain monetary control while reducing pressures on the exchange rate and to address prudential concerns in the presence of large, short-term inflows. The effectiveness of such controls is, however, a much debated issue — country experiences have varied, depending largely on the motivation and nature of controls and on country-specific characteristics such as the administrative capacity to implement them.

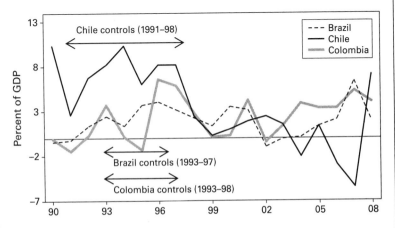

Figure 6.2
Net private financial flows (percentage of GDP)

Volume of inflows In general, capital controls are found to have little impact on the total volume of capital inflows and thus on currency appreciation. For example, the imposition of inflow restrictions by Brazil, Chile, and Colombia in the 1990s had no significant impact on total capital inflows, nor were pressures on the exchange rate alleviated (figure 6.2). In fact, over the course of their capital controls, the real effective exchange rate appreciated by about 5 and 4 percent annually in Brazil and Chile, respectively. In Thailand the real exchange rate started appreciating within a week after controls on short-term flows were imposed in December 2006. The most recent episode of controls in Colombia (during 2007–08) was also ineffective in reducing the volume of non-FDI inflows or in moderating the currency appreciation (Clements and Kamil 2009).

Box 6.1
(continued)

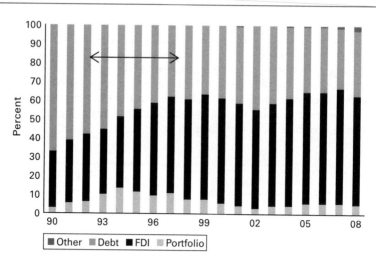

Figure 6.3
Chile: Composition of foreign liabilities (percent)

Composition of inflows   Controls on inflows, however, may alter the maturity structure and composition of inflows. In Chile, for example, controls seem to have been effective in altering the composition of inflows—short-term debt as a proportion of total liabilities declined, whereas the stock of FDI increased from about 34 percent in 1991 to 53 percent in 1998 (figure 6.3). Cardoso and Laurens (1998) and De Gregorio, Edwards, and Valdes (2000) find that the Chilean unremumnerated reserve requirement (URR) was also effective in tilting the composition of inflows away from short-term maturities. Similarly, after the URR was imposed in Colombia in 1993, the maturity structure of the private external debt stock changed significantly—the share of medium- and long-term debt increased to 70 percent of the total external debt stock in 1996, from 40 percent in 1993 (Ariyoshi et al. 2000).

Prudential concerns   Domestic financial stability concerns raised by large capital inflows are often addressed by introducing prudential measures either with traditional (administrative and market based) capital controls or as stand-alone measures. Such measures could be effective in reducing currency mismatches as well as in limiting debt inflows. For example, Malaysia introduced prudential requirements (e.g., the asymmetric open-position limits of banks) along with temporary capital controls to limit short-term inflows in 1994. The measures were effective in influencing the volume as well as composition of inflows in the short term. Similarly the strong prudential framework in place in Chile is considered to have played

Box 6.1
(continued)

> an important role in complementing capital controls to affect the composition of inflows (Ariyoshi et al. 2000). Croatia's imposition of prudential measures—including the marginal reserve requirement on bank foreign financing in 2004 to 2008—in response to concerns pertaining to the high credit growth triggered by capital inflows—was also effective in reducing external bank debt in 2006 to 2008 (Jankov 2009).
>
> An important issue highlighted by the experience of the EMEs is that the effectiveness of capital controls and prudential measures in terms of limiting inflows, changing their composition, and achieving the desired macroeconomic objectives hinges critically on countries' implementation capacity. In general, the controls' impact is short lived as markets adjust to them. A strong enforcement capacity as, for example, in Chile, is therefore needed to identify loopholes and prevent circumvention.

Multilateral dimensions, however, are integral to a balanced perspective on the appropriateness of using capital controls to manage inflows. While controls can be helpful to individual countries under certain conditions, their widespread use could have deleterious effects on the efficient allocation of investment across countries and harm prospects for global recovery and growth. Greater use of controls could also lead to crowding out of less distortionary policies to manage inflows, and contribute to contagion, with countries whose individual circumstances do not justify the use of controls choosing to adopt restrictions on inflows. Widespread adoption of controls could also contribute to widening of global imbalances, especially if restrictions were implemented by countries with undervalued currencies as a means to resist appreciation. Conversely, however, inasmuch as controls reduce countries' precautionary demand for reserves by curtailing inflows of "hot money" and especially risky forms of liabilities, they could contribute to reducing global imbalances and thus enhance systemic stability. A multilateral framework governing the re-imposition of controls, balancing the various considerations, could be helpful in managing possible cross-country spillovers.

The perspective of this chapter is thus that capital controls are a legitimate part of the tool kit to manage capital inflows in certain circumstances, but that a decision on their use should reflect a comparison of the distortions and implementation costs that they may impose and the benefits from regaining macro policy control and reducing financial fragility.

There is a need for a regular reassessment to ensure that capital controls remain the appropriate response as long as these are maintained. Moreover this chapter emphasizes that any use of capital controls should internalize to the extent possible the systemic dangers that could result from widespread adoption of controls by a large number of countries.

Notes

This chapter is largely drawn from Ostry et al. (2010). The views expressed herein are those of the author and should not be attributed to the IMF, its Executive Board or its management. The author thanks Olivier Blanchard for helpful discussions on these issues.

1. Controls may also be justified to mitigate financial-stability risks associated with (even persistent) inflows: see Ostry et al. (2011a, b) for a further discussion of this issue, which is not taken up here.

2. The vulnerability of emerging Europe in the wake of the recent crisis and the region's heavy dependence on foreign banking groups, particularly those from western Europe for capital, necessitated efforts (culminating in the Initiative for Coordination of European Banks) to induce parent banks to maintain exposures to their subsidiaries.

3. Other forms of sterilization include raising reserve requirements, which does not incur a fiscal cost (especially if reserves are not remunerated), though their excessive use can lead to undesirable financial disintermediation.

4. Cardarelli, Elekdağ, and Kose (2007) provide evidence that real appreciation and demand growth was more contained in countries that responded to capital inflows by pursuing a tighter fiscal policy. However, there is often a political temptation to avoid making necessary fiscal adjustments and to rely instead on capital controls.

5. The literature does not provide unambiguous evidence on the relative effectiveness/distortiveness of price-based versus administrative controls. Countries tend to use the types of controls they are most familiar with from past practice—the obvious advantage being easier implementation for both the authorities and the banking sector.

6. Excessive restrictions on banks could lead to disintermediation and proliferation of nonregulated financial institutions: see Wakeman-Linn (2007).

7. Such a policy will be less effective if foreign investors circumvent the restrictions, for example, by writing currency swap contracts.

8. To the extent that capital inflows to EMEs are driven by the policy environment in advanced economies, they too need to take account of the multilateral implications of their policies.

9. See Ghosh, Ostry, and Tsangarides (2010) for a discussion of how reducing the precautionary demand for reserves would contribute to systemic stability by helping narrow global imbalances and avoid a sudden tipping point in the demand for major reserve assets.

10. Risks of financial fragilities or asset price bubbles may actually be heightened in the case of more persistent flows. If prudential policies have little traction against those fragilities (e.g., because the flows bypass the regulated financial system as in the case of direct borrowing from abroad), capital controls may have a role to play even in the case of per-

sistent inflows: see Ostry et al. (2011a) for further discussion of this point, which is not taken up here.

11. One rule of thumb is that flows that push the real exchange rate toward equilibrium are more likely to be persistent than flows that contribute to overshooting. For an analysis of the cyclical behavior of different types of capital flows, see Becker et al. (2007), which argues that banking flows are much more prone to reversal than other types of inflows (portfolio and FDI).

12. See Cardarelli, Elekdağ, and Kose (2007), who find that among countries facing inflow surges, those with controls experienced smaller inflows—2 percent of GDP in episodes with "high" capital controls compared with 4 percent of GDP in instances where the country had no or low controls.

13. See Gallego, Hernández, and Schmidt-Hebbel (1999) and De Gregorio et al. (2000) for Chile; and Clements and Kamil (2009) for Colombia. Using a GARCH model, however, Edwards and Rigobon (2009) find that a tightening of controls led to depreciation of the nominal exchange rate within its band in Chile.

14. De Gregorio et al. (2000) find that capital controls allowed Chile's central bank to target a higher domestic interest rate over a period of 6 to12 months; Ma and McCauley (2008) and Hutchison et al. (2009) find that interest differentials are significant and persistent in China and India, which maintain more extensive capital controls. However, Ghosh, Ostry, and Tsangarides (2010) find significantly lower monetary autonomy in countries with fixed exchange rates compared with more flexible regimes, even in countries with relatively closed capital accounts.

15. See Ariyoshi et al. (2000), which examined the experience with capital controls of five countries (Brazil, Chile, Colombia, Malaysia, and Thailand) in the 1990s to limit short-term inflows. De Gregorio et al. (2000), Cardoso and Goldfajn (1998), Cárdenas et al. (2007), and Goh (2005) find that controls can lengthen the maturity of inflows. Of course, a finding of an effect on the composition of inflows belies the lack of a finding on aggregate volumes, unless one is willing to believe that substitution across types of inflow is perfect.

16. Note that FDI includes loans between a parent and subsidiary, as long as the parent has a controlling interest, where controlling interest is usually taken to be an ownership stake of at least 10 percent.

17. In a sample of about 200 crisis episodes in about 90 countries over 1970 to 2007, Gupta, Mishra, and Sahay (2007) report a similar result, namely that drops in output during crisis episodes are significantly lower if capital controls existed before the crisis.

References

Ariyoshi, Akira, Karl Habermeier, Bernard Laurens, Inci Ötker-Robe, Jorge Ivan Canales-Kriljenko, and Andrei Kirilenko. 2000. Capital controls: Country experiences with their use and liberalization. Occasional paper 19. IMF, Washington, DC.

Becker, Torbjörn, Olivier Jeanne, Paulo Mauro, Jonathan D. Ostry, and Romain Ranciere. 2007. Country insurance: The role of domestic policies. Occasional paper 254. IMF, Washington, DC.

Binici, Mahir, Michael Hutchison, and Martin Schindler. 2009. Controlling capital? Legal restrictions and the asset composition of international financial flows. Working paper 09/208. IMF, Washington, DC.

Cardarelli, Roberto, Selim Elekdağ, and Ayhan Kose. 2007. Managing large capital inflows. *World Economic Outlook* (October): 105–33.

Cárdenas, Mauricio, Julio Torres, Arturo Galindo, Camila Pérez, and Felipe Gómez. 2007. Controle de capitales en Colombia ¿Funcionan o no? *Debates de Coyuntura Económica* 70 (December): 1–46.

Cárdenas, Mauricio, and Felipe Barrera. 1997. On the effectiveness of capital controls: The experience of Colombia during the 1990s. *Journal of Development Economics* 54 (1): 27–57.

Cardoso, Eliana, and I. Goldfajn. 1998. Capital flows to Brazil: The endogeneity of capital controls. *IMF Staff Papers* 45 (1): 161–202.

Cardoso, Jaime, and Bernard Laurens. 1998. Managing capital flows—Lessons from the experience of Chile. Working paper 98/168. IMF, Washington, DC.

Carvalho, Bernardo S. de M., and Márcio G. P. Garcia. 2008. Ineffective controls on capital inflows under sophisticated financial markets: Brazil in the nineties. In Sebastien Edwards and Márcio G. P. Garcia, eds., *Financial Markets Volatility and Performance in Emerging Markets*. Chicago: University of Chicago Press/National Bureau of Economic Research, 29–95.

Clements, Benedict J., and Herman Kamil. 2009. Are capital controls effective in the 21st century? The recent experience of Colombia. Working paper 09/30. IMF, Washington, DC.

Concha, Alvaro, and Arturo J. Galindo. 2008. An assessment of another decade of capital controls in Colombia: 1998–2008. Presented at XIII LACEA Meeting, Rio de Janeiro, Brazil.

De Gregorio, José, Sebastian Edwards, and Rodrigo Valdes. 2000. Controls on capital inflows: Do they work? *Journal of Development Economics* 63 (1): 59–83.

Edison, Hali, and Carmen Reinhart. 2001. Stopping hot money. *Journal of Development Economics* 66 (2): 533–53.

Edwards, Sebastian. 1999. How effective are capital controls? *Journal of Economic Perspectives* 13 (4): 65–84.

Edwards, Sebastian, and Roberto Rigobon. 2009. Capital controls on inflows, exchange rate volatility and external vulnerability. *Journal of International Economics* 78 (2): 256–67.

Gallego, Francisco, and Leonardo Hernández. 2003. Microeconomic effects of capital controls: The Chilean experience during the 1990s. *International Journal of Finance and Economics* 8 (3): 225–53.

Gallego, Francisco, Leonardo Hernández, and K. Schmidt-Hebbel. 1999. Capital controls in Chile: Effective? Efficient? Working paper 59. Banco Central de Chile, Santiago.

Ghosh, Atish, Jonathan D. Ostry, and Charalambos Tsangarides. 2010. Exchange rate regimes and the stability of the international monetary system. Occasional paper 270. IMF, Washington, DC.

Goh, Soo Khoon. 2005. New empirical evidence on the effects of capital controls on composition of capital flows in Malaysia. *Applied Economics* 37 (13): 1491–1503.

Gupta, Poonam, Deepak Mishra, and Ratna Sahay. 2007. Behavior of output during currency crises. *Journal of International Economics* 72 (2): 428–50.

Hutchison, Michael, Jake Kendall, Gurnain Pasricha, and Nirvikar Singh. 2009. Indian capital control liberalization: Evidence from NDF markets. Working paper 2009-60. National Institute of Public Finance and Policy, Delhi.

Jankov, Ljubinko. 2009. Spillovers of the crisis: How different is Croatia? Presented at "Recent Developments in the Baltic Countries—What Are the Lessons for Southeastern Europe?" Oesterreichische Nationalbank, Vienna.

Kose, Ayhan, Eswar Prasad, Kenneth Rogoff, and Wei Shang-jin. 2006. Financial globalization: A reappraisal. Working paper 06/189. IMF, Washington, DC.

Larraín, Felipe, Raul Laban, and Romulo Chumacero. 1997. What determines capital inflows? An empirical analysis for Chile. Faculty research working paper R97–09. John F. Kennedy School of Government, Harvard University.

Le Fort, Guillermo, and Carlos Budnevich. 1997. Capital account regulations and macroeconomic policy: Two Latin experiences. Working paper 06. Banco Central de Chile, Santiago.

Lee, Jaewoo, Gian Maria Milesi-Ferretti, Jonathan D. Ostry, Alessandro Prati, and Luca Ricci. 2008. Exchange rate assessments: CGER methodologies. Occasional paper 261. IMF, Washington, DC.

Ma, Guonan, and Robert N. McCauley. 2008. Efficacy of China's capital controls: Evidence from price and flow data. *Pacific Economic Review* 13 (1): 104–23.

Montiel, Peter, and Carmen Reinhart. 1999. Do capital controls and macroeconomic policies influence the volume and composition of capital flows? Evidence from the 1990's. *Journal of International Money and Finance* 18 (4): 619–35.

Ostry, Jonathan D., Atish R. Ghosh, Karl Habermeier, Marcos Chamon, Mahvash S. Qureshi, and Dennis B. S. Reinhardt. 2010. Capital inflows: the role of controls. Staff position note 10/04. IMF, Washington, DC.

Ostry, Jonathan D. 2011. Are there "intelligent" capital controls? *East Asia Forum*. Available at: http://www.eastasiaforum.org/2011/06/26/are-there-intelligent-capital-controls.

Ostry, Jonathan D., Atish R. Ghosh, Karl Habermeier, Luc Laeven, Marcos Chamon, Mahvash S. Qureshi, and Annamaria Kokenyne. 2011a. Managing capital inflows: What tools to use? Staff discussion note 11/06. IMF, Washington, DC.

Ostry, Jonathan D., Atish R. Ghosh, Marcos Chamon, and Mahvash S. Qureshi. 2011b. Capital controls: When and why? *IMF Economic Review* 59 (3): 562–80.

Ostry, Jonathan D., Atish R. Ghosh, Marcos Chamon, and Mahvash S. Qureshi. 2012. Tools for managing financial stability risks from capital inflows. *Journal of International Economics*, forthcoming.

Reinhart, Carmen, and Todd Smith. 1998. Too much of a good thing: The macroeconomic effects of taxing capital inflows. In Reuven Glick, ed., *Managing Capital Flows and Exchange Rates: Perspectives from the Pacific Basin*. Cambridge, UK: Cambridge University Press.

Tamirisa, Natalia. 2004. Do macroeconomic effects of capital controls vary by their type? Evidence from Malaysia. Working paper 04/3. IMF, Washington, DC.

Valdes-Prieto, Salvador, and Marcelo Soto. 1998. The effectiveness of capital controls: Theory and evidence from Chile. *Empirica* 25 (2): 133–64.

Wakeman-Linn, John. 2007. Managing large scale foreign exchange inflows: International experiences. Unpublished manuscript. IMF, Washington, DC.

7 Capital Inflows and Policy Responses: Lessons from Korea's Experience

Kyuil Chung and Seungwon Kim

7.1 Introduction

After the late 1990s Asian currency crisis, the main policy framework that Korea adopted combined a free-floating exchange rate system and inflation targeting, together with a widening of financial liberalization. The theoretical background behind this policy scheme was the famous so-called trilemma,[1] which dictates that it is impossible to accomplish exchange rate stability, monetary policy independence, and free capital mobility simultaneously. Given the condition that financial markets in individual countries had been rapidly integrated into the international financial markets since the 1980s,[2] it seemed that the free-floating exchange rate system and inflation targeting was the best option Korea could choose. Since then, Korean policy makers have maintained this policy framework and considered this their starting point for policy-making. Under the trilemma framework, of course, this has implied an acceptance of high capital mobility.

From early 2000 through 2007 Korea experienced huge volumes of capital inflows, fueled by the nation's promising economic growth and stable inflation. In response to this surge in capital inflows, Korea took several measures: allowing exchange rate appreciation, intervening in the foreign exchange market and thereby building up its foreign reserves, liberalizing capital outflows, and so on. All were typical policy prescriptions under the Korean policy framework. During the 2007–08 global financial crisis, however, Korea was one of the countries experiencing the severest capital outflows. Whatever the reasons for this, it is evident that the existing tools are not entirely sufficient for countering the external shocks that the Korean economy can face.

This chapter first describes the stylized facts on capital inflows to Korea during the 2000s, and then explains the major policy responses to

them. Next it examines the effectiveness of Korea's foreign exchange
policy, especially related to capital outflow liberalization and foreign
reserve accumulation in terms of prevention and resolution of the
2008 liquidity crisis—the Korean version of the global financial crisis.
The chapter concludes with some policy lessons.

7.2   Capital Inflows and Policy Responses

7.2.1   Stylized Facts on Capital Inflows

Throughout the 2000s prior to the global financial crisis, Korea recorded
continuing large surpluses in both its current and capital and financial
accounts, although the capital and financial account did sometimes record
temporary deficits. As shown in figure 7.1, the twin surpluses in the Korean
balance of payments created a huge excess supply of foreign capital,
which imposed severe challenges to macroeconomic policy-making. Note
that even though the capital and financial account turned negative in the
second half of 2007, this did not receive any particular attention. Only
after the collapse of Lehman Brothers in September 2008 was it recognized that the capital and financial account deficit was not a temporary
one-off phenomenon.

Figure 7.2 shows gross foreign capital inflows to Korea during the
2000s, enabling us to identify three of their characteristics. First, while
capital inflows were relatively stable during the first half of the 2000s,
they increased rapidly from 2006 through the first half of 2008. The main

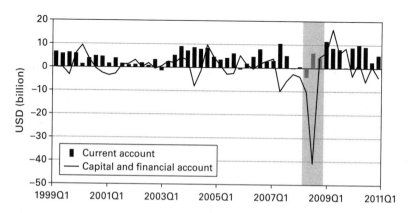

Figure 7.1
Balance of payments
Source: *Economic Statistics System (ECOS),* Bank of Korea

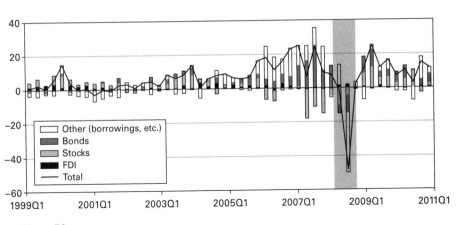

Figure 7.2
Foreign capital inflows
Source: *Economic Statistics System (ECOS)*, Bank of Korea

categories involved in this surge in foreign capital inflows were bond market and other (bank borrowings, etc.) investment, rather than equity-related investment. This implies as well that the large capital inflows resulted in a huge amount of foreign debt, which should have been addressed properly before eruption of the crisis. The combined burgeoning of investment in the bond market and of bank borrowings was related to the hedging activities in the banking sector, which will be explained in detail in section 7.3.

Second, throughout the 2000s, FDI accounted for a relatively small share of the capital inflows, while capital inflows related to portfolio investment (in stocks and bonds) and bank borrowings in contrast accounted for most of it. This composition implies that the capital inflows to Korea were very susceptible to external shocks, and that there was a high possibility of quick capital flow reversal in times of financial turmoil. We should note in this regard that bank borrowings were the largest item in the devastating deleveraging by foreigners during the global financial crisis.

Third, the gross capital inflows showed quite dramatic changes in around late 2008. After peaking in 2007, they quickly reversed in 2008, with a total outflow close to 50 billion US dollars (5 percent of annual GDP) in the fourth quarter of 2008. Capital inflows resumed again in 2009, however, to return to their pre-crisis 2007 level. This drastic volatility of capital inflows has been hard to combat in a small open economy like Korea's.

Table 7.1
Liberalization of capital flows in Korea

Dates	Measures
Dec 1997	• Adoption of free-floating exchange rate system • Full liberalization of corporate and government bond markets
May 1998	• Opening of all money market instruments (CP, CDs, RPs, etc.) • Removal of ceilings on foreigners' stock market investment (excluding investment in some state-owned enterprises)
Apr 1999	• Change in capital account transaction regulation, from positive to negative list system
Jan 2006	• Abolition of capital transaction licensing system, replaced by ex post reporting system
Mar 2006	• Removal of ceilings on outbound FDI by individual residents • Removal of restrictions limiting types and items of overseas securities investment by individual residents
May 2006	• Allowing of overseas real estate acquisition for investment purposes up to US$1 million
Feb 2007	• Raising of limit on acquisition of overseas real estate for investment purposes, from US$1 million to US$3 million
Jan 2008	• Abolition of reporting requirement for capital transactions up to US$50,000, and reduction of documents required for reporting

Source: Ministry of Strategy and Finance, Korea

The nation's promising economic performance was obviously the main factor contributing to the surge in capital inflows during the 2000s. However, the capital account liberalization boldly implemented by the Korean government after the Asian currency crisis also played an important role.

Table 7.1 highlights the main capital account liberalization measures taken after the Asian crisis. In December 1997, right after the crisis hit, Korea adopted a free-floating exchange rate system and fully opened its bond markets. Subsequently, in 1998, it liberalized its money market and removed its ceilings on foreigners' investment in the domestic stock markets. The most decisive measures then took place in 1999, when Korea changed its capital account transaction regulation from a positive to a negative list system, meaning that all capital account transactions could now be implemented freely, unless expressly forbidden by law.

Most of the liberalization measures in 2006 to 2007 revolved around capital outflows. To mitigate the adverse effects of capital inflows, Korea removed various restrictions on residents' investment in overseas assets. This will be explained in detail shortly as we discuss policy responses.

7.2.2 Policy Responses

There are in theory multiple policy options for combating a surge in capital inflows: monetary policy,[3] foreign exchange policy through foreign exchange market intervention and foreign reserve accumulation, and regulatory policy through prudential regulation and capital controls.[4] The trilemma mentioned earlier basically frames the policy responses chosen.

Since the inflation targeting adopted by Korea requires that monetary policy be used principally for inflation control, there has not been much room in monetary policy conduct for attention to capital inflows. More than that, in an open economy monetary policy can even create unwelcome side effects: an increase in interest rates to respond to capital inflows might induce further capital inflows due to widening of the interest rate differential between the domestic and overseas markets, while a decrease in rates might accelerate already existing inflationary pressures. Meanwhile under a free-floating exchange rate system it is generally believed that all external shocks are absorbed by flexible movement of the exchange rate, and that free capital mobility strengthens this automatic stabilization process further. Therefore the most viable option for mitigating the effects of external shocks is foreign exchange policy.

The policy options chosen by the Korean policy makers have reflected this situation. In other words, foreign exchange policy has been the first line of defense in response to surging capital inflows, with regulatory policy added complementarily. More specifically, in trying to lessen the negative effects of capital inflows, Korea accumulated a huge volume of foreign reserves first, and then liberalized capital outflows.

Figure 7.3 shows the movements of exchange rates and the balance of payments in Korea. As the combined current and capital and financial accounts recorded surpluses during the 2000s prior to the global financial crisis, the Korean Won continually appreciated against the US dollar. And although it is desirable to let the exchange rate fluctuate freely in the foreign exchange market, the Bank of Korea from time to time intervened in the market to prevent excessive exchange rate volatility, as a result accumulating a huge amount of foreign reserves. The nation's foreign exchange reserve holdings stood at over 250 billion US dollars (27 percent of annual GDP) just before the 2008 liquidity crisis. Figure 7.4 illustrates the steep increase in foreign reserves between 2000 and 2007.

In addition to exchange rate stability, the precautionary motive of self-insurance against another financial crisis has been an important factor

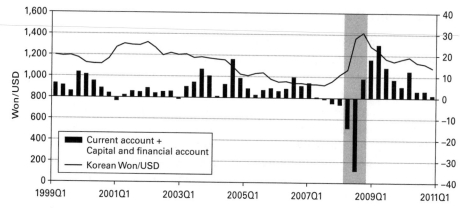

Figure 7.3
Exchange rate and balance of payments
Source: *Economic Statistics System (ECOS),* Bank of Korea

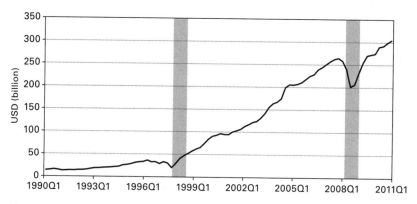

Figure 7.4
Foreign reserves
Source: *Economic Statistics System (ECOS),* Bank of Korea

behind the extraordinary growth in Korea's foreign exchange reserves. While there are various explanations for the Asian crisis that hit Korea in 1997, a shortage of international liquidity was the direct cause of the chaos that broke out. The level of foreign exchange reserves in Korea just prior to the crisis was around only 20 billion dollars (figure 7.4). To make matters worse, there was a perception among market participants, revealed afterward to have been prescient, that the amount of available reserves was actually far below that level. That perception led capital outflows to accelerate further. The learning effect from this experience drove Korea to subsequently build up an abundant level of foreign exchange reserves, to try to immunize itself from future crisis.

Another policy response to combat capital inflow problems is regulation. Theoretically regulatory measures involve such steps as prudential regulation and supervision, imposition of controls on capital inflows, and liberalization of capital outflows.[5] Of these three regulatory measures, Korea imposed a few microprudential regulations on the banking sector—for example, liquidity ratio requirements, guidance on foreign currency lending to residents, and ceilings on banks' overall (spot + forward) open foreign exchange positions. The microprudential regulations were undertaken very cautiously and minimally, however, since restricting the free flow of capital is considered undesirable. Korea preferred instead to actively liberalize overseas investment by residents.

As listed in table 7.1, the capital transaction licensing system was replaced by an ex post reporting system in 2006, which made capital transactions much easier to carry out. In the same year the restrictions on outbound FDI and overseas securities investment by individual residents were lifted. The ceilings on acquisition of overseas real estate for investment purposes were also raised, in 2006 and 2007. And the reporting requirements for capital transactions were further relaxed in 2008.

Figure 7.5 shows the trend of Korean residents' overseas investment during the 2000s. The most striking feature is the rapid increase seen from 2005. Capital outflows peaked in 2007, just before onset of the 2008

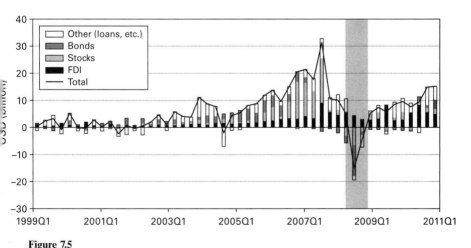

Figure 7.5
Overseas investment by residents
Source: *Economic Statistics System (ECOS),* Bank of Korea

liquidity crisis, at a level not since reached again even in 2011, three years after the crisis. As to the composition of these capital outflows, shown in figure 7.6, investment in foreign stock markets comprised the lion's share of overseas investment, FDI showed an increasing and stable trend, and bond market and other (bank lending, etc.) investment did not show any notable movements.

Unfortunately, and counter to its original intent, which had been to mitigate the negative effects of capital inflows, this capital outflow liberalization had an unexpected side effect. It actually led to a new wave of capital inflows, specifically short-term borrowings by banks. This will be explained in the next section, on the ultimate effectiveness of these measures.

7.3 Effectiveness of Policy Responses

7.3.1 Capital Outflow Liberalization

As described in table 7.1, various policy measures to promote capital outflows have been implemented since 2006. And investment by residents in foreign stock markets had accordingly risen substantially—from 0.5 percent of GDP in 2005 to 1.6 percent in 2006, and then to 5.0 percent in 2007 (figure 7.6).[6] Residents' direct investment overseas, after having been 0.5 percent of GDP in 2005, also increased to 0.8 percent in 2006 and 1.4 percent in 2007. Their overseas bond and other (bank loans, etc.) investments were meanwhile not much affected by the capital outflow liberalization.

However, as mentioned above, the liberalization of capital outflows caused an increase in banks' short-term borrowings. Here we first explain the mechanism behind this seemingly paradoxical behavior and then empirically analyze the phenomenon.

Figure 7.7 shows the mechanism of all related transactions. Asset management companies, which received individual residents' funds for overseas investment, purchased US dollars in the spot market and invested them in foreign financial markets. They then engaged in hedge trading through the sale of foreign exchange forward, for the main purpose of avoiding any losses caused by changes in exchange rates when their overseas investments matured.

In line with the increased selling of forward exchange contracts, domestic banks, as the forward exchange contract purchasers, needed to square their foreign currency positions by selling foreign currency in the

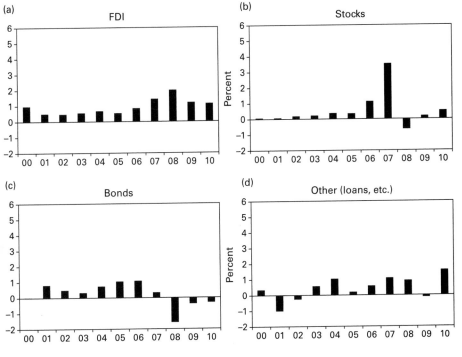

Figure 7.6
Capital outflows relative to GDP. (a) FDI; (b) stocks; (c) bonds; (d) other (loans, etc.)
Source: *Economic Statistics System (ECOS),* Bank of Korea

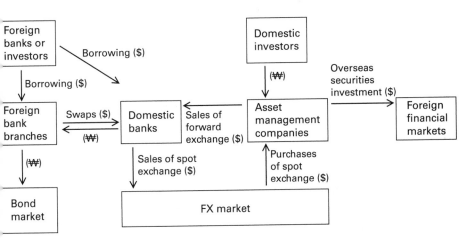

Figure 7.7
Foreign exchange flows related to overseas investment

Table 7.2
Overseas securities investment and related forward exchange sales

(billion USD)

	2005	2006	2007	2008[b]
Overseas securities[a] investment	11.1	24.1	50.1	−1.1
Net sales of forward exchange	1.5	13.1	27.2	3.7

Source: Yang and Lee (2008).
a. Securities include both stocks and bonds, but stocks account for the largest portion.
b. Due to data availability, the first half of 2008 is the only period having data.

spot market. As table 7.2 shows, asset management companies' net sales of forward exchange, which ultimately had to be squared by domestic banks, increased remarkably in 2006 and 2007.

The domestic banks procured the foreign currency they needed to square their positions either by entering into currency swap contracts with foreign bank branches in Korea or by borrowing directly abroad. The foreign bank branches, which borrowed the foreign currencies needed from their headquarters abroad, however, invested the Korean Won proceeds from their swap contracts with domestic banks in the domestic bond market. This way these forward exchange transactions contributed to increased short-term overseas borrowings by financial institutions in 2006 and 2007, and augmented the turmoil in the financial and foreign exchange markets during the 2008 liquidity crisis.

Moreover, by keeping the swap rate[7] much lower than the domestic –international interest rate spread, the overseas investment hedged by forward contracts contributed to persistent arbitrage transaction opportunities and massive inflows of foreigners' investment in the domestic bond market in 2006 and 2007 (figure 7.8). In addition to the sales of forward exchange by asset management companies, Korean shipbuilders sold huge amounts of forward exchange in 2006 to 2007, in natural consequence of the strong orders they were receiving from overseas. The banks' short-term borrowings in 2006, which were much greater than residents' overseas stock investments that year, as shown in figure 7.8, were owed to these very substantial additional forward sales.

From the perspective of individual institutions, hedging exchange rate risk is necessary and desirable. Overall, however, these transactions create unwanted negative effects, revealing the so-called fallacy of composition at work. What this means is that when we construct any policy measure to stem capital inflows, we must also consider the interconnect-

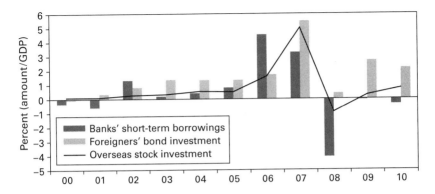

Figure 7.8
Overseas stock investment and related capital inflows
Source: *Economic Statistics System (ECOS)*, Bank of Korea

edness of the financial markets and the systemic risk that it causes. To put the same thing differently, we need to establish a macroprudential framework.

To empirically assess the effectiveness of Korean capital outflow liberalization, a VAR model is constructed using monthly data for January 2000 to December 2007. The model consists of five endogenous variables—overseas stock investment, banks' foreign borrowings, the Korean Won/US dollar exchange rate, the interest rate differential between Korea and the United States, and the Korean industrial production index. To control for global economic conditions and Korean shipbuilders' hedging transactions, which might have affected Korean banks' foreign borrowings, we add four exogenous variables: the US industrial production index, the M2 supply in the United States, the VIX index, and the total value of orders received by Korean shipbuilders. More details on the VAR estimation are provided in the appendix at the end of this chapter.

The empirical analysis focuses especially on the effects of overseas stock investment on domestic banks' foreign borrowings. Figures 7.9 to 7.12 show the impulse responses (with 95 percent error bands for a ten-month horizon) of banks' foreign borrowings to changes in overseas stock investment. As can be seen in figure 7.9, the relaxation of restrictions on overseas investment had a positive and significant impact on banks' borrowings abroad. Estimation of the accumulated impulse responses shows that the estimated positive effects peak in the second month and last for at least one quarter.

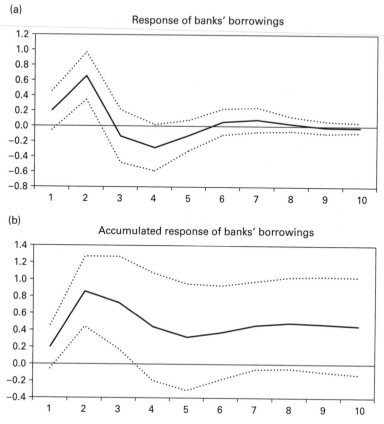

Figure 7.9
Responses of banks' borrowings to overseas stock investment. (a) Response of banks' borrowings; (b) accumulated response of banks' borrowings. The dotted lines represent 95 percent error bands, the solid lines the responses of each variable. The vertical units are percentages of GDP; the horizontal units are months.

We also divided total bank borrowings into long-term and short-term borrowings, and checked their responses. While the impact on long-term borrowings was small, the impulse responses of short-term borrowings were significantly large and lasted for four months. Estimation based on the term structure of foreign borrowings shows that the positive and significant effects on foreign borrowings are mainly due to the increase in short-term borrowings (figures 7.10 and 7.11). Last, there is no significant impact of overseas stock investment on the overall capital and financial accounts, implying that the capital outflows induced by the government liberalization policies were mostly offset by unintended capital inflows such as borrowings by banks (figure 7.12).

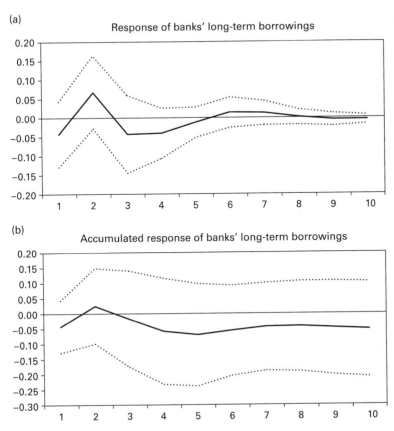

Figure 7.10
Responses of banks' long-term borrowings to overseas stock investment. (a) Response of banks' long-term borrowings; (b) accumulated response of banks' long-term borrowings. The dotted lines represent 95 percent error bands, the solid lines the responses of each variable. The vertical units are percentages of GDP; the horizontal units are months.

In sum, the VAR estimation shows that the capital outflow liberalization in Korea had little impact in lessening the adverse effects of capital inflows. At the same time it made the Korean economy more susceptible to external shocks by creating a new wave of short-term borrowings by banks.

7.3.2 Foreign Reserves

It had been generally believed that its large accumulation of foreign reserves could protect Korea even if there were another crisis. During the process of the recent crisis, however, it became clear that this belief

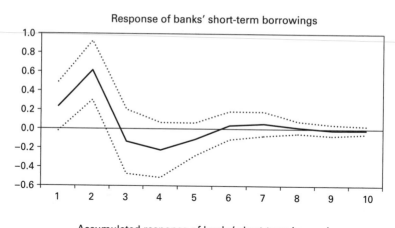

Response of banks' short-term borrowings

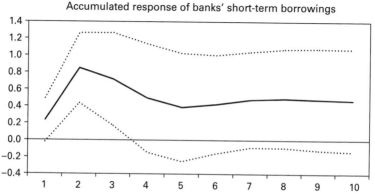

Accumulated response of banks' short-term borrowings

Figure 7.11
Responses of banks' short-term borrowings to overseas stock investment. (a) Response of banks' short-term borrowings; (b) accumulated response of banks' short-term borrowings. The dotted lines represent 95 percent error bands, the solid lines the responses of each variable. The vertical units are percentages of GDP; the horizontal units are months.

was false. The upper panel of figure 7.13 shows the movements of the Korean Won against the US dollar during the crisis period. In September 2008, after the collapse of Lehman Brothers, the exchange rate rose sharply. In addition to this depreciation of the Won, overseas borrowing conditions deteriorated dramatically. As shown in the lower panel of figure 7.13, the CDS premium and the spread on Foreign Exchange Stabilization Bonds[8] both skyrocketed on September 15, 2008, immediately after Lehman Brothers filed for bankruptcy protection.

Behind the outbreak of this liquidity crisis was a combination of factors, including panic and herding among foreign investors and certain structural weaknesses[9] in the Korean financial sector. We do not investi-

(a)

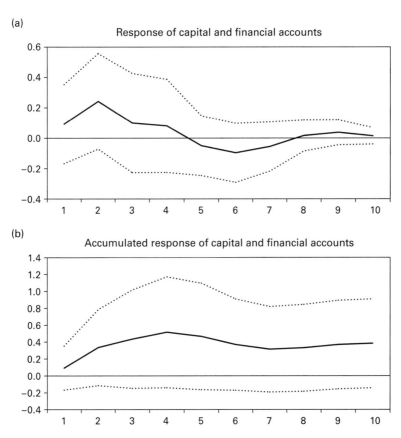

Figure 7.12
Responses of capital and financial accounts to overseas stock investment. (a) Response of capital and financial accounts; (b) accumulated response of capital and financial accounts. The dotted lines represent 95 percent error bands, the solid lines the responses of each variable. The vertical units are percentages of GDP; the horizontal units are months.

gate the causes of the crisis further here but focus instead on the effectiveness of the nation's foreign reserves in containing it.

To address the high level of instability and foreign currency liquidity crunch, Korean foreign reserve authorities initially provided foreign currency liquidity by using foreign reserves to financial institutions experiencing difficulties in overseas fund raising. From September to December 2008 the recorded changes in foreign reserves showed continuous large negative numbers, with the total amount of decline during those four months being close to 40 billion US dollars (16 percent of the reserves, upper panel of figure 7.14).

(a)

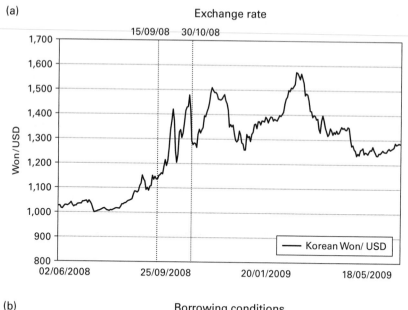

(b)

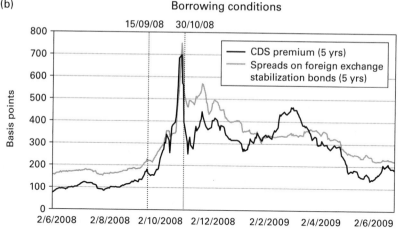

Figure 7.13
Exchange rate and borrowing conditions. (a) Exchange rate; (b) borrowing conditions.
Sources: *Economic Statistics System (ECOS),* Bank of Korea; Korea Center for International
Finance

(a)

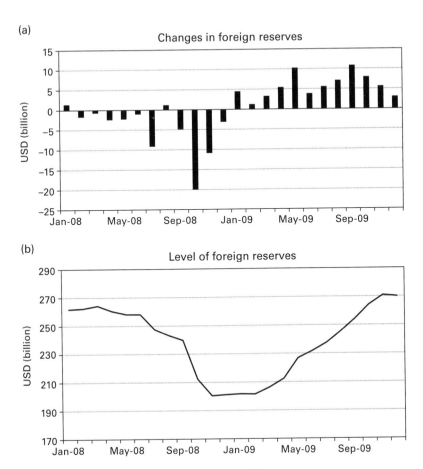

Figure 7.14
Foreign reserves. (a) Changes in foreign reserves; (b) level of foreign reserves
Source: *Economic Statistics System (ECOS),* Bank of Korea

When the level of foreign reserves reached close to 200 billion dollars, however, there was a reluctance to spend more foreign reserves to stabilize the foreign currency funding market. The main reason was the prevalent belief in the market that holding of sufficient reserves was essential to maintaining market participants' confidence in the Korean economy. The lower panel of figure 7.14 shows that the level of foreign reserves did not fall below 200 billion US dollars during the crisis period.

After realizing that the foreign reserves were no longer useful tools for foreign exchange market stabilization, Korean policy makers had to seek another war chest. An IMF credit line might have been one option, but the trauma associated with its IMF bailout program during the Asian financial crisis made Korea very reluctant to go to the IMF. In other words, this was not a politically feasible option.

Korea instead eagerly endeavored to secure a currency swap line with the US Federal Reserve, and this finally came into effect, for a total of 30 billion US dollars, on October 30, 2008. The initial date of expiry of the BOK-Fed swap was April 30, 2009, and it was later extended two times—ultimately until February 1, 2010. In December 2008 Korea reached two additional swap agreements, with Japan and China (table 7.3).

Table 7.3
Currency swap arrangements between Bank of Korea and other central banks

Country	Date of announcement	Ceiling	Expiration date
US	Oct 30, 2008	US$30 billion	Apr 30, 2009 → Oct 30, 2009 → Feb 1, 2010
Japan[a]	Dec 12, 2008	Yen/Won (US$20 billion equivalent)	Apr 30, 2009 → Oct 30, 2009 → Feb 1, 2010 → Apr 30, 2010
China	Dec 12, 2008	180 billion Yuan/38 trillion Won	3 years

Source: Bank of Korea.
Note: The Yen/Won swap arrangement was initially set up in May 2005, for an amount equivalent to US$3 billion. In December 2008 this amount was increased to US$20 billion equivalent, and the US$17 billion equivalent increase was later terminated in April 2010.

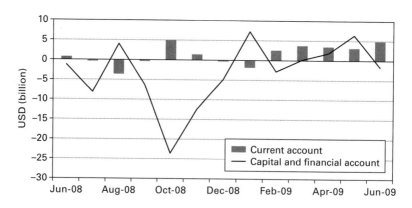

Figure 7.15
Balance of payments during crisis
Source: *Economic Statistics System* (ECOS), Bank of Korea

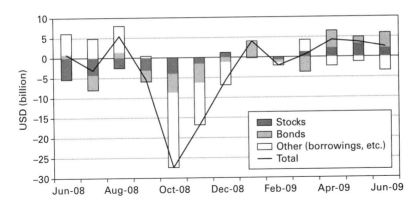

Figure 7.16
Capital inflows during crisis, by sector
Source: *Economic Statistics System* (ECOS), Bank of Korea

What was the market reaction to the BOK-Fed swap arrangement? After the swap arrangement was announced on October 30, 2008, the exchange rate and foreign currency borrowing conditions both stabilized quickly, as shown in figure 7.13, although some instability did still remain thereafter. Figures 7.15 and 7.16 show this more clearly. As seen in figure 7.15, after recording a huge deficit in October 2008, the monthly capital and financial account quickly recovered. The key to the restoration of capital inflows was the improvement in banks' borrowings (figure 7.16). And the Fed swap was instrumental in reversing investors' pessimistic outlook on the Korean economy.

7.4 Concluding Remarks: Lessons from the Crisis and New Policy Measures

The Korean economy quickly returned to positive growth from the third quarter of 2009, and there were a number of positive financial market developments: a stock market rally, the strengthening of the Korean Won, and the resumption of capital inflows. All these developments lead to the conclusion that overreaction and herding behavior had been one of the main causes of the 2008 liquidity crisis in Korea.

Korea has meanwhile learned a few lessons regarding policy measures for mitigating capital flow volatility. First, it is obvious that the combination of a free-floating exchange rate and free capital mobility is not enough to insulate emerging economies from external shocks. While it is evident that free-floating exchange rates play a key role in shock absorption during a crisis, a sudden reversal of capital flows can alone still pose serious threats to an emerging economy. In this regard an emerging economy planning future capital market opening should give meticulous consideration to the order and speed of such opening.

Second, it is important to note that the rational behavior of individual agents sometimes increases systemic risk as a whole, as shown by the expansion in Korean banks' short-term foreign borrowings during the period of capital outflow liberalization policy in Korea. And so, if financial transactions by individual banks create negative externalities, proper remedial action might be needed.

Third, accumulation of reserves is not a condition sufficient to protect the economy from crisis. During times of market turbulence, maintenance of reserves above a specific high level is critical to preserving foreign investors' confidence, meaning that not all of the reserves can be used to provide market liquidity. In this sense, a second line backup facility, for example, through bilateral or multilateral swap lines with other nations' central banks, is very crucial for emerging economies.

With these lessons Korea has now reshaped its policies in several ways. First, to reduce capital flow volatility, the Korean government has introduced a variety of new macroprudential policy measures. In October 2010 it newly established limits on the FX derivatives contracts of banks, to prevent systemic risks posed by short-term external debt.[10] Another policy measure, a macroprudential stability levy on banks' nondeposit foreign currency liabilities, was subsequently introduced in August 2011, to encourage banks' use of stable and long-term sources of funding.

Second, Korea has worked to improve the regional financial safety net, as a second line of defense against a possible sudden stop of foreign currency fund flows. The country expanded its currency swap arrangements with Japan and China in October 2011,[11] and amid the looming of another potential crisis originating from the eurozone, this is expected to help stabilize the financial and foreign exchange markets in East Asia.

The Bank of Korea Act was amended in August 2011, to provide the Bank of Korea with a new mandate for achieving financial stability besides price stability. Under the amended act, the BOK has enhanced access now to balance sheet information of both banks and nonbanks. The new act also eases the requirements for liquidity support provision by the Bank of Korea during times of emergency, while widening the scope of collateral eligible for this support. It is even possible now for profit-seeking enterprises to receive emergency liquidity from the Bank of Korea in exceptional circumstances.

It is too early to evaluate the effectiveness of these newly introduced policy measures. They may enhance the resilience of the Korean financial system, or they may bring short-term benefits while imposing long-term costs. It is therefore imperative to keep a few things in mind. First, continued efforts to strengthen a country's macroeconomic fundamentals are definitely needed. Developing the institutional framework, fostering transparency and consistency in regulation, and implementing sound macroeconomic policy are some examples in this regard. Second, one of the most important lessons from this global financial crisis is the extent of interconnectedness of the world we now live in. International capital flows are eventually determined by the interweaving of push and pull factors, and the effects of policies undertaken in individual advanced or emerging countries are not confined within their own territories but spill over to other regions. In this regard policy coordination among regions is a key prerequisite for a better and more prosperous world.

Appendix: Data and Empirical Methodology

Data

To assess the effectiveness of capital outflow liberalization, a VAR model is applied using monthly data for 2000 to 2007. Due to excessive volatility in the monthly data, three-month moving averages are used. There are five endogenous variables in the VAR estimation: overseas stock investment, banks' foreign borrowings,[12] the Korean Won/US dollar exchange rate, the interest rate differential between Korea and the United States, and the Korean industrial production index. The first two endogenous variables are included to estimate the impulse responses of capital inflows to capital outflow liberalization, and the last three are those most frequently employed in the literature as capital inflow pull factors. Overseas stock investment and banks' foreign borrowings are obtained from the Balance of Payments (BOP) Statistics and measured as percentages of GDP. The monthly GDP data are calculated by extrapolation from the quarterly data. The Korean Won/US dollar exchange rate is the log of the bilateral nominal exchange rate of the Won against the dollar. The interest rate differential is calculated from the difference between the 90-day Korean CD rate and the ninety-day US Treasury bill rate. The industrial production index is expressed in log levels.

In order to control for global economic conditions, three exogenous variables are added to the VAR model: the US industrial production index, the M2 supply, and the VIX index. To control for banks' foreign borrowings induced by Korean shipbuilders' forward hedging transactions, we also add the total value of orders received by Korean shipbuilders as an exogenous variable. The US industrial production index and M2 supply are expressed in log levels. The VIX index, defined as the implied volatility of at-the-money options on the S&P 500, is expressed in log levels and represents market participants' risk appetite. The total value of orders received by Korean shipbuilders is expressed as a percentage of GDP.

Empirical Methodology

According to the augmented Dickey–Fuller test, all variables with the exception of capital flows have unit roots. We thus use first differenced data in the VAR estimation. Considering the complex causalities and interaction effects among the five model variables, it is not easy to determine their proper ordering. Therefore, following the proposal of Pesaran and Shin (1998), we use the generalized impulse response function, which is unaffected by variable ordering. We check the sensitivity of the model by applying Cholesky decomposition and changing the order of the variables, but the results tend to not be sensitive to these changes.

Notes

The views expressed herein are those of the authors and do not necessarily reflect the official views of the Bank of Korea.

1. For more details on the trilemma, see Obstfeld et al. (2005) and Aizenman et al. (2008).

2. The IMF also urged aggressive financial market opening in Korea as a condition of its bailout program in 1997. Chopra et al. (2001) elaborate on Korea's restructuring process after the 1997 Asian crisis.

3. Fiscal policy can also be used complementarily to control aggregate demand pressure.

4. For details, refer to Ostry et al. (2010).

5. For more detailed explanation, refer to IMF(2010).

6. For analytical purposes, capital outflows here are reported as percentages of GDP rather than absolute figures.

7. The swap rate is defined as (forward rate – spot rate)/spot rate. Massive sales of forward exchange lower the forward rate, and the swap rate declines as a result.

8. The Korean government issues these bonds in the international financial markets to finance its Foreign Exchange Stabilization Fund, used for smoothing operations in the foreign exchange market.

9. The signs of financial sector deterioration cited included the rise in short-term foreign debt, the high loan-to-deposit ratio, and the increases in maturity and currency mismatches, all mainly caused by banks' short-term borrowings explained in section 7.3.1. Refer to Park (2009).

10. As of November 2011 the ceiling on the FX derivatives positions of domestic banks is set at less than 40 percent of their capital in the previous month. For foreign bank branches, it is less than 200 percent.

11. The total amount of the swap agreement with Japan was increased to US$70 billion equivalent, and that with China to 360 billion Yuan/64 trillion Won.

12. Banks' long-term borrowings, banks' short-term borrowings, and capital and financial accounts are alternatively used for the analyses shown in figures 7.10 to 7.12.

References

Aizenman, Joshua, Menzie D. Chinn, and Hiro Ito. 2008. Assessing the emerging global financial architecture: Measuring the trilemma's configurations over time. Working paper 14533. NBER, Cambridge, MA.

Chopra, Ajai, Kenneth Kang, Meral Karasulu, Hong Liang, Henry Ma, and Anthony Richards. 2001. From crisis to recovery in Korea: Strategy, achievements, and lessons. Working paper 154. IMF, Washington, DC.

International Monetary Fund. 2010. Global liquidity expansion: Effects on "receiving" economies and policy response options. In *Global Financial Stability Report (April)*. Washington, DC: IMF, 119–51.

Obstfeld, Maurice, Jay C. Shambaugh, and Alan M. Taylor. 2005. The trilemma in history: Tradeoffs among exchange rates, monetary policies, and capital mobility. *Review of Economics and Statistics* 87 (3): 423–38.

Ostry, Jonathan D., Atish R. Ghosh, Karl Habermeier, Marcos Chamon, Mahvash S. Qureshi, and Dennis B. S. Reinhardt. 2010. Capital inflows: The role of controls. Staff position note 04. IMF, Washington, DC.

Park, Yung-Chul. 2009. Global economic recession and East Asia: How has Korea managed the crisis and what has it learned? Working paper 409. Bank of Korea, Seoul.

Pesaran, M. Hashem, and Yongcheol Shin. 1998. Generalized impulse response analysis in linear multivariate models. *Economics Letters* 58 (1): 17–29.

Yang, Yang Hyeon, and Hye-Lim Lee. 2008. An analysis of the attractions of arbitrage transactions and of domestic bond investment by foreigners and Korean branches of foreign banks. *Bank of Korea Monthly Bulletin* (August): 55–89.

8 Policy Response to External Shocks: Lessons from the Crisis

Carlos Capistrán, Gabriel Cuadra, and Manuel Ramos-Francia

8.1 Introduction

The development of globalization in the last two decades has tightened financial and commercial linkages among economies. A consequence of this development has been a large increase in private financial flows across countries. Already a number of studies have documented that cross-border financial claims and direct foreign investment have experienced a significant growth (Kose et al. 2006), and according to the IMF, the amount of net private capital flowing to emerging economies increased from 90 billion US dollars in 2002 to 600 billion in 2007 (IMF 2010).

In general, capital inflows to emerging market economies have yielded several benefits for the recipient economies (Bosworth and Collins 1999). Among the most important, they allow economies with insufficient savings to have access to external resources to finance investment and promote growth. However, large surges of capital flows also pose significant challenges to the recipient countries. Apart from the concerns about excessive appreciation and unsustainable credit expansions, there is a risk of a sudden reversal in capital flows, with negative consequences for both financial stability and economic activity.

Emerging economies have often been subject to sharp reversals in capital flows, which sometimes reflect global factors such as sudden shifts in market sentiment among international investors, and sometimes domestic factors such as weak economic fundamentals in the recipient economies. Empirical evidence has effectively shown that such reversals, known as "sudden stops" in the economic literature, have had an adverse impact on domestic economies (Calvo 1998). In particular, such reversals in foreign financing force sharp contractions of domestic expenditure and production, real exchange rate depreciations, and reductions in both asset prices and credit to the private sector (Arellano and Mendoza 2002).

During the recent international financial crisis, the sudden increase in risk aversion among market participants following the events of September 2008, along with the deleveraging process in developed economies, led to a period of less access to international financial markets for emerging economies. This reversion in financial flows, coupled with a reduced demand for these economies' exports, negatively affected economic activity in emerging markets. From mid-2009 onward, after the sharp contraction of financial flows in late 2008 and early 2009, significantly loose liquidity conditions in the global economy, and better economic perspectives in emerging markets, contributed to a new episode of massive capital flows to these economies. This surge has raised concerns in the recipient economies. In particular, there are worries that these capital inflows could suddenly reverse. This could take place when the advanced economies start to withdraw monetary stimulus measures, or when a new episode of financial stress raises the level of uncertainty and risk aversion and therefore induces capital to move to safer places, suddenly affecting capital inflows to emerging economies. Indeed, since the beginning of August 2011, the sovereign debt crisis in Europe has led to a period of considerable stress in international financial markets. As a result there has been some reversal of capital flows in emerging markets. In this context, although a scenario of a sudden stop has not yet materialized, the probability of it happening has significantly increased.

In this setting an important issue for emerging economies' policy makers is how to respond to a sudden halt of external financing and its negative consequences for the domestic economy—in particular, the circumstances under which the authorities would be able to implement expansionary policies, such as loosening monetary policy and fiscal stimulus packages, to attenuate the adverse impact on economic activity. Using data for 104 countries for the period 1960 to 2003, Kaminsky et al. 2004 find evidence that in emerging and developing economies, episodes of capital outflows are associated with contractionary macroeconomic policies, and episodes of capital inflows with expansionary macroeconomic policies. These authors document that both monetary and fiscal policies tend to be procyclical in these economies, especially in times of financial stress, which exacerbate the output contraction. In the case of monetary policy, during a period of capital outflows it was a common practice among central banks in emerging economies to raise the interest rate in order to defend a fixed exchange rate (Kaminsky et al. 2004). As for procyclicality of fiscal policy, in an environment of weak institutions, Lane and Tornell (1999) and Frankel (2011) document that governments are usually not able to resist the political pressures to increase public spending, sometimes disproportionately, during economic expansions. In turn, when foreign financing disappears, they are typically forced to follow contractionary fiscal policies. These procyclical macroeconomic policies tend to exacerbate output volatility instead of moderating it (Frankel 2011).

However, during the recent financial crisis a number of emerging economies, especially those that have adopted sound monetary and fiscal policies in the years prior to the crisis, were able to implement countercyclical macroeconomic policies. Thus the experience of these economies during the recent crisis suggests that economies with relatively strong fundamentals had more capacity to provide monetary stimulus and expansionary fiscal packages. In this context the crisis reinforced the idea that an economy that follows prudent macroeconomic policies in normal times tends to be in a relatively better position to cope with the adverse consequences of a financial crisis (Fischer 2011). More generally, improved institutional frameworks built in times of economic growth may be the key to reducing the procyclicality of macroeconomic policies, and increasing the scope of countercyclical policies in times of economic distress.

In this chapter, to address these issues, we develop a small-scale macroeconomic model of the New Keynesian type that incorporates the possibility of a sudden reversal in capital flows as well as a fiscal policy rule. This model's simple analytical framework provides some insights as to the factors that would increase policy makers' flexibility in responding to adverse external shocks, such as a sudden stop in foreign financing. The numerical exercises illustrate how the margin of maneuver or to cope with negative shocks depends critically on the extent of credibility that the monetary and fiscal authorities enjoy, as well as on the condition of the economy when the shock hits.

In the case of monetary policy, a credible central bank's commitment to maintaining price stability over time gives it considerable flexibility to use monetary policy to ameliorate negative impacts on output. Nevertheless, if there is no commitment by the monetary authority or it lacks the power to keep inflation low and stable, then concerns about inflation, or even rising inflation expectations, could exacerbate the inflation rate. Under these circumstances the monetary policy could be constrained to counteract adverse external shocks. However, if the central bank's commitment is credible, and if this is reflected in a smaller pass-through from a nominal depreciation to the inflation rate, such as Taylor (2000) has argued, then the monetary authority may be able to implement large policy cuts without significant concern about a further deterioration in the inflation outlook.

As for fiscal policy, it is also critical to follow sound policies all of the time. That is, weak fiscal accounts and high public debt levels can significantly constrain the policy makers' capacity to implement fiscal stimulus packages. Under these circumstances an expansionary fiscal policy could raise fears about the long-term sustainability of public finances, and so have an additional negative impact on financial conditions. What is needed is an institutional framework that would encourage authorities to save the excess revenues during economic expansions to use them during economic downturns. For instance, higher transparency in fiscal management would make those authorities in charge of fiscal policy more accountable and could reduce the influence of interest groups on the allocation of public sector resources. It will also keep in check the procyclicality inclinations of fiscal policy makers (i.e., to increase public spending) and induce them to adopt prudent countercyclical policies (Cuadra and Sapriza 2011; Cuadra et al. 2010). A structural balance fiscal rule would be an example of such a fiscal policy framework that would allow authorities to implement a countercyclical policy without raising alarm about the sustainability of fiscal accounts.

Apart from the above-mentioned issues, another factor that influences whether an economic stimulus is plausible pertains to the conditions prevailing in the domestic economy at the time a sudden reversal of foreign financial flows takes place. For instance, an initial inflation rate above the central bank's target can severely limit the monetary authority's margin of maneuver so as to prevent a drop in output due to an abrupt loss of access to international financial markets. Clearly, under economic conditions characterized by the inflation rate staying in line with a country's inflation target, central banks have the flexibility to respond more aggressively, or at least to adopt a less restrictive monetary policy.

This chapter is organized as follows. Section 8.2 briefly describes the experience of emerging economies during the recent financial crisis. Section 8.3 presents a small-scale model with an external risk premium and a fiscal policy rule. Section 8.4 analyzes a number of exercises using this model and provides some suggestions as to the optimal policy response to external shocks. Section 8.5 presents some final remarks.

8.2 The Financial Crisis

Emerging market economies entered the recent international financial crisis with different initial conditions (Ghosh et al. 2009). Mainly less affected were a number of economies in Asia and in Latin America that a decade before the crisis had substantially improved their macroeconomic policy frameworks with sound fiscal and monetary policies, flexible exchange rate regimes, sustainable external accounts and, in many cases, large holdings of international reserves (IDB 2008). In some of these economies favorable terms of trade during that period considerably help strengthen their economic fundamentals.

As for macroeconomic policies, prudent fiscal policy management in these emerging economies helped eliminate the large and persistent budget deficits that had plagued them in the past. Fiscal prudence also helped reduce their public debt to GDP ratios. Moreover, since the decade of the 1990s, several of these emerging economies abandoned their fixed exchange rate regimes, replacing them with monetary policy frameworks aimed at achieving price stability. In some instances, an inflation-targeting regime was introduced. The monetary policy frameworks that were adopted, along with fiscal policy discipline, helped tame inflation and its volatility, as well as helped anchor inflation expectations.[1]

Given these conditions, it can be argued that when the global financial crisis materialized in 2007, these economies were in a relatively better position to deal with adverse external shocks than they were during previous financial crises and recessions. Unfortunately, progress in improving macroeconomic policy frameworks and, more generally, economic fundamentals, was not a generalized phenomenon. Indeed, prior to the crisis, some emerging economies in Eastern Europe experienced unsustainable private credit booms fueled by external financing that led to both large debt levels and foreign currency liabilities on their domestic balance sheets, making them highly vulnerable to capital outflows (Ghosh et al. 2009).

Although practically all emerging market economies faced tighter conditions to access external financing, the most affected were those with the worst economic fundamentals. As figures 8.1 and 8.2 in the appendix illustrate, those economies with higher inflation rates and larger current account deficits before the crisis tended to experience a greater widening in sovereign risk indicators following the sharp increase in uncertainty in mid-September 2008.

Hence, although the crisis was triggered by external factors, the severity of the shocks on each economy seems to have been related also, to some extent, to domestic elements. With the sharp rise in risk aversion among international investors, the larger the current account deficit was, the more likely the external accounts would be perceived as unsustainable, leading to a more severe adverse effect. Similarly, the higher the domestic inflation was, the more likely the market participants would lose confidence in the value of the domestic currency, with the negative impact intensified as a result.

It seems that market participants discriminated among the emerging economies and penalized more those that were in worse shape at the time. This evidence is consistent with the findings of Rangel and Ramos-Francia (2011) and Llaudes et al. (2010). Controlling for a number of factors, these authors find that those economies considered less vulnerable in 2007 suffered a less dramatic increase in sovereign spreads than economies regarded as more vulnerable. For instance, inflation-targeting economies with a lower cumulative inflation in the years before the crisis tended to experience a smaller increase in spreads.

It is also apparent that those economies that had created a sound macroeconomic framework based on fiscal and monetary discipline were most able to respond aggressively to the external shocks. In particular, it seems that policy makers in economies with weak fundamentals were less able to provide either expansionary fiscal packages or monetary stimulus measures. As shown in figures 8.3 and 8.4 in the appendix, monetary policy in those emerging economies with low inflation rates and small current account deficits could respond more positively. In particular, they implemented larger policy cuts during the two quarters after the events of September 2008. As for fiscal policy, figures 8.5 and 8.6 in the appendix illustrate that economies with stronger fiscal positions and lower public debt levels appeared able to provide larger fiscal stimulus packages.

From these facts it seems clear that initial conditions are an important factor in explaining why some economies were relatively less affected by the crisis, were able to implement countercyclical policies, or both. More generally, it could be argued that better macroeconomic policy frameworks in some economies increased the credibility of the monetary and fiscal authorities, so as the crisis erupted, their policy makers had more flexibility to stimulate their economies. In the next sections we proceed to illustrate these experiences using a small-scale macroeconomic model.

8.3   The Model

The small-scale New Keynesian model we employ corresponds to a type of model termed "hybrid" because it includes both forward- and backward-looking elements; the model is similar to the one used by Sidaoui and Ramos-Francia (2008).[2] However, in our model we incorporate the possibility of a sudden reversal in capital flows that can alter the prevailing fiscal policy.

As we mentioned previously, sudden stop episodes trigger sharp contractions in domestic absorption and output, leading to a depreciation of the real exchange rate. Sudden stop episodes can be driven by domestic factors such as weak fundamentals besides global factors such as an increase in risk aversion among international investors. Our model assumes that the trigger is a deterioration in market participants' sentiment, as reflected in a sharp increase in the risk premium. That is, the reversal in capital flows is incorporated as a shock to the risk premium, and is consequently an exogenous event.[3]

The model consists of five behavioral equations and one identity: a Phillips curve for inflation (equation 8.1), an IS equation for the output gap (equation 8.2), an uncovered interest rate parity condition for the nominal exchange rate (equation 8.3), a Taylor-type rule for the nominal interest rate (equation 8.4), a structural balance fiscal rule (equation 8.5), and an identity for the real exchange rate (equation 8.6). The dynamics in the model are driven by a risk premium shock that follows an AR(1) process (equation 8.7). In this gap model we use lowercase letters to indicate percentage deviations from the steady state values.

$$\pi_t = a_1 \pi_{t-1} + a_2 E_t \left(\pi_{t+1} \right) + a_3 x_t + a_4 \left(e_t - e_{t-1} \right), \tag{8.1}$$

$$x_t = b_1 x_{t-1} + b_2 E_t \left(x_{t+1} \right) - b_3 \left[i_t - E_t \left(\pi_{t+1} \right) \right] + b_4 q_t - b_5 \theta_t - b_6 f_t, \tag{8.2}$$

$$e_t = E_t \left(e_{t+1} \right) + i^* + \theta_t - i_t, \tag{8.3}$$

$$i_t = c_1 i_{t-1} + c_2 \pi_t + c_3 x_t, \tag{8.4}$$

$$f_t = \tau x_t, \tag{8.5}$$

$$q_t \equiv q_{t-1} + \left(e_t - e_{t-1} \right) - \pi_t + \pi^*, \tag{8.6}$$

$$\theta_t = \rho \theta_{t-1} + \varepsilon_t, \tag{8.7}$$

where π is the inflation rate, π^* is the external inflation rate, x is the output gap, e is the (log) nominal exchange rate, q is the (log) real exchange rate, i is the nominal interest rate, i^* is the external nominal interest rate, θ is the risk premium, f is the fiscal balance, and ε is iid with a normal standard distribution. Notice that in the model, trend inflation is assumed to be constant and equal to zero.

In the model the risk premium shock affects the economy through the following channels:

1. An increase in the risk premium triggers a nominal exchange rate depreciation (equation 8.3). In turn, the higher nominal exchange rate raises the inflation rate (equation 8.1). The pass-through from the nominal exchange rate to inflation depends on the value of a_4, which is assumed to be positive and lower than one.

2. Since there is not a complete pass-through from the nominal exchange rate to inflation, there is a depreciation in real terms (equation 8.6). In turn, the real exchange depreciation enlarges the output gap (equation 8.2). This positive effect can be rationalized by assuming that the change in relative prices associated with the real depreciation boosts net exports, which has a favorable impact on economic activity. But the increase in output generates inflationary pressures (equation 8.1).

3. There is a direct negative effect of the risk premium shock on the output gap (equation 8.2). Given the sudden increase in the cost of foreign financing, it can be argued that domestic agents have to adjust their spending patterns, which negatively affects output. This fact is well documented by a number of studies as a negative correlation between economic activity and sovereign risk indicators (e.g., Neumeyer and Perri 2005; Uribe and Yue 2006). By depressing economic activity, the risk premium shock exerts downward pressure on inflation.

In principle, depending on which of the effects above dominates, an increase in the risk premium can lead to different outcomes, namely inflation and a negative output gap, deflation and a negative output gap, or even inflation and a positive output gap.

As for the fiscal policy, the government follows a structural balance fiscal rule. Following Medina and Soto (2007), we define the structural balance SFB as the fiscal balance minus the cyclical fiscal income. The latter is the difference between the observed fiscal revenues and those revenues corresponding to the economy being at its potential level.[4]

$$SFB = f - \tilde{T},$$

$$\tilde{T} = \tau\left(X - X^{ss}\right),$$

where the uppercase letters X and X^{ss} represent the levels of current output and potential output, respectively. By this rule, fiscal authorities run a balanced structural budget over the business cycle. So there is a surplus (deficit) in the fiscal accounts whenever the output gap is positive (negative):

$$SFB = 0,$$

$$f = \tau(X - X^{ss}).$$

Given the structural balance fiscal rule, a negative (positive) output gap leads to a deficit (surplus) in the fiscal accounts. In turn, a fiscal deficit, which is associated with an expansionary fiscal policy, has a positive impact on economic activity (equation 8.2).[5] It can be argued that a parameterization with the fiscal balance, f, equal to zero can be interpreted as an economy where authorities keep a balanced budget over the business cycle, which would correspond to a balanced fiscal budget rule (or, equivalently in this model, b_6 equal to zero).

The values of the parameters we used in the numerical exercises fulfill the following criteria: First, the parameter values are similar to those used in the economics literature (Galí 2008; Sidaoui and Ramos-Francia 2008); that is, they are in line with empirical studies and make economic sense. Second, the parameters of the Phillips curve and the IS equation were chosen such that an increase in the risk premium would trigger a nominal exchange rate depreciation, an increase in inflation, and a negative output gap. Third, they satisfy the Blanchard–Khan conditions when the numerical exercises imply that the value of a parameter needs modifying. Finally, it is worth mentioning that our objective was to perform numerical exercises to gain insights as to the factors that would increase the policy makers' margin of maneuver in response to shocks rather than to calibrate a model matched to a specific economy. Table 8.1 in the appendix shows the parameter values used in this chapter.

Figures 8.7, 8.8, 8.9, 8.10, 8.11, and 8.12 in the appendix depict the dynamics of the model. The initial situation is an economy at its steady state, with an output gap equal to zero and inflation equal to the central bank's objective (zero in this model). As a sudden increase in the risk premium hits the economy, a nominal depreciation results, which tends to move inflation above the target. Simultaneously an incomplete pass-through from the nominal exchange rate to inflation leads to a depreciation in real terms.

Although it is assumed that real exchange rate depreciation has a favorable effect on economic activity, the negative direct effect of the risk premium dominates the positive effect through the real exchange rate. So there is a contraction in output. The central bank responds by loosening monetary conditions. However, given the initial hike in inflation, the initial policy rate cut is moderate. Later, the severe output contraction exerts downward pressures on inflation. This way the drop in inflation allows the monetary authority to implement a further reduction in the policy rate. Both inflation and the output gap overshoot their initial values, and finally all variables tend to converge to the steady state.

8.4   Policy Response to Sudden Reversals in Capital Inflows

In this section we perform a number of numerical exercises to illustrate how credible monetary and fiscal policy frameworks, as well as favorable initial conditions, can facilitate the adoption of countercyclical policies.

8.4.1   Credible Monetary Policy

We start with a baseline model to illustrate how a more credible central bank enjoys more flexibility to respond to the adverse effects related to an episode of a sudden reversal in capital flows, and the corresponding increase in risk premium. The case of a monetary authority with high credibility may be characterized by an economy with a lower pass-through from the nominal exchange rate to inflation than in the baseline scenario.

In open economies the exchange rate may affect inflation through different channels. First, economic agents consume not only domestically produced goods and services but also imported goods. To the extent that the latter are included in the consumer price index, there will be a direct effect of the exchange rate to the inflation rate. Second, in many cases imported intermediate goods are used to produce domestic goods. Thus fluctuations in the nominal exchange rate can affect the inflation rate through changes in the price of these intermediate goods. These can be interpreted as the first round effects of movements in the exchange rate on inflation.

However, apart from the above-mentioned effects, if the central bank's commitment to price stability is not credible and thus inflation expectations are not well anchored, a nominal depreciation may also influence domestic prices and thus inflation through second round effects. That is, if economic agents do not trust the monetary authority's commitment to maintain an inflation rate in line with price stability (or with its target, in case it has one), then given the rise in prices due to first round effects, they may revise their inflation expectations upward, leading to a widespread rise in prices and, consequently, to higher inflation levels.

In this context it can be argued that the higher the central bank's credibility is, the lower the persistence of inflation and the lower the pass-through (Taylor 2000). In fact the decrease in the pass-through in developed economies in the last two decades, and more recently in some emerging economies, has been attributed by some authors to the adoption of more stable and predictable monetary policies worldwide (Mishkin 2008).

In this section we regard an economy without pass-through as an economy with a fully credible monetary authority. Figures 8.13, 8.14, 8.15, and 8.16 in the appendix illustrate the impact of the risk premium shock on inflation, output gap, and real exchange rate, as well as the monetary policy response, for both the baseline model and the model without pass-through. In the latter, the depreciation of the nominal exchange rate does not lead to an inflation rebound. Rather, inflation falls due to the contractionary effect of the adverse risk premium shock. As for the output gap, the initial drop in economic activity is less severe in the model without pass-through. In particular, given the nominal depreciation, the lower inflation leads to a larger depreciation in real terms, which tends to attenuate the fall in the output gap.

Even though the output contraction is less acute, an inflation rate below the target allows the monetary authority to respond more aggressively with a larger policy rate cut. The central bank starts to increase the policy rate as inflation tends to return to its target and the output gap begins to close. In contrast to the baseline scenario, the dynamics of inflation and the output gap do not imply an important overshooting of these variables. That is, economic activity exhibits a more stable path, which may be associated with a smaller welfare loss due to the adverse external shock.

These results suggest that a central bank that is credibly committed to provide an environment of low and stable inflation over time has more capacity of maneuver in its response to adverse external shocks. In particular, it seems to be able to implement larger policy rate cuts than would otherwise be possible without significantly raising inflationary concerns. Furthermore, a credible monetary policy framework should seek to eliminate the trade-off monetary authorities face when assessing the appropriate policy response to an external shock that tends to depreciate the nominal exchange rate. On the one hand, tightening monetary conditions would contain inflationary pressures, but it may intensify the fall in output. On the other hand, a policy cut can contribute to boost economic activity, but it may lead to a higher inflation rate.

In this setting, it can be argued of course that the higher credibility of monetary authorities working at maintaining inflation in line with their price stability objectives not only contributes to successful monetary policy in times of economic growth and financial stability but also allows the central bank to respond aggressively in times of crisis (Orphanides 2010). Yet it is clear that central banks' credibility cannot be taken for granted. Credibility must be safeguarded. In particular, to establish a good reputation there is no better way than to see central banks delivering price stability over time.

Hence a lesson from the crisis is that institutional arrangements whereby central banks and monetary policy focus on price stability have been successful in anchoring inflation expectations and in preserving an environment of low and stable inflation.[6] Otherwise, institutions may lose credibility, even that gained by earlier favorable track records.

8.4.2 Credible Fiscal Policy

The adoption of fiscal stimulus packages to lessen the adverse impact of external shocks on domestic economies has been an important issue in the policy debate, especially during the recent international financial crisis (Eyzaguirre et al. 2009). In particular, it can be argued that a sudden reversal in capital flows may lead to a sharp adjustment in domestic expenditure, and consequently to a severe economic recession. Under these circumstances an expansionary fiscal policy can partially offset the contraction in private expenditures, and thus ameliorate the drop in economic activity.

Yet a relevant question is how to finance a fiscal stimulus package precisely at a time when external borrowing is more expensive and consequently there is a reduced access to international financial markets. That is, authorities may be significantly constrained by limited access to financing, and often, given a weak fiscal position and high public debt in an economy, a fiscal stimulus may not be feasible at all.

Furthermore the mere intention to run an expansionary fiscal policy may have an adverse effect on financial conditions and interest rates. For instance, the recent crisis has made clear that increases in fiscal deficits and public debt to GDP ratios associated with the adoption of fiscal stimulus packages can raise concerns about the long-run sustainability of fiscal policy, leading to even larger increases in sovereign risk. This concern is particularly relevant since widening sovereign spreads could reduce the effectiveness of fiscal policy to restart economic activity and preclude the adoption of additional fiscal measures to stabilize the economy.

These considerations are relevant for a number of emerging economies that experienced episodes of fiscal dominance in the past and do not have a long history of sound fiscal policies. Moreover often in these economies temporary surges in government revenues, such as oil windfalls, have been accompanied by sharp increases in public spending and external borrowing.[7] Under these circumstances the fiscal policy framework must allow authorities to save the extraordinary resources associated with surges in fiscal revenues during economic expansions and to use them to finance expansionary policies during recessions.

A possibility is a structural balance fiscal rule. As mentioned, the structural balance removes the cyclical component of fiscal revenues. Thus a rule aimed at maintaining a balanced structural budget over the business cycle would operate as an automatic stabilizer. For instance, whenever fiscal revenues are above the level of fiscal income corresponding to potential output, the government would run a fiscal surplus and accumulate assets. In turn, during economic contractions when fiscal revenues are below the level consistent with the economy operating at its potential, the fiscal authority will run a deficit. In this way governments could run countercyclical fiscal policies without raising concern about the sustainability of fiscal accounts.

Figure 8.17, 8.18, 8.19, and 8.20 in the appendix illustrate the dynamics of the policy rate, the output gap, inflation, and the real exchange rate when the economy is hit by a risk premium shock, for both the model with a structural balance fiscal rule, and the baseline model, which can be interpreted as a model with a balanced fiscal budget all the time. Since a structural balance fiscal rule implies a fiscal deficit whenever the output gap is negative, the fiscal authority would automatically provide a fiscal stimulus as economic activity deteriorates due to an adverse shock. The output contraction that results is then less severe.

More interesting, instead of immediately relaxing monetary conditions, the central bank would temporarily increase the policy rate in order to contain the inflationary pressures related to the depreciation of the nominal exchange rate. Later, as inflation subsides, the central bank would relax its monetary policy stance, supporting the fiscal authority in providing economic stimulus. Finally, the output gap, inflation, and the policy rate would return to their initial levels.

These results suggest that when an adverse shock, such as a sudden increase in risk premium, leads to both a negative output gap and an inflation rate above the target, the monetary authority would concentrate on the inflation problem, while the fiscal authority implements a countercyclical policy aimed at attenuating the adverse impact on output. Furthermore, with inflation no longer a concern, monetary policy would be used to complement the economic stimulus provided by the fiscal authority. That is, both authorities would move in the same direction to restart economic activity. In the baseline case, in contrast, monetary policy is less expansionary, and compensated by a fiscal expansion. We find the policy mix in the model with a structural fiscal balance to be associated with a lower volatility in economic activity. Using two instruments in a coordinated way, we find that the monetary policy rate and the fiscal budget would both contribute to the stabilization of the economy.

8.4.3　Initial Conditions

In our previous numerical exercises we assumed that the economy was at steady state when the increase in the risk premium occurred. That is, inflation was at the central bank's target and the output gap was zero. However, it should be noted that an adverse external shock, such as a sudden and sharp reversal in financial inflows triggered by global factors, can take place independently of the phase of the business cycle the domestic economy is going through. For instance, an economy can be hit by an external shock at a time when the inflation rate is either above or below the monetary authority's target for inflation. Clearly, the policy response would be different in each of these two situations. Thus the conditions prevailing in the economy when the sudden stop occurs also affect the scope of the economic stimulus.

Here we attempt to analyze how initial conditions can influence central banks' ability to respond to an episode of a sudden contraction in foreign financing. Figures 8.21, 8.22, 8.23, and 8.24 in the appendix depict how the economy evolves in two cases: when the initial inflation rate is above the central bank's target, and when it is equal to the target. The latter corresponds to the baseline model.

When the economy has a high initial inflation and is hit by an increase in the risk premium, the central bank will not be able to relax monetary conditions immediately, even as the negative shock leads to a negative output gap. Furthermore the high inflation would cause the central bank to increase the policy rate. Later, as inflation falls due to the output contraction and the monetary policy tightening, the central bank can implement policy rate cuts to support economic activity. From that moment on, the dynamics in both cases become similar.

8.5 Final Remarks

Volatile capital flows are endemic in the global economy. In the recent past emerging market economies have been subjected to sudden stops in capital flows, with negative consequences for their economic activities and financial stability. In particular, these economies have experienced reversals in financial flows that are associated with real exchange depreciation, adjustments in domestic expenditures, lowered output, falls in asset prices, and credit contractions. In light of the recent large capital flows going to emerging economies and the corresponding risk of an abrupt reversal in these flows, which has become more acute as a result of the European sovereign debt and banking crisis, a relevant issue for emerging economies' policy makers is how to cope with the negative impact of sudden stop episodes.

The recent experience of emerging markets economies during the global financial crisis suggests that those economies with better fundamentals are relatively less affected by adverse external shocks and are able to provide more monetary and fiscal stimulus. This chapter presents a small-scale macroeconomic model in order to rationalize these issues. The model incorporates the possibility of a sudden reversal in capital flows and a fiscal policy rule, and it provides a simple analytical framework to study the policy response to adverse external shocks such as sudden stops in capital flows. With this model we were able to analyze the role of credible monetary and fiscal policy frameworks in increasing policy makers' freedom to provide economic stimulus packages during episodes of financial crises.

On the one hand, a higher degree of central bank credibility associated with a lower pass-through from the nominal exchange rate to inflation would allow monetary authorities to implement larger policy rate cuts in bad times. On the other hand, a fiscal policy framework that induces authorities to save the extraordinary resources related to economic "booms" and to use them in bad times would allow policy makers to run a countercyclical fiscal policy. The increased margin of maneuver to provide monetary stimulus measures and expansionary fiscal packages leads to a more favorable evolution of economic variables. For instance, there is a less severe economic contraction, and also lower output gap volatility.

From these considerations one lesson from the recent crisis is that strong macroeconomic policy frameworks help maintain a stable macroeconomic environment in times of economic growth and also help authorities provide more stimulus in times of financial crisis. With this analysis we have attempted to take a step toward understanding the determinants of policy makers' capacities to cope with negative foreign shocks

Our results also suggest some factors behind the increasing margin of maneuver that policy makers might have had to respond to external shocks, such as that which some economies enjoyed through the recent crisis. We intend to complement our study with additional research on these issues. In particular, more sophisticated models would enable a more detailed analysis to be made on the propagation of external shocks and the policy responses to them. A richer model would also allow the analysis of other policy instruments such as macroprudential measures.

Appendix

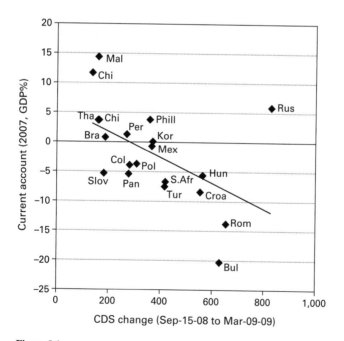

Figure 8.1
Current account versus CDS change. The countries included are Brazil, Chile, Colombia, Mexico, Panama, Peru, Bulgaria, Hungary, Poland, Russia, Turkey, Croatia, Romania, Slovakia, China, Korea, Malaysia, Philippines, Thailand, and South Africa.
Sources: IMF; Bloomberg

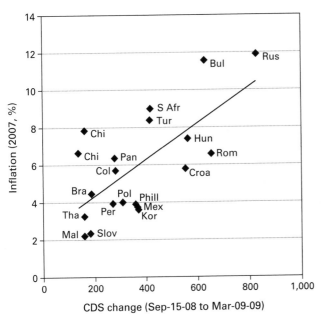

Figure 8.2
Inflation versus CDS change. The countries included are Brazil, Chile, Colombia, Mexico, Panama, Peru, Bulgaria, Hungary, Poland, Russia, Turkey, Croatia, Romania, Slovakia, China, Korea, Malaysia, Philippines, Thailand, and South Africa.
Sources: IMF; Bloomberg

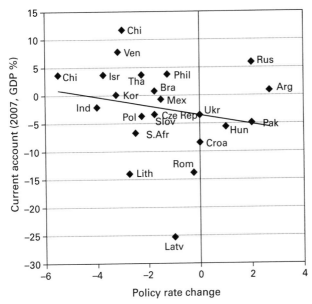

Figure 8.3
Current account versus policy rate change. The countries included are Argentina, Brazil, Chile, Mexico, Venezuela, Czech Republic, Hungary, Poland, Russia, Ukraine, Latvia, Lithuania, Croatia, Romania, Slovenia, China, India, Kores, Pakistan, Philippines, Thailand, South Africa, and Israel.
Sources: IMF; Bloomberg

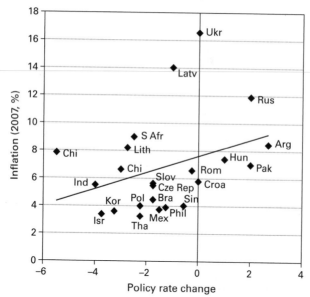

Figure 8.4
Inflation versus policy rate change. The countries included are Argentina, Brazil, Chile, Mexico, Czech Republic, Hungary, Poland, Russia, Ukraine, Latvia, Lithuania, Croatia, Romania, Slovenia, China, India, Korea, Pakistan, Philippines, Thailand, Singapore, South Africa, and Israel.
Sources: IMF; Bloomberg

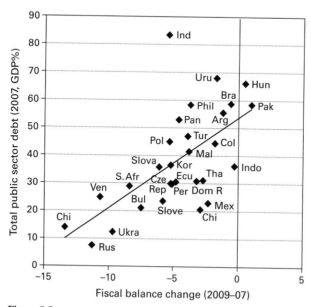

Figure 8.5
Public sector debt versus fiscal balance change. The countries included are Argentina, Brazil, Chile, Colombia, Dominican Republic, Ecuador, Mexico, Panama, Peru, Uruguay, Venezuela, Bulgarla, Czech Republic, Hungary, Poland, Russia, Ukraine, Turkey, Slovakia, Slovenia, China, India, Indonesia, Korea, Malaysia, Pakistan, Philippines, Thailand, and South Africa.
Sources: IMF; Bloomberg

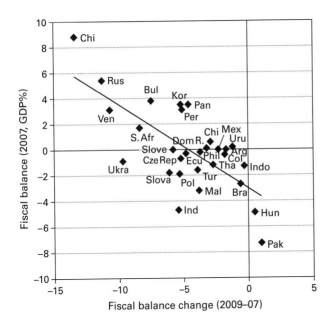

Figure 8.6
Fiscal balance versus fiscal balance change. The countries included are Argentina, Brazil, Chile, Colombia, Dominican Republic, Ecuador, Mexico, Panama, Peru, Uruguay, Venezuela, Bulgaria, Czech Republic, Hungary, Poland, Russia, Ukraine, Turkey, Slovakia, Slovenia, China, India, Indonesia, Korea, Malaysia, Pakistan, Philippines, Thailand, and South Africa.
Sources: IMF; JP Morgan Chase

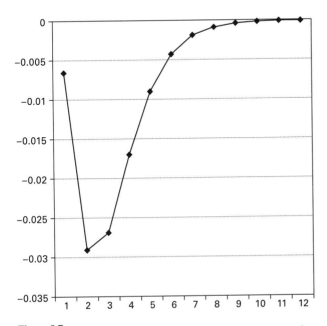

Figure 8.7
Policy rate

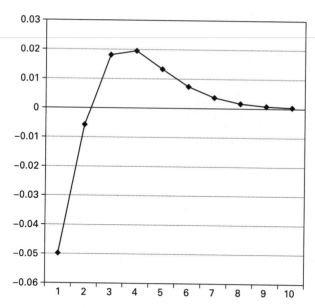

Figure 8.8
Output gap

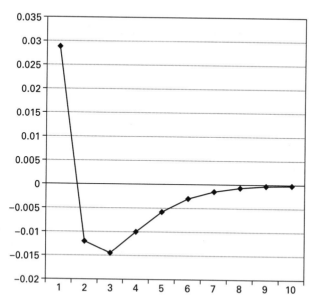

Figure 8.9
Inflation

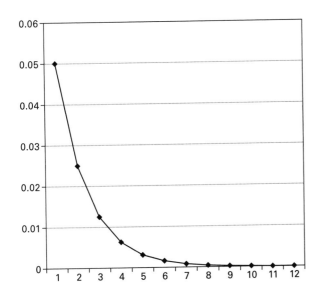

Figure 8.10
Risk premium

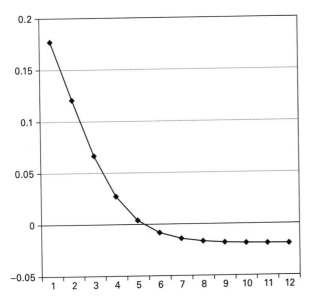

Figure 8.11
Nominal exchange rate

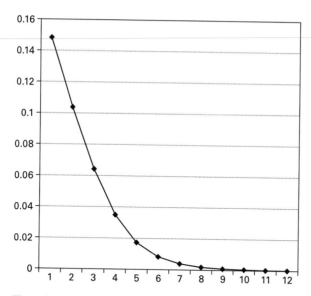

Figure 8.12
Real exchange rate

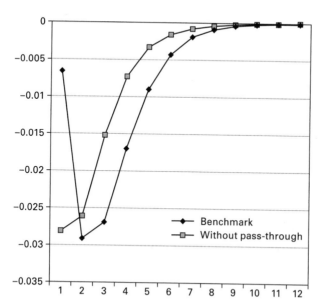

Figure 8.13
Policy rate

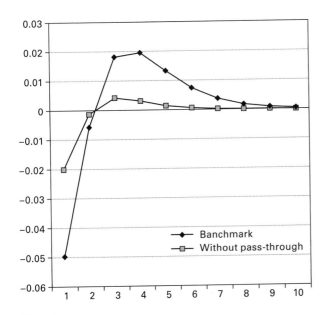

Figure 8.14
Output gap

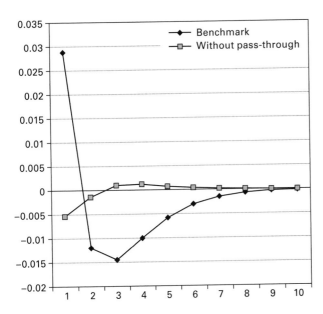

Figure 8.15
Inflation

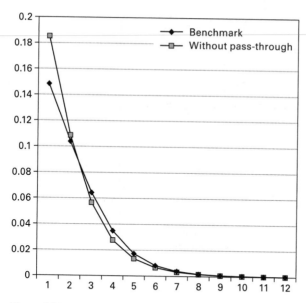

Figure 8.16
Real exchange rate

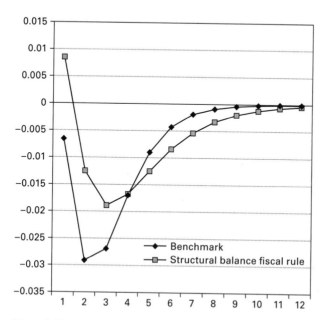

Figure 8.17
Policy rate

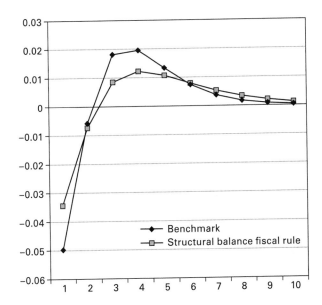

Figure 8.18
Output gap

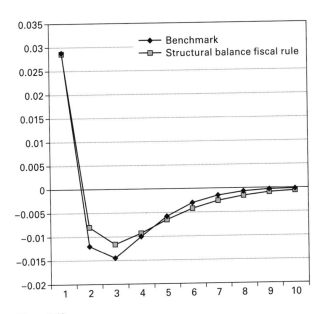

Figure 8.19
Inflation

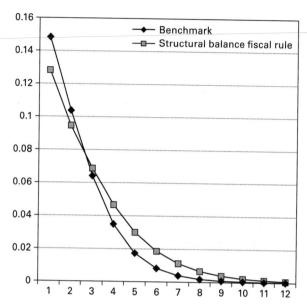

Figure 8.20
Real exchange rate

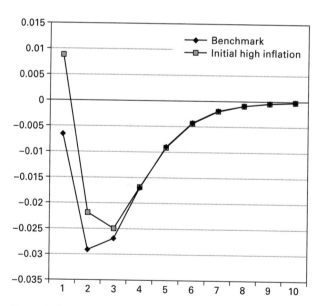

Figure 8.21
Policy rate

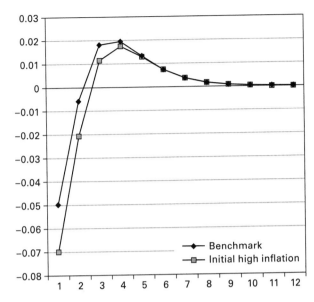

Figure 8.22
Output gap

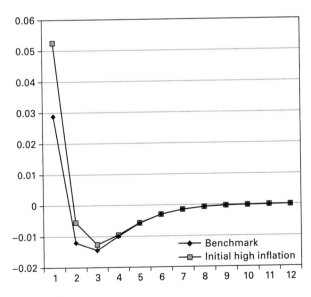

Figure 8.23
Inflation

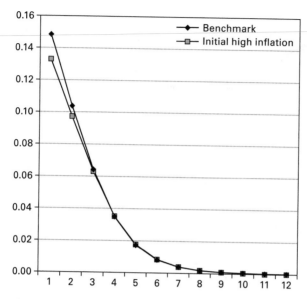

Figure 8.24
Real exchange rate

Table 8.1
Parameter values

Phillips curve		
a_1	0.25	Lag-inflation
a_2	0.25	Expected inflation
a_3	0.25	Output gap
a_4	0.25	Nominal depreciation
IS equation		
b_1	0.3	Lag output gap
b_2	0.6	Expected output gap
b_3	-0.04	Real interest rate
b_4	0.7	(Log) real exchange rate
b_5	-3	Risk premium
b_6	-2	Fiscal balance
Taylor rule		
c_1	0.8	Lag nominal interest rate
c_2	1.5	Inflation
c_3	1	Output gap
Fiscal rule		
τ	0.3	Tax rate

Note: According to the parameter values for the Phillips curve, either a higher lag-inflation or a higher expected inflation tend to increase the current inflation rate. In the same way, an increase in the output gap and a nominal depreciation are associated with a higher inflation rate. As for the parameter values for the IS equation, an increase in either lag output gap or expected output gap tends to increase current output gap. In turn, an increase in the real interest rate tends to decrease the output gap. A real exchange depreciation has a positive impact on the output gap, while an increase in the risk premium has a contractionary effect on output. Finally, increases in the fiscal surplus or decreases in the fiscal deficit are regarded as contractionary policies that tend to reduce the output gap. Regarding the Taylor rule, a higher lag nominal interest rate is associated with a higher current nominal rate. Finally, the monetary authority responds to an increase either in inflation or in the output gap by increasing the policy rate.

Notes

The chapter was presented at the Conference on "Lessons from the World Financial Crisis" held at the Bank of Israel in March 2011, at the Chief Economist' Workshop on "Monetary Policy, Macro-prudential Policy and Fiscal Policy: Interactions, Coordination and Policy Design" held at the CCBS Bank of England in May 2001, and at the Central Bank of the Republic of Turkey in November 2011. This chapter was prepared when Carlos Capistrán was working at Banco de México. The opinions in this chapter are those of the authors and do not necessarily reflect the points of view of Banco de México and Bank of America Merrill Lynch.

1. See Capistrán and Ramos-Francia (2009, 2010).

2. It is now customary to add lagged variables to New Keynesian models, usually to improve their fit to the data. "Hybrid" New Keynesian models can be found in Adolfson et al. (2008), Christiano et al. (2005), Del Negro et al. (2007), Galí and Gertler (1999), Galí et al. (2005), and Rudd and Whelan (2006), among others.

3. Similarly Gomez (2004) includes this type of shock in a gap model to analyze the "fear of floating" phenomenon under inflation targeting.

4. For simplicity, it is assumed that potential output coincides with the steady state level of output, and a fixed tax rate.

5. It is assumed that a fiscal policy framework based on this rule allows authorities to run a fiscal deficit in bad times without raising concerns about the long-run sustainability of fiscal accounts.

6. The severity of the recent financial crisis has brought about a debate on the suitability of central banks having a financial stability objective besides their price stability mandate. Effectively, central banks would need to consider developments in the financial sector when assessing monetary policy, and thus they may need to adopt such measures as lengthening the monetary policy horizon in order to be able to take into account adverse developments. However, this should not come at the cost of having a monetary authority less committed to price stability.

7. According to Lane and Tornell (1999), the lack of strong legal and political institutions in emerging economies led to a "voracity effect." That is, in good times a windfall in fiscal revenues intensifies the struggle for public resources among interest groups, leading to an excessive expansion in public expenditures and wasting extraordinary revenues.

References

Adolfson, Malin, Stefan Laseen, Jesper Lindé, and Mattias Villani. 2008. Evaluating an estimated New Keynesian small open economy model. *Journal of Economic Dynamics and Control* 32 (8): 2690–2721.

Arellano, Cristina, and Enrique Mendoza. 2002. Credit frictions and sudden stops in small open economies: An equilibrium business cycle framework for emerging market crises. Working paper 8880. NBER, Cambridge, MA.

IDB. 2008. All that glitters may not be gold: Assessing Latin America recent macroeconomic performance. Working paper. Inter-American Development Bank, Washington, DC.

Bosworth, Barry, and Susan Collins. 1999. Capital flows to developing economies: Implications for saving and investment. *Brookings Papers on Economic Activity* 30 (1): 143–80.

Calvo, Guillermo. 1998. Capital flows and capital-market crises: The simple economics of sudden stops. *Journal of Applied Econometrics* 1: 35–54.

Capistrán, Carlos, and Manuel Ramos-Francia. 2009. Inflation dynamics in Latin America. *Contemporary Economic Policy* 27 (3): 349–62.

Capistrán, Carlos, and Manuel Ramos-Francia. 2010. Does inflation targeting affect the dispersion of inflation expectations? *Journal of Money, Credit and Banking* 42 (1): 113–34.

Christiano, Lawrence, Martin Eichenbaum, and Charles Evans. 2005. Nominal rigidities and the dynamic effects of a shock to monetary policy. *Journal of Political Economy* 113 (1): 1–45.

Cuadra, Gabriel, Juan Sanchez, and Horacio Sapriza. 2010. Default risk and fiscal policy in emerging markets. *Review of Economic Dynamics* 13 (2): 452–69.

Cuadra, Gabriel, and Horacio Sapriza. 2011. Sovereign default risk and implications for fiscal policy. In Robert Kolb, ed., *Sovereign Debt: From Safety to Default*. Hoboken, NJ: Wiley, 303–308.

Del Negro, Marco, Frank Schorfheide, Frank Smets, and Rafael Wouters. 2007. On the fit of New Keynesian models. *Journal of Business and Economic Statistics* 25 (2): 123–43.

Eyzaguirre, Nicolas, Benedict Clements, and Jorge Canales-Kriljenko. 2009. Latin America: when is fiscal stimulus right? *Finance and Development* 46 (2): 48–49.

Fischer, Stanley. 2011. Central bank lessons from the global crisis. Unpublished manuscript. Bank of Israel, Jerusalem.

Frankel, Jeffrey. 2011. How can commodity exporters make fiscal policy and monetary policy less procyclical? Faculty research working paper RWP11–015. Kennedy School of Government, Harvard.

Galí, Jordi. 2008. *Monetary Policy, Inflation and the Business Cycle: An Introduction to the New Keynesian Framework*. Princeton:Princeton University Press.

Galí, Jordi, and Mark Gertler. 1999. Inflation dynamics: A structural econometric analysis. *Journal of Monetary Economics* 44 (2): 195–222.

Galí, Jordi, Mark Gertler, and David López-Salido. 2005. Robustness of the estimates of the hybrid New Keynesian Phillips curve. *Journal of Monetary Economics* 52 (6): 1107–18.

Ghosh, Atish, Chamon,Marcos, Crowe,Christopher, Kim, Jun Il, and Ostry, Jonathan. 2009. Coping with the crises: Policy options for emerging market countries. Staff position note 09-08. IMF, Washington, DC.

Gomez, Javier. 2004. Inflation targeting, sudden stops, and the cost of fear of floating. Unpublished manuscript. Banco de la República, Colombia.

IMF. 2010. Reserve accumulation and international monetary stability. IMF Policy paper. Washington, DC.

Kaminsky, Graciela, Carmen Reinhart, and Carlos Vegh. 2004. When it rains, it pours: Procyclical capital flows and macroeconomic policies. *NBER Macroeconomics Annual* 19: 11–82.

Kose, Ayhan, Eswar Prasad, Kenneth Rogoff, and Wei Shang-Jin. 2006. Financial globalization: A reappraisal. Working paper 06-189. IMF, Washington, DC.

Lane, Philip, and Aaron Tornell. 1999. The voracity effect. *American Economic Review* 89 (1): 22–46.

Llaudes, Ricardo, Ferhan Salman, and Mali Chivakul. 2010. The impact of the great recession on emerging markets. Working paper 10-237. IMF, Washington, DC.

Medina, Juan Pablo, and Claudio Soto. 2007. Copper price, fiscal policy and business cycle in Chile. Working paper 458. Banco Central de Chile, Santiago.

Mishkin, Frederic. 2008. Exchange rate pass-through and monetary policy. Working paper 13889. NBER, Cambridge, MA.

Neumeyer, Pablo, and Fabrizio Perri. 2005. Business cycles in emerging economies: the role of interest rates. *Journal of Monetary Economics* 52 (2): 345–80.

Orphanides, Athanasios. 2010. Monetary policy lessons from the crisis. Working paper 2010–1. Central Bank of Cyprus, Nicosia.

Rangel, Gonzalo, and Manuel Ramos-Francia. 2011. Revisiting the effects of country specific fundamentals on sovereign default risk. Unpublished manuscript. Banco de México, Mexico City.

Rudd, Jeremy, and Karl Whelan. 2006. Can rational expectations sticky-price models explain inflation dynamics? *American Economic Review* 96 (1): 303–20.

Sidaoui, José, and Manuel Ramos-Francia. 2008. The monetary transmission mechanism in Mexico: Recent developments. In *Transmission Mechanisms for Monetary Policy in Emerging Market Economies*. Basel: Bank for International Settlements, 363–94.

Taylor, John. 2000. Low inflation, pass-through, and the pricing power of firms. *European Economic Review* 44 (7): 1389–1408.

Uribe, Martin, and Vivian Yue. 2006. Country spreads and emerging countries: Who drives whom? *Journal of International Economics* 69 (1): 6–36.

IV THE CRISIS AND ITS LESSONS: SOME CASE STUDIES

9 Lessons from the Financial Crisis: An Australian Perspective

Jonathan Kearns

9.1 Introduction

The global financial crisis triggered a global recession, so severe it has been called the Great Recession. The recession has been notable not only for its depth in some countries but also for the exceptional degree of synchronization across countries.[1] All except three of the 34 OECD countries experienced two consecutive negative quarters of growth in late 2008 to early 2009, and only two avoided negative year-end GDP growth.[2] Australia was one of those fortunate countries. This chapter considers whether there are any lessons to be learned from Australia's experience in the face of such a large external shock. It first describes the macroeconomic policy and prudential regulation frameworks in Australia before the crisis, and then the fiscal and central bank policy responses during the crisis. Last, the chapter draws a comparison with Canada, a country that is similar in many ways but did experience a significant recession.

The IMF attributed Australia's good economic performance through the crisis to "a prompt and significant macro policy response to the global crisis, a healthy banking sector, and a flexible exchange rate," but importantly, also to strong demand for commodities from Asia (IMF 2010a: 3).[3] Australia had sound macroeconomic policy in the lead up to the crisis with the Australian government implementing fiscal policy that aimed to deliver a small surplus on average over the cycle. This resulted in declining levels of debt such that net debt outstanding was negative when the crisis hit. Monetary policy also provided a stable platform for the economy with an inflation target that had been in place for almost two decades delivering low inflation and stable inflation expectations. The policy response in Australia to the substantial negative economic shock in late 2008 was significant with a large fiscal stimulus and a large and rapid cut in the policy interest rate.

The fact that the economic shock in late 2008 emanated from a financial crisis means that postmortems of this episode require an examination of the framework for, and response of, both prudential regulation and the plumbing of central banking (open market operations and the central bank's balance sheet). The Australian banking system weathered the crisis well, remaining profitable and well capitalized with credit continuing to grow. Indeed, the four major banks retained their AA rating from Standard & Poor's through the crisis.[4] While other factors undoubtedly played a role, conservative prudential regulation had helped to shape the balance sheets of the Australian banks in such a way that they were in a good position to withstand the challenges of the crisis. Central banks have also featured prominently in the response to the crisis for the novel use of their balance sheets to support financial market functioning, and in some cases stimulate the economy. The Reserve Bank of Australia did not need to implement unconventional monetary policy, as the cash rate remained well above the zero lower bound. But it did modify its open market operations and expand its balance sheet in order to address dislocation in particular key financial markets.

Good economic policy was an important factor in Australia's remarkable performance through the crisis. However, good fortune also played a part. While there was a large global downturn, particularly in the developed economies of North America and Europe, many of Australia's trading partners, and China in particular, recovered quickly. More important than just their absolute rate of growth was the resource-intensive nature of their growth. Demand for commodities was very strong, leading the Australian terms of trade to be on average almost 10 percent higher in the period since the onset of the financial crisis in mid-2007 to late 2010 than it was immediately before.[5] Further, while virtually all economies experienced very large contractions in their exports, Australia's exports continued to grow through the crisis. In this chapter this good fortune is highlighted by a comparison with Canada, which experienced a sharp decline in GDP and larger increase in unemployment. Canada offers a natural comparison for Australia as it has similar institutional structures and is also a commodity exporter. Much like Australia, Canada has had a strong banking system that weathered the crisis largely unscathed, has had large fiscal and monetary stimulus, and has had a central bank that modified its operating procedures in response to financial market dislocation. However, Canada's close economic relationship with the United States and the type of commodities it produces contrasts with Australia's large exports to China, especially of bulk commodities.

9.2   The Policy Framework and Response in Australia

9.2.1   Fiscal Policy

The Australian government has had a policy of maintaining a small budget surplus on average since the mid-1990s. As a result the government's net debt was around –7.5 percent of GDP in mid-2007 (i.e., assets exceeded debt). Indeed, as the economy remained strong in the early stages of the financial crisis, the government had a budget surplus for 2007–08 of around 1.5 percent of GDP. With the dramatic change in the economic outlook following the collapse of Lehman Brothers in September 2008, the government announced its first fiscal stimulus package within a month. Three more stimulus packages were announced up to May 2009. The first phase of the fiscal stimulus was focused on making cash payments to households to provide immediate support to the economy (Henry 2009). The cash payments were distributed in the second half of 2008 and first half of 2009. Less than three months after the collapse of Lehman Brothers, in early December, approximately $8.5 billion (around 0.7 percent of annual GDP) began to be distributed to households (Gruen 2009b). The later stimulus spending had a greater focus on infrastructure packages (including school facilities, social and defense housing, and measures to improve energy efficiency) with payments planned from the first half of 2009 through to 2012.

Gruen (2009a) argues that the efficacy of the cash payments can be seen in the increase in retail consumption from when the payments were received in December 2008 (not when the package was announced). He also points to the increase in housing finance commitments as evidence of the positive demand created by the First Home Owners Boost, which provided financial incentives to first home buyers, particularly for new building. The Australian fiscal stimulus was large in comparison to other countries, which was noteworthy given the projected downturn was smaller. Gruen notes that the larger fiscal stimulus was possible because of the stronger starting debt position in Australia than in many other countries. The quick implementation of the fiscal stimulus was also important; a frequent criticism of activist fiscal policy is that the implementation lag is too long. Gruen argues that without the fiscal stimulus the economy would have contracted in the first two quarters of 2009, and that because of the more rapid impact for fiscal policy than monetary policy, fiscal policy provided a quicker stimulus when conditions rapidly deteriorated.

9.2.2 Monetary Policy and the Exchange Rate

The Reserve Bank was well into a tightening phase in mid-2007 and increased the cash rate three more times in response to rising inflation and limited spare capacity in the economy. With the cash rate peaking at 7.25 percent in early 2008, the Bank had a large margin to cut the policy rate in response to the escalation of the financial crisis and sharp downturn in economic activity in late 2008. Just three weeks after the collapse of Lehman Brothers, the Reserve Bank of Australia was the first central bank to cut by a large amount, 100 basis points.[6] This large cut broke with a pattern of gradualism in monetary policy; the Bank had not moved the cash rate by a full percentage point in a single move since the early 1990s. The Bank continued to cut the cash rate aggressively to a trough of 3 percent in April 2009. With the cash rate well above the zero lower bound the Bank at no time needed to engage in any unconventional monetary policy. From late 2009, the Bank gradually tightened monetary policy as the domestic economy regained strength. Overall, monetary policy through this episode continued to be forward-looking and countercyclical, as it always has been in the 18 years of inflation targeting. What was remarkable was the speed and magnitude of the cut in the cash rate in response to what was an unprecedented shock.

Having a floating currency also helped to cushion Australia from the crisis. The Australian dollar had been appreciating strongly in the lead up to the crisis consistent with the rising terms of trade from gains in commodity prices. After reaching a post-float high against the US dollar in July 2008, the Australian dollar depreciated sharply with the dramatic deterioration in global economic conditions, the associated fall in commodity prices and substantial reduction in risk appetite. The Australian dollar depreciated by almost 40 percent by late October to a low of around US60 cents. Despite the severe dislocation in most financial markets around this time, as with the other major currencies the market for Australian dollars continued to function relatively well. In October and November 2008 the Reserve Bank intervened on a number of occasions in response to dysfunctional and exceptionally illiquid market conditions. As demand for commodities and their prices rebounded, and the Australian economy recovered, the Australian dollar appreciated sharply reaching parity against the US dollar in October 2010. While the depreciation of the Australian dollar turned out to be relatively short lived, the floating exchange rate undoubtedly helped to cushion the Australian economy at the peak of the crisis.

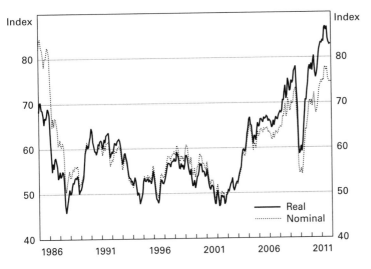

Figure 9.1
Australian dollar TWI. May 1970 = 100 for nominal; real indexed to equate post-float averages
Sources: RBA; Thomson Reuters; WM/Reuters

9.2.3   Central Bank Operations

The practice of open market operations in Australia, as elsewhere, was not widely understood outside of the central bank and, with hindsight, underappreciated prior to the crisis. Australian banks do not have required reserves, and so there is no reserves averaging, but banks need to hold nonnegative settlement balances (Exchange Settlement, or ES, balances) at the end of each day. This simple framework avoids any potential for seasonal pressure on the policy interest rate that can exist with reserve maintenance periods. ES balances are remunerated at the cash rate less 25 basis points, and overnight repurchase agreements (repos) are available at the cash rate plus 25 basis points and are used when banks face settlement problems (for technical reasons). This creates a corridor for the cash rate.

The Reserve Bank conducts open market operations every day to ensure that there is an appropriate supply of ES balances for the smooth operation of the cash market and that the cash rate remains at target.[7] Typically there is a system cash deficit, meaning the Bank needs to inject liquidity in the market, and so the Bank purchases securities under repurchase agreements (repos). There are different classes of securities accepted by the Bank, and counterparties specify the class of security when submitting bids. This enables the Bank to choose the shares of different classes of securities accepted in its dealing. The term of these repos is also at the Bank's discretion and is chosen each day to manage future system cash positions (see Baker and Jacobs 2010).

During the crisis the Bank made several changes to its open market operations (see RBA 2009b and RBA 2009c for summaries). Specifically, the Bank:

- increased the supply of ES balances,
- introduced a term deposit facility,
- lengthened the term of its repos,
- widened the pool of securities eligible for use in repos,
- conducted a larger share of its repos using private securities, and
- initiated a swap facility with the US Federal Reserve for institutions to receive US dollar funding.

Because of the nonprescriptive regulations governing the Bank's market operations, these changes could be made quickly at the discretion of Bank management without the need for new legislation and, with the exception of the term deposit and US dollar swap, without needing to create new facilities. This meant the Bank was able to immediately respond to rapidly changing conditions through the crisis. As seen in the bottom three panels of figure 9.2 and described below, the Bank's dealing actively responded to market pressures, demonstrated by the Bank Bill to Overnight Indexed Swap (OIS) spread (the top panel).

The increase in ES balances increased the supply of highly liquid risk-free assets when there was greater demand for such assets in response to the deterioration of market conditions and increased uncertainty. The supply of ES balances increased from its typical level of $750 million prior to the crisis, to average in excess of $8 billion at the peak of the financial crisis. The establishment of a term deposit facility, where banks could bid to deposit cash at the Bank—typically for terms of 7 to 14 days—also increased the supply of liquid risk-free assets, without excessively expanding the supply of ES balances (which could place downward pressure on the cash rate).[8] This facility was short-lived, being implemented in September 2008 after the increase in ES balances and being run down by February 2009 when demand eased. Increasing the supply of highly liquid risk-free assets was particularly important in Australia because of the small stock of government debt, and the fact that there were no short-term government securities on issue at the time.

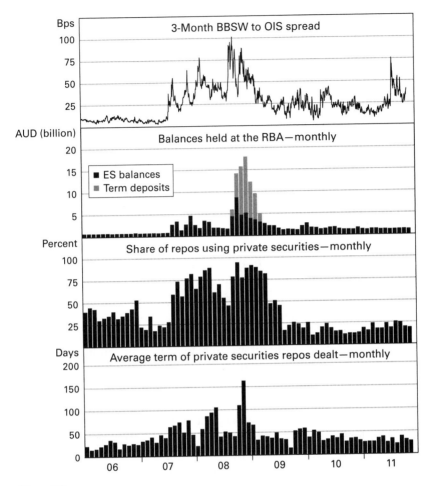

Figure 9.2
Reserve Bank open market operations.
Sources: AFMA; RBA; Tullet Prebon (Australia)

The lengthening in the term of repos enabled the Bank to provide its counterparties with more certain funding. It also encouraged institutions to hold longer term securities when the term of private securities issuance was shortening as a result of increased risk aversion (securities used in a repo must have a term at least as long as the length of the repo). Prior to the crisis, repos averaged less than 30 days, but the average increased to as much as 130 days, and some repos had a term as long as one year.

Making securities eligible for use in the Bank's repos increases their liquidity. Over the course of the crisis the Bank expanded the pool of eligible securities to include a wider range of commercial banks' securities, asset-backed securities (short and long term), and almost all securities with the highest short-term and long-term credit ratings. In particular, repo eligibility provided a boost for confidence in residential mortgage-backed securities (RMBS) and was seen to be a substantial selling point in the issuance of new RMBS. RMBS were greatly tainted during the crisis, despite Australian prime RMBS performing well with very few downgrades and no losses on rated tranches.

The increase in the share of repos conducted using private securities made it easier for financial institutions to fund their holdings of private securities, and so increased demand for private securities. The offsetting reduction in the share of Reserve Bank repos using public securities increased the relative supply of risk-free government debt available in the private market.

The US dollar swap the Reserve Bank of Australia (and other central banks) conducted with the Federal Reserve was initiated following equivalent arrangements the Fed made with major central banks to address US dollar funding shortages in non-US markets. The introduction of the facility did not reflect a shortage of US dollars in local financial institutions; rather it was to help address the problem in global markets of the dislocation of the US dollar swap market by increasing the supply of US dollars in non-US markets and time zones (CGFS 2010).

Since the Reserve Bank's policy interest rate remained well above the zero lower bound, the Bank did not need to undertake any form of quantitative easing. Nonetheless, the Bank's balance sheet did expand substantially with the increase in ES balances and term deposits, and the US dollar swap facility. These initiatives increased the Bank's total assets by over AUD$50 billion in late 2008, a sizable increase given the balance sheet had been around AUD$100 billion. As the crisis eased in early 2009, the expansion in the balance sheet unwound quite rapidly.

These timely initiatives were well received by the market and assisted with its smooth functioning. Kearns (2009) investigates whether the increases in ES balances, the term of repos and the share of repos using private securities reduced Bank Bill to OIS spreads. By considering how these spreads moved after the Reserve Bank's morning dealing, and controlling for movements in the Australian night when developments in Europe and the United States occurred, these measures were found to have marginally reduced Bank Bill spreads.

9.3 The Banking Sector and Prudential Regulation

Overall, the Australian banking system performed well through the financial crisis with banks remaining profitable and well capitalized. No Australian banks required capital injections from the government or direct support. Following similar initiatives in other developed economies, the Australian government guaranteed deposits and implemented a government-guarantee scheme for banks' wholesale debt issuance in October 2008 (see RBA 2009a; Schwartz 2010). Australian banks could issue government-guaranteed debt with a maturity of up to five years for a fee that varied with the credit rating of the bank. Deposits up to AUD$1 million were guaranteed for free, with deposits above this amount able to be guaranteed for the same fee as debt issuance. The guarantee scheme enabled Australian banks to issue debt at the peak of the crisis when markets were essentially shut to private issuance, and provided cheaper and more reliable access to term funding when the Australian banks were lengthening the term of their wholesale liabilities. At its peak, AUD$157 billion of wholesale liabilities were guaranteed, around 15 percent of banks' total wholesale funding. The guarantee scheme for wholesale debt was closed to new issuance in March 2010, with the guarantee on deposits less than AUD$1 million remaining in place until October 2011, when the financial claims scheme was modified to introduce a cap of AUD$250,000.

The four largest Australian banks have a current share of around three-quarters of total system assets. All four major banks retained their AA ratings from Standard & Poor's through the crisis—making them among the highest rated banks internationally, all the more so after many banks globally were downgraded. While the lower rated smaller banks experienced a larger increase in their cost of funds, they too came through the crisis in a sound state. Overall, lending practices in Australia were of a high standard before and during the crisis. There was only a relatively moderate pickup in bad and doubtful debts, although the downturn in the economy was also relatively mild (figure 9.3). As a result, and despite an increase in funding costs, Australian banks remained profitable with the major banks experiencing only a small dip in their return on equity.

As Davis (2011) discusses, another reason that Australian banks were well positioned at the onset of the financial crisis is that for some time credit growth had exceeded growth in deposits, leading them to borrow in offshore wholesale markets (fully currency and maturity hedged).

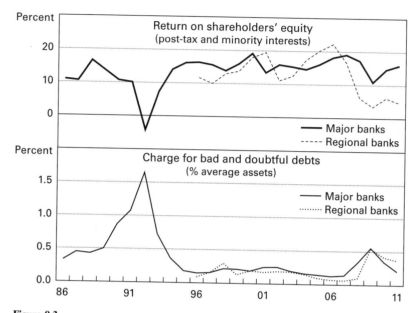

Figure 9.3
Bank profitability of institutions operating in Australia. From 2006 data are on an IFRS basis; prior years are on an AGAAP basis.
Sources: RBA; banks' annual reports and interim reports

Given this pattern of asset and liability growth, they had little incentive to invest in the high-yielding (but risky) securities that turned out to be at the heart of the crisis. As a result Australian banks had very small holdings of complex securities ("toxic assets") on their balance sheets. In the financial crisis borrowing in wholesale markets was considered to be risky for banks. The Australian banks mitigated this risk by relatively large holdings of liquid assets, and once the Reserve Bank made RMBS eligible for use in market operations, they securitized large stocks of on-balance sheet mortgages to create RMBS they retained.[9] This further liquefied their balance sheets, so that the Reserve Bank could provide large amounts of funding if needed.

Sound prudential regulation has also been highlighted as an important reason that Australian banks weathered the financial crisis. In 2009 the IMF noted that "Australian banks have coped well with the turmoil so far, largely because of robust supervision and regulation" (IMF 2009: 3). In Australia, prudential regulation of banks and other deposit-taking institutions has been the responsibility of a separate prudential regulator, the Australian Prudential Regulation Authority (APRA), since 1998.

While the responsiveness of the regulator during a crisis is critical, the regulator's actions before the crisis are at least as important in determining how the banking system performs in a crisis (Laker 2010b). APRA is a principles-based, rather than rules-based, regulator and it also supervises the consolidated entity. This reduces the incentive of banks to create complex structures or trades to circumvent regulations. One example of this is that APRA treated off-balance sheet vehicles as part of the institution, which limited the benefits to capital arbitrage through off-balance sheet financing such as asset-backed commercial paper—a market that experienced significant stress in the financial crisis.

APRA has a relatively conservative and proactive approach to regulation that, in part, reflects the lessons learned from previous failures and crises. Gruen (2009a) highlights the banking system losses in the early 1990s, which exceeded 5 percent of GDP, as helping to instill banking conservatism. The chairman of APRA, John Laker, similarly describes how the failure of the APRA-regulated insurer HIH in 2001 also led to more conservative and intrusive regulation (Laker 2010a). Important elements of supervision that he highlights are that APRA reviews most capital instruments issued, institutions need approval from APRA to buy back shares or to call capital instruments, and also to make changes to internal risk models. The conservative approach to supervision can be seen in APRA's rules regarding capital *before* the crisis: 80 percent of Tier 1 capital had to be of the highest form—ordinary shares and retained earnings—and APRA excluded from Tier 1 items such as intangible assets that have uncertain liquidation values. So, while the absolute level of Australian banks' capital was not high internationally prior to the crisis, the quality of that capital was, as APRA's rules were more conservative than Basel II rules (figure 9.4). Australian banks also issued new equity during the crisis, and demonstrated their strength by being able to do so into the private market at modest discounts. Laker also notes that APRA took the opportunity of the boom years to strengthen regulation, including adopting Basel II in 2008.

There are benefits to having a stand-alone prudential regulator that may be more likely to remain focused on lending standards and risk during boom years. Having the prudential regulator separate from the central bank has been criticized because of short-comings in coordination and cooperation between the organizations. This structure was not seen to have performed well in the United Kingdom, and is being reversed. However, in Australia this institutional structure did perform

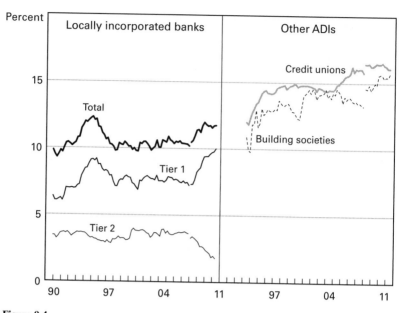

Figure 9.4
Capital ratios of consolidated global operations. Percent of risk-weighted assets; break in
March 2008 due to the introduction of Basel II for most ADIs
Source: APRA

well. Possibly this is easier with less complex banks and markets, but it
also reflects the close cooperation of the regulator and central bank and
efforts to foster a collaborative working arrangement between APRA
and the Reserve Bank with daily or intra-day conference calls at the peak
of the crisis, temporary staff transfers, and continual sharing of relevant
information.

Despite the good outcome in Australia, there are still lessons for the
financial system to learn from the crisis that are important for the prudential regulator. Laker (2009) identifies four:

• Risks can materialize very rapidly and substantially.

• Risks need to be clearly identified and well understood, for example,
asset-backed securities were not distributing risk beyond core financial
institutions to the extent assumed.

• Agency risk has been more pervasive than has appeared, and this was
highlighted in US subprime lending and securitizing and in some bank
remuneration practices.

• The importance of good governance cannot be understated.

The role of regulators is to continue to adapt to changing circumstances. The good performance of the Australian banking system is not a cause for complacency, and so Australia is participating in the formulation of, and has outlined a timetable to adopt, the new Basel III banking standards.

9.4   A Comparison with Canada

While the policy measures described above had a positive effect on the Australian economy, analysis of individual measures in isolation cannot establish the overall effect of policy initiatives versus other factors. One illustrative way to consider this is through a comparison of the outcomes in Australia and Canada.

Australia and Canada have many similarities, not just historically and culturally—being federal states with British origins and institutions—but also economically. While Canada has a somewhat larger population and so economy, GDP per capita is similar in the two economies, and both are relatively open economies with large exports of commodities. The two countries have similar sized primary production sectors, although Canada has substantially more manufacturing and Australia more mining (see Stevens 2009).

Both economies entered the global financial crisis with a history of inflation targeting with freely floating exchange rates and established fiscal policy rules. In both countries there was a strong policy response to the international economic and financial shocks. As seen in figure 9.5, both economies had a large fiscal stimulus. While the Australian discretionary stimulus was somewhat larger in 2008 to 2009, the change in the general government balance, and so overall fiscal stimulus (including the forecast automatic stabilizers), was remarkably similar. Both economies had a surplus of around 2 percent of GDP in 2007, with that projected to turn around to be a deficit of 4.5 to 5.5 percent of GDP. The IMF projected that this would lead to a deterioration in the government net debt by about 16 percent of GDP in Australia and about 11 percent of GDP in Canada (IMF 2010b), although more recent estimates point to a smaller increase in debt in Australia. The Canadian fiscal stimulus contained broadly similar elements to that in Australia: measures to boost consumer demand in the short term (tax reductions and credits) and also investment (investment incentives and infrastructure spending). There were differences in the composition and timeliness of the fiscal

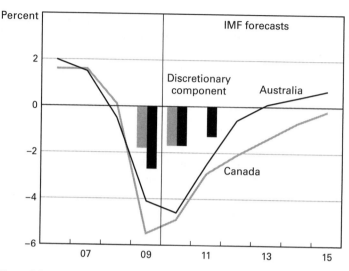

Figure 9.5
General government balance as percentage of GDP
Source: IMF (2010b)

stimulus that could have influenced their efficacy, but a detailed comparison is beyond the scope of this chapter.

Similarly both the Bank of Canada and Reserve Bank of Australia aggressively cut their policy interest rates (figure 9.6). The Canadian economy began to slow earlier, because of the weakening US economy, while the Australian economy continued to grow strongly through the early stages of the financial crisis, in part reflecting robust external demand from Australia's Asian trading partners. Consequently the Bank of Canada had begun to cut their cash rate at the time the Reserve Bank was still increasing the policy rate. But following the collapse in Lehman Brothers, and dramatic turn in global conditions, both the Reserve Bank and Bank of Canada aggressively cut policy. Altogether, both central banks cut their policy rates by 425 basis points, although the Bank of Canada may have cut more if it was not constrained by the zero lower bound, while the Reserve Bank of Australia had room for further cuts as the cash rate remained comfortably above zero.

Just as the Reserve Bank made some modifications, but not wholesale changes, to its market operations to improve market functioning so too did the Bank of Canada. The Bank of Canada introduced a term repo facility and broadened the range of collateral accepted in various facilities, much as the Reserve Bank did, and also broadened the range of institutions it dealt with (Longworth 2009). The summary in CGFS (2008)

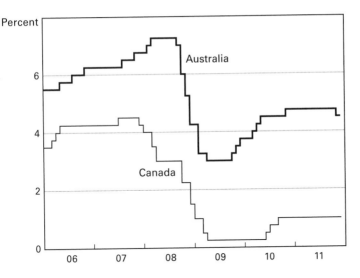

Figure 9.6
Policy interest rates.
Sources: RBA; Thomson Reuters

demonstrates the similarity in the changes made by these two central banks in their market operations in the first stage of the financial crisis.

Both economies also had well capitalized and profitable banking systems that did not need any injection of capital from the government. Canada has five major banks that account for around 90 percent of system assets, while Australia's four major banks currently account for around three-quarters of system assets. The two markets have similar regulatory structures with an independent principles-based prudential regulator that covers a broad range of financial institutions.[10] The Canadian regulator, Office of the Superintendent of Financial Institutions (OSFI), was also seen to be fairly conservative prior to the crisis. For example, similar to APRA, it required three-quarters of Tier 1 capital to be common equity. The strong performance of the banking systems in the two countries is neatly summarized by their share prices outperforming those in other major markets (figure 9.7).

KPMG (2010) compares the banking systems in Australia and Canada and attributes the good outcomes for the banking systems in both countries to a number of common factors, notably:

- lending standards weren't eased in the run-up to the crisis;
- banks had a low risk tolerance and conservative balance sheets in order to preserve their ongoing high profitability;

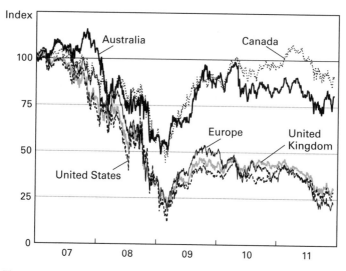

Figure 9.7
Banks' share prices, end December, 2006 = 100. ASX, Euro Stoxx, FTSE, S&P, and TSX
banking sub-indexes
Sources: Bloomberg; RBA

• banks' balance sheets were heavily weighted to domestic loans and in
particular low-risk housing lending; and

• by international standards, regulators in both countries have been proactive in prudential regulation.

Despite the broadly similar economic structures of the two economies,
including banking systems that continued to function well through the
crisis, and similar policy responses, the Australian economy fared much
better than the Canadian economy. GDP growth in Canada slowed from
late 2007, with the economy contracting from the December quarter
2008 (figure 9.8). The pace of growth of economic activity also slowed
substantially in Australia, but year-end growth remained positive throughout, with only one quarterly contraction in GDP recorded. Reflecting the
weaker economy, the pickup in the unemployment rate was also larger
in Canada (figure 9.9).

One obvious difference between the countries that has previously
been noted is that Canada has a close economic relationship with
the United States, which as a center of the crisis experienced a sharp
economic contraction, while Australia is more closely tied to Asia,
which was less directly affected and recovered quickly. High-growth
Asian economies, including China, Korea, and India, represent over 40

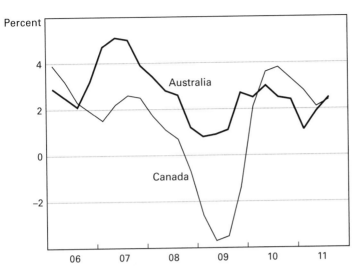

Figure 9.8
GDP growth, year-ended
Sources: Australian Bureau of Statistics; Thomson Reuters

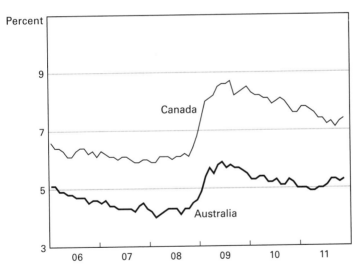

Figure 9.9
Unemployment rate
Sources: Australian Bureau of Statistics; Thomson Reuters

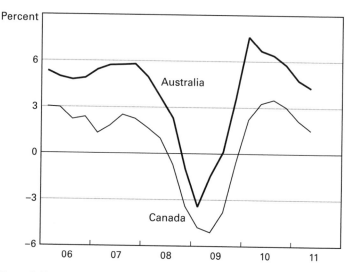

Figure 9.10
Major trading partner GDP growth, export-weighted and year-ended
Sources: Australian Bureau of Statistics; RBA; Thomson Reuters

percent of Australia's merchandise exports, and so the average level of Australia's trading partners' growth was higher leading into the crisis than it was for Canada, for which the United States is around three-quarters of merchandise exports (figure 9.10). While overall Australia's trading partners' economies contracted, their growth remained above that of Canada's trading partners, and they experienced a faster recovery.

What was seemingly more important was the nature of growth in Australia and Canada's trading partners. Globally manufactured trade experienced a precipitous decline. This affected Canada more than Australia because of its larger share of manufactured exports. In particular, Canada's automotive exports to the United States, which account for three-quarters of its automotive production, were affected by the contraction in demand for durable goods in the United States. Similarly some other Canadian exports were affected by areas of particular weakness in their largest trading partner, such as timber exports used in US house building. In contrast, trade in bulk commodities such as coal and iron ore, which are Australia's largest exports, did not decline like the trade in manufactured goods. Demand for these commodities was supported by the infrastructure construction as part of China's stimulus program. While the volume of Canada's exports declined by around 20

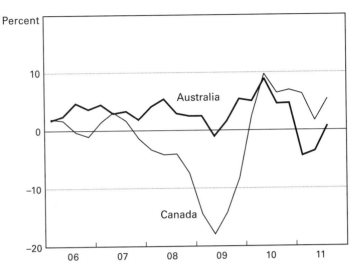

Figure 9.11
Export growth, year-ended, chain volumes
Sources: Australian Bureau of Statistics; Thomson Reuters

percent from peak to trough, broadly similar to the decline in global trade, Australia's export volumes grew strongly with year-end growth only dipping to zero in one-quarter (figure 9.11).

The strong growth in demand for minerals also led to sharp price increases that have pushed Australia's terms of trade higher (figure 9.12). The price increases have been spread across most of Australia's commodity exports, but iron ore and coal have made a particularly large contribution to the increase in the terms of trade. Their prices increased by 100 to 180 percent in US dollars from mid-2007 to late 2010, when they constituted around one-quarter of Australian exports.[11] From late 2008 both countries' terms of trade declined as commodity prices fell with the deterioration of economic and financial conditions. Australia's export earnings did fall substantially at this time, despite export volumes holding up, as Australia's export prices declined sharply. From the second half of 2009, prices of bulk commodities increased sharply causing Australia's terms of trade to surge once again. Overall, while Canada's terms of trade have averaged marginally below their mid-2007 level in the following period, Australia's terms of trade have averaged almost 10 percent higher. Given the Australian trade share of around one-quarter, this has made a substantial contribution to domestic income growth of over 2 percentage points.

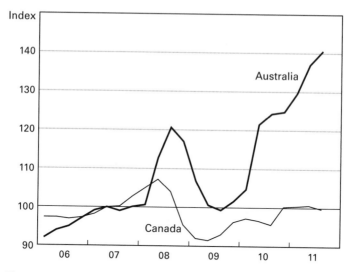

Figure 9.12
Terms of trade, June quarter 2007 = 100
Sources: Australian Bureau of Statistics; Thomson Reuters

9.5   Discussion of Lessons

Much of what helped Australia weather the global recession was done before the crisis. Establishing good economic policy was key:

• Inflation targeting had delivered credible monetary policy and stable inflation expectations, which in turn allowed the large cut in nominal interest rates to translate to a substantial cut in real interest rates.

• The exchange rate had been freely floating for close to twenty-five years at the onset of the crisis, and it performs an important role as a shock absorber for external shocks.

• Sustainable fiscal policy had delivered low government debt that allowed for a large fiscal stimulus; that is to say, there was plenty of "fiscal space."

• General economic reform, including of the labor market, created a flexible economy well placed to absorb shocks.

• Conservative, proactive, and principles-based prudential regulation had resulted in a highly rated banking system with healthy balance sheets of good quality domestic loans without complex and risky securities or trading strategies.

The macroeconomic policy response during the crisis was in many ways unprecedented, but it was not radical. The fiscal and monetary authorities followed standard countercyclical policy prescriptions; what was different was the speed and magnitude of the stimulus imparted on the economy. This not only had the standard stimulatory economic effects but also helped restore confidence, which had slumped following a chain of bad financial and economic news.

It is obviously critical that the prudential regulator is vigilant and responsive during a crisis, but the regulator's actions before the crisis in preventing a buildup in risk are at least as important in determining how the banking system performs in a crisis. Central banks were active during the crisis in adapting their open market operations. The framework that was found to be beneficial by the Reserve Bank of Australia was:

• having a simple yet flexible design for market operations, which not only works well in normal times but is robust to market disturbances; and

• having nonprescriptive regulations governing the actions of the central bank, so that it has the discretion to respond to market disturbances in a timely and transparent manner.

Good policy before, and during, the crisis played an important role in the performance of the Australian economy in the "global recession." Without it, Australia would have experienced a much more severe economic downturn. The comparison with Canada suggests that a broadly similar set of policies could similarly deliver a healthy banking system, but they cannot counteract all external shocks to the economy. Canada's close economic relationship with the United States exposed it to a much larger economic shock than that experienced by Australia. Clearly, good fortune also played a critical part in Australia avoiding a severe recession. Strong demand for bulk commodities such as coal and iron ore resulted in a remarkable export performance, both in volumes and prices, in comparison to other developed economies. Not only did this result in strong income growth and so stronger domestic demand, but in conjunction with the rapid and large fiscal and monetary policy response, it no doubt helped boost confidence at a time when confidence was key.

Notes

The views contained in this chapter are those of the author and do not necessarily reflect those of the Reserve Bank of Australia. This chapter was prepared for the Bank of Israel conference "Lessons from the World Financial Crisis," March 31 to April 1, 2011. The author thanks John Broadbent, Ellis Connolly, Luci Ellis, Alex Heath, Philip Lowe, Rick Mishkin, and Chris Thompson for helpful comments.

1. It is not uncommon for recessions to be international affairs. In the mid-1970s, early 1980s, and early 1990s most OECD economies experienced recessions. However, this recession is unique for the concurrence across countries. On those previous occasions some countries led others into recession by a year or two.

2. Poland and the Slovak Republic also avoided two consecutive quarters of negative growth. The Slovak Republic contracted by 7.6 percent in the March quarter 2009, resulting in negative year-end growth. Poland's year-end growth remained positive.

3. Similar assessments have come from domestic commentators and policy officials, for example, Henry (2009).

4. Standard & Poor's downgraded the four major Australian banks to AA– in December 2011 because of a change in their rating methodology.

5. While some studies date the start of the financial crisis as September 2008 (the collapse of Lehman Brothers), others refer to the crisis as having begun in August 2007 when many markets first became dysfunctional. Because central banks and regulators responded from this earlier date, in this chapter the period starting in August 2007 is taken to be the financial crisis.

6. The Reserve Bank board meets on the first Tuesday of the month, and so the scheduled October 2008 meeting occurred before most other central banks had their first policy meeting following the collapse of Lehman Brothers.

7. For more information on the Bank's open market operations, see Battellino (2007) and Debelle (2007).

8. Term deposits could be broken for same day value and so remained liquid.

9. See RBA (2009b). As discussed in Kearns and Lowe (2008), the small stock of government debt in Australia means that banks have to hold other financial institutions' debt as highly-rated liquid assets, so-called inside assets. Because of the small stock of government debt, in order to satisfy liquidity requirements consistent with Basel III, Australian banks will be able to establish a committed facility with the Reserve Bank that enables securities eligible in regular market operations to be used to obtain liquidity (see RBA 2010).

10. See Northcott, Paulin, and White (2009) for a summary of Canadian banks' performance through the financial crisis and the Canadian approach to prudential regulation.

11. Their share of the value of Australian exports has increased substantially to around two-fifths.

References

Baker, Alexandra, and Jacobs, David. 2010. Domestic market operations and liquidity forecasting. *Reserve Bank of Australia Bulletin* (December).

Battellino R. 2007. Central Bank market operations. Address to Retail Financial Services Forum, Sydney, August 28.

Committee on the Global Financial System (CGFS). 2008. Central bank operations in response to the financial turmoil. CGFS paper 31. Basel.

Committee on the Global Financial System (CGFS). 2010. The functioning and resilience of cross-border funding markets. CGFS paper 37. Basel.

Davis, Kevin. 2011. The Australian financial system in the 2000s: Dodging the bullet. In Hugo Gerard and Jonathan Kearns, eds., *The Australian Economy in the 2000s*. Sydney: Reserve Bank of Australia, 301–48.

Debelle, Guy. 2007. Open market operations and domestic securities. Address to Australian Securitisation Forum, Sydney, November 29.

Gruen, David. 2009a. Reflections on the global financial crisis. Address to the Sydney Institute, Sydney, June 16.

Gruen, David. 2009b. The return of fiscal policy. Address to Australian Business Economists Annual Forecasting Conference 2009, Sydney, December 8.

Henry, Ken. 2009. The global financial crisis and the road to recovery. Address to the Australian Institute of Company Directors, Sydney, September 23.

IMF. 2009. Australia: 2009 Article IV Consultation. IMF, Washington, DC.

IMF. 2010a. Australia: 2010 Article IV Consultation. IMF, Washington, DC.

IMF. 2010b. Fiscal Exit: From strategy to implementation. IMF Fiscal Monitor, November.

Kearns, Jonathan, and Philip Lowe. 2008. Promoting liquidity: Why and how? In Paul Bloxham and Christopher Kent, eds., *Lessons from the Financial Turmoil of 2007 and 2008*. Sydney: Reserve Bank of Australia, 139–72.

Kearns, Jonathan. 2009. The Australian money market in a global crisis. *Reserve Bank of Australia Bulletin* (June): 15–27.

KPMG. 2010. Canadian economy and major banks: A comparison with Australia. KPMG Financial Services Report (November). Amstelveen, Netherlands.

Laker, John. 2009. The Global financial crisis: Lessons for the Australian financial system. Address to Australian Economic Forum, Sydney, August 19.

Laker, John. 2010a. What makes "good" prudential regulation. Address to American Chamber of Commerce Business Briefing, Melbourne, August 25.

Laker, John. 2010b. Supervisory lessons from the global financial crisis. AB+F Leaders Lecture Lunch 2010, Sydney, December 8.

Longworth, David. 2009. Financial system policy responses to the crisis. Address to the Financial Markets Association of Canada, Toronto, March 12.

Northcott, Carol Ann, Graydon Paulin, and Mark White. 2009. Lessons for banking reform: A Canadian perspective. *Central Banking* 19 (4): 43–53.

Reserve Bank of Australia. 2009a. Box A: Government guarantees on deposits and wholesale funding. *Financial Stability Review* (March): 43–46.

Reserve Bank of Australia. 2009b. *Annual Report*. Sydney.

Reserve Bank of Australia. 2009c. Box E: Normalisation of domestic market dealing operations. *Statement on Monetary Policy* (November): 63–64.

Reserve Bank of Australia. 2010. Australian implementation of global liquidity standards. Media release. December 17. Sydney.

Schwartz, Carl. 2010. The Australian government guarantee scheme. *Reserve Bank of Australia Bulletin* (March): 19–26.

Stevens, Glenn. 2009. Australia and Canada: Comparing notes on recent experiences. Address to the Canadian Australian Chamber of Commerce Canada–Australia Breakfast, Sydney, May 19.

10 Lessons from the World Financial Crisis for the Central Bank of Norway: The Approach to Monetary Policy and Financial Stability

Sigbjørn Atle Berg and Øyvind Eitrheim

10.1 Introduction

Spillover effects from the emerging liquidity problems in dollar markets affected Norwegian banks adversely already in August 2007, and the escalation of the liquidity problems in September 2008 required immediate intervention by Norges Bank. Like many other small open economies, Norway has also been adversely affected by the global recession that followed the global financial crisis. But in an international perspective, the Norwegian economy and financial institutions have been less affected by the crisis than many other countries and their financial institutions.

There are still lessons we can learn from this turbulent epoch. Norway's approach to monetary policy, that of *flexible inflation targeting,* was already well established when the financial crisis hit. Norges Bank was therefore able to benefit from a credible and transparent framework for communication of its policy intentions during the crisis. The monetary policy reports from Norges Bank have, since 2005, contained contingent projections of future policy rates. When contingencies changed because of the crisis, it was relatively straightforward to account for the main factors behind the desired revisions of the interest rate path to guide financial market participants' expectations. One lesson was that monetary policy is more than setting the key policy rate. Appropriate and adequate liquidity measures were required to improve the functioning of the financial markets. The experiences from the financial crisis can help improve our understanding of the transmission mechanism, that well-functioning financial markets are crucial for the transmission channels to work properly. In our view, *flexible inflation targeting* proved to be a robust framework for monetary policy and successfully provided the necessary room for maneuver for Norges Bank in its pursuit of price stability and financial stability.

The international experiences have reminded us that inflation targeting per se is not sufficient, neither for price stability nor for financial stability. Financial stability in Europe has been threatened by contagion from the US crisis, but in countries like Ireland and Spain also by excessive domestic credit and property price growth. The need for macroprudential policies to handle financial imbalances has been clearly demonstrated. Furthermore the crisis highlighted the need for efficient resolution regimes for financial institutions, with lessons that are highly relevant in Norway. With the international scope of the systemically most important financial institutions, the need for multilateral cooperation for managing insolvencies and liquidity crises is evident. During the present crisis Norway benefited from the lessons learned from the Nordic financial crisis in the early 1990s. Nevertheless, the global financial crisis revealed serious weaknesses in the Norwegian policy framework for financial stability and made a strong case for Norges Bank to play a central role in the future policy framework, in particular in macroprudential regulation and the supervision of liquidity management at financial institutions.

10.2 Lessons for Monetary Policy

10.2.1 The Monetary Policy Regime in Norway

Monetary policy in Norway is based on inflation targeting. The inflation-targeting regime was formally introduced in 2001. The operational target is low and stable inflation, with annual consumer price inflation of approximately 2.5 percent over time. When the financial crisis hit Norwegian shores in August 2007, Norway benefited from its well-established and credible monetary policy regime. Several years with expansionary monetary policy had brought the headline consumer inflation quite close to the target level, and by 2007 the Norges Bank was already tightening its monetary policy to curb an excessive domestic demand that had materialized. As the financial crisis deepened following the collapse of Lehman Brothers in September 2008, inflation was still below, but approaching, the inflation target, and inflation expectations were well anchored (see figure 10.10 in the appendix). A long period of substantial petroleum revenues—and a clear savings plan—had provided Norway with considerable budgetary leeway. As a result fiscal policy could also be put to effective use during the downturn.[1]

Transparency of Interest Rate Policy

The interest rate is set by the Executive Board of Norges Bank, normally every sixth week, with a view to stabilizing inflation close to the target in the medium term. Three times a year, at every third monetary policy meeting, a monetary policy report is published together with the interest rate decision. In the report Norges Bank analyses the current economic situation and publishes its economic forecasts.

Most central banks communicate their future policy intentions indirectly through forecasts based on technical assumptions about monetary policy, and by giving signals about future interest rate decisions in policy statements and speeches. This helps market participants gauge *signs* of future interest rate changes, but leaves little if any indications of the *size* of the changes. During the early years of inflation targeting Norges Bank became gradually more open and transparent in its interest rate setting. From 2004 the bank started to publish its monetary policy intentions in the form of a separate section on monetary policy assessments in the bank's Monetary Policy Report. Since 2005 Norges Bank has published its own interest rate forecast, on which the reference scenario for the economic outlook is based. The projected interest rate path is conditional on the information Norges Bank has available at the time when the path is published. The interest rate projection represents a trade-off between concerns for bringing inflation closer to its target and concerns for stabilizing output and employment. The inherent uncertainty in the interest rate forecast is underlined by fan charts surrounding the baseline scenario. The fan chart reflects how unanticipated shocks may lead to alternative interest rate paths that better reflect these trade-offs.

Baseline Projections of the Key Policy Rate

The central banks in Norway and Sweden publish forecasts based on an explicit projection of the banks' policy rate on overnight sight deposits. Other central banks like the Reserve Bank of New Zealand and the Czech National Bank publish forecasts of the money market rate, typically on three months' horizon. Figure 10.1 shows the projected interest path in Norges Bank Monetary Policy Report 3/2010 (October 2010). An overall assessment of the outlook and the balance of risks at that time indicated that the key policy rate should be held at the current level over the coming quarters and then gradually be raised toward a more normal level.

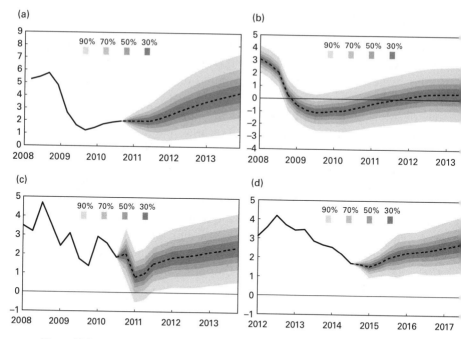

Figure 10.1
Baseline scenario presented in Norges Bank Monetary Policy Report 3/2010. (a) Projected key policy rate in the baseline scenario with fan chart, 2008Q1 to 2013Q4 (%). (b) Estimated output gap in the baseline scenario with fan chart, 2008Q1 to 2013Q4 (%). The output gap measures the percentage deviation between mainland GDP and projected potential mainland GDP. (c) Projected CPI in the baseline scenario with fan chart, four-quarter change 2008Q1 to 2013Q4 (%). (d) Projected CPIXE in the baseline scenario with fan chart, four-quarter change 2008Q1 to 2013Q4 (%). CPIXE is CPI adjusted for tax changes and excluding temporary changes in energy prices. As from August 2008, CPIXE is a real-time series.
Source: Staff Memos 7/2008 and 3/2009 from Norges Bank

Criteria for an Appropriate Interest Rate Path

The criteria used by Norges Bank to assess the interest rate reflect the general views and assessments of policy makers. These criteria can be summarized in four main points (for further details, see the box on page 22 in Norges Bank's Monetary Policy Report 2/2010 at http://www .norges-bank.no/en/about/published/publications/monetary-policy -report/210-monetary-policy-report/):

1. The interest rate should be set with a view to stabilizing inflation at target or bringing it back to target after a deviation has occurred. The specific time horizon will depend on the type of disturbances to which the economy is exposed and their effect on the path for inflation and the real economy ahead.

2. The interest rate path should at the same time provide a reasonable balance between the path for inflation and the path for overall capacity utilization in the economy. In the assessment, potential effects of asset prices, such as property prices, equity prices and the krone exchange rate on stability in output, employment and inflation are also taken into account. Assuming the criteria above have been satisfied, the following additional criteria are useful:

3. Interest rate adjustments should normally be gradual and consistent with the Bank's previous response pattern.

4. As a cross-check for interest rate setting, any substantial and systematic deviations from simple, robust monetary policy rules should be explained.

The two first criteria are optimality criteria for setting an appropriate interest rate. The optimal interest rate would move inflation toward the target level and represent a reasonable trade-off between the inflation concerns and the capacity utilization concerns in the economy. The next two criteria deal with concerns for *gradualism*, that the interest rate path should normally not be altered abruptly, and for *robustness*, that the interest rate path should give acceptable outcomes for inflation and output also under alternative albeit realistic assumptions on the functioning of the economy, and that any large and systematic deviations from simple stylized policy rules be accounted for.[2]

Starting from Monetary Policy Report 3/2007 the reports include a detailed discussion of factors that have contributed to the changes in Norges Banks projected interest rate path.

Factors behind Changes in the Projected Interest Rate Path

Figure 10.2, which is taken from Monetary Policy Report 3/2010 (October 2010), shows the factors behind changes in the interest rate path from the previous Monetary Policy Report (June 2010). At the beginning of the projected period, downward revisions of the price projections for imported consumer goods in foreign currency led to a drop in the interest rate. The central bank interest rate abroad had fallen, and the analyses in Norges Bank Monetary Policy Report 3/2010 were based on the assumption that foreign policy rates would remain low for a longer period than was earlier expected. This resulted in a lower interest rate path in Norway being projected, as a higher interest rate differential tends to cause a currency appreciation, and an inflation rate below the target.

10.2.2   Central Bank Policy Measures Taken during the International Financial Crisis

Two kinds of measures were taken to reduce the impact of the recent financial crisis on the Norwegian financial markets: (1) interest rate cuts

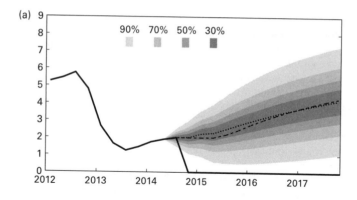

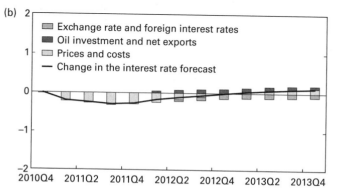

Figure 10.2
Factors behind changes in the projected interest rate path. (a) Key policy rate in the baseline scenario (dotted line) in MPR 2/2010 with fan chart and key policy rate in the baseline scenario (dashed line) in MPR 3/2010, quarterly figures, 2008Q1 to 2013Q4 (%). (b) Factors behind changes in the interest rate forecast since MPR 2/2010; accumulated contribution, 2010Q4 to 2013Q4 (%).
Source: Norges Bank Monetary Policy Report (MPR) 3/2010

and (2) central bank provisions to enhance the banking system's liquidity and to improve longer term funding for banks and nonfinancial enterprises. A detailed account of the measures is given in the Norges Bank's Annual Reports for the years 2007 to 2010, and here we will only briefly describe the main measures. The economic outlook changed abruptly in the fall of 2008 following the collapse of Lehman Brothers. As we explain below, the Norges Bank responded to this situation by altering its projected interest rate path. We will start by discussing the central bank's liquidity policy.

Liquidity Policy in Norway during the Financial Crisis[3]

The structural liquidity of the Norwegian banking system was, as usual, insufficient in this period as Norges Bank would routinely supply the extra liquidity.[4] When the financial turbulence reached the Norwegian money markets on August 9, 2007, Norges Bank responded by supplying liquidity. Additional liquidity was provided within the bank's normal practices for situations when money markets do not function satisfactorily.

The liquidity provisions from Norges Bank are normally through fixed-rate loans (F-loans) against collateral in the form of approved securities; see figure 10.3. During the early years of the crisis Norges Bank approved a wider range of securities as collateral in order to increase the banks' capacity to obtain central bank liquidity. Figure 10.3 shows that it was not until after the deepening of the financial crisis in September 2008 that the central bank deviated from normal procedures and supplied liquidity through F-loans with longer maturity (typically 2 and 3 months) and through foreign exchange swaps.[5] As a result the banks' overnight deposits in Norges Bank increased substantially in the fall of 2008 and were (on average) more than doubled until the fall

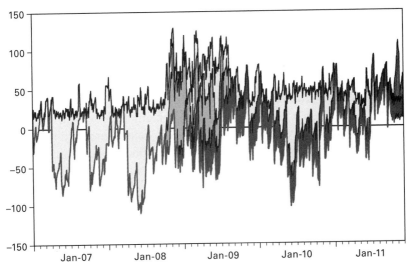

Figure 10.3
Liquidity in the banking system in Norway, 2007 to 2011. Banks' overnight deposits in the central bank (black line) and structural liquidity in absence of liquidity provision by the central bank (gray line). Bill NOK. Supply of central bank liquidity through F-Loan auctions up to 3 months maturity (white shaded area), 3 to 24 months (light gray shaded area) and 24 months + (dark gray shaded area).

of 2009. Since then overnight deposits have stabilized, although at a higher level than before the crisis.

Foreign exchange swaps are used when Norges Bank is not able to supply adequate liquidity through F-loans. All banks active in the Norwegian money market can participate, not just banks established in Norway. In the wake of the Lehman bankruptcy on September 15, 2008, investors' fears of new losses increased, with the result that liquidity in money markets virtually disappeared. Because of the shortage of dollar liquidity, Norwegian banks stopped quoting prices in the Norwegian money market on Tuesday, September 16. Norges Bank then decided to offer US dollars against collateral in NOK for a one-week foreign exchange swap. NOK 5bn were allocated. After this, prices were again quoted in money markets. The foreign exchange swap was rolled over one week later for the same amount. At the end of September Norges Bank, together with a number of other central banks, agreed on a credit facility with the US Federal Reserve. Under this agreement Norges Bank could draw up to USD 15bn if needed. The agreement applied until April 30, 2009, and was later extended to 30 October 2009.

Norges Bank continued to provide short-term loans, as is customary and natural for a central bank. But in line with the practice in many other countries, the average maturity of the outstanding volume of loans was temporarily increased. Moreover Norges Bank took the initiative to arrange a special swap whereby banks could exchange covered bonds (OMFs in Norwegian terminology) for treasury bills. These swaps were made on the government's balance sheet and not by the central bank. Because of this arrangement, the central bank did not provide long-term loans to banks on a large scale—unlike in many other countries where the central bank supplied liberal amounts of long-term liquidity.[6]

What distinguishes the management of the financial crisis in Norway from that of many other countries is, in our view, that the medium-term financing of the banking sector, when needed, is to be provided by the government and not by Norges Bank. We could draw a parallel to solvency support, which should also be a government responsibility. Such delimitation of Norges Bank's responsibilities is important and anticipates the extraordinary measures, with broad democratic backing in this regard, of the government and the Parliament (Storting). Thus avoided has been the kind of criticism that was leveled at Norges Bank when it provided funding for distressed banks in the late 1980s.[7]

One old lesson that was re-learned this time is that dependence on foreign funding can threaten the stability of a financial system even where the banks are not initially distressed financially. Norges Bank has therefore encouraged banks to choose more robust funding strategies. Norwegian banks no longer have the option to take on substantial liquidity risks in the expectation that Norges Bank will bail them out whenever foreign funding flops. Such expectations of central bank bailout create incentives for excessive liquidity risks over the long term and thus a market distortion.

Under the prevailing liquidity management system, before October 3, 2011, Norges Bank's deposit rate set the floor for short-term money market rates. The main advantage of a floor system is that the interest rate policy can be detached from monetary aggregates; see Keister et al. (2008). The central bank can accommodate the amount of liquidity demanded by the banking system without pushing short-term money market rates below the lowermost policy rate. Hence the interest rate can be set in accord with the monetary policy goals while the quantity of liquidity in the banking system is free to float to other goals, such as financial market stabilization. Bernhardsen and Kloster (2010) discuss the pros and cons of a floor versus a corridor system for liquidity management.[8]

The interest rate on F-loans is normally determined by price auctions and will typically be close to the key policy rate. Figure 10.4 shows the overnight deposit rate (the key policy rate) and the overnight lending

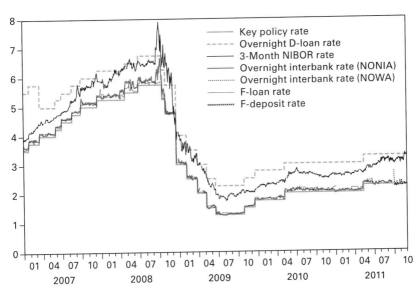

Figure 10.4
Key policy rate and other short-term interest rates in Norway, 2007 to 2011.

rate at the central bank together with overnight interest rates in the money market and the interest rate on F-loan and F-deposit auctions. Note that the interest rate on the F-loans remained quite close to the key policy rate during most of the period. A weighted average of overnight rates in the interbank market (NONIA), as recently reported in Akram and Christoffersen (2011), also most of the time remained quite close to the key policy rate, except at the peak of the crisis in the fall of 2008 when the weighted average of overnight rates increased almost as much as the three-month NIBOR rate spread.[9]

A particular feature of the Norwegian money market is its close connection to the US money market. Norwegian interbank rates are derived from the rates of interbank loans in US dollars swapped with Norwegian kroner (NOK) in the FX-swap market. Given this background, it would be interesting to learn whether the spillover from US money market premiums has been more pronounced in Norway than elsewhere. Forward exchange premiums can provide insight as to why money market premiums differ across European currencies; see Bernhardsen et al. (2009). Their main argument is that the excess supply of term liquidity in dollars relative to the excess supply of term liquidity in other currencies has had an impact on the domestic money market premium relative to that on USD via the term FX market.

This relationship is illustrated in figure 10.5. In the upper panel, we have plotted three-month money market premiums for NOK and SEK (Swedish kroner), and in the lower panel, we have plotted two series for three-month dollar premiums and the covered interest rate parity (CIP) deviations for NOK and SEK (calculated as the difference between actual forward premiums and the theoretical forward premiums under covered interest rate parity for NOK and SEK).[10] In normal times we would expect the CIP deviation to be small and stay near zero. The premium facing a bank would then be the same in both the domestic market and the dollar market and reflect its credit risk. Any CIP deviation is therefore related to the (relative) liquidity situation in the money markets. In times of market stress with increased liquidity risk and counterparty risk the CIP would deviate significantly and persistently from zero. Bernhardsen et al. (2009) develop a simple model where CIP deviations reflect a relative excess supply of USD to domestic (European) currencies.

We focus on these three observations in figure 10.5. First, we note that the money market premiums on NOK and SEK observed in the top panel of figure 10.5 are considerably lower than the dollar premiums in

(a)

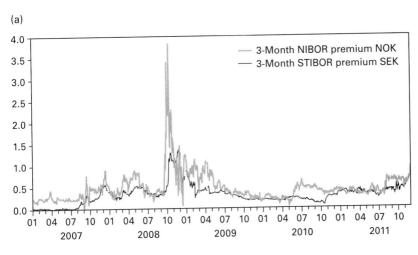

(b)

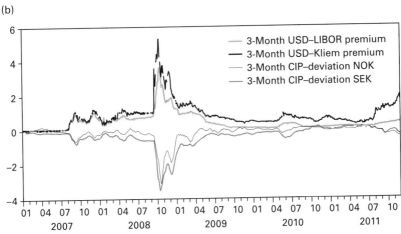

Figure 10.5
(a) Money market premiums on NOK and SEK (three-month money market rates minus expected key policy rates). (b) Three-month dollar premiums, notably the difference between three-month dollar rates (LIBOR and Kliem rates, respectively) and expected policy rates (OIS rates), and deviations from covered interest parity (CIP) calculated as the difference between actual forward premiums and the theoretical forward premiums under covered interest rate parity for NOK and SEK.

the US money market in the lower panel—in particular, after the bankruptcy of Lehman Brothers in September 2008. This difference seems to be connected to the CIP deviations in the forward FX markets for SEK and NOK reported in the lower panel of figure 10.5. We see a small negative shift in the CIP deviation for NOK and SEK already in August 2007. This can be associated with a positive shift in the demand for dollar. Then we note the large negative shift in the CIP deviation after September 15, 2008, when relative excess demand for dollar is strongly exacerbated. The lower premiums for SEK observed in the top panel of figure 10.5 correspond to larger negative CIP deviations for SEK than for NOK. The CIP deviation reverts after Fed responds to the crisis in the fourth quarter of 2008 and in the spring of 2009 with ample injections of USD liquidity—in particular, through facilities supporting the commercial paper market.

Second, we note that the NOK premiums remain persistently higher than SEK premiums throughout the entire period. Theoretically, this would translate back to the differences in the supply of central bank liquidity between the two countries. According to the model presented in Bernhardsen et al. (2009) a more ample supply of central bank liquidity in SEK relative to NOK would be consistent with the faster reversion to zero of the CIP deviation for NOK relative to that of SEK, as can be observed in 2009. This seems to be consistent with a strong commitment made by the Swedish Riksbank to supply liquidity with longer maturities in 2009 and 2010. While Norges Bank has typically supplied liquidity using F-loans with less than one-month maturity since mid-2009, the extraordinary liquidity measures taken by the Swedish Riksbank were first phased out in late 2010. This seems to be consistent with the observation in figure 10.5 that the negative CIP deviation for SEK reverts to zero and the premium for SEK increases toward levels closer to the premium for NOK.

Third, we note that the NOK money market premium measured by three-month NIBOR premiums after 2008 seems to be better represented by the higher Kliem dollar premiums than the LIBOR dollar premiums;[11] for example, see the shift upward in the three-month NIBOR premiums in mid-2010 following the Greek sovereign debt crisis and the recent sovereign debt crisis in Europe. Bernhardsen et al. (2009) argue that the LIBOR dollar rates underestimate the funding costs (in dollar markets) for European banks and suggest that brokered dollar rates like the Kliem rate may be closer to the actual funding costs for European banks.[12] Thus we may associate the recent shift upward in the Kliem premium with the increased credit risk in Europe. This feeds more directly into the money market spreads in Norway than in Sweden. We need, however, to also account for potential differences in liquidity policy. The shift upward in the three-month NIBOR premium relative to the seemingly unchanged three-month money market premiums on SEK (and EUR) is consistent with a relatively tighter liquidity policy in Norway. This is indicated by forward NOK deviation remaining close to zero in the latter half of 2010, whereas there a shift toward zero occurs in the forward deviation for SEK, pushing the SEK premium upward. More work is needed to fully understand the conditions of the money market premiums following the financial crisis. It is of special interest to study how much impact the change in the liquidity supply regime in Norway as of October 2011 has had on the relative money market premium in Norway as compared with Sweden.

Interest Rate Policy in Norway during the Financial Crisis

The factors behind changes in the interest rate path since the beginning of the financial crisis are reported for selected Monetary Reports summarized in figures 10.11 through 10.14 in the appendix. Each figure shows the projected interest rate path of the corresponding Monetary Policy Report together with a 50 percent fan chart interval and updated values of daily key policy rates and the three-month NIBOR interest rate. We also plotted the previous interest rate path projected by Norges Bank and the corresponding factors behind changes in the interest rate path. We are interested, in particular, in the changes to the interest rate path made during the fall of 2008 and spring of 2009. By focusing on the changes in the interest rate path we can judge how Norges Bank evaluated the incoming economic news over the course of the financial crisis.

The monetary policy reports of Norges Bank have grouped the factors behind interest rate changes in five categories: (1) prices, (2) foreign interest rates and exchange rates, (3) demand, internationally and domestically, (4) interest rate premiums, and (5) interest rate smoothing. In the policy reports of 2007 and the first half of 2008 the predominant monetary policy concern was to bring the interest rate back to a normal level—in small infrequent steps. The tightening phase had already lasted for some time and inflation was gradually approaching its target level from below. From the time when the financial crisis hit the Norwegian shores in August 2007 and until the deepening of the financial crisis after the collapse of Lehman Brothers in September 2008, the main concern in setting interest rates was to prevent inflation rate increases. The cycle of tightening continued into 2008, and was accelerated in the summer of 2008 following the high increase in many commodity prices including oil prices. The economic outlook changed abruptly in the fall 2008 following the Lehman collapse. Norges Bank reduced the key policy rate in both September and October 2008 before an updated interest rate projection was published in Norges Bank Monetary Policy Report 3/2008 at the end of October. Figure 10.11 shows a strong downward shift in the interest rate path, predominantly explained by a negative shift in economic activity (demand) but also by the sizable negative contributions from interest rate premiums and a desire to accelerate the cut in interest rates (negative interest rate smoothing). The economic outlook continued to deteriorate, and at the interest rate meeting on December 17, 2008, the Executive Board decided to cut the key rate with unprecedented 175 basis points; see figure 10.12. The Board also presented an extra set of projections that explained the new downward shift in the interest rate path with a strongly negative shift in demand and lower expected inflation rates.

The flow of negative news continued in the first quarter of 2009 and in the Monetary Policy Report in March 2009 Norges Bank presented a further shift down in its interest rate projection. The main factors behind this change (see figure 10.13) were the lower international central bank rates and the lower demand. This projected path was followed until the summer of 2009 when the key rate reached its lowest level of 1.5 percent. The interest rate path was subsequently revised slightly upward, with 25 basis points in the June report and another 50 basis points in the October report of 2009. Among the factors behind the increase was a reversal of the unusually high money market premiums. But upward revisions in estimates of economic activity (demand) and higher inflation also contributed positively. The widened interest differential against Norway's trading partners and the NOK appreciation between the June and the October report resulted in a negative contribution from foreign interest rates and exchange rates to the projected change in the interest rate path.

In March 2010 the interest rate path was adjusted slightly downward due to the lower international forward interest rates and a stronger NOK. In June 2010 the continued downward adjustment in the international forward interest rates at longer maturities continued to push the interest path downward. In addition there were now marked increases in the money market premiums following the European government debt crisis. Norges Bank still expected money market premiums to gradually revert to a more normal level. And the concern for avoiding abrupt and unexpected changes in the key policy rate (criterion 4) suggested that the temporary rise in money market premiums should be disregarded. This interest rate smoothing is shown in figure 10.14. On balance, the interest rate path was adjusted downward some 50 basis points from 2011 onward. In October 2010 the interest rate path was adjusted slightly downward due to lower than expected inflation.

In its Monetary Policy Report 3/2010, Norges Bank noted that the key policy rate in Norway had been very low for a fairly long period. The Bank also stated that the consideration of guarding against financial imbalances, which could trigger abrupt and sharp falls in output and inflation somewhat further ahead, suggests that the key policy rate should not be kept low for too long.

The experiences gained during the crisis have shown that the monetary policy framework was nevertheless sufficiently robust to remain fixed. Even in such extreme circumstances the interest rate policy could be explained by referring to the same set of factors that were in place before the crisis. It is fair though to say that the premium of the money market rate above the policy rate took on a larger importance than it normally would.

Although the main disturbances originated abroad, Norway was affected early in the course of the financial crisis through a money market with close connections to the US dollar swap market. During the first phases of the crisis there was serious concern for the functioning of short-term money markets. The direct dependence on the USD money markets is an issue we still have to consider thoroughly, to see whether that dependence should be modified and, if so, how we should do it.

10.3   Lessons for Financial Stability

10.3.1   The Norwegian Financial Sector during the Crisis

Norwegian financial institutions held very small volumes of troubled assets, and their portfolios were not significantly impaired during the international financial crisis. But Norwegian institutions were affected by the general breakdown of the international money and capital markets. The largest Norwegian banks depended on market funding from foreign counterparties, and experienced problems rolling over their funding after the Lehman Brothers collapse. The liquidity problems rapidly spread to the rest of the financial system.

Internationally, a large number of banks got into solvency trouble, and the markets started paying more attention to counterparty risk and the capital adequacy of counterparties. The markets developed a narrow focus on tangible common equity capital (core tier 1), while disregarding capital that might not be available for covering losses on a going concern basis. The regulatory standards for capital adequacy were largely considered uninformative and were ignored by the markets. Banks started to worry about their own liquidity reserves and became very reluctant to lend except on very short term to other banks. Volumes in the interbank markets were reduced and became more concentrated on short maturities. This affected the funding of Norwegian banks and called for higher capital levels in much the same way as for all other banks operating in international markets.

In December 2008 Norges Bank proposed a government fund for capital injections to banks. The Norwegian State Finance Fund was set up in the spring of 2009 and offered two different forms of capital to the banks. The window for applications was from May to September 2009. During that period the market conditions improved substantially, and less than 10 percent of the fund capital was actually paid out. In particular, the larger banks found other sources of new capital. They still benefited from the longer window of funding opportunities created by the state fund.

While the crisis did not have a dramatic impact on the Norwegian banking sector and the Norwegian economy, the international experiences made us think more carefully about the soundness of our regulatory framework. We already had a special resolution regime for banks, but the experiences of other countries convinced us that it needed updating. Our resolution regime had worked relatively well in the early 1990s, but even then we had not been able to make senior or junior bank creditors bear any part of the losses. This option should be introduced to provide the banks with reasonable risk-taking incentives and to avoid that a financial crisis turns into a sovereign debt crisis.

It was clear to us that our policy tools to contain systemic risk in the financial sector were inadequate. We had long seen property prices and household and corporate debt growing rapidly, creating what we believed might be a bubble; see figure 10.6. Interest rate policies could not be efficiently used since inflation targeting required a relatively low policy rate.

Our discussion of lessons will be organized around these topics. We first look in detail at the broad field of macroprudential policies; then we turn to the specific issue of resolution regimes. Any resolution regime applicable to multinational institutions will involve cross-border cooperation, and we conclude by discussing cross-border issues in a broader context.

10.3.2 Macroprudential Policies

BIS defines macroprudential policy as "the use of prudential tools with the explicit objective of promoting the stability of the financial system

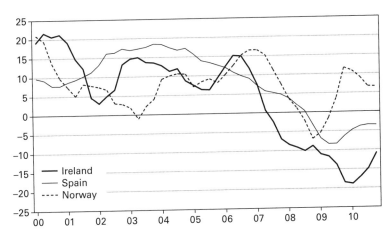

Figure 10.6
Annual property price growth rates, 2000 to 2010. All dwelling types.
Source: BIS property price statistics

as a whole, not necessarily of the individual institutions within it. The objective of macroprudential policy is to reduce systemic risk by explicitly addressing the interlinkages between, and the common exposures of, all financial institutions, and the procyclicality of the financial system."[13]

The international crisis has provided convincing evidence for the need of macroprudential policy. The stated purposes of such policy are to make the banking sector more resilient to the next financial crisis and to reduce the probability of a crisis reoccurrence. The classical theories of financial crises stress the role of credit and asset price growth in building imbalances and making a system vulnerable to negative shocks, which may ultimately trigger a crash and full crisis. Kindleberger (1978) and Minsky (1986) describe how the strong incentives for credit growth in the early part of the financial cycle can quickly turn into incentives for deleveraging. This happens when the credit volumes have reached some unsustainable level, and it is usually triggered by some negative news causing asset prices to fall.

While this is a basic insight and well known to regulators, it is extremely difficult to draw the right policy conclusions from that insight. The turning point of the cycle cannot be identified ex ante. The regulators are likely to be aware that vulnerabilities are accumulating in the financial system. But there may be a very long time lag before the vulnerabilities materialize into a crisis. And there is no certainty that a crisis will actually materialize; the vulnerabilities may dissolve for other reasons. This uncertainty about the consequences makes it extremely difficult for the regulators to act in the face of developments that in the short term look very desirable both for the financial sector and for its customers. The developments prior to the recent crisis are perfect illustrations of that problem.

Countercyclical measures for the medium term constitute one important and interesting part of macroprudential policies. The set of medium-term macroprudential instruments most relevant for the Norwegian economy includes higher temporary capital requirements in terms of the countercyclical buffer, loss provisioning beyond realized losses, and restrictions on loan to value (LTV) and loan to income (LTI) in the home mortgage market.

The Basel Committee on Banking Supervision has issued guidance for how the countercyclical buffer should be operated.[14] The main recommendation is that we should look at the credit-to-GDP ratio and consider introducing a buffer requirement when the ratio is significantly higher than its long-term trend. Figure 10.7 shows how that recommendation would have worked in the (mainland) Norwegian economy: The credit to GDP ratio has been more than 10 percent above the long-term trend for the past ten years, which would have implied a buffer requirement at the maximum level of 2.5 percent. This illustrates that looking only at this particular ratio is not sufficient. It would, for instance, have been hard to argue for a maximum countercyclical buffer requirement as we worried about reduced bank lending in 2009. A more thorough analysis of the financial balances will be required for managing the buffer requirement.

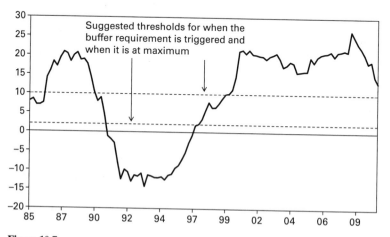

Figure 10.7
Credit (C3) to GDP. The gap to trend was calculated using a one-sided Hodrick–Prescott filter with lambda equal to 400,000 for mainland Norway, 1985Q1 to 2010Q4
Sources: Statistics Norway; International Monetary Fund; Norges Bank

In response to this challenge Norges Bank Financial Stability has reorganized to set up a new Macroprudential Department. The focus will be on the relationships between asset prices and debt, also separately for the household and the corporate sectors. There is no doubt a tight relationship between house prices and household debt volumes. In the models we have for the Norwegian economy we find that the house price growth Granger causes credit growth. There is also likely to be a similar relationship between the prices of commercial property and corporate debt, but that has been much less explored.

The countercyclical buffer could work as a circuit breaker if bank capital were effectively rationed. Truly effective rationing would occur if banks were not able to raise new capital at any acceptable price. That will rarely happen during an upturn. More likely the banks will be able to market their loan business as profitable and worth funding. There would still be a cost to the issue of new shares, with the existing value to shareholders somewhat watered down. This makes us believe that there will be some moderating effect from a countercyclical buffer requirement.

Restrictions on mortgage lending would have a direct effect on credit volumes. The effect on house price inflation is a more open question. We have done some back-of-the-envelope calculations that suggest the effect would be limited. There are additional doubts due to the numerous ways that credit restrictions can be circumvented, such as by side collateral or guarantor allowances. Recommended LTV and LTI levels for new mortgages were introduced by the Norwegian FSA in early 2010, but these have so far not been fully observed by the banks.

The bottom line is not a very optimistic one: it is hard to imagine that any medium-term macroprudential policy could work nearly as efficiently as high interest rates. And even the interest rate would have a limited effect after a credit bubble has started feeding an asset price bubble. The arithmetic of expected capital gains can be very powerful once a price bubble is under way.

A more promising policy may be to build some sort of automatic stabilizer into the credit-generating process. Financial crises are usually the result of vulnerabilities being slowly accumulated over a long period of time. Stabilizers would work before a boom takes off, and so reduce the probability of the takeoff materializing. What we have in mind are permanent measures to make rapid credit growth less profitable to the banks. This could, for instance, be high permanent requirements for core tier 1 capital, requirements for routine ex ante loss provisioning, requirements for more long-term funding of loans, or some combinations of such measures.

The Spanish dynamic provisioning system can be seen as an alternative to countercyclical buffers. Dynamic provisioning has one major advantage, namely that banks will automatically accumulate larger reserves whenever the loan growth rate is high. There is no need for discretionary intervention from the regulator. But other countries have been reluctant to follow the Spanish example because it can be seen as conflicting with the mark-to-market accounting principle. Our view is that the reporting of provisions under the Spanish model is very transparent and avoids any such conflict. There is now work under way to restate the international provisioning framework by allowing provisioning for expected losses. The precise contents of that term have still not been defined, but it could go some way toward the Spanish model. Notice, however, that the actual loss provisions made in Spanish banks were not sufficient to make them immune to the collapse of the country's huge property price bubble. There may be even better reasons to be worried that provisioning for expected losses will prove insufficient when a crisis occurs.

The net stable funding ratio in Basel III has been proposed as a liquidity requirement, but it could also work as an automatic stabilizer. Shin and Shin (2011) has demonstrated that financial crises are often preceded by large increases in banks' dependence on market funding. Figure 10.8 shows the growth of market funding in Norwegian banks as property

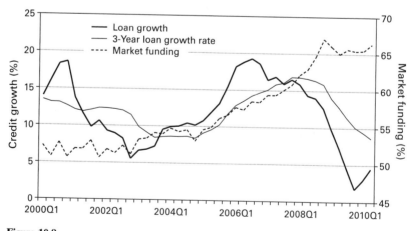

Figure 10.8
Credit growth (left-hand axis) and market funding (right-hand axis) in Norway, 1990 to 2010
Source: Statistics Norway

price inflation took off from 2004. Since short-term market funding is generally cheaper and more easily available than long-term funding, a requirement for some minimum long-term funding may work as a check on credit growth.

The instruments available for macroprudential policies are to a very large extent the same as those already used in microprudential supervision and regulation by the Financial Supervisory Authority (FSA). In Norway this authority is organized outside the central bank. This institutional setup imposes some limits on what Norges Bank can do. While Norges Bank can potentially create some macroprudential instruments based on its role as liquidity provider, the Bank will mainly have an advisory role on financial stability issues.

An important part of Norges Bank's responsibilities for financial stability will be to provide a macroprudential perspective on supervision and regulation. Norges Bank has long been producing biannual Financial Stability Reports where we present our analysis of systemic risks to the Ministry of Finance, the Financial Supervisory Authority, the banking system and the general public. We believe that the kind of analysis we are providing in these reports will be an important contribution to the design of macroprudential policies.

We also have an ambition to help with specific advice on the use of macroprudential instruments that we do not control. Our advice will span a wide field from short-term measures to the long-term regulatory framework. The procedures for determining macroprudential policies should observe some of the same principles as monetary policies. Accountability would require that one institution be clearly responsible for any intervention. Committee decisions do not satisfy this principle. Norges Bank must make its recommendations in public, by writing open letters to the Ministry of Finance and the FSA. A report from the Ministry of Finance on macroprudential policy has recently been published.[15] The report proposes that Norges Bank be given full responsibility for decisions on the countercyclical buffer requirement in Norway.

The second important principle is transparency. We intend to expose the full analysis behind any suggested interventions. For the predictability of macroprudential policies, it is important that these analyses be understood and accepted as relevant by the banking sector. If the banks understand our analytical framework, the need for actually using macroprudential tools may well be reduced: the banks will more likely behave in a way that does not call for government intervention.

10.3.3 Resolution Regimes

Lehman Brothers was the only large bank that was allowed to fail openly during the international financial crisis. That failure created such disorder in the markets that all other large banks in trouble were later rescued in some way or another. The most common form of government intervention was the injection of capital to maintain the troubled bank as a going concern. Bank shareholders lost some money and bank management was in some cases replaced. But senior creditors did not lose their money in any single case, and even holders of subordinated debt were most often protected. The market expectations that creditors will be protected in a crisis were certainly strengthened. This creates the well-known moral hazard situation of creditors paying too little attention to the risk exposure of banks. For that reason banks will obtain market funding at a lower cost than they would without the implicit government guarantee.

There is an obvious case for trying to change these market expectations. Governments have long been trying to downplay the probability of government rescue, but that has naturally little effect when rescues have become the typical solution for troubled banks. The strength of market expectations is exemplified by the twin ratings that large banks get from their rating agencies, with the stand-alone rating typically three notches below the rating that takes expected outside support into account; see table 10.1.

The moral hazard problem can be mitigated if creditors were made to believe that they would be likely to lose money in a bank failure. The most direct way to eliminate the implicit guarantee to creditors would be the introduction of a well-defined resolution regime where creditors get about the same protection as they would in a normal bankruptcy in

Table 10.1
Moody's ratings of the largest Scandinavian banks in March 2011

Bank	Credit rating	Stand-alone rating	Difference
Danske Bank	Aa3	C	3
DnB NOR	Aa3	C	3
Svenska Handelsbanken	Aa2	C+	3
Nordea	Aa2	C	3
SEB	A1	C-	3
Swedbank	A2	D+	3

the nonfinancial sector. The regime would need to spell out in great detail how this can be combined with retaining systemically important functions as going concerns. Such clarity will probably be an absolute precondition for making the resolution regime credible.

The resolution regimes mandated by the FDICIA bill of 1991 in the United States and by the UK Banking Act of 2009 provide useful examples.[16] The resolution authorities in these countries have a number of options. They can close the bank and pay out the insured deposits; the entire bank or parts of it can be sold to another bank, or transferred to a bridge bank for later sales or closure. Another option is full-scale nationalization of the entire bank or parts of it. While such a resolution regime also involves some unknowns for creditors, it resembles a standard bankruptcy procedure where creditors' interests are handled according to the normal legal priorities. Some uncertainty about the feasibility will remain, however, as long as the procedures have not been applied to large bank failures.[17] The largest banks handled by the resolution regimes so far has been Washington Mutual with total assets of about 200 billion USD in the United States and Dunfermline Building Society with total assets of about 3.3 billion GBP in the United Kingdom.

Norway does have a special resolution regime, but one that is in need of modernization. The present regime can easily handle smaller banks that can either be closed or sold to an interested buyer. This was the solution used for one branch and one subsidiary of Icelandic banks during the recent crisis. Notice, however, that such solutions tend to protect creditors in full and thus do not take care of the moral hazard problem.

Moreover capital injection or nationalization remains as the most likely feasible option for a troubled bank that has systemic importance and must therefore be maintained as a going concern. This solution does implicitly protect bank creditors. Taking a bank into receivership is not feasible as it would imply immediate expulsion of the bank from the payment system. That can naturally be fixed by imposing changes in the contracts governing this system. But the present regime also does not define which instruments can be used to handle a bank taken into receivership. There is a need to expand the resolution tool kit, at least by including the option of establishing a bridge bank, and to be able to divide the bank and its creditors into systemic and nonsystemic parts. Only the systemic functions should always be protected. The Norges Bank has been looking into this resolution issue and has presented its recommendation in an open letter to the Ministry of Finance; see table 10.2.

Table 10.2
Norges Bank recommendations for a viable resolution regime

1	Living wills
2	More relevant trigger values for supervisory intervention
3	Supervisory authority to break up a failed bank
4	Supervisory authority to establish a bridge bank
5	Guaranteed deposits to be paid within two days
6	Well-defined procedures for nationalization
7	The bail-in option should be clarified

The Norges Bank recommendations include that banks should be required to produce a recovery and resolution plan ("a living will"). The resolution plan must demonstrate that the bank can be split up in a sensible way in case it has to be taken into receivership. This may require organizational changes to achieve a more transparent and divisible structure.

The present law does provide both soft and hard triggers for the supervisor to intervene in a troubled bank. However, the hard triggers are only reached long after the bank has ceased to meet the minimum capital requirement. There is an obvious need to rethink the trigger levels. The soft triggers leave much up to the supervisor, both in terms of defining when they are reached and in terms of what the supervisor should be doing. It would be useful to spell out more precisely what the main options are. There may even be a need to make clear where the resolution authority is going to be.

The present law does not give a resolution authority an explicit mandate to break up the bank and sell parts of it. Such a mandate would be essential in order to impose some losses on creditors. The evident benchmark is that creditors should not be treated less favorably than they would in a bankruptcy, but also not much more favorably. Achieving this balance is perhaps the most important and most complicated element in a good resolution regime.

Breaking up a large troubled bank will only be feasible if it can be done over time. A weekend is normally not sufficient. The resolution authority will thus need a mandate to establish a bridge bank, as routinely done by the FDIC in the United States. The FDIC always has an empty shell ready for a failing bank, and the FDIC has the skilled manpower to step in and take over a distressed bank. This level of preparedness is much more difficult to maintain in a small economy where there are typically many years between bank failures. But there should at least be a realistic emergency plan for taking a bank into receivership and freezing its liabilities.

10.3.4   Cross-border Issues

The big unresolved issue in crisis resolution is how cross-border banking organizations should be handled. The most obvious example from the recent crisis is again Lehman Brothers, which had thousands of subsidiaries and branches in a large number of countries. Its bankruptcy is being handled according to US law. This has led to some frustration in other jurisdictions involved, where it is felt that US interests are given priority in the settlement process.

Fortis Bank was a somewhat smaller financial institution with activities mainly in the Benelux countries, where it was considered systemically important in each of the countries. When it ran into trouble in 2008, its Dutch operations were nationalized by the Dutch government, whereas its Belgian operations were taken over by the Belgian government and sold to BNP Paribas. The rescue operations followed national boundaries with very little cooperation between the authorities of the two countries.

In both of these cases there were conflicts between the governments of the two countries, both of which had legitimate interests in the operations of the same bank. These examples are not unique. It seems that similar conflicts would arise if other banks with large cross-border operations should fail. The key question would be how the costs of a rescue operation should be shared. Ex ante agreements on this have proved difficult to obtain, perhaps because what constitutes a fair share of the burden depends on the exact circumstances of the failure. And when a failure occurs, there is no time to sit down and discuss. Immediate action is needed to avoid panic among depositors and investors. National rescue operations are then the only alternative.

The Norwegian banking market is dominated by one large domestically held bank. But subsidiaries and branches of Danish and Swedish banks have about one-third of the market. The distinction between subsidiaries and branches may not be important since subsidiaries under European law can always be transformed into branches. Norwegian authorities would seem to be in a favorable position by only having to relate to the authorities of two neighboring countries. However, even in this narrow Scandinavian setting there is no clear understanding of who should take responsibility in the case of a large bank failure.

There is no lack of work in this area. Researchers have pointed out that there cannot be an open international banking market if supervision, regulation, and crisis resolution remain national.[18] The obvious recommendation in today's market is to establish supranational regulation and supervision, and supranational resolution regimes. The Basel process aims to harmonize bank regulation, and within the European Union there is now some progress toward common supervision through what is called supervisory colleges. But all efforts to create a common resolution regime have so far become stranded on the question of who should pay the bill.

What exist are vague recommendations from the Financial Stability Board (2009) and the Basel Committee (2010a) on how countries should harmonize their national resolution regimes and negotiate ex ante burden sharing agreements for banks operating in multiple jurisdictions. In the Scandinavian context this issue has been discussed for years with very little concrete output. The European Union is presently undertaking a harmonization initiative,[19] and exploring options to make bank creditors bear part of any losses through a new "bail-in" mechanism. This may take some pressure off the burden-sharing issue, though not eliminate the problem.

Spain and Switzerland are examples of home countries whose banks largely use subsidiaries for their foreign activities. New Zealand is an example of a country that has required foreign (Australian) banks to set up subsidiaries for their operations in the country. This protection naturally comes at a cost. No doubt, the funding and operating costs of cross-border banks will increase, and lending will be more expensive. Requiring local establishment by subsidiaries may be in conflict with the common internal market project in the European Union, but it seems to be the only viable option for handling cross-border banks in an orderly and predictable fashion.

Cross-border banks may also constitute a problem in more normal periods, if one country wants to introduce discretionary macroprudential regulation. A basic problem is that asset price inflation can be fueled by foreign as well as domestic lenders. Macroprudential restrictions on lending need to apply to all lenders in a jurisdiction if they are to be effective. This is acknowledged by the Basel Committee in its proposal for countercyclical buffers. The Committee proposes that once a jurisdiction introduces a buffer requirement, the regulators from other jurisdictions should impose the same buffer requirement for all lending to this first jurisdiction, whether the loans are from a branch located within that jurisdiction or are cross-border loans.

However, this Basel proposal only applies to one of the tools in the set of possible macroprudential tools. This countercyclical buffer requirement is not necessarily the most efficient instrument to use, since it will in most cases only be introduced when the credit boom has taken off. Our perception is that higher capital requirements in normal times, or in the early stages of the credit cycle, will very likely be a more efficient instrument for leaning against a credit boom. And permanent capital requirements on lending, including IRB risk weightings, should still be the responsibility of the home jurisdiction authorities. Pillar 2 can be used to impose higher capital requirements for domestic banks, but there is no possibility for the host country to impose the same requirements on foreign banks' lending in the same market.

LTV or LTI limits may in some cases be imposed on all banks operating in a jurisdiction. The clause that makes this possible is the concern for "the public good, that the limits on lending be in the interest of consumers. A concern for financial stability is not a valid reason under European law. New Zealand appears to have met a similar legal problem when they introduced a temporary add-on to the risk weightings on mortgage loans in 2009. Regulators often do not have to authority to intervene for macroprudential reasons. This must obviously be rectified.

There is an obvious rationale for applying the same reciprocal rule that is proposed for the countercyclical buffer to any tools that a jurisdiction may want to use to lean against a credit boom. But this is in conflict with the principle of free entry in the EU common internal market. The EU Commission has therefore been exploring an alternative where only the home authorities can impose the countercyclical buffer, with no regard for the interests of the host jurisdictions. Norges Bank and the Norwegian FSA have duly protested against this alternative.[20]

Researchers at the University of Warwick published a report in November 2009 with the heading "In Praise of Unlevel Playing Fields."[21] The concern of EU competition authorities and bankers has long been the opposite: that a level playing field should be an important goal of the international regulatory system. Accordingly no banks should face stricter regulations than their competitors from other countries.

A level playing field is a key objective for the EU internal market. This may partially explain why bank regulators have, to a large extent, accepted the bankers' argument and avoided regulations that are not largely in line with common practice in other countries. A related consideration is the desire of regulators not to put their national banks at a competitive disadvantage. But the consequence of such attitudes among bank regulators is evidently that regulatory restrictions will tend toward the lowest acceptable level in any one country, even when there are good reasons for stricter regulations in some or all countries.

There are nevertheless some exceptions to this rule. The Swiss rules have always been stricter than required by the minimum defined in the

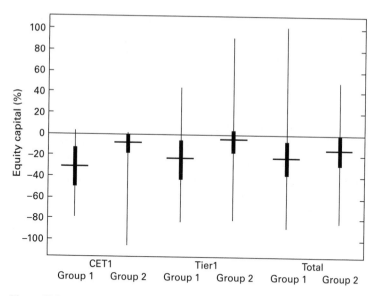

Figure 10.9
Changes in common equity tier 1: Results of the comprehensive quantitative impact study
in December 2010. Shown are the new definitions for tier 1 and total capital: medians and
spreads for large banks (group 1) and medium-sized banks (group 2)
Source: BCBS

Basel accords. The Norwegian authorities have also deviated by imposing a narrower definition of tier 1 capital than that of most other countries. Under Basel II up to 50 percent of tier 1 can be hybrid capital,
but the Norwegian limit has been 15 percent. Furthermore, under Norwegian law, tax-deferred assets and minority interests are deducted in
full from equity capital. This is more restrictive than even the new tier
1 definition proposed as part of Basel III. Figure 10.9 illustrates that
the new definition will substantially reduce the eligible capital of many
international banks. The effect on Norwegian banks will, however, be
negligible.

Even in Norway the general tendency is that banks can successfully
argue that they need the same regulatory framework as their foreign
competitors. One case where the Norwegian FSA explicitly accepted the
argument was the easing of the Basel I risk weightings on home mortgages in 2001. The differences to competing jurisdictions have been kept
at a minimum.

The Swiss example yet illustrates that a level playing field is not necessary for the survival and efficient functioning of the national banking
industry. Banking is very much about soft information, which is not easily

exchangeable. The trend toward commoditization of banking that we saw prior to 2008 is probably not the way forward.

10.4 Conclusions

The lessons for monetary policy can be summarized very briefly. During the global financial crisis Norway benefited from having a well-established and credible monetary and fiscal policy regime in place prior to the crisis. Monetary policy has been, throughout the crisis, conducted within the same framework that had been well established prior to the crisis. This seems so far to have provided a robust framework to handle the sequence of disturbances that hit the Norwegian economy during the course of the crisis

The early effect on the Norwegian money market could have partly been due to its close connection to the dollar swap market. During the first phases of the crisis, concerns for the functioning of short-term money markets took center stage. This posed some challenges that we should be looking into.

Monetary policy is more than setting the key policy rate. In Norway appropriate and adequate liquidity measures were required to improve the functioning of the financial markets. This part of monetary policy bordered on financial stability policies, and the measures taken were sufficient to avert the immediate negative effects on the financial sector. Further actions at a later stage ensured that the Norwegian banking sector would be largely unscathed by the international crisis

But we did learn a few lessons from the experiences of other countries. We had to think deeply about how we could have handled the financial sector problems that other countries faced in 2008 and 2009. We understood that the low interest rate environment had created bubble-like developments in our own national debt and property markets, and that there was a need to look more creatively for macroprudential instruments. We also understood that the resolution regime we have had since our banking crisis of around 1990 left much to be desired. And we were again given good reasons to think about the issue of cross-border banking.

On the cross-border banking issue, any progress will depend on the broader European developments. But on our own banking issues, Norges Bank has taken initiatives for an upgrading of the policy frameworks. We are trying not to miss the opportunity that the international crisis has provided.

Appendix: Figures

(a)

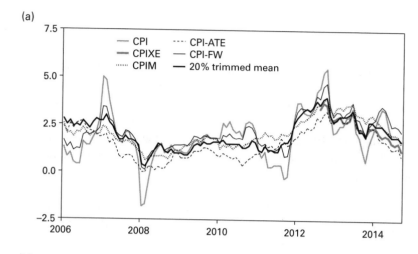

(b)

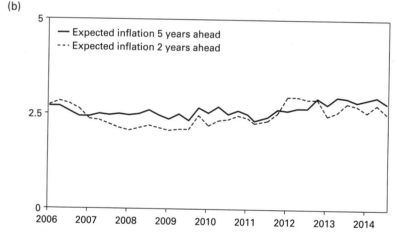

Figure 10.10

Consumer price inflation in Norway, 2002 to 2010, and expected consumer price inflation, two and five years ahead. (a) CPI-ATE is CPI adjusted for tax changes and excluding energy products; CPIXE is CPI adjusted for tax changes and excluding temporary changes in energy prices. (Real-tiem figures; see Staff Memos 7/2008 and 3/2009 from Norges Bank.) CPI-FW is CPI adjusted for frequency of price changes. (See box Economic commentaries 7/2009 from Norges Bank.) CPIM is a model-based indicator of underlying inflation. (See Economic commentaries 6/2010 from Norges Bank and box on page 31 therein, Statistics Norway and Norges Bank.) (b) Average of expectations of employer/employee organizations and economists (financial industry experts, macro analysts, and academe). (Sources: TNS Gallup and Perduco.) The charts are from the Norges Bank Monetary Policy Report 3/2010.

(a)

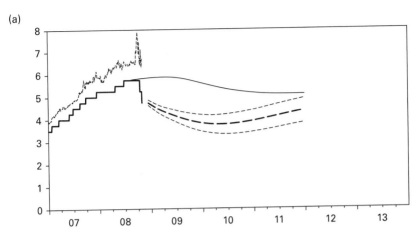

(b)

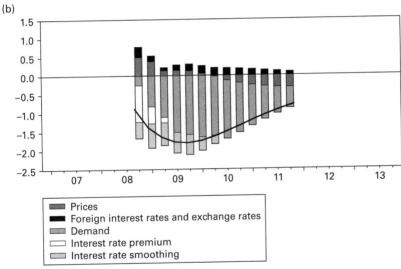

- Prices
- Foreign interest rates and exchange rates
- Demand
- Interest rate premium
- Interest rate smoothing

Figure 10.11
(a) Projected interest rate path for the key policy rate (dashed line) in Monetary Policy Report 3/2008, with 50 percent fan (dotted lines), and (b) the main factors behind the changes since the path in Monetary Policy Report 2/2008. In (a) the thin solid line is the projected path from the previous Monetary Policy Report.

(a)

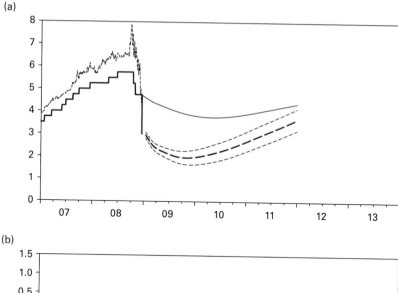

(b)

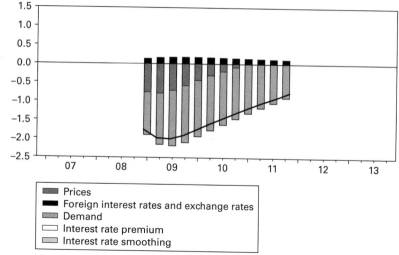

Prices
Foreign interest rates and exchange rates
Demand
Interest rate premium
Interest rate smoothing

Figure 10.12
(a) Projected interest rate path for the key policy rate (dashed line) from December 17, 2008, with 50 percent fan (dotted lines), and (b) the main factors behind the changes since the path in Monetary Policy Report 3/2008. In (a) the thin solid line is the projected path from the previous Monetary Policy Report.

(a)

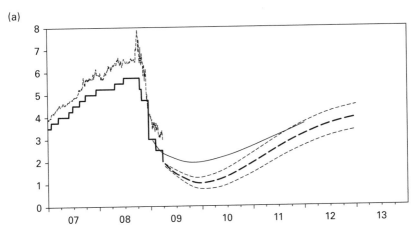

(b)

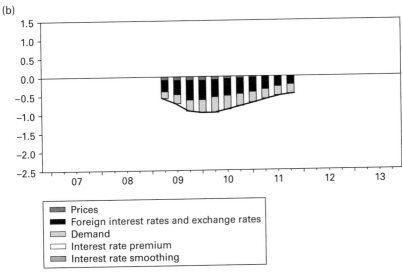

Figure 10.13
(a) Projected interest rate path for the key policy rate (dashed line) in Monetary Policy Report 1/2009, with 50 percent fan (dotted lines), and (b) the main factors behind the changes since the path from December 17, 2008. In (a) the thin solid line is the projected path from the previous Monetary Policy Report.

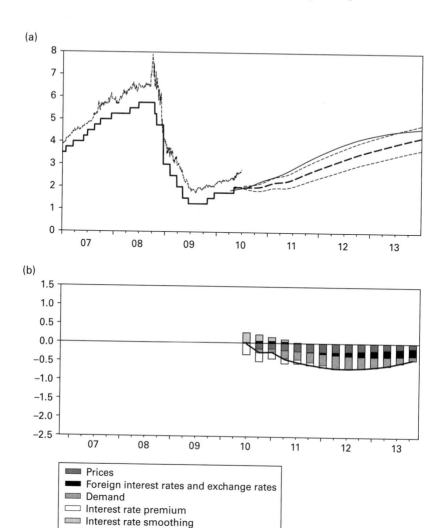

Figure 10.14
(a) Projected interest rate path for the key policy rate (dashed line) in Monetary Policy Report 2/2010, with 50 percent fan (dotted lines), and (b) the main factors behind the changes since the path in Monetary Policy Report 1/2010. In (a) the thin solid line is the projected path from the previous Monetary Policy Report.

Notes

1. When the inflation target was formally introduced in 2001. the government also presented some new guidelines for fiscal policy. The guidelines stipulate that the government budget deficit should, over time, be equivalent to the expected return of the capital in the Government Pension Fund Global—more in bad times, less in good times.

2. See Holmsen et al. (2008) for further discussion of these criteria for an appropriate interest rate path. An example where the criteria are applied is provided on page 18–19 in Norges Bank Monetary Policy Report 3/2010 .

3. This section draws heavily on the material presented in Bernhardsen et al. (2009). We have extended the empirical analysis to cover the period after their study ended in August 2009.

4. On October 3, 2011, a new liquidity management system was introduced in Norway. A set volume of bank reserves in Norges Bank (a quota) will bear interest at the key rate. Deposits in excess of this quota will bear interest at a lower rate. Under the previous floor system, Norges Bank would typically provide reserves via fixed-rate loans (F-loans). Under the new system, Norges Bank will also drain reserves via fixed-rate deposits (F-deposits). As necessary, Norges Bank can also execute fine-tuning operations in order to rapidly change the amount of reserves in the banking system.

5. As an extraordinary measure to help fund smaller banks during the fall of 2008 and spring of 2009, Norges Bank also supplied two longer term F-loans with two and three years' maturity, respectively (the dark gray shaded area in figure 10.3).

6. As an extraordinary measure, in connection with the establishment of the swap facility, two- and three-year fixed-rate loans specially designed for small banks were allotted.

7. After the currency crisis in the spring 1986, Norges Bank provided substantial amounts of loans to the banks to prevent a rise in money market rates. The loans, which were unsecured, were kept on Norges Bank's balance sheet when solvency problems at the banks began in 1987. Norges Bank was later criticized for providing these loans. In one instance Norges Bank ended up providing income support when a savings bank experienced solvency problems. The Ministry of Finance immediately submitted a report to the Storting (Report No. 24, 1989–90) where the Ministry of Finance wrote: "The write-down of loans from the central bank may . . . represent an active use of central government funds that should be deliberated in the Storting in advance." The Standing Committee on Finance and Economic Affairs endorsed this view, and the resolution received final approval only after the Storting had deliberated the matter.

8. See Norges Bank's website for a detailed account of the decision behind the new system for liquidity management at http://www.norges-bank.no/en/price-stability/liquidity-management/the-liquidity-management-system/#decision.

9. It is possible to observe overnight interbank rates below the key policy rate. As both Akram and Christoffersen (2011) and Bernhardsen et al. (2009) observe, because only banks with a head office or branch in Norway are allowed to take part in Norges Bank's deposit and lending facilities, foreign operators with a surplus of NOK have to make deposits at other banks with access to Norges Bank's facilities. Banks with access can deposit excess liquidity with Norges Bank at its deposit rate and may therefore accept excess liquidity from foreign banks only at a lower rate.

10. The theoretical forward premium is calculated on the basis of the Overnight Indexed Swap (OIS) rates on dollar and domestic currencies (NOK and SEK), respectively.

11. Kliem is a dollar rate quoted by the broker Carl Kliem in Frankfurt. Bernhardsen et al. (2009) report that during the financial crisis Norwegian banks claimed that the USD LIBOR tended to underestimate their actual costs of interbank borrowing in USD. The banks pointed to the Kliem rates as a better reflection of the true dollar borrowing costs for European banks.

12. See, for example, Baba and Packer (2008, 2009) and Baba et al. (2009) for further discussion of European swap markets for US dollar.

13. From a speech given by Jaime Caruana on April 23, 2010.

14. Confer BCBS (2010b).

15. The Ministry's consultation paper on "Macroprudential policies" (in Norwegian only) was submitted on January 27, 2012, and has been circulated for comments from interested parties.

16. The German Bundestag has approved a similar resolution regime for German banks on October 28, 2010.

17. A *Financial Times'* editorial on February 1, 2011, states: "While some countries have acquired the legal powers to keep crucial bank operations going while allocating losses, this has not yet been made credible and workable in practice."

18. See, for example, Schoenmaker (2011).

19. http://ec.europa.eu/internal_market/bank/crisis_management/index_en.htm.

20. Norges Bank and Finanstilsynet's letter of November 19, 2010, to DG Internal Market and Services, Banking and Financial, Conglomerates Unit: "Response to the European Commission's Consultation on Countercyclical Capital Buffer."

21. Warwick Commission (2009).

References

Akram, Q. Farooq, and Casper Christophersen. 2011. Norwegian overnight interbank interest rates. Staff memo 01/2011. Norges Bank, Oslo.

Baba, Naohiko, and Frank Packer. 2008. Interpreting deviations from covered interest rate parity during the financial market turmoil of 2007–2008. Working papers 267. BIS, Basel. Available at: www.bis.org.

Baba, Naohiko, and Frank Packer. 2009. From turmoil to crisis: Dislocations in the FX swap market before and after the failure of Lehman Brothers. Working paper 285. BIS, Basel. Available at: www.bis.org.

Baba, Naohiko, Robert N. McCauley, and Srichander Ramaswamy. 2009. US dollar money market funds and non-US banks. *BIS Quarterly Review* (March). Available at: www.bis.org.

Basel Committee for Banking Supervision. 2010a. Report and recommendations of the Cross-border Bank Resolution Group—final paper. BIS, Basel.

Basel Committee for Banking Supervision. 2010b. Guidance for national authorities operating the countercyclical capital buffer. BIS, Basel.

Bernhardsen, Tom, Arne Kloster, Elisabeth Smith, and Olav Syrstad. 2009. The financial crisis in Norway: Effects on financial markets and measures taken. *Financial Markets and Portfolio Management* 23: 361–81.

Bernhardsen, Tom, and Arne Kloster. 2010. Liquidity management system: Floor or corridor? Staff memo 04/2010. Norges Bank, Oslo.

Financial Stability Board. 2009. *FSF Principles for Cross-border Cooperation on Crisis Management.* Basel: FSB.

Holmsen, Amund, Jan F. Qvigstad, Øistein Røisland, and Kristin Solberg-Johansen. 2008. Communicating monetary policy intentions: The case of Norges Bank. Working paper 20/2008. Norges Bank, Oslo.

Keister, Todd, Antoine Martin, and James McAndrews. 2008. Divorcing money from monetary policy. *FRBNY Economic Policy* (September 8): 41–55.

Kindleberger, Charles P. 1978. *Manias, Panics, and Crashes: A History of Financial Crises.* Hoboken, NJ: Wiley.

Minsky, Hyman P. 1986. *Stabilizing an Unstable Economy.* New York: McGrawHill.

Shin, Hyun Song, and Kwanho Shin. 2011. Macroprudential policy and monetary aggregates. Working paper 16836. NBER, Cambridge, MA.

Schoenmaker, Dirk. 2011. The financial trilemma. *Economics Letters* 111: 57–59.

Warwick Commission. 2009. Praise of unlevel playing fields. University of Warwick.

11 Israel and the Global Crisis: Events, Policy, and Lessons

Jacob Braude

11.1 Introduction

The effects of the global crisis on the Israeli economy and its financial system were severe, though less so than in most other developed countries. The evolution over time of the crisis in Israel roughly followed that of the worldwide crisis. Thus, while certain effects were evident even before Lehman's collapse, the crisis peaked at the end of 2008 and the beginning of 2009, and hesitant recovery began in the second quarter of 2009.

Several factors helped mitigate the adverse effect of the crisis on the Israeli economy. These included the timing of the crisis, which followed five years of rapid growth, and certain features of the economy and of its financial system, among them a conservative banking system that is subject to tight regulation, a conservative mortgage market, and the virtual absence of complex assets. These factors helped prevent the development of over-leveraging and a real estate bubble in Israel during the years prior to the crisis.

The financial markets in Israel reacted right at the onset of the crisis in July 2007. However, since the economy at that time was considered relatively immune to the crisis, the reaction was moderate in comparison to subsequent developments. During the last quarter of 2008 as the global crisis intensified, prices of shares and corporate bonds in Israel dropped sharply; volatility and risk spreads soared; the cost of credit increased and the raising of capital by the business sector came to almost a complete halt; and the economy's risk premium rose. However, Israel's financial institutions, including the banks, showed resilience relative to the intensity of the crisis; they remained stable and none collapsed.

The last quarter of 2008 and the first quarter of 2009 constitute the peak of the crisis in Israel as in other countries with respect to developments in the financial markets and in real economic activity, the fears and uncertainties that existed, and the policy response. Although in retrospect the financial system in Israel withstood the storm, there were real concerns at the time regarding the stability of some financial institutions and the continued proper functioning of the financial system. The recovery of the markets in Israel began toward the end of the first quarter of 2009, along with the recovery in global markets, and gained momentum over time.

The impact of the crisis was primarily felt in the nonbank credit market, which essentially stopped functioning and became the major source of risk for Israel's financial system during the crisis. The interactions between the crisis in this market and large-scale redemptions from provident funds led to public pressure on the government and to the creation of a limited government safety net for pension savings, which was not used eventually.

The effect of the global crisis on real activity in Israel intensified gradually. While the rapid growth of the economy continued during the first half of 2008, there was a turnaround in the second half of the year and the economy slid into recession. GDP growth was negative in the last quarter of 2008 and in the first quarter of 2009. Growth resumed in Israel in the second quarter of 2009, with the start of the global recovery, and it accelerated in the subsequent months. Thus the economy suffered a significant, though short-lived recession, and its effect was more moderate than in other developed countries and relative to the concerns that prevailed at the height of the crisis. The eventual relatively moderate effect on the Israeli economy was the result of policy measures abroad that helped to contain the global crisis, successful policy measures taken in Israel during the crisis, and several features of the Israeli economy described below.

The top priority of economic policy in Israel was to maintain the stability of the financial system and the financial institutions and to ease the liquidity and credit shortage. The policy response was vigorous and contributed both to moderating the effect of the crisis on the economy and the financial system, and to the relatively rapid recovery. Monetary policy played a central role, involving unprecedented monetary expansion during the crisis and the use of unconventional tools for quantitative easing. These included the purchase of government bonds, in addition to the purchase of foreign currency which had begun earlier in order to increase foreign exchange reserves and in view of the appreciation of the shekel. The response of fiscal policy was more restrained, though the tax revenue automatic stabilizers were allowed to operate in full and the government introduced several programs to ease credit constraints. The statements by policy makers of their confidence in the resilience of the banking system and their willingness to take additional steps if needed helped to calm the markets.

During the crisis the Supervision of Banks focused on strengthening capital adequacy in the banking system and improving its risk management, in line with long-term processes that it had engaged in prior to the crisis. It also concentrated on closely monitoring the exposure of the banks to developments in Israel and abroad, particularly exposure to foreign assets and large borrowers in Israel, on increasing transparency with regard to their exposure, and on intervening when necessary.

As recovery gained momentum in the later part of 2009, policy makers were increasingly concerned with the need to strike a balance between supporting the recovery and preventing undesirable developments, such as an excessive rise in real estate prices.

There are important lessons to be learned for reducing the risk of a crisis occurring, for the early detection of its development, and for reducing vulnerability to a crisis. These lessons highlight the need for macroprudential policy based on an integrative view of the financial system, the importance of a high level of capital adequacy, and the need to improve risk management in all financial institutions and the regulation of those institutions. Particular attention should be given to the supervision of nonbank entities, instruments and markets.

Additional lessons concern policy management during a crisis and upon emerging from it. These underline the need for quick and determined action in order to stabilize systemically important financial institutions, including nonbank entities, and to inject liquidity into the financial system and relevant institutions. This is in addition to the need for a quick and large-scale response by monetary policy, which includes quantitative tools. The crisis also underlined the importance of maintaining fiscal discipline in good times. Such discipline contributed, among other things, to the ability to pursue countercyclical fiscal policy during the recession.

This chapter describes Israel's experience with the crisis during the period 2007 to 2009. Section 11.2 describes the crisis in Israel and the policies adopted. Section 11.3 discusses the lessons from the crisis that are most relevant to Israel.

11.2   The Crisis in Israel

11.2.1   The Israeli Economy prior to the Crisis

The global crisis hit Israel after five years of rapid growth, which began with the exit from the previous recession in 2001 to 2003 (figure 11.1)

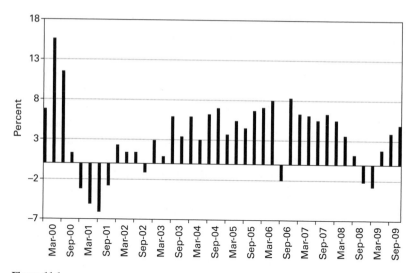

Figure 11.1
Rate of GDP growth (quarterly, seasonally adjusted, annual rates of change)
Source: Based on Central Bureau of Statistics data

and which was supported by global economic prosperity, an improvement in the security situation (during most of the period), and growth-oriented macroeconomic policy. These were reflected in many positive developments, some of which peaked at the beginning of 2008: a high level of economic activity, very low unemployment, a surplus in the current account of the balance of payments (figure 11.2), a high rate of saving and a large cumulative decline in the public debt-to-GDP ratio (figure 11.3), a booming capital market, a high level of foreign direct investment, a decline in the economy's risk premium and a rise in its credit rating, high profits in the business sector, and an increase in the resilience of the banking system. In addition, and in contrast to many developed economies, a bubble in real estate prices had not developed in Israel in the years prior to the global crisis. Thus the economy was in a favorable situation prior to the crisis, although this was not enough to spare it altogether.

In the years preceding the crisis, the financial system in Israel underwent some far-reaching transformations, as a result of, among other things, wide-ranging reforms including the "Bachar" reforms.[1] These processes contributed to the development of new markets, particularly regarding nonbank credit and had important advantages. However, a gap was created between the pace of developments in the markets and the

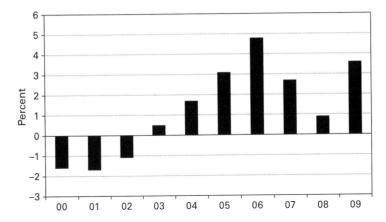

Figure 11.2
Current account of the balance of payments (percentage of GDP)
Source: Central Bureau of Statistics

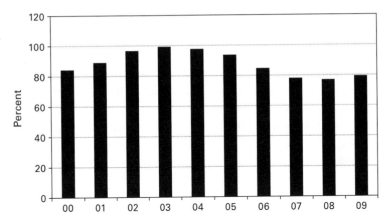

Figure 11.3
Gross public debt (percentage of GDP)
Source: Bank of Israel

rate of adjustment of the regulation and supervision of the nonbank markets and financial institutions—which now represented a larger share of the financial system. This gap increased the vulnerability of Israel's financial system to the global crisis.

A prominent development in that respect during this period of prosperity was the rapid growth of the corporate bond market (figure 11.4). The share of corporate bonds rose significantly both in the financing of the business sector and in the public's asset portfolio, including long-term

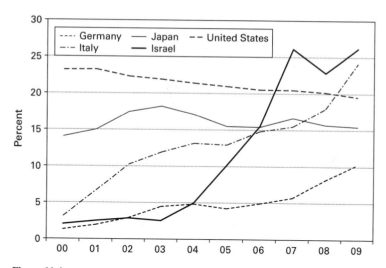

Figure 11.4
Ratio of the balance of corporate bonds to GDP (percentage of GDP). Bonds of domestic
companies were issued on the domestic market; bank and insurance company bonds and
structured bonds are excluded.
Sources: BIS Quarterly Review; IMF data

saving. The development of the nonbank credit market provided significant advantages; however, it was not accompanied by the development
of an appropriate infrastructure within financial institutions for the evaluation and monitoring of credit risk nor by an adequate development of
a regulatory infrastructure and institutional restrictions on this credit,
which increased the risk of the economy's credit portfolio. For example,
it was possible in Israel, in contrast to other countries, to issue corporate
bonds without there being an appropriate level of corporate governance
in the issuing companies. During the crisis this market experienced a
major shock, particularly in the case of bonds for the financing of real
estate investments abroad, and corporate bonds became the focus of risk
in the Israeli financial system, as well as a major factor in the contraction
of sources of financing for the business sector.

The development of the corporate bond market interacted with
changes that occurred at the same time in the public's asset portfolio,
including pension savings. These include an increase in the share of
negotiable assets, whose values vary with market fluctuations, including
corporate bonds, in the household portfolios. Many savers were apparently not sufficiently aware of the implications for the level of risk of
their savings, particularly regarding provident funds. Against this back-

ground, there were large-scale redemptions of provident funds during the crisis. Due to their major role in the corporate bond market, this situation exacerbated the crisis in that market and was a major factor in the decision to create a "safety net."

Against the background of the major changes undergone by the financial system, the conservatism of the banking system in Israel, which is closely regulated, stood out. During the years of prosperity prior to the crisis, the banks had been forced to make the necessary adjustments to meet the requirements of the Supervision of Banks. These adjustments were intended to increase the stability of the system and reduce its vulnerability: there had been an improvement in their resilience and their performance, as reflected in high levels of profitability, in the level of capital adequacy, and in a reduction in credit risk. These characteristics were of major benefit to the financial system and the economy as a whole during the crisis.

As described below, the effect of the global crisis on the Israeli economy and the financial system was relatively moderate. This was partly due to favorable cyclical factors prior to the crisis and its relatively short duration. However, it was mainly the result of a number of the economy's basic characteristics:

• *Features of the financial system.* Conservative management of the financial institutions, particularly the banking system (which is subject to tight and meticulous supervision), the underdeveloped interbank market, the lack of complex asset and securitization markets, and a conservative mortgage market that also contributed to a stable housing market. As a result excessive leverage, a real estate bubble, and complex assets—all of which were major factors behind the global crisis—did not develop in Israel prior to the crisis. Households maintained a high rate of saving and avoided overleveraging, in general, and with respect to mortgages, in particular. Furthermore the economy's overall debt burden (public and private) was low relative to other countries.

• *An ongoing surplus in the current account.* The surplus was primarily due to the rise in national saving, and a balanced structure of the economy's foreign assets and liabilities.

• *Credibility of the monetary policy and of the price stability environment.*

• *Credibility of fiscal policy based on fiscal discipline and the continuing and significant reduction in the ratio of debt to GDP.*

11.2.2   Events and Policy in Israel during the Crisis

From the Onset of the Crisis in July 2007 until September 2008

The first indications in Israel of the global crisis appeared in its financial markets. In the second half of 2007, volatility and risk spreads in the local financial markets increased, particularly in the case of bonds in the real estate industry, and the prices of financial assets stopped rising. The first part of 2008—until September—saw an intensification of some of the effects of the crisis on the financial markets, as well as fluctuations in the assessments regarding its overall impact on the economy. For example, share prices lost about 20 percent of their value in the first quarter of 2008 but rebounded toward the middle of the year.

The prevailing perception in the financial markets in Israel at this stage was that the effect of the global crisis on the domestic economy would be smaller than in the developed economies. This was reflected in share prices, the real appreciation of the shekel at the end of 2007 and the beginning of 2008, the continued flow of foreign investment into Israeli securities, and in the repatriation of investments by Israelis abroad. Furthermore the economy continued to grow rapidly at the end of 2007 and during the first half of 2008. This perception was also reflected in the 2009 budget approved by the government in August, which did not include any particular response to the crisis. However, tax revenues began to fall already in mid-2008, which was one of the earliest signs of the crisis' effect on real activity.

The trend in the Bank of Israel interest rate changed several times during this period. This occurred against the background of the moderate effect of the crisis on the financial markets and continued rapid growth, which were accompanied by an increasingly inflationary environment, a sharp appreciation in the exchange rate, and changes in the assessments of the expected effect of the crisis on the economy and its timing. Additionally the Bank of Israel began purchasing foreign currency at the time, which was motivated by the need to increase foreign exchange reserves and later on by the sharp appreciation of the shekel.

Even before the crisis, the Bank Supervision Department worked to increase the resilience of the banking system, in part due to the recognition that during a period of prosperity preparations should be made for a slowdown. At the beginning of 2007, it advanced a three-year plan to implement the Basel II principles for upgrading the banks' frameworks for risk management, monitoring, and corporate governance. In addition it required the banks to adopt an upward path for capital adequacy that would lead them to a capital ratio of at least 12 percent by the end of 2009.

With the onset of the global crisis in the summer of 2007, the Bank Supervision Department concentrated on assessing the banks' exposure to the financial instruments that were at the core of the crisis and found that this exposure was limited. Starting from March 2008, with the crisis at Bear Stearns, monitoring of the banks was tightened, and banks were required to take extra precautions. These included the re-evaluation of risks, strengthening of their capital, preparation of contingency plans to raise additional capital, and so forth. A clear example of the Bank Supervision Department's measures at that time was its actions that led one of the largest banks in Israel (Bank Hapoalim) to reduce its holdings of certain MBS assets. The Bank Supervision Department took additional measures at that time that by September 2008 left the banking system with a low exposure to sophisticated foreign financial assets and reinforced it against the possibility of deterioration.

The Peak of the Crisis: September 2008 until the End of the First Quarter of 2009

The situation in Israel, both in the financial markets and in the real economy, changed dramatically with the worsening of the global crisis following the collapse of Lehman Brothers in September 2008. The indications in the financial markets were numerous: the prices of shares and corporate bonds fell sharply and volatility increased significantly; risk spreads in the credit market (both the bank and nonbank markets) rose sharply, thus raising the price of credit in the economy; the raising of capital by the business sector came to almost a complete halt; the economy's risk premium rose; financial investments by foreign residents dropped; and the profitability of the business sector, including that of banks and insurance companies, declined and the value of bank shares dropped sharply. Volatility also increased significantly in the foreign currency market and following a large appreciation in the first half of 2008, there was a substantial depreciation of the shekel in the second half. This depreciation was in large part due to the intervention by the Bank of Israel in the market (as well as the strengthening of the dollar worldwide), and it helped moderate the effect of the global crisis on Israeli exports. The changes in the capital markets reflected not only the actual deterioration of the situation but also the increased fear of a further worsening of the effect of the crisis on the economy and the financial system. There was a significant turn for the worse in real activity as well, and the economy moved from rapid growth to recession. Thus, during the last quarter of 2008 and the first quarter of 2009, growth was negative, such that GDP fell by 2 to 3 percent each quarter (seasonally adjusted annual rates).

The nonbank credit market was the most affected component of the local financial system and became the focus of risk in the system. The primary market shrank and during the second half of 2008 disappeared almost completely. Yields on corporate bonds and their risk spreads rose sharply, and the dispersion of yields and volatility grew significantly. Spreads increased in all the industries and all the ratings, particularly in the low ratings, and in the real estate industry, in which a significant part of the funds raised were used for investment abroad (figure 11.5). The reaction of the nonbank credit market reflected the concern that a significant part of the credit raised in previous years would not be redeemed on time and that large companies might default. This concern was also driven by the concentrated structure of ownership and control in Israel,

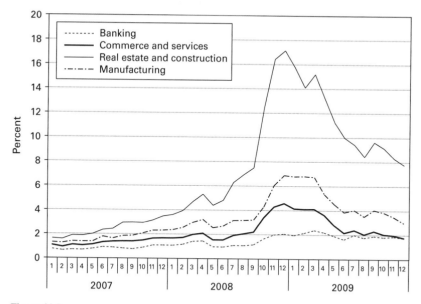

Figure 11.5
Gap between yields on CPI-indexed corporate bonds and yields on CPI-indexed government bonds, by industry (monthly average). The gap is calculated as the difference between the weighted average yield to maturity on CPI-indexed corporate bonds, excluding convertibles, with a yield to maturity of up to 60 percent and with an average duration longer than six months, and the yield on Galil-type government bonds with an average duration of five years.
Source: Bank of Israel

which could have spread the crisis from the real estate industry to other industries.

The increase in yields in the corporate bond market was partly the result of the dramatic acceleration in redemptions from mutual funds and provident funds, which achieved unusually negative yields in the second half of 2008. The large withdrawals forced the funds to sell off assets in large quantities, including corporate bonds, thus increasing their yields. The possibility of a further increase in the redemptions, which would have exacerbated the deterioration in the financial markets and in particular the market for corporate bonds, and the fears among the public of a decline in the value of its pension savings constituted a major concern among policy makers at the end of 2008 and led to the announcement of a "safety net" as described below.

Total credit to the nonfinancial private sector continued to grow during the crisis although at only a moderate rate. The availability of bank credit at this time eased the effect of the crisis on households and the business sector and emphasized the banking system's continued functioning and its role in the provision of credit during the crisis. Nevertheless, total credit to the business sector declined, and the risk premium on credit to this sector rose significantly in 2008. Bank credit to households expanded rapidly both in 2008 and 2009 and, together with the high rate of private saving, helped smooth consumption. The expansion in mortgages helped preserve the level of activity in residential construction. The policy adopted in the financial markets, including the sharp cut in the Bank of Israel interest rate, helped ease the credit shortage throughout the crisis.

Although the stability of the banking system was maintained throughout the crisis and none of the banks went bankrupt, 2008 and the beginning of 2009 were a difficult period for the banks in Israel: their profits declined and their market values dropped sharply. In some banks the crisis led to the realization of losses on mortgage-backed securities abroad, and to a drop in the repayment ability of firms and households in Israel, which required an increase in loan-loss provisions and large write-offs. Still, the ability of the business sector to raise capital in the nonbank market declined and most of the demand for credit shifted to the banks. This was reflected in, for example, the provision of bank credit to the real estate industry, which had previously been a heavy user of nonbank credit. At the same time the banks were required to continue the process of adopting Basel II rules and to increase their capital adequacy ratios.

Aside from the pre-crisis factors that contributed to the resilience of the financial system, in general, and that of the banks, in particular, several factors that were at work during the crisis contributed to the success of the Israeli banking system at this time: the steps taken by the Supervisor of Banks, an expansionary monetary policy, the provision of government guarantees for the raising of capital by the banks (even though they were not utilized), and the declarations of the Governor of the Bank of Israel and the Minister of Finance that the public's deposits were assured.

As in the developed countries, exports and nonresidential fixed capital formation dropped sharply, though in contrast private current consumption and investment in construction in Israel grew moderately. The drop in economic activity in Israel was concentrated in imports, while the decline in GDP was smaller. The decrease in activity led to a substantial reduction in tax revenues and to an increase in the public deficit and debt.

The main channel through which the crisis affected the real economy was the fall in demand for exports. Total exports of goods and services from Israel in the first quarter of 2009 were about 20 percent lower than in the third quarter of 2008.

The profitability of exports was also eroded due to the major appreciation of the shekel during 2007 and early 2008 (figure 11.6). In 2009 the

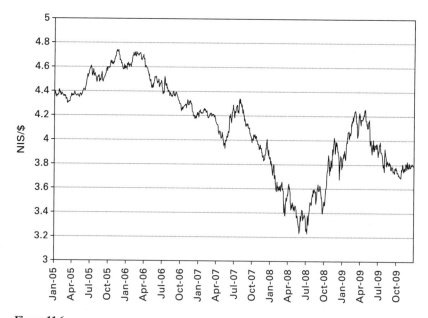

Figure 11.6
Shekel/dollar exchange rate
Source: Bank of Israel

shekel depreciated somewhat (on average), which was the result of opposing forces: a moderate decline in domestic relative to foreign demand and growth in the current account surplus worked toward an appreciation while the purchase of foreign currency by the Bank of Israel worked toward a depreciation. Some of the changes in the exchange rate in 2009 were apparently also the result of changes in the assessment of Israel's relative resilience. Foreign investment in Israel also declined during this period. The real depreciation and the improvement in the terms of trade at the height of the crisis eased the situation of exporters.

Households reduced consumption and increased their rate of saving at the end of 2008 and the beginning of 2009. The high level of private saving, the low level of leverage among households prior to the crisis and the relatively cheap and available credit during the crisis—which was partly due to the expansionary monetary policy and the fact that the banking system continued to function normally—enabled the smoothing of current consumption. The sharp drop in the purchase of durables primarily affected imports while its effect on GDP was small.

The labor market reacted quickly to the crisis. At the end of 2008 and beginning of 2009 there was a sharp drop in the demand for labor. However, the drop in labor input was primarily in form of fewer work hours per employee. This allowed fewer layoffs so that the number of employed fell only slightly and the increase in unemployment (from a low of 5.9 percent in the second quarter of 2008 to 7.9 percent in the second quarter of 2009) was moderate in comparison with the situation in other developed countries. The fall in the real wage together with a stable level of labor productivity led to a decrease in unit labor costs. This contributed to the stabilization of corporate profits, which was particularly important in view of the credit difficulties.

Activity in the construction industry remained almost unchanged. The housing market, which during the previous decade had experienced price declines and a low level of activity, saw an increase in demand and prices during the crisis. This was due partly to the expansionary monetary policy, and in contrast to the situation in other countries it thus had a stabilizing effect in Israel during the crisis.

The declining prices of raw materials, especially oil, during the crisis improved Israel's terms of trade significantly and thus moderated the effect of the crisis on the economy. Together with the sharp decline in the volume of imports, it also worked to increase the surplus in the current account significantly (figure 11.2), which contributed to macroeconomic stability.

Policy Response at the Height of the Crisis

The policy response at this time reflected the fact that the last quarter of 2008 and the first quarter of 2009 constituted the peak of the crisis in Israel, in terms of both the actual situation and the fears and uncertainty. It is important in this context to distinguish between developments viewed ex post and the situation as it was perceived in real time, particularly at the peak of the crisis. Although with hindsight the financial system in Israel withstood the shocks with relative success and none of the financial institutions collapsed, there were real fears at the time, including concerns for the stability of financial institutions and the proper functioning of the financial system. The policy implemented during the crisis should therefore be viewed not only against the background of actual developments, as known in retrospect, but also in terms of the difficulty in knowing the actual situation in real time and the uncertainty and fears of a further deterioration that prevailed at the time. Furthermore the eventual outcome in terms of the various aspects described above and the overall relatively mild effects of the global crisis on the Israeli economy are partly due to the policy measures taken during the crisis.

Policy during this period focused on maintaining the stability and continued functioning of the financial system and the financial institutions, easing the liquidity shortage and preventing the creation of a liquidity and credit crunch, preventing deflation, and mitigating the threat to real activity and preparations for dealing with an additional deterioration. Policy had to balance the need for a quick and effective reaction with the desire to avoid steps with negative consequences in the long term.

The features of the crisis and the policy objectives influenced the nature of the policy response: it was rapid and large scale, included broad intervention in the financial markets, and involved the use of a wide variety of tools, including unconventional ones. Monetary policy played a major role as did measures taken by the Bank Supervision Department and other regulatory authorities. Fiscal policy was less active, due in part to the lack of an approved budget, and it focused on the provision of guarantees and credit. Statements by officials regarding the resilience of the financial system, the measures being taken, and their willingness to take additional steps were meant to calm the public and the markets and to prevent behavior that would exacerbate the situation.

Following are the main policy measures taken at this time:

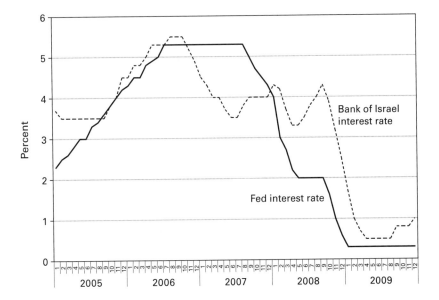

Figure 11.7
Bank of Israel and the Fed interest rates (monthly average)
Sources: Bank of Israel; US Fed

Aggressive monetary expansion—interest rate cuts and additional tools. Monetary policy played a central role in the policy response at this stage of the crisis. The Bank of Israel adopted a highly expansionary monetary policy and also expanded its use of other tools. The rate of interest was cut drastically—two of the cuts were carried out on unscheduled days—from 4.25 percent in September 2008 to 0.5 percent in April 2009, the lowest level ever reached and close to the floor of zero (figure 11.7). The Bank took additional steps: at the end of 2008, it announced several monetary measures to improve liquidity and to reduce its cost; in February 2009, the Bank began purchasing government bonds in the secondary market in order to influence yields in long-term ranges as well.

Continued purchase of foreign currency. The Bank of Israel continued to purchase foreign currency in the amount of $100 million per day (the scale of purchases had been expanded already in July). This helped induce a depreciation of the shekel, thereby moderating the adverse effect of the crisis on exports, in view of the fall in world trade.

Statements regarding the stability of the banking system and the protection of depositors. The Governor of the Bank of Israel declared that the banking system was stable and that the Bank of Israel was prepared to assist the banks with all the tools available to it and to the extent required, with the intention of protecting depositors, but that at the moment this assistance was not necessary. The Prime Minister also expressed his confidence in the banking system. The Minister of Finance declared that the government would stand behind the stability of the financial system and that although Israel does not have deposit insurance, the Bank of Israel and the government have essentially provided such insurance to the banks' depositors in all past cases.

Actions taken by the Bank Supervision Department. Although the banks in Israel did not experience a liquidity crunch, the crisis emphasized the need for cautious management of liquidity risks. Therefore the Bank Supervision Department tightened its reporting requirements with respect to this type of risk, monitored developments continuously, and intervened when necessary. For example, in October 2008 the Bank of Israel canceled the permit given to an Israeli bank to purchase a bank in eastern Europe.

The Bank Supervision Department at this time also focused on credit risks, the condition of the large borrowers, and the degree and quality of disclosure. It issued instructions regarding disclosure requirements in financial reports, valuation of financial instruments, and bank credit. Consequently the banks provided wide disclosure regarding their exposure to risks and this increased public confidence in them.

The Bank Supervision Department during this period also placed special emphasis on shoring up the banking system's capital. The requirement to achieve a capital adequacy ratio of 12 percent was maintained in view of the effects of the crisis on banks worldwide, an analysis of the system's capital structure, and the results of stress tests. During 2008 the banking system increased its balance-sheet credit to the public significantly, and there was concern that this increase might lower the quality of the system's credit. However, a capital adequacy ratio target of 12 percent at the end of 2009 was perceived as likely to constrain the expansion of bank credit and lead to a credit shortage. As a result there were increasing calls to trim back the capital adequacy requirement. It should be emphasized that at that time there was much uncertainty with regard to the duration and intensity of the crisis. The decision to continue to strengthen capital adequacy was also a result of the concern that there might be an additional deterioration in the markets and in the repayment ability of large borrowers. An additional step to reinforce the system's capital was an announcement by the Bank Supervision Department that the payments of dividends by banks would require the approval of the

Supervisor of Banks. This essentially prevented the distribution of dividends for that year and reinforced the system's capital.

Additional measures to stabilize the financial markets and to ease the credit and liquidity constraints included:

A government "safety net" for pension savings. In December 2008 the government announced a program (the "safety net") to protect part of the pension savings of individuals close to retirement whose pension savings had lost significant value during the crisis. The plan was intended to soothe public concern regarding the value of these savings, to halt the redemptions from the provident funds, and to stabilize the corporate bond market. It followed the wave of redemptions from the funds and the concerns that further redemptions would exacerbate the situation. The safety net was put in place with relative speed and thus helped calm the markets and avoid further deterioration.

Government guarantees to the banks for raising capital. This program was created in view of the halt in the raising of capital in the capital market during the second half of 2008, the inability of the banks to satisfy all the demand for credit and the fact that they were being required to continue increasing their capital adequacy ratio. The program was intended therefore to expand the supply of bank credit, build up the banks' capital, and reinforce the stability of the system. The plan took a long time to set up and eventually the banks did not utilize the guarantees. Nevertheless, its very existence demonstrated that the government was standing behind the banks and this reinforced public confidence in them.

Creation of investment funds. In view of the freeze in nonbank credit and the large expected redemptions of corporate bonds, it was decided to create investment funds ("Manof funds") with the participation of the government and the private sector. The funds were intended to expand nonbank credit through the recycling of debt and debt settlements. Only little use was made of the three funds that were created in early 2009 and following the recovery in the corporate bond market, no additional funds were created.

Setting up tools for debt settlements in the bond market. Since appropriate tools for dealing with a crisis had not yet been created in this market, the Israel Securities Authority initiated the appointment of "credit officers." Their role was to assist companies that had issued bonds and needed to negotiate debt settlements. This measure helped achieve the numerous debt settlements that were needed during 2009.

Additional measures to deal with the credit shortage included the expansion of funds for assistance to small and medium-sized businesses and to exporters. There were delays in the implementation of some measures and their criteria for granting assistance were sometimes complicated and not sufficiently flexible.

The response of fiscal policy to the crisis—even at its peak—was moderate in comparison to both the reaction of monetary policy in Israel and the reaction of fiscal policy in the developed countries. The intensification of the crisis occurred simultaneously with the development of a political crisis in Israel so it was at the height of the crisis that Israel lost the ability to approve the State Budget for 2009. The government was thus forced to operate until July 2009 on the basis of the 2008 budget,[2] which was not formulated to deal with the crisis. However, the moderate reaction at that time also reflected the intentional caution of the government with respect to a hasty increase in expenditure. Still, the budget deficit increased (figure 11.8) as the government allowed the tax revenue automatic stabilizers to operate to their full extent and these were significant, given the sharp drop in tax revenues. Spending-side automatic stabilizers were not activated, as there are virtually no such mechanisms in the Israeli budget.

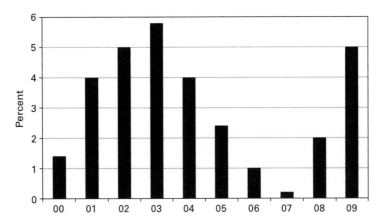

Figure 11.8
Budget deficit (percent of GDP). Excluded are the Bank of Israel's profits and extended credit.
Source: Bank of Israel

In conclusion, the policy undertaken, along with the factors described above, contributed to moderating the effect of the crisis on the economy and on the financial system and to the relatively quick recovery. The relatively mild effect of the crisis, together with the caution exercised in choosing the policy measures, also minimized the long-term costs of the policy response. The government did not purchase assets, including "toxic" ones, and the public debt grew only slightly during the crisis.

The Recovery: The Second Quarter of 2009 and Subsequently

By the beginning of the second quarter of 2009, the crisis had passed its peak in Israel. As signs of recovery appeared abroad, a gradual recovery began in Israel as well, first in the financial markets and a short time later in real activity as well.

The recovery in the local financial market began in March 2009, along with that in the global markets. Share and bond prices rose sharply and at higher rates than in the developed countries; the issue of shares increased; the issue of corporate bonds was resumed; and financial investment by foreign residents grew. There was a decrease in volatility in the markets, in the economy's risk premium and in spreads in the corporate bond market although they did not return to their pre-crisis levels.

The long-term real rate of interest on government bonds declined in 2009 following its temporary rise at the peak of the crisis, and at the end of the year it reached a historic low. The short-term real rate of interest also reached a historic low and even became negative, reflecting the expansionary monetary policy. The low rate of interest and the near-zero yields on conservative investments also encouraged the public to take out new mortgages, particularly un-indexed floating interest rate shekel mortgages, in order to purchase homes, some of them for investment purposes.

During 2009 there was a significant improvement in the financial ratios of the banks and insurance companies, which was due to the improvement in economic activity and in the capital markets, and to the increases in capital designed to meet regulatory requirements and even beyond that.

After two quarters of decline in GDP, positive growth was recorded in the second quarter of 2009. The recovery accelerated during the second half of the year. By the end of 2009, GDP and private consumption were higher than their pre-crisis levels, while exports, imports, and investment were still much lower.

The resumption of growth was based on the start of the global recovery, the relatively favorable conditions of the economy, the fact that it had been affected only moderately by the crisis, and the expansionary monetary policy in Israel. Contributing to this on the supply side was the fact that firms and banks had not collapsed during the crisis and there were no massive layoffs. Expansionary monetary policy and the renewal of corporate bond issues improved the availability of credit to the business sector. The effect on the exchange rate of the Bank of Israel's intervention in the foreign exchange market helped exports. The rise in the value of financial assets, the low rate of interest and the improvement in the labor market contributed to the growth in private consumption. The high rate of private saving and low household leverage also supported the rapid expansion of consumption with the improvement in consumer confidence.

During 2009 the rise in house prices, which had begun at the end of 2007, accelerated and the number of housing starts grew. House purchases grew significantly and many of them were for investment purposes. These developments raised the question of whether a bubble had evolved in the real estate market in 2009 and stressed the challenge facing monetary policy during the exit from the crisis, in view of the particularly low Bank of Israel interest rate. An examination of the trends in housing prices shows that despite the sharp increases, there was no bubble in 2009.

Although with hindsight one can identify a process of acceleration in the recovery of the economy during 2009, at the time there was considerable uncertainty as to the robustness of the recovery and its sustainability. This uncertainty constrained growth in employment and investment and influenced the gradual nature of the process to trim back monetary expansion.

The improvement in the Israeli and global economies, together with the uncertainty with regard to the recovery, represented a challenge to the Bank of Israel. Thus it had to fine-tune monetary policy to take into account these changes, an increased inflationary environment and the need to prevent the development of bubbles in asset prices, including those of real estate, without jeopardizing the fragile recovery and in the context of still very low interest rates worldwide. Accordingly, in August 2009 the Bank of Israel began a gradual process of reducing the scope of monetary expansion. This process was carried out in three consecutive stages. First, the Bank announced that it was ceasing the purchase of government bonds; following that, in August, the intervention policy in the foreign currency market was modified, such that the daily fixed purchases were replaced by a policy of intervention in the event of unusual movements or disorderly conditions in the foreign exchange market; and finally, in September, the Bank began gradually raising the rate of interest.

During the first half of 2009 there was a substantial increase in unindexed variable interest rate shekel housing loans. Although this was found at the time to be negligible in terms of its effect on the stability of the banking system, the Supervisor of Banks issued a clarification to the banks that an increase in the shekel rate of interest would be liable to create problems in repayment, and they were therefore asked to exercise caution when marketing variable interest rate housing loans. In addition the Bank Supervision Department continued the process of assimilating Basel II rules and the adoption of additional steps to improve risk management and to reinforce the system's capital.

The State Budget for 2009–10 was approved in July 2009 after a new government was formed. For the first time in Israel this was a two-year (actually one and a half year) budget. It was approved after the crisis had peaked and it had become clear that its effect on Israel was relatively moderate and there was no need for substantial fiscal stimulation. The deficit targets for these years were raised to match the predicted fall in tax revenues. The actual deficit in 2009 totaled about 5 percent of GDP, about 1 percent of GDP less than the updated ceiling.

11.3   Lessons from the Crisis

The processes that led to the crisis, the events during the crisis, and the policies adopted to deal with it have produced numerous lessons that are relevant to all the areas of policy: policy directly concerning the financial system and its stability, monetary policy, and fiscal policy.

The lessons can be divided into two main categories: (1) lessons for reducing the risk of a crisis developing, for its early detection and for reducing the vulnerability to it, and (2) lessons for policy during a crisis and during the exit stage.

There are three main points regarding prevention and early detection:

1. A policy is needed for maintaining financial stability and reducing the risk of a crisis, which is based on an overall view of the financial system and the interrelationships among its components. This underlines the

importance of macroprudential policy that would reduce systemic risk in the financial system.

2. The crisis has highlighted the importance of high capital adequacy and the need to improve risk management in all the financial institutions— banks and nonbanks—and in their monitoring. In particular, there is increased awareness of the importance of regulation and monitoring of nonbank institutions, instruments, and markets, both for their own sake and with regard to the exposure of the banks to the nonbank-related risks.

3. Sound macroeconomic policy is important. The experience of the various countries during the crisis has once again underlined the importance of maintaining over time both fiscal discipline and credible monetary policy that supports price stability.

The main lessons for policy during a crisis concern the need for a rapid and determined response in order to stabilize systemically important financial institutions, including nonbank institutions, and to inject them with liquidity, as well as the need for a rapid and broad response by monetary policy including a variety of quantitative tools. This highlights the key role of the central bank in dealing with a financial crisis, alongside the measures that the government and other authorities should take.

Following are the main lessons for policy divided into the two aforementioned categories and a number of general lessons for policy management during a crisis. The discussion is limited to lessons relevant to Israel.

11.3.1   Lessons for Financial Stability

Minimizing the Risk of a Crisis Developing and Early Detection of a Crisis

Macroprudential Policy
• *The importance of maintaining systemic financial stability.* A policy is needed that strengthens the resilience of the financial system against shocks and mitigates the effect of shocks that originate in this system on the rest of the economy. It is not sufficient to ensure the stability of a particular financial institution or financial market; rather an overall perspective is needed of all the components of the financial system, namely banks, nonbank financial institutions, financial markets, and payments and settlement systems, and the interrelationships among them. This policy should include the following: the development of tools for early detection of risks to the financial system, such as the development

of bubbles in asset prices, overexpansion of credit and the excessive narrowing of credit spreads, and the improvement of the capability to deal with these risks; the identification of systemically important financial institutions, including nonbank institutions and the tightening of supervision over them (which is particularly important in Israel in view of the relative size of the local institutions and the degree of concentration); the imposition of pro-cyclical capital requirements and provisions in these institutions in order to strengthen their resilience during recessions and to restrain the expansion of credit and the growth in risk in times of prosperity; and the performance of stress tests for financial institutions and for the financial system as a whole in order to identify weak spots and to estimate their resilience during a crisis.

Banks

• *The importance of tight and meticulous bank supervision, comprehensive regulation of the banking system, and a willingness to act if necessary.* Several features of the supervision of banks in Israel contributed significantly to the resilience of the banking system. This supervision is characterized by tough ongoing inspections and the imposition of a comprehensive and conservative regulation in many areas. These are manifested in, among other things, the scope of audits and the examination of business deals, sometimes even their approval in real time, as well as limits on exposure to a single borrower or group of borrowers, restrictions on exposure to particular industries, and limits on the introduction of complex instruments. The crisis has again demonstrated the importance of the willingness of the Supervision of Banks to act quickly and with determination when needed, including the modification of regulatory requirements in real time and intervention in specific business deals and in the operations of the banks.

• *The strengthening of the regulatory capital framework, corporate governance, and the quality of risk management.* The level of capital in the banking system and its quality should be raised further in view of the regulatory developments worldwide (e.g., from the Basel Committee and the Financial Stability Board) and there is a need to strengthen the banks' corporate governance and risk management, an area in which weaknesses also appeared in Israel. The Bank Supervision Department's activities in this context include the requirement to appoint a chief risk manager, as well as to maintain a risk management ability, the formulation of a compensation policy, the improvement of the functioning of the Board of Directors and the Executive and preparing for the adoption of up-to-date international standards for the measurement and monitoring of liquidity risk.

Nonbank Financial Institutions

• *Monitoring of nonbank financial institutions and the formalization of the central bank's ability to supply them with liquidity when needed.* The global crisis has shown that the central bank may need to provide liquidity to nonbank financial institutions as well as the banks and to also serve as their lender of last resort. Therefore there is a need to identify systemically important financial institutions and to tighten supervision over them. The circumstances and conditions under which the central bank may inject these institutions with liquidity should be defined and a formal framework for their ongoing reporting to the central bank should be created. The new Bank of Israel Law provides the legal infrastructure for this.

• *Improvement in capital adequacy and risk management in insurance companies in Israel.* The instructions of the Solvency 2 Directive regarding insurance companies are expected to be applied in Israel starting in 2012. This is particularly important in view of the growing role of these companies in the Israeli financial system and the crisis which emphasized the contribution of a stable capital structure to the stability of financial institutions.

• *Pension savings.* The crisis has highlighted the problematic nature of the pension savings industry and, in particular, provident funds, from which significant savings can be withdrawn at short notice. In periods of uncertainty, withdrawals from the funds accelerate, thus increasing the pressure on the financial markets. Measures are needed, such as incentives for transferring accumulated funds from provident funds to pension funds from which money can be withdrawn only after retirement.

   An additional problem underlined by the crisis is that most of the money accumulated in provident funds is managed in general tracks, without any correspondence between the age of the saver and the level of risk implicit in his assets. A crisis in the markets is therefore likely to severely affect fund members who are close to retirement age. Provident funds should be required to maintain default tracks for investment, to which members will be channeled automatically according to their age.

Regulation of the Financial Markets

• *The corporate bond market.* This market constituted the major risk in the Israeli financial system during the crisis. This was the result of its rapid development, which outpaced the creation of an infrastructure for the monitoring of credit risk in the financial institutions and was not accompanied by the development of a supervisory infrastructure and institutional constraints. Supervision of long-term institutional investors who are active in the nonbank credit market has since been tightened, and they have been instructed to improve their investment procedures for corporate bonds. This should be accompanied by increased transparency with regard to the quality of the bonds even after they are issued and by close supervision of institutional investors, which will allow the early detection of any unbalanced growth in credit to high-risk sectors. The Israel Securities Authority has also made some regulatory modifications since the crisis, and it is promoting additional legislation that will increase the responsibility of bond trustees and upgrade corporate governance in companies that have issued bonds.

· *The derivatives market in Israel.* This market, which was at the core of the global crisis, hardly existed in Israel prior to the crisis. It is important to develop this market in Israel, though with caution and while implementing the lessons learned in other countries and creating an appropriate legal infrastructure. Among other things, it is important to develop a securitization market and a CDS market, though they should be limited to simple products, and the transparency of the risk implicit in them should be ensured. There is a need to introduce both more stringent supervision of over-the-counter nonstandard transactions and reporting requirements, in order to monitor the volume of such transactions and the types of exposure.

Regulatory Authorities
· *Improvement in the structure of the supervisory authorities and the upgrading of coordination, cooperation, and exchange of information between them.* It would also be worthwhile to concentrate the overall responsibility for financial stability in the Bank of Israel and to add to its responsibility the monitoring of the stability of all financial institutions. This is in view of, among other things, the need that arose in other countries for the central bank to provide liquidity to nonbank financial institutions and to act as the lender of last resort for them as well.

Additional Lessons
· *Addressing excessive leverage and real estate bubbles at an early stage.* Unbalanced developments in the credit and real estate markets, including the exceptionally high increases in the rates (and not just the levels) of leverage and asset prices, are a major risk factor in the creation

of financial crises. They need to be addressed through a variety of policy areas: financial stability, supervision of the banks and monetary policy.

• *Improving the structure of incentives in the financial system.* The structure of incentives in the financial system encouraged excessive risk-taking in many countries. This was also the case in Israel, particularly in the nonbank credit market and in the activity of financial intermediaries. Measures are needed such that the structure of incentives, in particular, among systemically important institutions, does not encourage excessive risk-taking. This includes the determination of appropriate standards for executive compensation. Accordingly, during 2009, the Supervisor of Banks and the Commissioner of the Capital Market required that the banks and institutional investors establish a compensation policy that rewards long-term performance. Additional measures should be considered if the incentive structure continues to constitute a major risk.

• *Reducing concentration in the economy.* The high rate of concentration in the Israeli business sector in both real and financial activity and the control of a significant portion of economic activity by a small number of business groups increase systemic risk. Supervision of these groups should be reinforced and disincentives to form such groups should be created.

• *Rating companies.* The global crisis exposed deficiencies in the conduct of rating companies, and regulation in this area is being modified abroad. In Israel as well, the regulation of rating companies was not appropriate and they were not subject to sufficient supervision. The Israel Securities Authority is currently advancing legislation in line with the conclusions being drawn abroad, while new directives by the Commissioner of the Capital Market require institutional investors to design an independent process for evaluating investments.

Addressing Crises Once They Begin

• *During a crisis, institutions that represent systemic risk need to be dealt with immediately.* In such a situation there is a need to act immediately and with determination in order to stabilize the financial system, including the stabilization of systemically important institutions. In addition formal mechanisms should be created for the orderly liquidation of institutions that are not going to be stabilized. Frameworks should be created for resolving a situation in which a bank is in distress (a "resolution mechanism") and the legal framework should be amended in order to, among other things, expand the set of actions that the authorities may take when a bank is in such a situation. The measures should ensure the uninterrupted functioning of the institutions or the transfer of their activity to other institutions. This needs to be done without shielding the owners of the institutions from the drop in the value of their assets, so as to reduce the moral hazard that may result from stabilization measures.

• *Establishing frameworks for early intervention when there is concern of a bank in distress.* The legal framework for dealing with a bank in distress should be amended, while strengthening the powers of the Governor and the Supervisor of Banks with regard to early intervention when there is concern for a bank's stability.

11.3.2 Lessons for Monetary Policy

Mitigating the Risk of a Crisis Developing

• *Importance of the credibility of monetary policy.* The ability of the Bank of Israel to reduce the rate of interest and the interest rate gap with other countries to a particularly low rate emphasizes the importance of maintaining price stability and monetary policy credibility during normal times. The reduction of interest rates worldwide also contributed to this ability; however, without the credibility that had been built up over previous years, it would have probably been difficult for the Bank to maintain this policy throughout the crisis without undermining stability.

• *Greater weight in monetary policy to financial stability.* Monetary policy should not focus exclusively on price stability. It should also consider in a timely manner risks that are evolving in the financial system — including risks in the credit and real estate markets. The challenge of striking the balance between these considerations was highlighted in Israel during the exit from the crisis in view of the effect of the low interest rate on real estate prices.

Addressing a Crisis

• *Monetary policy's major role in the rapid response to a crisis and in addressing it.* Under the appropriate circumstances an aggressively expansionary monetary policy should be adopted. The speed of response and its intensity are highly important. Monetary policy can be implemented with a near-zero interest rate by including quantitative tools that can amplify its effect and reduce interest rates all along the yield curve.

Monetary policy has been effective in dealing with the crisis, particularly in easing the credit and liquidity shortage and in preventing a slide into a deflationary spiral.

• *Purchase of government bonds by the Bank of Israel in the secondary market.* This measure was effective and led to a certain decrease in yields on government bonds. The purchases did not undermine the credibility of the Bank of Israel since, among other things, they were restricted to the secondary market and were perceived as an exceptional and temporary measure.

• *Intervention in the foreign currency market.* It is possible to intervene in this market over an extended period of time and on a large scale through the purchase of foreign currency (the feasibility of intervening through the selling of foreign currency is not symmetric). The intervention was instrumental in moderating irregular fluctuations in the exchange rate and in preventing an overappreciation of the shekel during part of the period and thus apparently helped cushion exports from the effect of the crisis.

• *Optimal size of foreign currency reserves.* The crisis led to a reassessment worldwide of the optimal size of foreign currency reserves and emphasized the advantages in maintaining them at a high level. This is all the more important as markets become increasingly open to international capital flows, and in view of the size of these capital flows and the high level of exposure of financial institutions to foreign currency risk. The Bank of Israel's purchase of foreign currency, which began in March 2008, even before the intensification of the crisis, significantly increased its foreign currency reserves and thus reinforced the resilience of the economy to the crisis, apart from its contribution to moderating the appreciation of the shekel.

11.3.3 Lessons for Fiscal Policy

• *Increasing expenditure.* During the crisis it was difficult for governments both in Israel and abroad to increase public expenditure quickly; hence in the immediate run monetary policy has an advantage.

• *Guarantees.* Fiscal resources can play a central role even in the short run in alleviating the liquidity and credit shortage by providing guarantees.

• *Maintaining fiscal discipline in normal times.* It has again been shown that fiscal policy's ability to respond in a crisis depends on the preexisting levels of the debt and the deficit. During the crisis, the benefits of the improvement in Israel's fiscal situation in recent years became evident. During past crises in Israel, the yields on government bonds surged with the increase in the deficit and the government was forced to reduce it. In contrast, during the recent crisis, it was possible, due in part to the favorable fiscal situation, to allow the tax revenue automatic stabilizers to work unhindered with an accompanying increase in the deficit. Therefore the government should continue to maintain fiscal discipline and a downward path for the debt.

11.3.4 Overall Lessons for Policy Management during a Crisis

• *Speed of response.* The crisis illustrated the importance of the authorities' speed of response. This is needed to deal not only with actual developments but in some cases with changes in expectations and forecasts as well, even though they have not yet been realized.

• *Adopting a variety of measures.* A wide variety of measures may be required for several reasons, including the high level of uncertainty in real time regarding the actual situation and the effectiveness of any particular measure; and the need to deal with a large number of problems, including some that the authorities do not deal with in normal times or in which it is unlikely to foresee that the involvement of the authorities would be required.

• *Long-term considerations and exit strategy.* Policy during a crisis should also take into account long-term considerations, including the implications for the size of the public debt and for the government's future liabilities due to guarantees that it has provided, as well as potential distortions resulting from the intervention in the markets. It is important to outline the conditions and the manner in which special intervention will be ended. Accordingly intervention should focus on steps of a temporary nature and it is important that they be perceived as such by the public.

• *Early preparations for dealing with a crisis.* These should include contingency plans, a legal infrastructure to be used by the regulatory authority during a crisis, an infrastructure to ensure operational capability during a crisis (e.g., payments and settlement systems), and simulations of crises to test the functioning of the authorities.

Notes

This chapter is based on chapter 1 of a special report published by the Bank of Israel (Braude, Erdman, and Shemesh 2011).

1. The "Bachar" reforms, implemented in 2005, constituted primarily the separation of the provident and mutual funds from the banks.

2. According to the Law if the new budget has not been approved by the parliament, the government may spend each month one-twelfth of the previous year's (price adjusted) budget.

Reference

Braude, Jacob, Zviya Erdman, and Merav Shemesh. 2011. *Israel and the Global Crisis 2007–09,* ed. Zvi Eckstein, Stanley Fischer, and Karnit Flug. Jerusalem: Bank of Israel.

12 Prolonged Dislocation and Financial Crises

Frank Browne and Robert Kelly

12.1 Introduction

As it happens, Ireland's property-boom-turned-banking-bust had little to do with its membership of the single currency.

—Philip Stephens, *Financial Times*, 23rd November 2010.

The chapter argues that the four peripheral countries in the euro area in which we include Ireland, Spain, Greece, and Portugal, all four of which have already experienced a severe financial crisis or have experienced some financial market turbulence and are seen as being vulnerable to a full blown financial crisis (i.e., Spain), are special among euro area member states in the following sense. They were all coming from economic backgrounds that were characterized by lower standards of living and lower price levels than those that prevailed in the core of the monetary union at the time when they adopted the euro. The euro area core is taken to be represented by Germany, France, the Netherlands, Belgium, Austria, and Luxembourg. Ongoing convergence to the core levels of these variables was driven in part by labor market dynamics, along with the single currency and full, or near full, integration of many financial markets covering the monetary union. This, along with the ECB's single monetary policy had the effect of bestowing very similar nominal interest rates on all the member states of the monetary union. This created two nominal distortions that have impacted the nontraded (NT) sector of these economies and have had the effect of creating serious dislocation (explained in detail below) in these peripheral countries.

The first of these distortions was the wedge that was driven between the real wage and labor productivity in the NT sector by centralized collective wage agreements. This impacted inflation in the NT sector. It reinforced a Balassa–Samuelson effect that was also probably exerting upward pressure on NT sector inflation. The second distortionary effect was the wedge that was driven between the actual real cost of capital and the marginal product of capital in the NT sector by an exogenous monetary policy setting of the nominal interest rate, which prevented nominal interest rates from responding to rising NT sector expected inflation and therefore drove the corresponding real rates in the NT sectors of the peripheral countries to very low and, in most cases, negative values for prolonged periods. The chapter argues that this particular economic and institutional configuration contributed to the severe financial stress experienced by these peripheral countries. There were many other aspects to the crisis in Ireland and many complex factors driving the distortions that led to the crisis (not least of which was lax regulation). We do not revisit this well-trodden ground again since it is all dealt with thoroughly in the Honohan (2010), Regling and Watson (2010), and Nyberg (2011) reports on the financial crisis in Ireland.

Although we are arguing that there were two nominal distortions impacting on the NT sector of the economy, coming respectively from nominal wage setting and nominal interest rate setting, the effects of these distortions are captured in just one variable, which we call economic dislocation. The neoclassical growth model derived on the basis of consumer optimization says that the golden rule level of the capital stock occurs when the (real) interest rate (r) equals the steady state (real) growth rate of output (g). This interest rate is equal to the marginal efficiency (productivity) of capital less the rate of depreciation of the capital stock (δ). Anything, an unfavorable dynamic, for example, that drives a wedge between the actual real rate of interest and the actual real growth rate for a prolonged period of time will cause serious dislocation by driving the capital stock (the housing stock in this context) away from its golden rule level. The idea is that prolonged economic dislocation leads to a severe misallocation of resources, and when the future pattern of demand that was initially anticipated by this allocation ultimately fails to materialize, asset price collapses (mostly property in the Irish case) and financial instability ensues.

The dislocation variable is therefore measured as the difference between the actual real growth rate and the actual real interest rate in the NT sector of the economy. A stylized fact of monetary union is that this variable has tended to be very large and persistent for most of the peripheral countries. The longer the duration of this dislocation, the greater is the misallocation of resources and the greater is the ultimate threat to financial stability. We therefore propose using the cumulative difference between these two variables over time as our single measure of economic dislocation and as a leading indicator of financial instability.

We believe that this dislocation drove misalignments in prices and imbalances in quantities in a whole array of economic variables, especially in asset markets and, within asset markets, especially in property markets. The longer this dislocation lasted the bigger and more threatening these misalignments and imbalances became and the greater the ultimate catastrophic fallout for the banking system and broader economy. Much of the analysis here has a close affinity with Maurer (2010) and Black (2010).

A popular measure of the damage done by financial instability is the output lost due to the disruption in the economy. In this chapter we show that our measure of economic dislocation can account for this output loss. Anticipating our results, we find a significant relationship between our measure of economic dislocation and subsequent output loss across countries. We can comfortably infer that this relationship is one of causality. This is because all of the variation in the cumulative dislocation variable occurs chronologically prior to (indeed years before) the output losses being incurred.

The forces of dislocation tend to creep into the system insidiously and tend to be nontransparent. And even if they were transparent, they might not elicit a policy response. After all, who can be against high growth and low real interest rates (the two variables comprising our dislocation measure)?

Different speeds of integration as between financial markets on the one hand and the markets for goods and services on the other, when countries are starting from quite different positions, can result in divergent developments across these countries in their real economies as well as in their banking and broader financial systems. It can, and we argue did, throw up a configuration of economic forces, stemming from institutionally determined nominal distortions that, we think, contributed in important ways to the boom/bust cycle in Ireland and possibly in the other peripheral countries that have experienced or are currently in the process of experiencing severe financial markets turbulence.

Developments in cross-border banking clearly show sharp differences in the extent to which different segments of the financial system are integrated internationally (see ECB 2010). Integration in retail banking markets has been very slow, indeed close to nonexistent, while that for wholesale funding and debt securities markets has been very fast if not actually complete at the time the crisis was triggered. However, these differences mean that households can only achieve international portfolio diversification via securities markets. They cannot achieve diversification across asset classes by diversifying their deposit holdings internationally. International portfolio diversification (driven by the objective of reducing the home country bias in portfolios) therefore occurs at the expense of deposits. Since bank loan markets are not integrated either (at least as far as households and small firms are concerned), international portfolio diversification leaves the banking system with potentially a large funding deficit. In sum, differences in the degree of cross-border integration in markets can give rise to problems. In this case it saw banks substituting volatile (and relatively expensive) wholesale funding for relatively stable (and cheaper) retail funding. This, along with the banks' exposure to property, has been one of the biggest sources of vulnerability of the Irish banking system in the lead up to the financial crisis. Examples where banking systems have been weakened by prior programs of financial liberalization are legion. Ireland is no exception in this regard (see Browne and Kennedy 2010).

In section 12.2, we look at policy aspects of these distortions and their dislocational effects. In sections 12.3 and 12.4, we discuss converging standards of living in the context of labor market distortions and converging price levels in the context of capital market distortions, respectively. Our proposed measure of overall dislocation, reflecting both of these distortions, is introduced in section 12.5. Section 12.6 discusses the measure of dislocation. In it we also look briefly at how our cumulative dislocation variable measures up against cumulative private sector credit growth and cumulative bank funding deficits over the boom period. This is followed by our econometric results examining the relationship between cumulative dislocation and subsequent crisis-driven output losses. Section 12.7 concludes the chapter.

12.2 Preamble on Policy

A probable factor militating against any effective policy action to preempt the crisis in euro area peripheral economies was that the configuration of NT sector variables was not seen as a force for dislocation. The confluence of forces driving the NT sector was, in a sense, a once-off phenomenon. There was no precedent therefore for saying that some very dangerous macroprudential vulnerability would later emerge from it. A problem of perception arose from the fact that all the ingredients into the maladjustment in the NT sector of the economy, our dislocation measure, could easily have been construed as having been good for the overall health of the economy—and were invariably so construed at the time. Indeed many of them were part of agreed domestic and international economic policy agendas, salient examples being monetary union and the single market.

Specifically, economic convergence of living standards and price levels were to be welcomed. Monetary union was deemed almost universally to be a very favorable development for Ireland and the other peripheral countries. A policy of low interest rates pursued by the ECB in the interests of a sluggishly performing euro area economy as a whole were also welcomed in Ireland as a positive factor for the economy. This combination yielded robust overall growth. But it also produced a hugely dangerous dislocation in the economy. What were apparently very benign developments contained inherently unsustainable and dangerous elements whose confluence was far from favorable in the long run as is now painfully evident.

A number of other factors, especially in policy settings, tended to exacerbate the maladjustment in the NT sector of the economy. A wave of financial market liberalization preceded the boom–bust in the Irish property market and, along with fiscal policy in general and tax settings in relation to the property market in particular, helped reinforce these distortions. These are discussed in detail in Browne (2004) and Browne and Kennedy (2010) and are not considered further here.

Given the context, one would expect that the same factors would have affected all of the peripheral countries in the monetary union and not just Ireland. This we show to be the case to a greater or lesser extent. In general, the size of the cumulative distortion was bigger for the so-called peripheral countries (in our case, Ireland, Spain, Portugal, and Greece) than for the core countries (identified here as Germany, France, the Netherlands, Austria, Belgium, and Luxembourg). But it was biggest of all for Ireland.

The story here is not just a question of price and standard-of-living convergence within a monetary union with a single stance of monetary policy. It is also about monetary policy being too loose even for the requirements of the core (as evidenced by inflation accelerating beyond target and asset price booms) and, by a measure, for the requirements of the peripheral countries. This loose monetary policy was probably also helped along by a very loose monetary policy in both the United States and Japan that encouraged carry trades and had the effect of diffusing the excess liquidity created in these countries around the world.

12.3   Converging Standards of Living and Labor Market Distortion

12.3.1   Converging to the Core

Real convergence, as reflected in standard of living convergence patterns among euro area member states of the euro area, is depicted in figure 12.1, both before and after the start of monetary union in January 1999. After the start of monetary union, Portugal and Spain continued to converge but at a slower pace than in pre–monetary union. Greece's rate of convergence accelerated after it adopted the euro as did Ireland's rate of convergence after the start of monetary union. Ireland overshot the core in 2000. So catch-up growth was in evidence for all of the peripheral countries but was especially robust for Ireland.

Although all countries have been affected to a greater or lesser extent by the financial crisis and recession, Ireland was the most affected and the start of the reversion to the core was immediately apparent in 2008.

12.3.2   Labor Market Distortion in the NT Sector

In our description of the typical peripheral economy in the euro area, the link between real convergence (in standards of living) and nominal convergence (price levels) has to be made, specifically the channels through which real convergence affects the price level. In this context, by the Balassa–Samuelson effect, it would be assumed that a country experiencing catch-up growth enjoys more rapid convergence in produc-

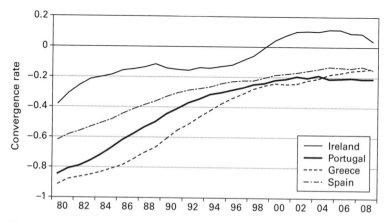

Figure 12.1
Standard-of-living convergence for EU periphery countries

tivity levels in the traded goods (T) than in the nontraded goods (NT) sector of the economy. With perfect labor mobility between these sectors, the real wage increases warranted in the T sector tend to spread to the NT sector where real wages are also pushed up. Since the level of productivity in the NT sector is assumed to be lower, the tendency for real wages to be equalized can only happen if NT prices increase leading to an increase in the overall price level. This regularity is reflected in the relationship between the price level and the overall GDP per capita in purchasing power parity (PPP) terms. Cross-country evidence for this relationship is robust (see figure 4.4 in Lein et al. 2009). For EU countries, Lein et al. obtain an elasticity of the relative price level to the relative GDP per capita level (in PPP) of about 0.92 for the period 2000 to 2007.

This diffusion of wage increases would also tend to be reinforced by centralized collective wage bargaining of the type that was practiced in Ireland over the relevant time period.[1] The labor market distortion in the nontraded-goods sector arises from having a nominal wage imposed on it by this collective bargaining process that is higher than the productivity in that sector. Equalizing nominal wages across these two sectors in a situation where the productivity in the T sector exceeds that in the NT sector can only be achieved by an acceleration of the inflation rate in the NT sector.

12.3.3 Modeling the Labor Market Distortion

We make some simplifying assumptions. We start by assuming that the T sector is on a par with the rest of the world in terms of both standards of living (i.e., real wages) and price levels. Since it is integrated into the rest of the world economy and would typically be a price taker, this is not an unreasonable assumption. The standard of living in the NT sector is lower, in fact typically much lower. However, through labor mobility between the sectors or via centralized collective wage bargaining, the nominal wage in the NT sector is brought up toward that in the T sector.

The general price index of the peripheral country (expressed in logs) is

$$P_c = aP_T + (1-a)P_{NT}, \tag{12.1}$$

where P_T and P_{NT} are the price indices in the T and the NT sectors and a is the share of T goods in the consumption basket. The equilibrium prices in the T and NT sectors are assumed to be equal to the ratio of the respective wages to productivity levels. In logs this is

$$P_T = W_T - q, \tag{12.2}$$

$$P_{NT} = W_{NT} - z, \tag{12.3}$$

where q and z are the (logs of) the levels of productivity in the T and NT sectors. Substituting (12.2) and (12.3) into (12.1), we get

$$aW_T + (1-a)W_{NT} = P_c + aq + (1-a)z. \tag{12.4}$$

Imposing immediate convergence (equality) of nominal wages, brought about by centralized collective bargaining, we get

$$W_{NT} = P_c + aq + (1-a)z,$$

or

$$\frac{W_{NT}}{P_c} = aq + (1-a)z. \tag{12.5}$$

Equation (12.5) is what we call the NT distortionary real wage, where

$$\frac{W_{NT}}{P_c} = z \tag{12.6}$$

is the nondistortionary real wage, since it equals productivity in the sector. Since $q, a > 0$, the nondistortionary real wage is lower than the distortionary wage. The size of the distortion is therefore equal to the difference between the real wage in equations (12.5) and (12.6), which is $a(q - z)$, namely the share of the traded good in the consumption basket multiplied by the difference in productivity between the traded and nontraded sectors (see De Grauwe (1991) for an analysis along similar lines). So the cumulative distortion arising from this exogenously imposed nominal wage in the NT sector is the sum of the individual period distortions for as long as the distortion lasts:

$$\sum_{i=0}^{N} a_{t-i}(q_{t-i} - z_{t-i}). \tag{12.7}$$

12.4 Converging Price Levels and Capital Market Distortion

The type of mechanism at work is best understood in the context of the following simple model. It also continues with the assumption that the T sector is essentially the same as the world economy. The nominal rates of interest in the two sectors can be described by simple Fisher relationships

$$R_T = r_T + P_T^E, \tag{12.8}$$

following the convention that the large R is the nominal and the small r the real rate of interest, and

$$R_{NT} = r_{NT} + P_{NT}^E \tag{12.9}$$

We are assuming that the full Fisher effect pertains in both sectors of the economy. The distortion here arises from the single stance of monetary policy, which imparts the same nominal interest rate in the euro area (i.e., traded) and the NT sectors of the economy (i.e., $R_T = R_{NT}$). Imposing this equality on equations (12.8) and (12.9) obtains

$$r_T - r_{NT} = P_{NT}^E - P_T^E. \tag{12.10}$$

We start from equilibrium and assume that there is no expectation of an appreciation of the real exchange rate, that is, $\left(P_{NT}^E - P_T^E \right) = 0$, which implies that $r_T = r_{NT}$. However, the Balassa–Samuelson effect, along with the effects of centralized collective nominal wage agreements, drives the price level convergence via an appreciation of the real exchange rate, which is assumed to lead to an expectation of further increases in the real exchange rate, $P_{NT}^E - P_T^E > 0$.

This implies a corresponding increase in the real interest rate differential as reflected in equation (12.10), that is, ($r_T - r_{NT} > 0$). Since r_T is the world (or euro area) real interest rate and is therefore exogenous to the peripheral country, the only way an increase in the real interest rate differential can be maintained is for the real rate of interest in the NT sector to continue to fall. So r_{NT} has to fall to compensate for the appreciation of the real exchange rate such that it remains consistent with the exogenously set nominal rate (R_{NT}).[2]

As we have just seen, there is a good deal of empirical support for the Balassa–Samuelson proposition that price levels tend to be correlated with standards of living. It is therefore not surprising that the pattern of nominal convergence, as reflected in the price levels for the euro area periphery relative to that of the euro area core, follows similar patterns, with some qualifications, to that of the respective standards of living noted above.

12.4.1 A Destabilizing Force

It is quite clear that such a development in the NT sector of the economy is, potentially, a situation of dynamic instability. First, unavoidable market-driven price level convergence and the effects of centralized collective wage agreements cause the real exchange rate (P_{NT}/P_T) to appreciate. Second, given the exogeneity of the traded sector (world) real interest rate, the NT real rate of interest has to fall. This increases the profitability of investment in this sector (notably in property). Therefore demand in this sector rises, and given the inevitable inelastic supply in this sector (unlike in the T sector), an acceleration in the NT sector inflation is the inevitable outcome. As NT inflation re-accelerates, so does the expectation of more of the same, and given the virtual exogeneity of the nominal rate of interest, R_{NT}, the real rate (r_{NT}) falls even further. Indeed it can become substantially negative. With more economic activity being generated in the NT sector more NT inflation is likely, and again even a lower real rate of interest and a bigger gap between NT growth and the real interest rate. This dynamic could have been mitigated to the extent that workers in the T sector would have been attracted into the NT sector moderating growth in that sector. However, the scope for this type of labor mobility would have been limited given the very different skills sets required in the respective sectors (with the T sector requiring highly skilled workers and the NT sector requiring only low skilled workers for the most part). The spiraling nature of dynamic instability was suggested in the early 2000s by Honohan and Lane (2003), who say: "The fall in real interest rates in those countries with larger-than-average inflation is a potentially destabilising force. It sustains spending levels and hence upward demand pressure on prices in exactly the countries that already have relatively high inflation, hence working against the factors that tend towards inflation convergence." (p. 372)

With escalating pressures of convergence, and an exogenous (and at the time very low) nominal rate of interest for the NT sector, the NT sector of the peripheral euro area economy was subject to dynamic instability. Given the sheltered nature of the NT sector, the forces of international competition could not have been brought to bear directly to constrain inflationary growth.

Indeed, in the Irish case, and to a lesser extent, in the two other peripheral countries of Spain and Portugal, what has added force to the mechanism outlined above is that these countries, which adopted the euro at its inception, were starting from substantially undervalued real exchange rates. At the euro introduction in 1999, the constant nominal exchange rate made the relative price level of members more transparent.

12.5   Departing from the Golden Rule—Measuring Overall Dislocation

The Ramsey growth model derived on the basis of consumer optimization says that the golden rule level of the capital stock (K^*) occurs when the real interest rate (r) equals the steady state (real) growth rate of output (g). This interest rate is equal to the marginal efficiency (productivity) of capital [$MP(K)$] less the rate of depreciation of the capital stock (δ). The steady state growth rate is equal to the sum of the rate of technical progress (x) and the rate of population growth (n). Accordingly, given that $K = K^*$ when the interest rate equals the steady state growth rate, we can write

$$r = MP(K^*) - \delta = n + x = g.$$

Although there are also some limitations to this model, it is intuitive and serviceable for our purposes here. The rate of interest is the natural or equilibrium rate, since it clears the market for loanable funds. The interest rate may also be used to find the steady state rate of growth (g) as the "warranted" growth rate, in accord with Harrod's terminology. We could even say that when the warranted growth rate is equal to the equilibrium real interest rate, the golden rule level of the capital stock prevails.

Since the golden rule, or optimal, capital stock requires that the steady state (or equilibrium) (real) interest rate (r) and the steady state (real) growth rate of output (g) be equal, the further the actual real interest rate falls below the equilibrium level and the further the actual growth rate exceeds this steady state level, the further the economy departs from the optimal capital stock (in the NT sector, in the current context). It is, as we will see below, a matter of fact that there were egregious departures from this golden rule in Ireland (and in Spain and Greece, but not in Portugal) from the start of monetary union.

Implicit in the convergence of living standards, via the Balassa–Samuelson effect, are increases in NT growth even in the presence of a distortion where the real NT wage exceeds NT marginal productivity of labor. This distortion can be exacerbated by centralized collective wage agreements, which can push real wages further up relative to productivity in the NT sector. Clearly, as has happened, NT growth can be driven to higher levels than would be warranted if the distortions did not exist. That part of growth that is driven by economic activity that arises as resources are in the process of being misallocated is not sustainable and is therefore in "excess" of true sustainable, or warranted, growth rate.

12.5.1   Coordination Failure

The intuition behind our dislocation measure is that coordination failure was the leading cause of the boom–bust cycles in the peripheral countries in the following sense. Firms responding to the very low actual real interest rate environment were not producing to meet consumers' future consumption preferences, although they would not have known this. In fact they were producing far too much in the NT sector of the economy. The rate at which industry in the peripheral countries was transforming the current NT sector output into future output (i.e., the marginal rate of transformation in production, or MRT) was out of kilter with the rate at which the household sector wanted to substitute current consumption for future consumption of this output (i.e., the marginal rate of intertemporal substitution in consumption, or MSC). In other words, the growth rate was out of kilter with the time preferences of households as investors. More important, the growth rate exceeded the equilibrium real interest rate.

In theory, in keeping the MRT aligned with the MSC, the real equilibrium interest rate helps coordinate the plans of corporate producers and consumers and obviates any intertemporal coordination failures in the process. When this rate is subjected to prolonged distortions, it cannot perform such an indispensable function. In the unique circumstances of European monetary union, the actual interest rate departed from the equilibrium rate for very prolonged periods in the NT sectors of the peripheral countries, boosting the capital stock (especially in relation to property) beyond required levels, with catastrophic consequences.

The nonfinancial corporate sector received a distorted signal from the household sector (i.e., the very low, and indeed occasionally negative, actual real interest rate) rather than the correct signal (i.e., the equilibrium real interest rate). The natural, though misguided, response to this signal was to produce more than the household sector wanted for future consumption. The result was a very serious coordination failure. Because of the institutional and structural features of the Irish economy and likely also of other euro area peripheral economies at the time, the household sectors in these economies were unable to convey their intertemporal consumption preferences to the corporate sector. The other peripheral countries in the euro area were subject to similar distortions and problems but to a lesser extent. Tax incentives applying to some NT business areas in Ireland (especially property) reinforced the distortions.

Our proposed measure of dislocation is the difference between the actual growth rate and the actual real interest rate in the NT sector. The bigger the wedge is between the growth rate and the real interest rate and the longer it is sustained, the more severe is the economic dislocation, the more critical is the misallocation of resources, and the more wrenching is the adjustment needed when asset prices inevitably collapse. The theory is therefore that prolonged economic dislocation drives financial weakness and the associated loss in output.

The size of the ultimate distortion was exacerbated by the fact that investor funding was available in almost indefinitely large amounts even at the low real rates of interest. Banks from the core eurozone countries were eager to lend to borrowers in the periphery (mainly via their banks), knowing the dearth of domestic (i.e., core country) borrowers who were facing high real rates of interest and knowing that they would be repaid in euros that would not be devalued.

12.5.2   Costing Financial Instability

While a variety of measures have been used to proxy the costs of banking crises, probably the most widely adopted is the lost national output on account of a crisis. A lot depends on whether the cost of a crisis is seen as temporary or permanent. If the productive fabric of the economy is damaged permanently, losses continue into the indefinite future and naturally tend to be very large. The cumulative median output loss discounted in the presence of permanent steady state effects has been estimated at 63 percent of pre-crisis GDP across all studies undertaken (see Basel Committee on Banking Supervision 2010). Haldane (2010) provides a range of estimates for the current banking crisis based on the fraction of output losses likely to be permanent (i.e., 25 percent, 50 percent, and 100 percent). He derives a minimum of 90 percent loss, but this could reach a maximum loss of 350 percent of 2009 GDP if all of the output losses were to turn out to be permanent.[3] For the present exercise we assume pragmatically (though somewhat audaciously) that all losses are temporary but can last for several years.

Of course, in principle, some adjustment should be made for the fact that the pre-crisis measured GDP was distorted by the bubble economy, which was producing output for some of which there was then no demand, nor even future demand. If some adjustment for this could be made, then the output losses (reckoned as a percentage of GDP) would be even higher.

However, this methodology does not factor in the fact that there might, in any case, have been a normal cyclical downturn (likely tempered by the Great Moderation) if the financial crisis had not happened. This would point to somewhat lower costs than are usually estimated.

Our estimate of output loss is recursive to our dislocation variable since the latter is chronologically prior to the former. If the latter is a significant determinant of the former, then it would be, unequivocally, a leading indicator.

12.6   Graphical and Econometric Evidence

12.6.1   Graphical Evidence

Although our theory is stated in terms of variables relating to the NT sector of the economy, data limitations prevent testing of the theory for the NT sector. Therefore the empirical application uses data for the whole economy and not just the NT sector.[4]

We assume that an increase in the rate of growth increases the return on the capital stock and that the current real rate of interest is a good indicator of the cost of the (debt) funding for the investment required to obtain this rate of return. If the return on capital and the real rate of interest are not equal, then the neoclassical model points to strong forces bringing the two back into alignment. If, for example, the return on capital (as proxied, let us say, by the per capita growth rate) were greater than the real rate of interest, then additional investment would be profitable, and there would be an incipient excess demand for loanable funds to invest. The demand for loanable funds increases until the rate of interest is driven into equality with the real growth rate per capita. It is argued here that this equilibrating mechanism did not operate smoothly in the peripheral countries of the European monetary union from the time of its inception to the start of the financial crisis.

This is clear from the accompanying plots in figure 12.2. With the exception of Portugal, there were prolonged, large and systematic, discrepancies between the real GDP growth rate and the real interest rate for the peripheral countries. For Spain, this divergence lasted for nine years from roughly the start of monetary union in quarter one of 1999 to roughly the start of 2008. For Ireland, the span of the divergence was similar to that for Spain lasting from the start of monetary union to

(a)

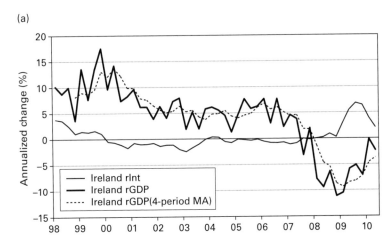

(b)

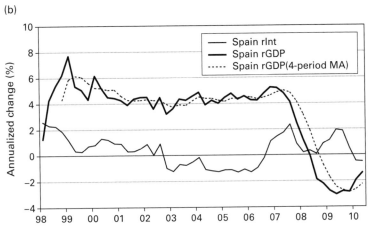

Figure 12.2
Prolonged economic dislocation

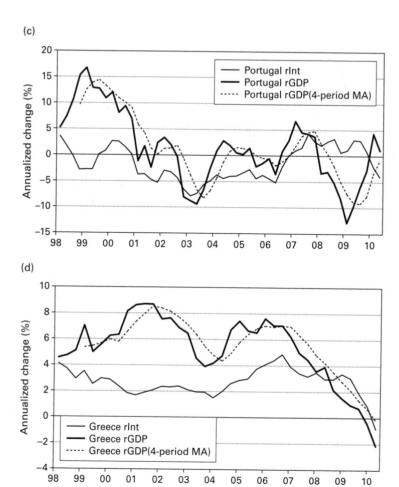

Figure 12.2
(continued)

roughly the middle of 2007 (the start of the crisis) but the cumulative difference is much bigger (note the difference in scale). For Greece, the divergence lasted seven and a half years from roughly the start of 2001 to quarter three of 2008. Note that the real interest rate in these cases was negative for long periods of time. However, our model cannot easily account for the financial pressures besetting Portugal, where our measure of economic dislocation indicates that inflation there was very short-lived, and credit growth was moderate (averaging only 8 percent per annum in the five years leading up to the crisis). From this comparison, it appears that Portugal belongs with the stable economies in the monetary union rather than to the distressed periphery.

Figure 12.3 gives a scatter plot of our cumulative dislocation variable for the period 1999 to 2007 as compared with the cumulative private sector credit growth for the same period. Some have argued that this latter variable is close to the best indicator of future financial system weakness. The correlation is remarkable. High (low) values of the cumulative dislocation variable are associated with high (low) values for the cumulative private sector credit growth variable. The dynamic instability in the peripheral economies was fed by, or at least accommodated by, credit growth.

Figure 12.4 presents further corroborating evidence of our cumulative dislocation measure being a fairly good indicator of imbalances in the

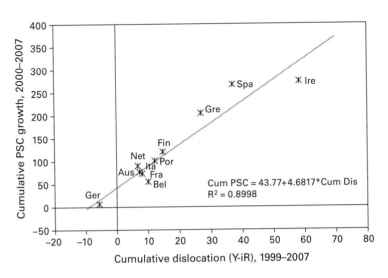

Figure 12.3
Scatter plot of cumulative dislocation and cumulative PSC growth

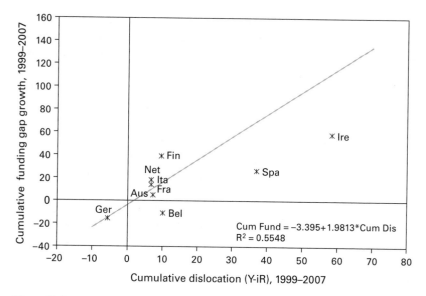

Figure 12.4
Scatter plot of cumulative dislocation and cumulative funding gap growth

financial sector. This also shows a positive correlation of the cumulative dislocation variable with the cumulative growth in the banks' funding deficit from 1999 to 2007. For low values of the prolonged distortion variable, the cumulative funding gap was negative (i.e., that country's banks were net lenders in the wholesale funding market). Germany is the outstanding example of this. At the other extreme is Ireland for which the prolonged dislocation seems to have been a driving force for both cumulative credit growth and the cumulative funding gap. It is clear that credit growth was so strong that it could not all be satisfied by domestic retail deposit flows.

The clincher here is whether the prolonged distortion variable can account for the banking crisis and the cumulative loss of output arising from the crisis. The evidence presented in figure 12.5 is supportive of this. The bigger the prolonged dislocation is, the more severe the subsequent financial crisis as reflected in the output losses stemming from the crisis. It would also seem from the figure that output losses increase more than proportionately in response to prior increases in the extent of economic dislocation.

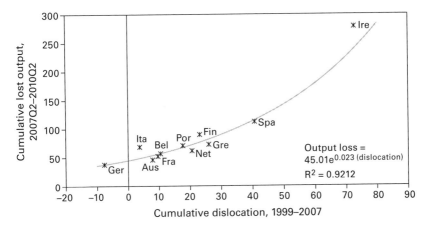

Figure 12.5
Scatter plot of cumulative dislocation and cumulative lost output

12.6.2 Econometric Evidence

Since we are looking at dislocation being prolonged in time and then giving way to financial instability and output losses that are also prolonged in time, we have in effect only one observation per country. So our econometric tests relate to an examination of this relationship across countries. Initial inspection of the data suggests that the relationship between prolonged distortions and cumulative output losses is nonlinear. We propose a double-log (exponential) relationship. We added a number of countries to the sample (see figure 12.6) in order to test if this is a phenomenon unique to European monetary union. The additional countries are selected based on data availability over the sample period. By increasing the number of countries to 57, it also improves the degrees of freedom for hypothesis testing.

The explanatory power of the specification is about 50 percent. Our cross-country empirical results would suggest that our dislocation variable is a good leading indicator of financial instability (figure 12.6). Our theory points to the bulk of these countries falling into either quadrant 2 or 4 in figure 12.6. Indeed almost 80 percent of them do. With a few exceptions, the countries that don't are very close to the boundaries of quadrants 2 and 4. A simple regression of cumulative output loss (COL) for the period of the crisis (i.e., 2007Q3 to 2010Q3) against our leading indicator of financial instability (CD, i.e., the cumulative difference between the growth rate and the real interest rate) for the period 1999Q1 to 2007Q2) for all 57 countries in our sample is

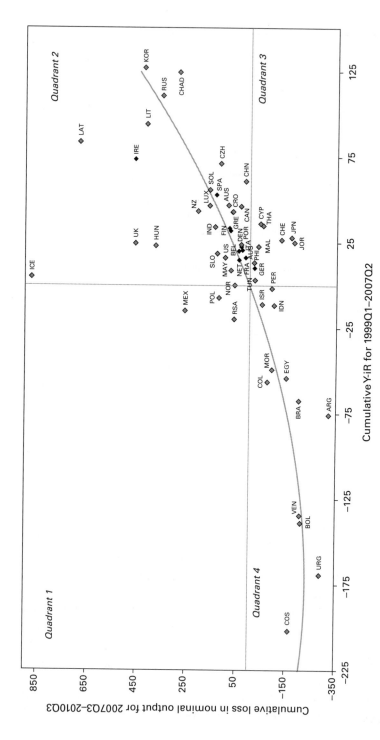

Figure 12.6
Scatter plot of cumulative dislocation and cumulative lost output

$COL_i = 36.3 + 2.19CD_i$,

$\qquad (1.84) \quad (7.17)$

$R^2 = 0.48; F(1/54) = 51.4$,

$i = 1, \ldots, 57$ countries.

The scatter plot of countries in figure 12.6 suggests that this relationship might be nonlinear. To test for this, we add a squared term in the CD variable to our specification with the following result:

$COL_i = -0.45 + 2.63CD_i + 0.008CD_i^2$,

$\qquad (0.02) \quad (7.63) \qquad (2.81)$

$R^2 = 0.55; F(1/54) = 38.4$,

$i = 1, \ldots, 57$ countries.

These results support the notion that our dislocation measure has predictive power for future output losses. Indeed it is possible that the graphical and econometric evidence presented here understates the strength of the relationship. This is because for some countries the CD variable is signaling danger without that danger having yet materialized. Our results also suggest that as the cumulative distortion gets bigger, the subsequent cumulative losses in output become proportionately greater. This is another reason for paying particular attention to this dislocation variable from a financial stability perspective.

12.7 Conclusions

Many of the judgments on the optimality of common currency areas seem to be made on the basis of the steady state of monetary union after all adjustments are complete. The results of this chapter suggest that there may be serious pitfalls for monetary union during the process of convergence to this steady state.

The broad macroeconomic and convergence story for Ireland within the EU and subsequently within EMU has a number of noteworthy features. First, it faced an asymmetry in convergence as between money and capital markets (where convergence was virtually instantaneous), on the one hand, and in the market for goods and services (where convergence was sluggish), on the other. Second, it faced a monetary policy where the cyclical nature of the Irish economy would have played no role, given its insignificant size relative to the whole of the euro area, and that it was targeted at the cyclically weak countries of the core. In this environment the real cost of debt capital failed to respond to escalating domestic demand pressures in the nontraded sector of the Irish economy. This had the effect of suppressing a natural self-correcting market mechanism in this sector. In fact the real rate of interest was either falling or, as in the first decade of the new millennium, stuck at or below zero. It should, of course, have been rising sharply given the robustness of growth in the nontraded sector of the economy. The perverse behavior of the real interest rate in the nontraded sector of the economy led to dynamic instability in the domestic economy and contributed to the boom and bust in the property market. The source of the falling real rate was the inability of the nominal rate, set by monetary policy, to capture the effects of accelerating nontraded goods price inflation and inflation risk premia.

The combined effect of this economic and institutional setting appears to have suppressed a natural self-correcting market force, namely suppressed an increase in the real interest rate that would have choked off additional domestic demand and brought the growth rate into alignment with the equilibrium real interest rate. This is exactly what tended to happen in the past in Ireland (and presumably in the other three peripheral economies) before financial market liberalization and the adoption of the euro.

There were other additional factors operating to reinforce this unstable dynamic. One of the most potent was fiscal policy. The higher growth in the periphery tended to boost government revenues. In the Irish case, budget surpluses were used in part to pay off government debt, giving yet another fillip to the dynamic. The strong inverse relationship between private and public sector indebtedness would further suggest that the trend reduction in the public debt ratio encouraged Ricardian effects on private sector indebtedness. Lowered income taxes increased disposable income, boosting demand and growth even more in the nontraded sector and adding to dislocation.

Indeed, in accounts of the underlying factors behind Ireland's financial crisis, surprisingly little attention has been paid to the unprecedented configuration of economic and institutional forces to which we draw attention here and which, according to our account, played a big role in driving economic and financial dislocation resulting in systemic disruption.

The graphical and econometric results reported in this chapter corroborate our argument that nominal distortions impacted the nontraded sector of peripheral euro area economies (including Ireland) and, through a convergence of standard of living and price levels toward those of the core euro area countries drove a misallocation of resources, overinvestment (especially in property), and subsequent collapse.

We use a cumulative dislocation variable to suggest the types of distortions that affected the nontraded sectors of peripheral euro area economies. We can therefore account for the very rapid growth in bank credit and banks' funding deficits as well as for the output losses following the bust. However, given the limited number of observations (only one per country), these results have to be treated cautiously. Nevertheless, when the sample was expanded to include non-eurozone countries, the overall theory continued to be upheld by the data. We could conclude that while our cumulative distortion variable is an important driving force of future financial instability, it does not appear that this phenomenon is any more robust than it appears to be in our overall sample of 57 countries.

It is clear from our analysis that misalignment in the real interest rate should be recognized as an early warning indicator of dislocation in the real economy. This finding suggests that more research and analysis should be devoted to homing in on a better and more accurate estimate of the equilibrium or warranted real interest rate, especially for the nontraded sector of the economy. It would also be important to have time-varying estimates of this equilibrium rate, ideally along with time-varying confidence intervals and the corresponding real interest rate misalignment as other financial stability tools.

Variations in the differential between the actual and equilibrium real interest rates take the form of prolonged misalignments (as happened in both directions in the housing market boom and bust), then the likely outcome is widespread resource misallocation, with businesses either not producing enough to meet demand or producing to meet demand that is not going to materialize.

The sources of financial instability, to which we bring attention here, grew imperceptibly over time and did not appear on the radar of policy makers (after all, who can be against high growth and low real interest rates?) That has made this source of dislocation all the more insidious and treacherous from a financial stability and overall economic policy perspective.

For Ireland, joining a monetary union created special problems for its policy makers. It may be worthwhile to speculate as to why Ireland was affected by the crisis so much more severely than some of the other peripheral countries. We think that the impact was exceptionally big in Ireland because, first, the size of the dislocation was exceptionally large;

second, the Irish banks had been exceptionally dependent on foreign wholesale funding, which in turn was related to the size of the dislocation and dried up almost completely during the crisis; and third, with all the banks being affected, the credit crunch was pervasive in closing down virtually the only channel of intermediation in the economy. Effectively a robust negative feedback loop resulted from the real economy to banks' balance sheets.

It would appear that the financial market turmoil affecting countries on the periphery of monetary union goes well beyond the issue of reckless lending and feckless borrowing in these countries and the inadequacies of the regulatory framework governing the banking system, although these were important ingredients. The finger of blame also has to be pointed to an unprecedented configuration of economic and institutional forces whose interaction threw up a dangerously unstable dynamic that culminated in severe financial instability.

Notes

The authors wish to acknowledge the very help comments of Mike Leahy and other participants at the Bank of Israel's conference on Lessons from the World Financial Crisis.

1. In the Irish case it is unlikely that labor mobility per se was sufficiently strong to substantially push up NT wages. The degree of substitutability between traded and non-traded labor was likely limited. It is more probable that the enlarged capacity for centralized collective wage bargaining ratcheted up NT real wages toward those prevailing in the T sector.

2. Some other reasons why the real interest rate in the NT sector fell are that the exchange risk premium, following a history of devaluation of the Irish pound, disappeared from interest rates and the liquidity premia in domestic interest rates also fell sharply with the integration of the Irish money and short-term debt market with those in the rest of the euro area following the adoption of the euro.

3. Cumulative output loss is measured as the difference between actual GDP and forecast GDP using an ARIMA $(1, 1, 1)$ framework beginning in 2007Q4.

4. While no data are available on NT output and prices, the services sector may be a good proxy for the NT sector. Data would appear to be available on overall services sector output and prices. Lane (2006) reports data that show that inflation differentials to have been substantially larger across the services sectors of the 12 euro area member states from the start of monetary union in 1999 until 2004 than they were for goods in all categories. The biggest increases were for Ireland (an annual inflation rate of 5.5 percent), Portugal (4.4 percent) and Spain and Greece (3.8 percent each). The increases in the cost of services in the core countries were consistently substantially less: Germany (1.4 percent), France (1.9 percent), Belgium (2.1 percent), Austria (2.2 percent), and Luxembourg (2.7 percent). The Netherlands is an exception at 3.4 percent. We suspect that if the data sample were to be extended up to end of 2007, these differences would be greater. This also means that the growth in real interest rate differential would also be greater as between NT sectors of the

member states of the monetary union. Our work is continuing on a way to test the theory using data relating to just the NT sector of the economy.

References

Basel Committee on Banking Supervision. 2010. *An Assessment of the Long-Term Economic Impact of Stronger Capital and Liquidity Requirements.* Basel: BIS.

Black, S. W. 2010. Fixing the flaws in the eurozone. Mimeo.

Blanchard, Olivier, and Stanley Fischer. 1989. *Lectures on Macroeconomics.* Cambridge: MIT Press.

Browne, Frank. 2004. Fundamental and non-fundamental influences on the housing market. Central Bank and Financial Services Authority of Ireland. Mimeo. Published as thematic article in 2004 Financial Stability Report of the Central Bank and Financial Services Authority of Ireland.

Browne, For, and G. Kennedy. 2010. Explaining Irish house prices with a focus on the recent boom/bust. Central Bank of Ireland, Dublin.

De Grauwe, P. 1991 *International Money Post-war Trends and Theories.* Oxford, UK: Clarendon Press.

ECB. 2010. *Financial Market Integration in Europe.* Frankfurt: European Central Bank.

Haldane, A. 2010. The 100 billion question. Speech at the Institute of Regulation and Risk, North Asia (IRRNA), Hong Kong, March 30.

Honohan, P., and P. Lane. 2003. Divergent inflation rates in EMU. *Economic Policy* (October): 18, 37, 357–394.

Humphrey, T. M. 2002. Knut Wicksell and Gustav Cassel on the cumulative process and the price-stabilising policy rule. *Federal Reserve Bank of Richmond Economic Quarterly* 88 (3): 59–83.

Lane, P. 2006. The real effects of European Monetary Union. *Journal of Economic Perspectives* 20 (4): 47–66.

Leijonhufvud, A. 1991. *Natural rate and market rate.* The New Palgrave, vol. 3. London: Palgrave Macmillan, 1002–1100.

Lein, S., M. Leon-Ledesma, and C. Nerlich. 2009. The link between real and nominal convergence: The case of the new EU member states. In R. Martin and A. Winkler, eds., *Real Convergence in Central, Eastern and South-eastern Europe.* London: Palgrave Macmillan, 65–97.

Maurer, Rainer Willi. 2010. The eurozone crisis: A simple theory, some not so pleasant empirical calculations and an unconventional proposal. Working paper. Hochschule Pforzheim University.

Contributors

Enrique Alberola Banco de España

Harun Alp Central Bank of the Republic of Turkey

Sigbjørn Atle Berg Norges Bank

Jacob Braude Bank of Israel

Frank Browne Central Bank of Ireland

Carlos Capistrán Bank of America Merrill Lynch

Kyuil Chung The Bank of Korea

Gabriel Cuadra Banco de México

Zvi Eckstein Interdisciplinary Center Herzliya-IDC

Øyvind Eitrheim Norges Bank

Selim Elekdağ International Monetary Fund

Stanley Fischer Bank of Israel

Karnit Flug Bank of Israel

Jonathan Kearns Reserve Bank of Australia

Robert Kelly Central Bank of Ireland

Seungwon Kim The Bank of Korea

Jonathan D. Ostry International Monetary Fund

Huw Pill European Central Bank

Manuel Ramos-Francia Banco de México

Helene Schuberth Oesterreichische Nationalbank

Frank Smets European Central Bank

Claudio Soto Central Bank of Chile

Carlos Trucharte Banco de España

Juan Luís Vega Banco de España

Index